T0287025

Mega-Urban Regions in
Pacific Asia

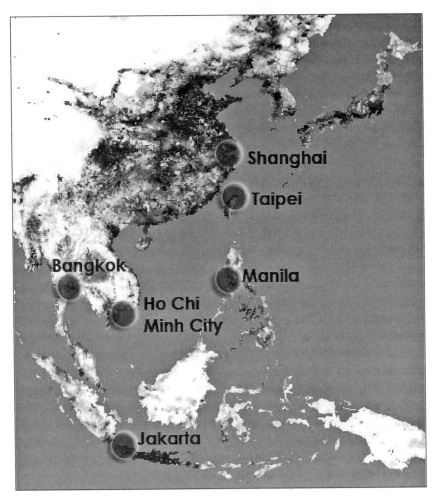

Mega-Urban regions included in this study

Mega-Urban Regions in Pacific Asia

Urban Dynamics in a Global Era

Edited by

GAVIN W. JONES & MIKE DOUGLASS

NUS PRESS
SINGAPORE

© 2008 NUS Press
National University of Singapore
AS3-01-02, 3 Arts Link
Singapore 117569

Fax   : (65) 6774-0652
E-mail : nusbooks@nus.edu.sg
Website : http://www.nus.edu.sg/npu

ISBN 978-9971-69-379-4 (Paper)

All rights reserved. This book, or parts thereof, may not be reproduced in any form or by any means, electronic or mechanical, including photocopying, recording or any information storage and retrieval system now known or to be invented, without written permission from the Publisher.

National Library Board Singapore Cataloguing in Publication Data

Mega-urban regions in Pacific Asia: urban dynamics in a global era / edited by Gavin W. Jones & Mike Douglass. – Singapore: NUS Press, c2008.
p. cm.
Includes bibliographical references and index.
ISBN-13: 978-9971-69-379-4 (pbk.)

1. Asia – Population. 2. Migration, Internal – Asia. 3. Asia – Social conditions. I. Jones, Gavin W. II. Douglass, Mike.

HB3633.A3
304.6095 – dc22   OCN213300083

Front Cover: Squatters along railroad tracks, in the background is Baiyoke Tower II, Bangkok (2004)
Back Cover: (left to right)
1. A new urban core of Bangkok emerging since the mid-1980s (2005)
2. The globalising skyline of the Bangkok MUR (2005)
3. The advent of the automobile age, Bangkok (2005)
(Photos were taken by Mike Douglass.)

Typeset by: International Typesetters Pte Ltd
Printed by: Vetak Services

Contents

Tables, Figures and Boxes

FIGURES

BOXES

Preface

A century ago, New York, London and Paris were the world's largest cities. In recent times, though, London and Paris have been left far behind in population by the largest cities in Asia. Since the end of World War Two, the populations of the largest cities in Southeast Asia have multiplied many-fold, and their transformation into mega-urban regions has been extraordinarily rapid. We need to understand better the dynamics of growth of these cities, which now play such an important role in spearheading economic and social change in the countries of the region.

The book is the result of close collaboration with researchers and their institutions in six countries: Indonesia, Thailand, the Philippines, China, Vietnam and Taiwan, who were brought together to study the dynamics of change in mega-urban regions focusing on six cities: Jakarta, Bangkok, Manila, Shanghai, Ho Chi Minh City and Taipei, based on analysis of 1990 and 2000 population census data.

The aim of basing such a study on the rich but relatively inaccessible unpublished data on metropolitan regions from the population censuses in the different countries had long been an aim of the first editor, whose work in the different countries of the region over time had put him in close contact with the agencies conducting censuses in these countries. It required colleagues in each country to collabourate in accessing the data, deciding on standardised approaches to enable comparative analysis, analysing the data and writing the reports. Long-term work in the region by the two editors enabled us to identify appropriate collaborators who shared our enthusiasm for the project. The team was able to gain access to unpublished census data enabling it to study change in these MURs in ways that were never possible before.

Funding, however, proved a difficulty, and for some time it seemed that this ambitious team project would be consigned to the category of good ideas never realised. With great gratitude we therefore record our debt to the Andrew W. Mellon Foundation, and in particular Carolyn Makinson, who saw the value in our project and provided the funding needed to secure and analyse the data and hold the workshops needed to iron out analytical issues and present preliminary findings. We trust that this book justifies the confidence the Foundation expressed in us.

Whether such a detailed comparative study utilising census data to analyse the dynamics of change in mega-urban regions can ever be repeated is not clear. The level of organisation needed is daunting. The future of census taking in the region is also uncertain due to the recent tendency for the data collected through censuses to be less detailed, particularly in relation to the labour force. This being the case, we are particularly pleased to be able to bring this study to fruition.

Our thanks go to many people. First, to our country collaborators who worked with us throughout the project and who authored the chapters on each mega-urban region in this book. Second, to the census officials who supplied the data (and in the cases of Indonesia and the Philippines were part of our analytical team). Third, to our research assistants without whom the delays in completing the book would have been much greater: Ng Kian Boon in Singapore, who sadly passed away before the book was completed, Hao Thien Nguyen and Haina Lee in Honolulu. Fourth, to our colleagues from different countries who met with us in a conference in Singapore in June 2004 to comment on our presentations of findings from the study and to discuss policy implications. Fifth, to our universities — the Australian National University, the National University of Singapore and the University of Hawaii — which provided the academic atmosphere, the flexible work situation, and the willingness to administer the grant, all of which enabled the project to be conducted efficiently and in an academically rewarding manner. Special thanks go to Milisa Haberschusz, area manager of the Demography and Sociology Programme at the Australian National University, who was most helpful in carrying through the administrative matters even after the first editor had moved to Singapore.

Finally, we would like to thank our wives, Henny and Etsuko, for their unfailing understanding and good humor when faced with our absences and — even when present — our limited attention span.

Gavin Jones & Mike Douglass
Singapore, Honolulu

Contributors

Gavin W. Jones is Professor in the Asia Research Institute, National University of Singapore, where he is research team leader on the changing family in Asia. After completing his PhD degree at the Australian National University (ANU) in 1966, he joined the Population Council, where he worked first in New York, then in Thailand and Indonesia. He returned to Australia to work with the Demography and Sociology Programme at the ANU for 28 years, serving as head of programme for a six-year period, and conducting a wide range of research mainly on Southeast Asia, notably on nuptiality, fertility, urbanisation, the demography of educational planning, and labour force analysis. He has published a number of single-authored and jointly-authored books, many edited books, and about 130 papers in refereed journals or as book chapters. He has also played an active role as a consultant in the region, working in particular with planning agencies in the integration of population in development planning. He has served as member or chair of IUSSP scientific committees dealing with urbanisation and with population and development. He is currently Chair of the Council of CICRED, the organisation bringing together the world's centres of demographic research, located in Paris. He is editor of the new journal *Asian Population Studies*, published by Routledge.

Mike Douglass is the Director of the Globalisation Research Centre and a Professor and former chair of the Department of Urban and Regional Planning at the University of Hawaii (UH) at Manoa. He holds a Ph.D. in Urban Planning from UCLA. A specialist in planning in Asia, he has joined numerous research and planning projects and has been a consultant for international development agencies as well as national and local governments in Asia. His current research includes: the urban transition and spaces of democracy; world cities and mega-urban region dynamics; international migration and global householding; livable cities. Awards and honours include: Excellence in Research award from the College of Social Sciences, UH (2001–2); Canada Research Chair (2001); Fulbright Senior Specialist (from 2001); Visiting Professor and Scholar at Stanford University (2000); Perloff Chair in Urban Planning at UCLA (1996). The University of Hawaii identifies him as one of its "90 fabulous faculty".

Jarunun Sutiprapa received a bachelor's degree in Architecture from Chulalongkorn University and an M.Sc. in Urban Planning at the Asian Institute of Technology, Bangkok, Thailand. In 1988 she participated in a Training Course on Regional Development Planning at the National Land Agency, Japan. From 1993–97 she studied in the School of Environmental Planning, Faculty of Architecture, University of Melbourne, Australia, where she received her Ph.D. Her professional experience includes Physical Planner on Master Plan of Chulalongkorn University (1980–81); Urban Planner, the Specific Plan Division, Department of Town and Country Planning, Thailand (1982–87); Policy and Plan Analyst, the Urban Development Coordination Division, Office of the National Economic and Social Development Board (NESDB), Thailand (1987–2001); Policy and Plan Analyst, the Spatial Development Office, Office of the NESDB, Thailand (2001–2), and Policy and Plan Analyst, Office of the Suvarnabhumi Airport Development Committee, Office of the NESDB, Thailand (2002–present).

Paranee Watana received a B.A. in Economics from Chulalongkorn University and an M.A. in Demography from the Australian National University. Her professional experience has been as a Policy and Plan Analyst, Office of the National Economic and Social Development Board (NESDB), Thailand (1976–present) where she is presently Chief, Strategic Social Policy Group, Quality of life and Social Development Office, Office of the NESDB, Thailand.

Preeya Mithranon received her bachelor's degree in Mathematics from Khon Kaen University and a Master of Arts in Demography from Chulalongkorn University. From 1981 to the present she has been working as a Statistician at National Statistical Office (NSO), Thailand. She is now Chief, Social Statistics Analysing and Forecasting Group, Statistical Forecasting Bureau, National Statistical Office, Thailand. She is responsible for planning, conducting and analysing NSO data using demographic methods and statistical techniques and summarising findings that are particularly concerned with the interpretation of demographic and socio-economic statistics obtained from population censuses, surveys and other sources. She also participated in preparing Thailand Population Projections (2000–25), especially on the population-based fertility, mortality and migration data.

Chanpen Taesrikul received her bachelor's degree in Statistics and Master's degree in Demography from Chulalongkorn University. From 1975–95 she was a Policy and Plan Analyst, Population Sector, Population and Manpower Planning Division, NESDB, Thailand. In 1996 she was a Policy and Plan Analyst, Human Resource Planning Division, NESDB. From 2003 to the present she has been a Policy and Plan Analyst, Macro Economic Planning Office, NESDB.

Si Gde Made Mamas has recently retired after a long career with the Central Statistical Board in Jakarta, Indonesia, where he was the leading demographer and closely involved in planning all aspects of population censuses, intercensal surveys and other surveys. He gained his Ph.D. at the University of Hawaii, and was involved in joint research with colleagues there — notably with Geoffrey McNicoll in analysing Indonesian demographic trends. He has published many academic papers dealing with Indonesian demography, and in recent years particularly dealing with megacities in Indonesia. He is also working on a history of census taking in Indonesia since 1961, the earliest census of the Independence period.

Rizky Komalasari has an M.Sc. in Environmental Engineering from the Bandung Institute of Technology and a MURP degree from the Department of Urban and Regional Planning at the University of Hawaii. She has been involved in numerous projects related to livable cities in Southeast Asia.

Rachel H. Racelis was born in the Philippines and has resided in Metro-Manila for over 25 years. She obtained her bachelors (Statistics) and masters (Economics) degrees from the University of the Philippines, and her doctoral degree (Economics) from the University of Hawaii. Her main areas of research include: internal population migration; household structures and household projection methodologies; health care financing; sectoral expenditure estimation, analysis and projections; and projection methodologies for development planning. She is currently a professor at the School of Urban and Regional Planning, University of the Philippines.

Paula Monina G. Collado was born in Manila, Philippines. She obtained her bachelor's degree (Management) from Ateneo de Manila University, her masters degree (Applied Statistics) from the Polytechnic University of the Philippines (PUP) and a diploma (Demography) from the Cairo Demographic Center, Egypt. She has worked in government since graduation from the university. She is an expert in population and housing censuses, labour force, gender statistics and strategic management. She has served as consultant to various government agencies and international organizations. Ms. Collado is currently the Deputy Administrator of the National Statistics Office (NSO), Philippines.

Dang Nguyen Anh is a senior researcher and head, Department for Population Studies at the Institute of Sociology, Hanoi, Vietnam. In addition to managing and supervising the Department's administrative affairs, he participates actively and coordinates a wide range of research activities dealing with issues of social development, population and family, human migration and labour mobility, health transitions and interventions research. Anh is also a guest lecturer at the National University of Hanoi and the University of Social and Human Sciences in Ho Chi Minh City. He is an editorial member of the *Population and Development Journal* published by Vietnam's Committee for Population, Family and Children. He has served as an advisory member of the General Statistical Office, the Ministry of Health, the National Assembly's Committee for Social Affairs, and Vietnam Women's Union. He has conducted research projects and consultancies for a number of international organisations, donors and NGOs, and is involved in an institutional strengthening network with other countries in the Asian region. Anh graduated from the National Economic University of Hanoi and obtained both M.A. and Ph.D. degrees in sociology from Brown University, USA. He is currently a national coordinator of the Asia-Pacific Migration Research Network (APMRN) in Vietnam.

Li-ling Huang is an assistant Professor at the Architecture Department and Graduate School of Media Space Design at Ming Chuan University, Taiwan. She received her Ph.D. in Urban and Regional Planning at National Taiwan University. Her research interests are concerned with urban governance and globalisation studies. She is currently conducting research on the social life and community spaces of migrant workers in Taipei. She recently published "Urban Politics and Spatial Development: the Emergence of Participatory Planning in Taipei", in R.Y Kwok, ed., *Globalising Taipei* (Routledge, 2005).

Yu Zhu is Research Professor, School of Geography, and Deputy Director, Centre for Population and Development Research, Fujian Normal University. He is a Council Member of China Population Association, Member of CPA's Committee on Migration and Urbanisation, and Vice President of Population Association of Fujian Province. He earned his M.Sc. in human geography from East China Normal University, and his Ph.D. from the Demography Programme at the Australian National University. His research interests straddle the two disciplines of demography and human geography, focusing on issues relating to urbanisation and migration, and especially China's new urbanisation patterns since the era of reform and opening-up. Between 1985 and 1995 he worked with East China Normal University in Shanghai, and then with Fujian Normal University in Fuzhou. From 1995 to 2003 he was with the Demography Programme of ANU, first as a Ph.D. student, and then as a programme visitor and a postdoctoral fellow. Returning to Fujian Normal University in 2003, he has been continuing research on China's migration and urbanisation, while continuing to be involved in international collaborative research. He has published a book, book chapters, and numerous papers in both major international and leading Chinese journals.

Trung Quang Le is a researcher at the Centre for Natural Resources and Environmental Studies at Vietnam National University, Hanoi. He has participated in research and consultancy on projects on ethnic minorities and resources in upland areas, as well as studies on traditional craft villages in Red River Delta area of Vietnam. Having a B.Sc. degree in Environmental Management from the Vietnam National University at Hanoi and Master degree — sponsored by the East West Centre, Honolulu, Hawaii — in the Department of Urban and Regional Planning of the University of Hawaii at Manoa, focusing on Rural and Regional Planning.

Cameron Kawika Lowry is a graduate researcher at the Department of Urban and Regional Planning, University of Hawaii-Manoa. His research/consulting is in two broad areas of mediation and geographical information systems applications. He holds a bachelor's degree in East Asian studies and geography from Macalester College and a Master's in Urban and Regional Planning with a research focus on civil society and nation building.

Hao Thien Nguyen is a doctoral student in the Department of Urban and Regional Planning at the University of Hawaii at Manoa (UHM), and a Graduate Research Assistant for the Globalisation Research Centre. Before pursuing the programme at UHM, he worked as a researcher at the Institute of Sociology, under the Vietnam National Centre for Social Sciences and Humanities in Hanoi. His main concerns include issues of population and development, internal and international migration, poverty, urbanisation and environment, and decentralisation in the developing world. Hao received a Bachelor of Sociology at the College of Social Sciences and Humanities from the National University of Hanoi, Vietnam. He has been awarded the Harvard-Yenching Institute's Scholarship from Harvard University to pursue the Doctorate Programme in Urban and Regional Planning. He has co-authored several publications.

Anh Nguyen Pham is currently pursuing a master's degree in Urban and Regional Planning at the University of Hawai'i at Manoa. Her interests focus on issues of community development, urban service provision, environmental management, and livability in Pacific Asia. She was an Asia-Pacific Leadership Fellow at the East-West Centre and holds a B.A. in both Japanese and Asian Studies from California State University, Long Beach.

Nghi Dong Thai is a doctoral student in the Community & Culture Psychology programme at the University of Hawaii-Manoa. She holds a B.A. from the University of Nebraska-Lincoln and received her M.A. from the University of Hawaii-Manoa. Currently, she serves as a Student Reviewer for the *American Journal of Community Psychology* (*AJCP*) and will be a Guest Co-Editor for a forthcoming special issue of the AJCP. She has also served as an Editorial Reviewer for a *Special Issue on Asian and Pacific Islander Youth for Crime and Delinquency*. Nghi Thai has been a lecturer for the Departments of Psychology and Family and Consumer Sciences at the University of Hawaii-Manoa. In 2003, she was recognised as an "Up and Coming Female Trailblazer in Community Psychology". Her research interests include youth gangs, juvenile delinquency, and violence as they pertain to immigrant populations.

Hernani Yulinawati is a lecturer and researcher in the Department of Environmental Engineering, Trisakti University, Jakarta, Indonesia. Her work focuses on environmental quality management, especially air quality management and air pollution control engineering. She has also been responsible for an air quality labouratory and research on air pollution. Yulinawati has a bachelor's degree in environmental engineering from Trisakti University and a Master of Urban and Regional Planning at the University of Hawaii-Manoa. Currently, she is pursuing a doctoral degree at the Department of Urban and Regional Planning at the University of Hawaii-Manoa. The focus of her research is on integrating air quality management with land use and transportation planning.

1

Introduction

Gavin Jones and Mike Douglass

Mega-Urban Regions and Asian Urbanisation

The latter half of the twentieth century was a period in which the percentage of the world's population living in urban areas rose from 30 per cent to 47 per cent. In Asia, the rise (from a lower base) was even faster: from 17 per cent to 37 per cent. The latter half of the twentieth century was also a period in which total populations in Asia grew enormously. Putting these two facts together, the absolute numbers of Asians living in urban areas increased astronomically. Though the real meaning of urban and rural has been increasingly contested (Champion and Hugo 2004), the reality of an increasing proportion of Asia's populations living in urban areas is clear.

Urban areas differ greatly in size, from the urban villages included under the urban rubric in the Philippines and Indonesia, to vast metropolitan areas such as Metro Manila and the Special Region of Jakarta (DKI Jakarta). Large cities with populations exceeding five million constitute only 13.8 per cent of the urban population in the world in 2000, or 16.2 per cent in Asian countries (United Nations 2003). Even if the cut-off size of cities is reduced to half a million, cities above this size hold only 47.5 per cent of the world's urban population, and 50.2 per cent of Asia's. This serves to emphasise that the study of smaller cities and towns has not received the attention it deserves in studies of Asian urbanisation.

On the other hand, the proportion of population residing in very large cities is considerably understated by these official figures, because many places defined as small towns or even medium sized cities lie, in reality, within the mega-urban region focusing on a very large city. Kuala Lumpur, the highly under-bounded capital of Malaysia, is a good example. Its population

1

is 1.38 million according to the United Nations data, although a true urban agglomeration estimate would put the figure at more than four million, and would incorporate in the Kuala Lumpur urban agglomeration not only many small towns, but also Petaling Jaya, accorded fourth place in Malaysia's urban hierarchy although it is merely a suburban extension of Kuala Lumpur, and Klang, accorded fifth place. Thus official data not only greatly underestimate the size of the country's main metropolis, but also distort the true picture of Malaysia's urban hierarchy.

Viewed from this perspective, it is not only the smaller cities and towns in Asian countries that are under-researched. At the other end of the spectrum, the mega-urban regions (MURs) of Asia also deserve serious attention from researchers, but they have tended to give undue emphasis to large cities as officially defined. Certainly, there has been some attention to the phenomenon of MURs (sometimes termed extended metropolitan regions) in Asia, notably the work of McGee and others (Ginsburg, Koppel and McGee 1991; McGee and Robinson 1995). Such studies drew inspiration from the seminal study of Vining (1986), but placed emphasis on what were seen as special features of the phenomenon when it was taking place in regions of dense agricultural population. What are lacking, however, are studies which systematically examine the structure and dynamics of change in MURs, recognising the reality of different zones within the MUR which play different roles, and which disaggregate the overall pattern of change into the sharply differing patterns specific to each of these zones. The lack of such studies appears to result partly from a lack of attention to the conceptual issues, but also from the tyranny of official definitions of metropolitan areas and the availability of statistical data only for these areas, which has deterred researchers from exploring in detail the dimensions of the mega-urban regions which extend far beyond the officially defined metropolitan areas.

As will become clear in this book, such MURs are not only very large in population and area, but they are even more important when their key roles in the economic and social life and the governance of the countries in which they are situated are taken into consideration. Their share of national output is well in excess of their share of population, they are at the forefront of their countries' cultural and intellectual life, and they are the focus of international trade, commerce and political relations. Their massive scale and heavy and concentrated use of resources raise a host of environmental issues.

This book discusses six large mega-urban regions located in Pacific Asia: those focusing on the cities of Bangkok, Ho Chi Minh City (HCMC),

Jakarta, Manila, Shanghai and Taipei. The reason for the choice of the first four was that they are the only MURs in Southeast Asia. Others — Kuala Lumpur, Surabaya, Bandung, Yangon, Hanoi, Cebu and Davao City, for example — may develop into MURs in time, but have not yet reached the scale or population required for such designation. The other two — Taipei and Shanghai — are included to give a more comparative assessment for the Southeast Asian ones. Shanghai, like Ho Chi Minh City, represents an accelerated urban transition in a "transition economy"; Taipei represents a more "mature" phase of MUR development that is becoming post-industrial.

Urbanisation at the Turn of the Millennium

To set the growth of the MURs in context, we need to examine the trends in urbanisation in the countries or regions in which they are located. This is done in Table 1.1, which indicates that the level of urbanisation differs widely in the countries and regions we are concerned with in this book. On the whole, they are less urbanised than the world as a whole, because the world figure is lifted by the much higher levels of urbanisation in Europe and North and South America. But Taiwan's level of urbanisation approaches that of these Western countries, whereas Vietnam's is much lower.

The figures on urbanisation in Table 1.1 should be treated with a degree of caution, because they accept national definitions of urban areas.

Table 1.1 Changes in Urban Population Share and Numbers, Selected Countries and Regions

Country or Region	Percentage Urban				Urban Population (millions)			
	1950	1975	2000	2030 (proj.)	1950	1975	2000	2030 (proj.)
Indonesia	12.4	19.4	42.0	67.7	9.8	26.0	88.9	187.8
Thailand	16.5	23.8	31.1	47.0	3.2	9.8	19.0	35.4
Philippines	27.1	35.6	48.1	n.a.	5.4	14.9	36.8	n.a.
Vietnam	11.6	18.8	24.3	43.2	3.2	9.1	19.0	46.9
China	12.5	17.4	35.8	60.5	69.5	161.4	456.2	877.6
WORLD	29.1	37.3	47.1	60.8	733	1,516	2,857	4,945

Source: United Nations 2004. Figures for the Philippines for 2000 are from the official 2000 Population Census report. The 2030 projections for the Philippines are not shown because the UN's projected figures are based on an incorrect figure for 2000.

Thus the level of urbanisation in the Philippines is exaggerated compared with that of Thailand, because the Philippines uses very generous criteria in allocating urban status to particular localities, whereas the criteria used in Thailand serve to understate the real level of urbanisation (Jones 2004: 115–7).[1]

The absolute numbers living in urban areas are shown in the right-hand panel of Table 1.1. The dramatic increase in urban populations in the second half of the twentieth century, noted above, is readily apparent, whether we focus on the rise in Indonesia from 10 million to 89 million, in Thailand from three million to 19 million, or in China from 70 million to 456 million. The rise in urban populations projected to 2030 is equally impressive: in Indonesia from 89 million to 188 million, in Thailand from 19 million to 35 million, and in China from 456 million to 878 million.

The mirror image of the sharp increase in urban populations is the deceleration in growth of rural populations. Indeed, the historically crucial point where rural population peaked and then started to decline appears to have been reached first in Taiwan in the late 1960s, then after a long lag, in China, Indonesia and Thailand by the early to mid 1990s. In the Philippines and Vietnam, however, this point appeared to be still a long way off. Still, as noted in the studies to follow, large populations classified as rural, but lying within the shadow of the six megacities, are deeply affected by urbanising influences.

The four Southeast Asian mega-urban regions have some important elements in common. Three of them — Jakarta, HCMC and Manila, were colonial creations, serving as entrepots, and although Thailand was not colonised, Bangkok served a somewhat similar role during the period when colonising forces dominated the region. These cities grew to megacity status because the large population of the country in which they were located enabled one very large city to develop. This is why they exceed the populations of other cities with colonial origins, such as Kuala Lumpur, Singapore and Phnom Penh.

We have witnessed demographic inflation by a factor of ten or more in the built-up areas of these Southeast Asian MURs since 1950. This remarkable growth — from "million cities" to "ten million cities" is surely one of the most amazing occurrences in a half-century marked by many amazing occurrences. Yet the growth has been relentless rather than dramatic. Those living through it, and adjusting almost daily to the changing urban environment, were not as aware of the transformation in scale and built environment as were those visiting every ten years or so.

Mega-Urban Regions in an Era of Accelerated Urban Transitions

The accelerated urban transition in the open economies of Pacific (East and Southeast) Asia from the late 1960s brought hundreds of thousands of migrants annually to a select number of city regions. By the year 2000 the largest of these urban agglomerations had reached well beyond their administrative boundaries to form extended mega-urban regions extending more than 50 kilometres into satellite city and peri-urban areas. With residential populations of 15 million or so in their built-up areas, three of these MURs (Jakarta, Manila and Shanghai) have joined the league of the largest urban agglomerations in world history.

The chapters that follow focus on the 1990–2000 period of change in the six Pacific Asia MURs listed above. At the national scale, the analysis seeks to address a long-standing and highly debated question of whether processes of spatial polarisation have reached a peak and are now attenuating or, to the contrary, continuing unabated. The technical issue that has been lost in this debate is how to measure the size of these very large agglomerations. Data supplied by the United Nations Population Division and used in the widely cited World Bank *World Development Reports*, for example, use administrative boundaries rather than actual agglomeration size to demarcate the area and population size of what is typically listed as the "largest city". This privileges politically demarcated boundaries over the actual size of an urban agglomerations defined as the furthest reach of a contiguous daily field of an urban region.[2]

Given that many, if not most, very large urban agglomerations in the world have spread beyond their administrative boundaries, this confusion is not simply a technical one. By using administrative boundaries, both the size and rate of growth of major urban agglomerations are systematically understated. Many metropolitan areas are defined by boundaries that once encompassed not only the city proper, but also suburban areas and rural areas into which city planners expected urban growth to spread. As the metropolis grew, the core area frequently had relatively slow growth (at least of its night-time population, the population recorded in population censuses), and the outer areas faster growth, but at that time both core and outer areas were contained within the administratively defined metropolitan boundary. As a result, the growth of the metropolitan population took account of both the slower growth in the core and the faster growth in the periphery.

As the metropolis expanded, however, most of the remaining rural areas were transformed and the built-up area expanded to the metropolitan boundary. After that, the process of suburbanisation and the location of housing estates and industrial developments took place largely outside the metropolitan boundary. Thus the peripheral areas with faster population growth are in many cases located almost entirely outside the metropolitan boundary. In such a circumstance, the slow growth of the metropolitan population does not necessarily mean that the growth of the mega-urban region as a whole is slowing.

Together, the smaller size and lower rates of growth attributed to major urban agglomerations lead to the larger mistaken conclusion that these cities have stopped growing, and thus a "polarisation reversal" or "trickle-down" effect has overcome backwash effects of the urban transition in a global age. Major deductive leaps are thus based on a simple error of interpretation.

Using a common methodology to measure the effective size of urban agglomeration based on density, non-agricultural employment and contiguous space, the studies in this book seek a more rigorous empirical analysis of the question of whether economic growth and development foster greater spatial concentration or a deconcentration and more even spread over national territorial space. The studies of the six MURs show that in some cases the actual agglomeration size can be twice that indicated by data using the administrative boundaries of core municipalities. The general findings are that the era of accelerated urban transitions is producing giant mega-urban regions having neither historical precedent nor perceptible turning points. Polarisation continues in varying degrees in all cities, including the higher income economy of Taipei. With residential populations ranging from five to more than 20 million, each was garnering larger shares of the national population, signalling a more advanced process of spatial polarisation driven as much by global linkages as by domestic factors. Economic accounts show even higher concentrations of economic power in these MURs, with some being the locus of half or more of the national GDP and even higher shares of foreign direct investment.

At the same time, the process whereby the major mega-urban regions covered in this study dominated their countries' urban scene is showing signs of changing, with the urban population as a whole growing faster than the MUR in a number of cases. This faster growth of the non-MUR urban population may reflect a number of factors: for example, the effects on choices made by governments, enterprises and individuals of the diseconomies of agglomeration, more effective decentralisation of economic activity and the growth-dampening effect of particularly low birthrates in the megacities. It may also, however, reflect the understatement of the population of the

MUR, even within the wider boundaries used to define them, as a result of a number of factors: notably, the difficulty of enumerating the highly mobile populations of these complex and densely populated metropolises, and a tendency to miss large numbers of temporary migrants, both because they do not always have fixed residences and because the definitions applied in the census to determine where mobile populations should be recorded leads to systematic under-recording of the city population. Thus there is an element of uncertainty regarding the faster increase in the non-MUR urban population.

To further illuminate the spatial dynamics under investigation, each MUR is divided into core, inner and outer zones to assess within each the patterns of migration, natural population growth, employment and human capital as measured by educational attainment over the 1990–2000 decade. Among the most interesting patterns is the finding that in several MURs the core zone is reaching below replacement fertility which, coupled with the suburbanisation of significant segments of the middle class, means that migration of lower income workers and households has become the principal source of core zone population growth. While this might be reminiscent of some Western experiences, the Pacific Asia pattern is different in a number of ways. For example, all of the core zone populations except that of Taipei (and Jakarta in the 1995–2000 period) are still increasing, and in some MURs are still increasing in their shares of MUR population. Core zone population densities are also very high and continue to support a vibrant inner city economy. In some cases, notably Manila, the urban middle class remains concentrated in the core despite massive expansion of the MUR over the past few decades.

Variations in population dynamics over the three zones of each MUR are substantial, indicating how life chances and human welfare outcomes of the urban transition are also variegated over space. The most basic indicator of all is mortality: expectation of life at birth varies sharply between the zones in some of the MURs, reflecting higher incomes, higher education and better access to health facilities in the core. Yet within the core itself, health conditions vary sharply according to socio-economic group. As the chapter on livability shows, access to schools, health centres and the full panoply of public services as well as community infrastructure such as lanes, drainage, piped water and electricity have a precipitous decay from core to outer zone. While the inner zone tends to be the area of new middle class prosperity in the form of gated communities and shopping malls, outer zones tend to fall beyond municipal boundaries and lack even the most basic urban infrastructure despite the large urban population increases they are experiencing.

The movement of people over space reflects the desire to improve access to the social and economic benefits associated with urbanisation. The studies show, however, that trade-offs exist in making spatial choices. Poorer households might find higher chances of employment in the urban core, but the high land prices in this zone typically relegate them to crowded, environmentally degraded living spaces. Suburbanisation for the middle class brings more spacious housing, but results in worsening the environment by idling in congested traffic along long commuting corridors. Expansion of the city into the third zone can prove to be the most disruptive of rural community life even while it brings the promise of economic growth and higher access to urban services.

Not only space but also time factors influence the dynamics of these massive urban regions. As a result of massive diurnal, weekly and seasonal population movements, the "population" of a metropolis or its component zones is in a constant state of flux. Commuting from the bedroom areas in the inner and outer zones brings millions to and from the core on a daily basis. There is a weekend exodus of the better-off to getaway areas such as the Puncak near Jakarta, mountain resorts around Taipei, and coastal areas on both sides of the gulf of Thailand, accessible from Bangkok. Seasonally, key festivals such as *lebaran* or Chinese New Year see massive movements out of the MURs to regions of origin of large proportions of their populations. The "downside" of living in such massive cities is apparent to all at these times, as transport systems cannot cope with these peaks of movement, and even the wealthy cannot fully escape traffic delays and frustrations.

The forces underlying the tremendous transformations underway in the mega-urban regions are complex. Some are related to improved health care, social stability and other factors that created conditions for a pronounced surge in population growth rates following World War Two, decolonisation and the advent of what has been called "developmental states" with governments taking on the mantel of active promoters of economic growth.

Pacific Asian MURs in their International Context

Aside from the point made earlier — namely, that Jakarta, Manila and Shanghai now rank among the largest of the world's largest mega-urban regions — there is no attempt in this book to set the trends and structure of these regions in the context of the trends and structure of such regions in other parts of the world. The reason why this is not attempted is not only that such a comparative analysis would be an enormous undertaking.

More to the point, such a comparison is not possible, because the kind of analysis undertaken in this book — the systematic analysis of the dynamics of population and employment change within MURs over the decade of the 1990s, utilising a zonal structure, has to the best of our knowledge simply not been attempted for MURs in other parts of the world. Thus for example, whereas Simmonds and Hack (2000) analyse the emerging forms of global city regions with a strong emphasis on infrastructure development, they neither attempt to define boundaries of zones outside official metropolitan areas, nor do they conduct a systematic analysis of population change. The major recent overview of city chance from a demographic perspective, while presenting fascinating data for cities such as Mexico City and Sao Paulo, relies on an earlier version of our present study (Jones 2002) in highlighting the value of a zonal analysis of demographic change in large city regions (National Research Council 2003: 19). The authors had clearly not been able to draw on any comparable study elsewhere.

Much as a comparison of the findings of our study with those in other regions is needed, therefore, we cannot provide such a study for the simple reason that the comparable analyses for other regions have not been conducted. It is our hope that the analysis conducted in this book, which required voluminous data custom-produced from Censuses a decade apart for zones in six MURs, will spur comparable efforts in other parts of the world, so that over time useful comparable analysis will become possible.

Organisation of the Book

The book consists of 11 chapters, six of which are chapters on each of the mega-urban regions, and the remainder of which are introductory and comparative chapters.

Chapter 2. The Morphology of Mega-Urban Regions Expansion

In addition to internal changes, changing global-local dynamics are of increasing importance in urban dynamics. Chapter 2 traces these changes as they have affected the region in general and with specific reference to the cities under study in this book. Up to the 1960s, most Pacific Asia countries were integrated into the world economic system as suppliers of primary products and raw materials. Core urban regions served as entrepot port cities for the export of timber, minerals, and cash crops. Often expanding through a "double-squeeze" on agriculture in the form of high prices for agricultural inputs and suppressed prices for basic food to keep urban wages low, the cities remained relatively small in population size even through the long history of high colonialism. It was the colonial system, however, that brought many of the current MURs into existence as the logic of the global economy favoured ports over inland capital cities. Rangoon (Yangon), Saigon (Ho Chi Minh City), Batavia (Jakarta), Hong Kong and Singapore are among the better known cities that emerged as key commercial centres in the 1600–1950 colonial era.

Beginning in the late 1960s, the rise of newly industrialising countries — most of which are in Pacific Asia — thoroughly transformed the space-economy of these city regions and their nations. Accelerated rural urban migration toward urban manufacturing and service occupations added to the then rapid increases in national population growth rates to propel principal urban regions into the megacity realm of millions of inhabitants. With Pacific Asia being integral to the "new international division of labour" characterised by a shift of labour-intensive assembly and manufacturing segments of production from the North to the South, select open economies in the region experienced the true beginning of their transition to urban-based economies and societies. Taiwan was among this group, which also included Korea, Hong Kong and Singapore. By the mid-1980s other Pacific Asian countries — Indonesia, Malaysia, Thailand, and, to a lesser extent, the Philippines — formed a second wave of urban export-oriented miracle economies.

A decade later, the globalisation of finance capital and the appearance of global franchise outlets began an intensive process of urban restructuring that came to a peak with the 1998 economic crisis. Multiple crises followed, with a mixed pattern of economic recovery among the cities under study. Governments have responded by promoting these MURs as candidate "world cities", which has further directed national public and private resources toward investments in their built environment.

Urban-centred economic growth and crises have been sources of political change and reform as well as social and demographic change. The urban transition is directly associated with the formation of urban middle and working classes that have been the source of the rise of civil society in national political life. The deep political reforms toward elected governments that reached high levels through Pacific Asia from the mid 1980s could not have been effected without the mobilisation of these urban classes. Globalisation as a process of widening access to information and knowledge contributes to political reform, though not always in a linear way.

Chapter 3. Comparative Dynamics of the Six Mega-Urban Regions

These globally-linked transformations have interplayed with demographic variables in ways that have had direct, if sometimes contradictory, impacts on the political life of cities and nations. At a national-international scale, the advent of below replacement fertility in higher income countries and even core zones of middle income countries has spurred increases in international migration from other countries in Asia. This has led to public policy dilemmas over issues related to multiculturalism and ethnic diversity. With most receiving countries either believing themselves to be ethnically homogeneous or otherwise giving favour to ethnic majority groups, the current moment in the urban transition is marked by policies seeking to abstract the labour power of global migrant workers without accepting them as citizens or even permanent residents. Given the powerful and seemingly inexorable force of demographic trends of declining fertility rates and rapidly ageing societies, the share of foreign workers in the urban work force will continue to climb, making this one of the most socially important issues of the coming decades.

At a more local intra-MUR level demographic shifts are also playing a decisive role in patterns of employment and welfare. Family structures are changing along with spatially differentiated natural population growth rates. A decisive ageing of populations is occurring in every country, and this plays out variably over space.

This chapter summarises the methodologies used in the MUR studies discussed in the remainder of the book, including the delineation of the zones, and presents basic comparative findings. For example, in all cities (except Manila) fertility rates are very low, and thus migration critical in growth. There are commonalities in the sex and age patterns of migration into the MURs from other parts of the country, and clear differences between these longer-distance flows and the flows within the MUR, particularly that from the core to the inner and outer zones. At the same time, migration patterns do differ between the different cities. For comparative purposes, each study is based on c1990 and c2000 population census data to:

- define the zones using census data on density and non-agricultural employment in contiguous administrative areas in and around the metropolitan core.
- show the share of each mega-urban region in the national population
- measure the area, population, density and population growth rates of the zones

- study population, migration, educational and employment patterns in each zone

What emerges from these comparative dynamics are some interesting commonalities, but also substantial differences in aspects such as population densities, growth and decline within the core, and migration patterns to the zones, implying that each mega-urban region must be considered as a unique case, even before the sharp differences in political structures are considered. The following six chapters therefore present the specifics of mega-urban region dynamics in more detail for each case study.

Chapter 4. Bangkok — from Royal City to Skyscraper Metropolis

In terms of urbanisation, Thailand has two notable features. First, it has long been considered as a largely rural country. But the low rate of urbanisation in Thailand is somewhat of a myth, resulting from the urban definitions used. Second, it has only one dominant city: Bangkok. Bangkok is one of the world's most notable primate cities, holding a population 11 times larger than the populations of the second, third and fourth cities combined (Jones *et al.* 1996). Bangkok's population has increased remarkably over the past several decades. Aircraft approaching Don Muang, 24 kilometres to Bangkok's north, in the 1960s, flew over paddy fields and canals. Now the approach to Don Muang reveals a mixture of housing estates, roads lined by shops, factories, temples, universities relocated from the central city, and residual agricultural areas.

Unlike some of the other cities included in this study, Bangkok has few natural barriers to outward expansion in all directions. It does reach the Gulf of Thailand to the south, but aside from that, there are no hills or lagoons to hinder the spread of its suburbs in any direction. Partly for this reason, and partly because the Central Plain of Thailand has never been particularly densely populated, Bangkok has lower population densities than the other cities included in this study. As the seat of the monarchy and the location of Thailand's main palace and temple complexes, it symbolises the Thai nation to Thais to a greater extent than other cities included in this study symbolise their nation. It is a vibrant, 24 hours a day city, aspiring to world city status.

Chapter 5. Jakarta — Southeast Asia's Largest MUR

Jakarta — as Batavia — already had a population of 27,000 in 1673, though it had only grown to 70,000 in 1850 (Abeyasekere 1987: 19–20; 52). It therefore has a long history as the premier city of what later became Indonesia, although it needs to be borne in mind that at the beginning of the twentieth century, its population had reached only about 115,000, and it was more or less matched in size by Surabaya. Massive population growth occurred only after independence in the late 1940s, but since that time Jakarta has grown to be South-East Asia's largest city. Actually, it is contested in this status by Manila, because Metro Manila's population exceeds that of DKI Jakarta by some one and a half million, but as shown in Chapter 3, if an inner zone is added to both cities following similar criteria, Jakarta's population exceeds that of Manila.

Jakarta has expanded in all directions except north, where its growth is blocked by the ocean. It has absorbed the towns of Bekasi, Bogor and Tangerang, which serve to form secondary nodes in an expanding metropolis whose built-up area spreads to and beyond each of them. There is the potential in time for Jakarta's urban extremity to link up with Indonesia's third largest city, Bandung, located some 180 kilometres. away to the south-east. As shown in Chapter 5, migrants have come to Jakarta from throughout Indonesia, most of them, though, from other parts of Java. The inner zone, as well as receiving a substantial share of such migrants, has also received large numbers of migrants from the core, moving to the affordable housing and expanding employment opportunities in this zone. These combined sources of migrants have pushed up the inner zone's growth to exceed that of the inner zone of any of the other cities in this study. The environmental impacts and transportation difficulties of such growth in an economy as poor as that of Indonesia's — notwithstanding Jakarta's status as the wealthiest part of that economy — are discussed in Chapter 5 as well as in the chapter on livability — Chapter 10.

Chapter 6. Manila — Continuing Magnet of Rural-Urban Migration

Manila has dominated the Philippines' urban scene over centuries, since the Spanish made it the capital of their newly acquired dominion in 1571. Its strategic location astride the main transport routes in the large and fertile island of Luzon gave it an advantage over any potential rivals. Despite Manila's devastation during World War Two, its locational advantages and "path dependency" ensured that it would be restored as the Philippines' capital and centre of power following the ending of hostilities. Subsequently, economic policies (a long period of import-substitution industrialisation) and political realities reinforced its position of primacy.

In some ways, Manila's dominant position in the Philippines' urban hierarchy is surprising. Like Indonesia, the Philippines is an archipelago, and distance and transportation difficulties favour the growth of substantial regional cities. Nevertheless, among the six cities studied, Manila's domination of its country's urban hierarchy is second only to Bangkok's. Moreover, its share of the Philippines' total population outranks even Bangkok's share of Thailand's population.

The expansion of the Manila mega-urban region has necessarily been on a north-south axis, because of the limits to east-west growth posed by Manila Bay to the west, Laguna de Bay to the east and hilly areas to the north-east. The direction of this expansion has been assisted by transportation links, though cause and effect are difficult to separate. Manila today covers a vast area, is marked by stark contrasts in living conditions between its poor and its wealthy, and faces massive transportation problems in getting its far-flung population from their places of residence to their places of work.

Chapter 7. Ho Chi Minh City and Doi Moi Renovation

Ho Chi Minh City, formerly known as Saigon, was the capital of the French protectorate of Indochina from 1862 to 1954, and of the Republic of Vietnam until the unification of Vietnam in 1975, after which it lost its administrative functions to Hanoi. It is a relatively young city compared to Hanoi, dating back only 300 years. The elongated shape of Vietnam and its two dominant, densely population "cores", the Red River delta in the north and the Mekong Delta in the south, more or less determine that whatever administrative arrangements are put in place, Hanoi and HCMC will both be large cities vying for supremacy. Saigon's growth spurt began after the end of World War Two, when significant population displacement took place from the countryside as a result of the French-Vietminh and American wars, and the migration of one million people from the north in 1954–55. By unification in 1975, its population had reached 3.5 million. This increased very little over the following decade and a half, because of the exodus to other countries and the government-organised movement to rural areas. But over the 1990s, the transition from a command to a market economy initiated by the new economic policies of *Doi Moi* led to renewed growth, and the population reached 5.2 million in 1999, or possibly 7 million if unregistered migrants are included. The speed of this growth and its unplanned nature raised concerns about increased social inequality within the city and between the city and rural areas.

HCMC's expansion is limited by its deltaic location, with water barriers hindering growth in some directions. Its main extension is to the north, into

Binh Duong and Dong Nai provinces. This was partly the result of geography: these areas were largely outside the area of seasonal inundation. It was also partly a legacy of war: for security reasons, only one national highway into the Mekong delta was maintained and developed during the American war, and roads and bridges into Bien Hoa, site of American military bases, were expanded. However, the longer-term direction of industrial expansion is hard to predict. Southward expansion is currently occurring, but much will depend on development of transportation routes and industrial estates. Whatever the exact form of metropolitan expansion, the potential for very rapid growth in the near future is clear. Vietnam's level of urbanisation remains low, its economic growth has accelerated, and if other countries' experience after reaching an urbanisation level of 25 per cent is any guide, rapid urbanisation can now be expected. As the key locus of industrial activity in the country, the HCMC MUR stands to capture a substantial part of this urban population growth, provided that the physical barriers to expansion can be overcome and the long-term political rivalry with the north is not allowed to hinder its growth.

Chapter 8. *Taipei into a Post-industrial City*

Taipei began its urban transition earlier than the other MURs represented in this book. It completed its demographic transition and reached very low fertility levels, resulting in a total reliance on migration for its population growth. It also completed its industrial transitions ahead of the others, entering the post-industrial economy stage and thus displaying trends that are not yet prominent among the other MURs, including a shift in occupational structure from an industrial city to a post-industrial metropolis. In the 1990s Taipei was transformed into a city based on producer service and hi-technology industry (with linkages with Shin-Chu Science Park). Interestingly, Taipei has not been a target of shopping malls or global retail/franchise outlets and fast food shops. This is now changing, however, particularly with urban renewal around Taipei 101, among the world's tallest buildings, and the Hsin Yi shopping complex and financial district in the centre of the city, which has become a showcase of its global ambition.

Taiwan has moved into a service economy that is consolidating much of the economic activity in an expansive corridor from Taipei along the eastern coast to Kaohsiung. With the fast train linkage to Kaohsiung, opened in 2006, the vast majority of Taiwan's population are located along a corridor with two to three hours travel time from end to end.

A third element of the Taipei MUR is the growing presence of foreign workers and, most recently, of international marriages. One-third of all new marriages in Taiwan now have one spouse who is not a citizen of Taiwan. The future of Taipei will be as an amenity-oriented, service driven and multi-cultural city.

Chapter 9. Shanghai Opens to the World Economy

In the 1920s and 1930s Shanghai was China's window to the world in a way that Beijing could not hope to match. The economic links between China and the outside world were very much concentrated in Shanghai, seen then as China's most Westernised city. After the communist victory in China, though, Shanghai's growth was severely constrained by the government strategy of "strictly control the size of large cities", the sharp edge of which was the control of movement of people through the registration system, which restricted their access to food and housing if they moved to other areas. The one child policy was also totally successful in Shanghai, leading to the inability of its population to increase through the excess of births over deaths.

Thus Shanghai's population barely increased during the 1960s and 1970s. However, after the economic reforms of the late 1970s, Shanghai increasingly consolidated its earlier position, along with Beijing, as China's financial, technological and cultural hubs. At present, according to a recent survey by the Chinese Academy of Social Sciences, other major cities in China can only match them in the field of manufacturing. Shanghai has been targeted for major investment, symbolised by the construction of an ultra-modern, high-rise city centre in Pudong, and is increasingly seen as China's "world city". It is the undisputed centre of the more "avant garde" aspects of changing Chinese urban culture.

Chapter 10. Assessing the Trends: Livability in a Global Age

Three realms of livability are discussed in this chapter: lifeworld, personal well-being and environmental well-being in the mega-urban regions, and where possible, attention given to the situation in each zone within the MUR. Lifeworld is the most under-researched, which is unfortunate given that the decline in public, green and civic spaces has serious consequences for community life. Increased spatial separation along class lines has exacerbated this trend. On the positive side, however, personal well-being is typically better in the MURs than in other cities and in rural areas, with lower levels of poverty and better healthcare and education. At the same time, the MURs are not a very benign environment in which to be poor. As for environmental well-being, all the MURs display poor environmental quality, the degradation of environments seemingly surpassing government capacity to provide environmental infrastructure and services. Major differences can be observed in provision of environmental infrastructure and open space between slums and other low-income areas and areas housing the more affluent.

The urban cores provide a pronounced richness of lifeworlds, and higher levels of personal well-being. However, they have the lowest levels of environmental well-being. The inner zone suffers from poor lifeworlds, with fragmented and enclosed neighbourhoods and shopping malls, but rapidly improving levels of personal well-being in terms of health and educational facilities. The outer zone typically has more traditional lifeworld spaces, but changes are occurring in the directions already experienced in the inner zone. By highlighting these three realms of livability in the MURs, the study may stimulate greater public policy focus on these issues and concerted efforts for improvement.

Chapter 11. The Urban Future

The purpose of the discussion in this chapter is to draw from the commonalities and differences in these aspects to sketch plausible pathways into the future in the growth, morphology and national and global roles of these MURs. The view taken is that while each MUR seems to be encountering similar forces shaping patterns of growth and change, no city faces a pre-destined future. While major transitions of many types — demographic, economic, environmental, urban — are at play and suggest a number of transformations that are common to all cities, these do not amount to a single development path for all cities. The analysis shows that in terms of livability and economic prospects, variations are significant even among cities that are at a similar point in their urban and demographic transitions.

Three factors cut across these transitions to lead to significant variations in livability and prosperity. First, in an era of political reform towards more participatory forms of governance, among the many key defining differences guiding cities toward the future is governance. Second, changes in the global economy and how that plays out differentially among countries constitute powerful influences on the patterns and human outcomes of MUR expansion. The turbulences of the past decade — the finance crisis, collapse of the "dot. com" "new economy", and even epidemics such as SARS — are likely to continue to occur in unexpected forms and impacts on a given city.

Third, with regard to the global economy, of special importance to the cities under discussion are the changing international patterns of competition within Pacific Asia. Specifically, political reforms in China opening it to the world economy beginning in the 1980s have begun to influence changes in economic structures of other countries in the region. Many of the labour–intensive assembly and light industry propelling urbanisation in Southeast Asia in the 1970s and 1980s have been shifting to China, leaving other national economies and their cities to search for new foundations for economic growth and resilience.

Projecting the evidence of the past decade into the future is thus made with a great deal of caution. The purpose is not to predict any one future but rather to reveal the dynamics at play as they might extend into the future in variant ways. A further purpose is to link the analysis of population data with the normative questions of livability of cities (Chapter 10), including personal well-being, environmental integrity and community lifeworlds. As more shares of the population reside in the mega-urban regions over time, this purpose takes on increasing importance in national well-being.

Notes

1. Happily, it was possible to update the figures in Table 1.1 for the year 2000 for the Philippines from those presented in United Nations, 2004 to the more realistic figures resulting from the population census. United Nations (2002) was still using the old, greatly underestimated figure for Thailand in 2000 (19.8 per cent), but gave a more realistic figure in United Nations (2004). For the Philippines, however, the United Nations continued to use a projected figure for 2000 (58.6 per cent), but the actual increase in urbanisation, as shown in Table 1.1, turned out to be much less.

2. The term urban agglomeration is often contrasted with conurbation or metropolitan area composed of many nodes of different scale. Here this distinction is not being made. Rather, the intention is to measure the effective size of the respective city regions as dense clusters of activities and flows over space. The United States Bureau of Census, for example, groups areas together into a metropolitan area (MA) comprising a large population nucleus, together with adjacent communities that have a high degree of economic and social integration with that nucleus, which is defined by daily flows of commuters. A related concept is the Consolidated Metropolitan Statistical Area (CMSA), which is defined as an MA with more than one million persons composed of a cluster of counties that have very strong internal economic and social links (Source: US Census Bureau 2005).

2

The Morphology of Mega-Urban Regions Expansion

Mike Douglass and Gavin Jones

Overview

This chapter explores the geography of MURs and addresses on-going debates about the nature and form of their transformations, with particular emphasis on the 1990–2000 decade. Its major premise is that the emergence over the past four decades of the Pacific Asia MURs is best understood as part of an intensifying process of globalisation of urban economies and city life. Through these decades urban economies have become more open to global impulses while the magnitude of global flows of capital has itself expanded in quantum terms.[1] In addition, over time additional circuits of global capital have successively integrated into urban economies, first as rural commodity flows and later through direct investment in urban-industrial production followed by the appearance of global retail consumption, and, finally, the opening of domestic banking systems to global finance. By the year 2000 all of these major forms of global capital had directly linked with the MUR economies under study, making their future prospects interdependent with those of other city regions around the world.

This layering of global dynamics over MUR economies and societies has had a transformative impact on the scale, pace of expansion, and form of each MUR. From relatively small entrepot cities channelling cash crops and raw materials to the world economy, each has now joined the league of the largest urban agglomerations in the world. In the process, their urban landscapes have been radically reconstructed with modern transportation infrastructure, industrial platforms, suburban housing, shopping complexes, and other urban functions on a scale and complexity that defy any simple classification as "Third World" or "developing country" urban regions.

This observation opens discussion to debates about the distinctiveness of the MURs represented in the chapters of this volume. Are they uniquely Asian (McGee 1991)? Or are they all blending into one megalopolis form similar to the Boston-Washington or Los Angeles-San Diego complexes of cities (Webber 2000)? There are no simple answers to these questions. Not only do all MURs exist within their respective historical contexts that differentiate, for example, Shanghai from Manila; all are also differentially linked to the world economy, which is itself dynamically transforming through time. Rather than trying to stylise cities by broad world geographies — the Asian city vs. the Latin American, African or Western city, for example — the discussion that follows in this and subsequent chapters falls more into a "local-global" framework allowing the distinctiveness of each city to be revealed in light of its own history and in a globalisation context.

Similarities among MURs do, of course, exist, and identifying them is as important as distinguishing each from the others. Yet, as the decade under study shows, history is not linear, global-local outcomes are varied, and many factors are at play in the morphology of MUR expansion in Pacific Asia. Demographic variables and transitions are among the most powerful of these factors.

The Demography of MUR Growth and Expansion

The latter half of the twentieth century — the period during which the MURs of Pacific Asia grew to massive proportions — was also the period in which population growth in the region reached its highest rates, peaked and then began to slow. The demographic transition in the region — the transition from a regime of high fertility and mortality rates to a much more efficient regime of low fertility and mortality rates — ran its course in this half century, a transition that was collapsed into a much shorter space of time than was the case in the West. The overall growth of population during this period was immense. In Southeast Asia, population almost trebled from 178 million in 1950 to 522 million in 2000. In East Asia (dominated by China), the population "only" grew by 2.2 times, but absolute growth was greater because the initial population base was larger. Observers were so worried about the "population explosion" that a movement to slow population growth through family planning programmes gained great momentum in the late 1960s and in subsequent decades

(Jones and Leete 2002). Though this movement undoubtedly played an important role in slowing population growth in the region, the rapid economic development and expansion of education probably played a greater role in lowering fertility.

In the countries and regions in which the MURs studied in this book are located, the demographic transition ran its course over the last half of the twentieth century, with total fertility rates dipping below replacement level in the 1980s in Taiwan and the early 1990s in Thailand and China, and remaining only slightly above replacement level at the end of the century in Indonesia and Vietnam. Only in the Philippines was replacement fertility still a long way off, as a result of a complex of factors, including a poor record of economic development and the role of the Catholic church in impeding family planning programme efforts.

The demographic transition brings with it changes in the age structure of the population, including the "demographic bonus" of lowered dependency rates (usually measured roughly by the ratio of those aged 0–14 plus those aged 65+ to those in the working ages 15–64), and, towards the end of the half century, the beginnings of a sustained rise in the share of the elderly (aged 65+). The "demographic bonus" undoubtedly assisted these countries to achieve their rapid economic development through the 1970s, 1980s and 1990s (Mason 2001). The contrast with countries such as Pakistan or Nepal, where fertility rates remained high, was marked. However, in the rapidly ageing societies of Pacific Asia, a new pattern of increasing dependency of the non-working elderly on the labour force is now quickly increasing in magnitude.

The large cities were the front runners in the demographic transition. Their mortality rates were the lowest in their respective countries, and their fertility rates fell faster and further than elsewhere. As shown in Table 2.1, fertility rates fell to dramatically low levels in all the cities covered in this study, except Manila. Despite this, most of their populations were still capable of growing through natural increase, because their age structures were still weighted towards the reproductive ages. There were two reasons for this. The first was the delay in the smaller birth cohorts, resulting from lowered fertility, growing up to reach the reproductive ages. This is in fact another manifestation of the "demographic bonus", which resulted in a disproportionate share of their populations being in the younger working ages. The second reason was that their reproductive age populations were being replenished by migration, which tended to be concentrated in the young adult ages.

Table 2.1   Fertility Rates, Metropolitan Areas Compared with Rest of the Country, Southeast and East Asian Countries

City	Year	TFR of the Metropolitan Area	TFR of Whole Country
Jakarta	1991	2.18	3.22
	2000	1.78	2.34
Bangkok	1984–87	1.60	2.23
	1991	1.41	2.41
	2000	1.16	1.81
Manila	1993	2.76	4.09
	2000	2.80	3.50
Ho Chi Minh City	1999	1.40	2.50
Taipei	1991	1.37	1.72
	1996	1.45	1.77
	2001	1.21	1.40
Shanghai	1990	1.29	2.00
	2000	0.70	1.60

Source: **Jakarta** 1991: own children method from IDH Survey. Refers to 3 years before the survey 2000: Rele method from 2000 Census. Refers to 3 years before the Census. **Bangkok** 1984–87: Hirschman *et al.*, 1994. Estimate based on 1987 Demographic and Health Survey, 1991 Survey of Population Change. **Manila** 1993: Population and Health Survey, 2000: 2003 Demographic Survey. Refers to 1998 to early 2001 period. **Ho Chi Minh City** — personal communication from Dang Nguyen Anh. **Taipei**: Freedman *et al.*, 1994, Table 6; other data provided by Ching-Lung Tsay.

Variations in this pattern appear among the MURs. In Shanghai, faced with perhaps the lowest fertility rate of any major city in the world, the population is no longer capable of replacing itself, and in Taipei and Bangkok, a similar situation is about to be reached. Increasingly, then, the continued growth of population in the core of the mega-urban regions and in the zones surrounding them will be dependent on continuing in-migration from other parts of the country. There is still a considerable "pool" of rural population in most of the countries or areas where these cities are located, particularly in Southeast Asia since their levels of urbanisation range from little over 30 per cent in Thailand to about 50 per cent in the Philippines.[2] There is therefore still considerable potential for continuation of the urban-rural migration flow that has fuelled the growth of these cities in the past. Increasingly, however, they will need to rely on flows of migrants from other urban areas in the country or from abroad.

Rural depopulation has long been underway in the higher income economies of Pacific Asia such as Japan, Korea and Taiwan. In response to labour shortages in lower wage occupations in these countries, international migration is already becoming crucial to the viability of their MUR economies (Douglass 1999). Even at a lower per capita gross domestic product (GDP), Bangkok has also become a destination for significant numbers of workers from its neighbouring countries. In contrast, the Philippines, which currently has approximately 20 per cent of its labour force working abroad, has become increasingly dependent on remittances from its emigrant workers to sustain its national economy. Indonesia and China are also supplying millions of migrant workers to other countries, many of which are in Pacific Asia.

One other point needs to be mentioned regarding the demographic dynamics of mega-urban regions. There is often a marked gradation in fertility rates between the core of the MUR — typically the official metropolitan administrative region — and the zones surrounding it, especially the outer zone. Jakarta is perhaps the most dramatic case of this. As will be discussed in more detail in Chapter 5, the total fertility rate in the 1995–2000 period is estimated to have ranged from 1.8 in the core region of Jakarta to 2.5 in the inner zone and 3.4 in the outer zone. This is an enormous range given that all areas lie within the one mega-urban region. The high rate in the outer zone reflects the young ages at marriage and high fertility levels that have characterised the local populations of these areas (the Bantenese, Sundanese and Betawi). Though the rates for these ethnic-linguistic groups are changing with social and economic development, it is probably more the lowering of their percentage of the population in the inner and outer zones by immigration from the core and from other parts of Indonesia that has had the greater effect in lowering fertility rates in the zones, particularly the inner zone.

Other important factors include technological changes, notably the arrival of the automobile. Accompanying the expansion of the urban middle class, these and other fossil fuelled vehicles have been among the most important contributors to urban sprawl, air pollution, the economics of suburban mall development, and the push on governments to privilege them over pedestrian walkways. The automobile late-comers of Shanghai (Chapter 9) and Ho Chi Minh City (Chapter 8) are now at the early stage of this transformation, which is one reason why both are currently the most compact of the MURs under study.

Historical imprints and more localised socio-political developments contribute to the localisation of global influences on MUR morphology.

Despite their marginalisation by global functions, pre-capitalist and colonial landscapes are still prominent in such MURs as Bangkok and Ho Chi Minh City, although they have been substantially muted in Jakarta and Manila. Political reforms occurring in all the countries in question have also impacted on the role of government in guiding MUR morphology. This is particularly the case in the so-called transitional economies of China and Vietnam in which private land markets are now being allowed to begin to flourish for the first time since the advent of their socialist governments. Along with the collapse of the Soviet Union in 1989, the explicit moves to embrace the market economy in China and Vietnam in the 1980s represent a significant moment in the political economy of urban policy. The intention was no longer to create alternatives to the capitalist city but rather to create alternatives within its logic. The development of the city would no longer be directed by a state-driven command economy, but would instead be guided by the state within a market system. With neoliberal reforms to further open economies to the world system also pushing ahead in other Pacific Asian economies, by the 1990s the economic context for urban policy in all the MURs was global rather than local.

Pacific Asia MURS in a Globalising Urban System

Among the most compelling assessments of contemporary urbanisation and MUR formation are those from literature on global/world cities, which posits that global urban networks are emerging from the confines of the nation-state as the spatial system articulating the world economy (Friedmann 1986, 1996; Knox and Taylor 1995; Clark 1996; Sassen 1991).[3] Composed of cities as nodes interconnected by flows of information, goods, services and decision-making power, this network allows for an intensification of interaction around the world at a scale and pace that have no historical precedent (Castells 2000).

The construction of this emergent global urban system is localised by the necessity to engage governments and local actors in the production of the urban landscape, much of which calls for substantial investment in such public goods as roads, environmental infrastructure, and basic services needed to routinise and sustain the daily functioning of a market economy. Public intervention in the built environment of the city constitutes one of the most important distinguishing features in comparing the MURs. In some, for example, historic preservation has been given significant attention due in part to the continuity of pre-capitalist institutions, such as the constitutional monarchy and Buddhist *sangha* in Thailand that continue to maintain royal palaces and build impressive temples in Bangkok (Chapter 4). In others, the state continues to play a formidable role in planned urban modernisation, as exemplified by the construction of the Pudong area of Shanghai, a new city equivalent to the size of Shanghai itself (Chapter 9).

In bringing their own histories, political systems, cultural institutions, demographic structures and other endowments to a particular moment, cities occupy varying positions in the emerging global urban network.[4] This variability is not simply internally constructed but is also the outcome of their linkages to various global modes or circuits of capital at different historical *times*. Together, the variations in local-global interaction and the junctures at which key modes of capital have gained global reach have a telling impact on the morphology of cities, both in their size and rates of expansion as well as in their physical structuring.

As shown in Figure 2.1, from colonial times to the present four key modes have formed primary linkages with Pacific Asia MURs. They are: (1) primary commodity production and resource extraction; (2) labour-intensive export-oriented industrialisation (EOI), (3) global retail consumption, and (4) global

Figure 2.1 Globalisation and MUR Formation in Pacific Asia

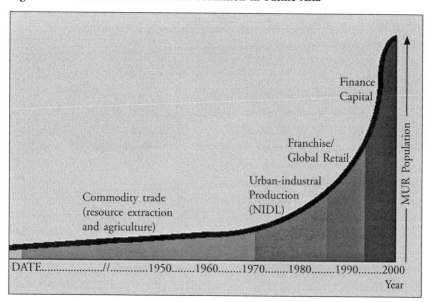

Source: The authors.

finance capital. The latter three are all associated with the accelerated urban transition experienced in Pacific Asia and the great magnitude of population increases this has brought to MURs. In terms of urban restructuring, global consumption and finance capital channelled into urban land development have been the most profound.

Primary Exports with Slow Urbanisation

In the case of Pacific Asia, as in most of the colonial world, from pre-colonial times until the 1960s global economic linkages were mostly contained within commodity trade characterised by manufactured goods produced in the North and agriculture and raw material extraction comprising the export economies of the South or the so-called Third World. The outcomes of these linkages on urbanisation and the formation of proto-MURS were widely observable. Although national urbanisation levels remained low the dominance of one city over the national urban system was almost everywhere apparent.[5] This city was typically the site of the country's major gateway port to the world economy, with many created through colonial linkages at the expense of inland and other cities that had dominated pre-colonial settlement systems. Called "primate cities", the would-be MURs of the seventeenth to mid-twentieth century in Pacific Asia were not "engines of economic growth" but were instead conduits for rural surplus extraction. Their economy and thus population size were also limited by this position in the national economy. Most remained well under 1 million in population even into the 1960s.

The New International Division of Labour

The impetus for the first round surge in population growth of the MURs was twofold. First, as discussed above, national population growth rates experienced a substantial wave of growth after World War Two, and cities began to expand rapidly on the basis of natural population increases. In the case of the MURs, however, a new era of massive rural-metropolis migration was initiated by the rapid inclusion of a select number of Pacific Asia economies into a second form of linkage with global capital described by the phrase, "new international division of labour" (NIDL) (Fröbel and Kreye 1980). The advent of the NIDL on a world scale in the late 1960s saw a deep de-industrialisation of the fordist factory system in North America and Europe parallelled by a shift of its labour-intensive assembly and manufacturing components to a small number of "newly industrialising economies" in Pacific Asia and elsewhere.

This global shift was enhanced by equally basic changes in government attitudes toward foreign investment. From positions of non-alignment and aversion to transnational capital in the early post-colonial years, by 2000 more than 150 countries had adopted policies to attract foreign direct investment (FDI), which not only include tax holidays and other subsidies to specific enterprises but also investments in economic infrastructure such as export processing zones to attract FDI. In 1970 only ten countries had signed on to these pro-TNC policies (UNCTAD 2001).

In the intensifying competition to gain segments of global capital for EOI the number of successful countries has been quite limited. Most are located in Pacific Asia (Douglass 2000), and include the first generation "newly industrialising economies" (NIEs) of Korea, Taiwan, Hong Kong and Singapore followed a decade or so later by Malaysia, Thailand, Indonesia and the Philippines. Vietnam and China began their efforts to join this group in the 1980s. Thus not only are most of the successful EOI countries in Pacific Asia, but also most Pacific Asian countries have joined the ranks of the successful EOIs. In all cases where EOI has taken root, accelerated urbanisation and spatial polarisation have become the most prominent features of the space-economy (Friedmann 2002). Concerning levels of urbanisation, in 1950 the urban population of Pacific Asia accounted for only 15 per cent of the population, totalling approximately 140 million people; in the year 2000 it was approaching 50 per cent of the population with almost one billion people — a sevenfold increase — living in urban places (UN 2001). During the same period, hundreds of thousands of migrants begin to move to the MURs, which had become the national centres for EOI.

The rise of the first generation of export-oriented industrialising "Tiger" economies of Taiwan, Hong Kong and Singapore was driven by FDI from North America and Europe. South Korea also oriented its EOI to Europe and North America, but did not rely on FDI; instead, it nationalised the banking system and channelled funds into creating the giant family run corporations (*chaebol*) that continue to command the Korean economy. The MURs in the Southeast Asian economies of Thailand, Malaysia, Indonesia and the Philippines were targets for light industry in textiles and garments, but they did not yet become centres for electronics or heavy industry (except for Malaysia in the case of electronics).

By 1980 the polarising effects of global linkages were evidence in all of the countries under review. Figure 2.2 uses estimations for MUR populations that combine populations of districts/provinces contiguous to the principal city with those of the principal city (Vining 1986; Douglass 1991). The

Figure 2.2   MUR Share of National Population by Per Capita GNP

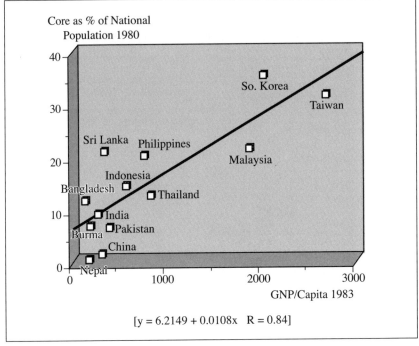

Source: Douglass (1991) using Core population (1980): Vining 1986, pp. 1–46. All other data (1980–83): World Bank, *World Development Report 1985.*

purpose of this approach is to better account for the actual size of the urban agglomeration, which had by that time typically spread beyond official municipal boundaries. It shows that as per capita income increases, so does primacy. Moreover, the countries shown to have the highest levels of primacy are those that had successfully adopted EOI strategies.

Table 2.2 uses the same data to show that in the four cases, MUR population growth rates proceeded ahead of national population growth rates, resulting in MUR shares of national population increasing in each. Shares of the total urban population also increased in each. Bangkok, which is among the most primate cities in the world, increased from ten times in 1900 to 50 times the size of the second largest city, Chiang Mai, in 1980 (Bronger 1985; Moriconi-Ehrard 1993). Table 2.3 shows that population shares severely underestimate MUR shares of other attributes of development and power.

Table 2.2 Population of Mega-Urban Regions, 1960, 1970 and 1980

Country or Territory/ MUR	Principal Mega-Urban Region					National Growth Rate		Population Share of MUR in Nation (%)		
	Population			Growth Rate (%)						
	1960	1970	1980	1960–70	1970–80	1960–70	1970–80	1960	1970	1980
Indonesia/Jakarta	6.7	9.2	13.0	3.2	4.9	2.1	2.3	10.6	12.1	14.3
Philippines/Manila	4.1	6.4	9.6	4.5	4.1	2.9	2.7	15.3	17.6	20.1
Taiwan/Taipei	2.2	3.7	5.7	5.3	4.3	2.1	1.9	20.6	25.4	31.7
Thailand/Bangkok	2.6	3.7	5.5	3.7	4.2	2.9	2.3	9.8	10.7	12.5

Notes: *Java only. Years 1960, 1970, 1980 for all countries except the following: Indonesia in 1961, 1971, 1981; West Malaysia in 1957, 1970, 1980.

Source: Core populations: Vining 1986; population growth rates: World Bank 1985; for Taiwan: Asian Development Bank 1986; Indonesia/Jakarta growth rate 1970–80: BPS 1980.

In the mid-1980s, FDI in electronics and other labour-intensive manufacturing began flooding into the Southeast Asian economies of Malaysia, Thailand, Indonesia and, to a lesser extent, the Philippines from new sources — Japan and the first generation NIEs. The impetus for the surge in export-oriented manufacturing in the economies occurred with "endaka", the sudden doubling of the value of the Japanese yen *vis-à-vis* the U.S. dollar in 1985, which undermined the viability of exports of labour-intensive products from Japan. With currencies also revaluating in Korea, Taiwan and Hong Kong, corporations in these countries joined with Japan's transnationalising companies to begin a sustained offshore redeployment of low-wage production into Southeast Asia.

By the late 1980s, the "transition economies" of China and Vietnam were also providing export-processing zones in coastal cities in explicit policy attempts to join this process.[6] Within all the countries and territories that were able to shift from agrarian to urban-industrial based economies, the sites for the rise of export-oriented manufacturing economies turned out to be exceptionally limited to one or a few rapidly growing mega-urban regions.

Table 2.3   Concentration of Population and Activities in Selected Cities of Asia

Indicator	Bangkok 1980	Manila 1980	Seoul 1980	Shanghai 1981
Population (mn.)	5.2	5.9	8.4	6.1
Ratio to 2nd City	49:1	10:1	3:1	1.1:1
Ratio to 3rd City	59:1	12:1	5:1	1.2:1
Share of nation (%)				
Energy consumed	62	60	n.a.	n.a.
Mfg. employment	70	73	25	5
Value mfg. production	>70	70	22	11
Private bank investments	>70	n.a.	64	n.a.
National bank hq's	100	100	100	n.a.
GDP	27	32	31	7
Motor vehicles	47	47	41	n.a.
Telephone connections	74	75	42	5
Universities	54	34	44	n.a.
University students	92	62	46	7
Doctors	67	n.a.	50	3
Hospital beds	n.a.	41	50	2
GDP/cap: rest of nation	3:1	3:1	2:1	6:1

Source: Dirk Bronger 1985.

Statistics for that time indicate that the MURs had come to account for half or more of the national GDP (World Bank 1996).

Global Consumerism and Finance Capital

From the 1980s to the economic crisis of 1997 all of the MURs witnessed a heroic leap in urban restructuring that was based on the confluence of two new forms of globalisation: global retail consumption and finance capital. By the mid-1980s the urban transition in Pacific Asia — even in the second generation Southeast Asian EOI economies — had created a broad urban middle class of sufficient size and wealth to begin to attract what can be called a circuit of consumer franchise and retail capital that began to saturate cities in Pacific Asia in a surprisingly short space of time. From almost no presence in the 1970s, the magnitude of global franchises is now vast, ranging from ubiquitous fast food restaurants such as MacDonald's, KFC and Burger King to upscale Starbucks coffee shops, Euro-design clothing stores, "big

Figure 2.3   Shopping Malls and Superblocks in Jakarta, 2001

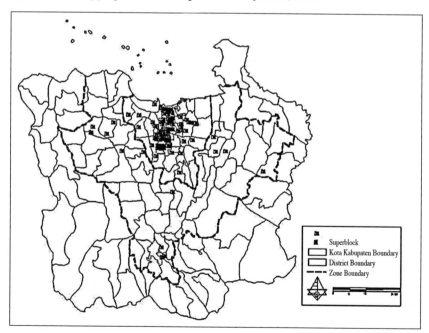

Source: M. Douglass.

box" outlets, hotel chains, car rental companies, internet providers, and even Disneyland and Universal Studio theme parks. The growth in the number of malls alone has been extraordinary. In the case of Jakarta, for example, in 1970 there was not a single mall in the city. As shown in Figure 2.3, by the year 2001, more than 70 malls and an additional 20 superblock shopping and business complexes had been completed in the Jakarta MUR mostly since 1980.

In addition to a growing number of potential urban (mostly MUR) customers for global consumption, the reconstruction of MURs from the mid-1980s also received tremendous impetus from two other events. One was the spread of Japan's bubble economy to Pacific Asia following *endaka*, which created large speculative investments in urban land development. The second, equally momentous contributor was the opening of Pacific Asia banking systems to global finance, especially short-term bank deposits. With land speculation reverberating off skyrocketing stock prices, and exchange rates unofficially maintained at *status quo* by Asian governments, billions of dollars of short-term investment flowed into the region in just a few years. This was made possible by banking reforms pushed by Western countries to open Pacific Asia to finance capital.[7] Instead of being channelled into industrial growth, the bulk of the sudden influx of capital went to urban development projects (Bello 1997:1).

The outcome of these events was an unprecedented MUR land development boom (Douglass 2001). Much of the activity was directed at

Figure 2.4   Bangkok "Manhattan Skyline" Rises in the Core

Source: M. Douglass.

the urban core in an effort to transform older low-rise structures into world city hubs. In Bangkok, for example, between 1990 and 1997 at least 65 buildings higher than 30 stories were completed — an average of almost ten per year (Siam Future Development 2002) (Figure 2.4). Equal numbers were being constructed in other MURs. Suburban housing also enjoyed explosive expansion. Again, in the Bangkok MUR from 1993 to 1997 an average of 150,000 new housing units were being constructed per year (Sopon 2002).

At the end of 1997, the bubble burst with catastrophic results. Some 350,000 housing units were unoccupied in the Bangkok MUR (Sopon 2002), and as late as 2001 at least 230 tall buildings remained uncompleted in the metropolis (Herron 2001).[8] Among the greatest fiascos was Muang Tong Tani (MTT), a planned new city 40 kilometres from the heart of Bangkok that was intended to house and provide work for at least 1 million people. "Bigger than Ghent, Salzburg or Cork", it was the largest ever construction contract in the Global South (Kristof and Sanger 1999:1). With the crisis the project came to a halt (Figure 2.5) with almost no occupants for the buildings and housing units built at the cost of $1 billion (*New York Times* 1999). All the other MURs also found themselves with some of the world's tallest buildings juxtaposed to slums and uncompleted buildings in great number (Figure 2.6). Yet the decade of the 1990s as a whole will also be known as one of the most prodigious periods in the production of urban space in the region.

Figure 2.5   Muang Thong Thani Ghost Town Rises in the Distance in Inner Zone of the Bangkok MUR

Source: M. Douglass.

From Industrial Platforms to World Cities

In the following chapters, analysis of change in the MURs is largely based on the 1990 and 2000 census in each country. As discussed above, the 1990–2000 decade represents one of great extremes of boom, bust and possible recovery; assessing this decade using just two points in time can lead to tendencies to assume straight line pathways. Moreover, the 1997 crisis has been followed by a series of further crisis coming from unexpected sources: the crash of the "new" dot.com economy in 2000, the 9/11 terrorist attack on the United States in 2001, the Bali bombings in 2002, the SARS epidemic and U.S. attack on Iraq in 2003 all had serious dampening effects on Pacific Asia economy.

One of the most important turning points in the morphology of the MURs came as an outcome of the 1997 crisis. This was initiated through fundamental neoliberal reforms required by the International Monetary Fund as a condition for receiving billions of dollars of bailout loans. In addition to privatising a host of public services and institutions, including famous national universities, tariff and non-tariff barriers to trade and foreign investment were eliminated or weakened as a means to promote economic growth through international economic competition. The result of this sea change in public policy has been a heightening of intercity competition for global investment (Douglass 2002). This has led to yet another round of what can be called intentional world city formation, which entails government support of urban mega-projects as symbolic as well as functional elements of MUR landscapes intended to promote to the highest ranks of an emergent global urban hierarchy.

The list of urban mega-projects seeking to transform MURs into world cities is impressive. Taipei has just completed the world's tallest building called Taipei 101 for the number of storeys it has. Ho Chi Minh City is developing Saigon South on 3,300 rural acres of land that is intended to create a completely new city for 140,000 people complete with a large export processing zone just four kilometres from the centre of the MUR.

The Thai Government has at least six major urban development projects aimed at transforming the core into a global service and management centre. Figure 2.6 shows the Rama III Global Finance and Commercial Centre proposed for the inner city. Likewise, Figure 2.7 is a proposal for a huge transportation centre in Pahon Yothin, the old railroad terminal of northern Bangkok. Both proposals reveal heroic urban architecture with little reference to the city's culture or history and on a scale that dwarfs daily human activity.

Figure 2.6   Proposed Global Finance and Commercial Centre, Rama III, Bangkok Core

Source: Department of City Planning, Bangkok Metropolitan Administration, 2002.

Figure 2.7   Bangkok Metropolitan Transport Hub, Pahon Yothin, 2003

Source: State Railway of Thailand, 2002.

Shanghai is among the most ambitious of all the MURs in terms of global mega-projects. It is now constructing the next world's tallest building, and has inaugurated a magnetic levitation rail service connecting the city to its new international airport. The most spectacular addition to the city is Pudong, a massive city and export processing zone covering an area of 522 square kilometres, or more than the size of city of Shanghai itself (Figure 2.8). It is expected to house over 650,000 residents.

Conclusions

As described in Chapter 1, for the purposes of better comparatively assessing the changing morphology of the MURs, each is divided into core, inner and outer zones. Looking at the past several decades of change within and among these zones shows discernable commonalities as well as contrasting experiences among the Bangkok, HCMC, Jakarta, Manila, Shanghai and Taipei MURs. The patterns can be summarised by the following points:

    a. While Taipei has passed through the EOI phase of morphological change focusing on inner zone export processing zones, airports and marine ports connected by trunk roads, Bangkok, Manila and Jakarta remain in the heart of this process. Shanghai and HCMC have only just begun it. For Taipei, much of the inner zone is now subject to conversion to amenity-oriented weekend activities, and with the opening of the high-speed rail line linking it to Kaohsiung in only a few hours, it is on the cusp of experiencing the most extensive expansion of a MUR among the six MURs studied.

    b. The most thorough morphological transformation of most MURs came in the mid-1980s to 1997 period when global retail combined with global finance to remake core zones of the MUR, vastly expand suburban housing, and in-fill existing transportation corridors with shopping centres, commercial buildings, condominiums, and service functions.

    c. HCMC and Shanghai are the most compact of the MURs. Most of their urban expansion is still contained within the core and inner zones of the cities. Yet they are also the most likely to experience rapid expansion in the near future. Both have positioned themselves for accelerated EOI-led growth through massive public investments in export processing zones and infrastructure. Shanghai's Pudong is one of the largest export processing zones in the world. More than half of all foreign direct investment in Vietnam is accruing to the HCMC MUR.

d. Demographic factors are having a dampening effect on the expansion of MURs. While globalisation continues to centre national development on the MURs, which continue to accrue larger shares of the national population, demographic transitions that are leading to slower overall population growth mean that overall MUR (and urban) growth rates are slowing down as well.

e. As the demographic transition proceeds, migration will once again become the source of MUR growth, particularly in urban core zones, most of which are now at or below replacement fertility. Manila, in a country that continues to have relatively high population growth, is the principal exception to this pattern.

f. The future of most MURs will be one of slower population growth, but technological advances in transportation, particularly high-speed rail systems and expressway development, are likely to see the incorporation into their daily urban field of areas now lying far outside them.

Asking what form the MURs will take in the coming decades returns the discussion to the question of whether they are somehow distinct from experiences in other parts of the world. The U.S., with its automobile dependent cities and hollowed out core zones, is often portrayed as the most relevant pattern of expansion for the equally automobile dependent MURs of Pacific Asia. If this is the case, then the future of Pacific Asia MURs will see a shift from monocentric extended metropolitan configurations to multi-centred urban regions with decentred spatial flows. In such a "post-metropolis" (Soja 2000) setting, exopolis interaction among "edge cities" (Knox 1993) is likely to be as great or even greater than interaction with the old metropolitan core. Outer zones that in the Pacific Asia MURs are still quite rural in character will become urban fields without visible distinctions between what is rural and what is urban.

Some MURs, such as Jakarta, show a discernable multi-centre pattern of expansion and daily flows. This is in part due to the successes of urban development policies seeking to anchor inner zone development around the growth poles of Tangerang, Bekasi, Depok and Bogor. Others, such as Shanghai, HCMC and even Manila continue to be monocentrically expanding. The exopolis pattern of decentred growth is yet to emerge in the MURs, which might seem improbable given their huge sizes that are in

Figure 2.8   Pudong, Shanghai

Source: Wikipedia, 2007. "Image: Shanghai_Pudong_Skyline.jpg" <http://en.wikipedia. org/wiki/Image: Shanghai_Pudong_Skyline.jpg> [4 Dec. 2007].

Figure 2.9   Satellite View of the Built-up Area of the Bangkok MUR c. 2000

Source: NASA for satellite photo. Bangkok 1890 added by authors.

some cases double the population of the southern California conurbations surrounding Los Angeles. In contrast to Los Angeles, the metropolitan region of Tokyo, which now has a population of over 30 million, has remained monocentric largely due to the vast complex of commuter trains and subways capable of bringing millions of people into the core zone on a daily basis.

While the future pattern of the MURs is not certain, a few outcomes appear to be more likely than others. One is that half or more of residential population increases in the future will be in the further reaches of the inner zone and into the outer zone (Webster and Muller 2002). The morphology of all the MURs will continue to show core areas turned into office and commercial uses that displace residential populations, with transport corridors extending ever further afield to bring suburban and peri-urban commuters to work in them every day. Because existing administrative arrangements result in the most rapidly growing areas lying outside of official municipal boundaries, this eventuality is largely unanticipated in public planning.

More peripheral areas are instead left to a chaotic process of private land development initiatives that are readily seen today in the form of factories and expensive housing estates appearing as enclaves in agricultural areas that otherwise have little or no provision of basic urban and environmental infrastructure such as sewerage, drainage, water treatment, feeder roads, or public services such as health centres and secondary schools. Given that much, if not most, of the population increases in the MURs in the future will be in the outer zone, one of the contributions of the following chapters is to point toward the need to better anticipate this eventuality through the provision of serviced land for housing, public spaces and amenities, and finer, local networks of roads and streets to help put in place a physical template for private sector development.

Figure 2.9 shows the transformation in scale of Bangkok over a little more than a century from a walled royal city of about 500,000 people at Rattanakosin to a mega-urban region of over ten million people. The satellite photograph shows the core to be intensively filled in, but as development moves into the inner and outer zones, its expansion takes on the form of corridors and radial trajectories along major trunk roads. As Bangkok continues to grow in population and urban functions, these radials will be in-filled with housing, shopping centres, and perhaps satellite cities. Although the demographic transition will inevitably slow Bangkok's rate of growth, leaving its population expansion increasingly dependent on domestic and international migration, global linkages are nonetheless likely to continue to focus on this MUR as the most dynamic engine of economic growth. The other MURs discussed in the following chapters show variations of this pattern and expectation. For all the MURs, interpreting the implications of this phenomenal urban process as it contextuates the daily life experiences of MUR residents will be a leading issue in public policy in Pacific Asia's first urban century.

Notes

1. By the 1990s two-thirds of world trade was within transnational corporate networks rather than among national economies. From 1970 to 1997 the net flow of foreign direct investment into developing countries increased from under $5 billion to $150 billion (UNCTAD 1999).
2. In Taiwan, the percentage urban is higher — 77 per cent.
3. This new spatial layering does not, of course, mean the demise of the nation-state. As noted by Sassen (1998) and many others (Harvey 2002), just as the nation-state is losing many of its power of global flows of capital and information, it is strengthening its power in other aspects, notably in the realm of policing of citizenry.
4. As summarised by Webber (2000:280), "All metropolises are global ... all are connected with all others in real time ... they are all interlinked parts of an integrated international urban system.... Despite their geographic separation, Bangkok's economy is a subset of the world economy in which San Diego, São Paulo, Tokyo, the Randstad and the rest are also subsets".
5. Vietnam was an exception, with two city nodes — Hanoi and Saigon, resulting from the extremely elongated shape of the country, and the location of the fertile deltas of the Red River and of the Mekong in the extreme north and south of the country, respectively.
6. At the same time, it should be noted that many other countries, such as Burma, Laos, Cambodia, Brunei, did not follow this path.
7. By 1996 of the total debt in corporate financing in Thailand 30 per cent was through short-term loans. The estimated total short-term debt among firms in mid-1997 was $46 billion, which greatly exceeded the country's $31 billion in international reserves (Asia Development Bank 1998).
8. The resulting economic collapse was registered in 1998 with the Thai economy shrinking by 8 per cent. In terms of investment in land development projects, assets worth 100 dollars in June 1997 were worth 25 dollars by Sept. 1998 (Sachs 1999).

3

Comparative Dynamics of the Six Mega-Urban Regions

Gavin Jones

As mentioned in Chapter 1, the key objective of the comparative studies of the six MURs covered in this book was to study their growth dynamics over the 1990–2000 period, using a zonal approach. This chapter presents basic comparative findings of the mega-urban region studies, after summarising the methods used to delineate the zones. In each case, the foundation for the study was the utilisation of special tabulations from the 1990 and 2000 rounds of population censuses, produced for these zones. Even with access to this rich and detailed set of data, it was not possible to generate fully comparable data for the six cities, because of differences in definitions of variables between the cities, differences in definitions between the two censuses for the same city, and deficiencies in the quality of the data. Nevertheless, access to the data for the six cities has provided us with unique opportunities for comparative study, which we have attempted to utilise to the fullest extent possible.

Delineation of the Zones

The basic contribution of the study is in analysing the dynamics of change in population, migration and employment between zones in the MUR, and relating these to the broader forces acting on MUR change. Basic to the study, then, was the delineation of zones according to criteria with some analytical meaning. Based on experience with earlier studies of some of the same cities (Jones, Tsay and Bajracharya 2000; Mamas, Jones and Sastrasuanda 2001),

41

it was known that such delineation of zones needs to be based as closely
as possible on application of certain criteria, but that the practicalities of
applying the delineation meant that the task required art as much as science.
The method of delineating the zones could not be fully standardised between
MURs, because of the availability of useful data for some MURs that was
unavailable for others.

Basically, the method used was to define the zones using census data
on population density and non-agricultural employment in contiguous
administrative areas in and around the metropolitan core. The aim was to
adhere as closely as possible to the following criteria:

Core:
Population density should exceed 5,000 per square kilometre

Inner zone:
Population density should exceed 1,000 per square kilometre.[1]
Percentage of employment in agriculture should be less than ten per cent

Outer zone:
In most cases, the outer zone represents the remainder of the administratively defined regions surrounding the core and the inner zone; for
example, for Shanghai, the remaining parts of Shanghai Municipality;
for Jakarta, the remainder of the Jabodetabek area (which, in addition to
the Jakarta special region, comprises the kabupaten of Bogor, Tangerang
and Bekasi and the cities of Bogor, Tangerang, Bekasi and Depok);
for Manila, the remainder of the provinces of Rizal, Laguna, Cavite,
Batangas, Pampanga and Bulacan. In the cases of Bangkok, Taipei and
HCMC, the boundaries of the outer zone were defined at the district
level. The aim was normally to exclude areas with more than 40 per
cent of employment in agriculture. But this could be overridden in some
cases, in order to adhere to administrative boundaries that would provide
ease of access to other data useful in assessing urban trends.

In the case of Jakarta, the availability of data giving an "urban score" for
every village provided the basis for mapping patterns of villages according to
"degree of urbanity" to assist in drawing the border between the inner and
outer zones (see Mamas, Jones and Sastrasuanda 2001). This classification
used the following three indicators:

1. demographic (population density)
2. economic (percentage of agricultural households)

3. urban facilities (whether a village has schools, health facilities, a market, a bank, asphalt roads, electricity and other facilities)

Each indicator is scored from one to ten. If the sum of these scores exceeds 20, the village is considered urban, if below 18 rural; if the sum is 18, 19 or 20, the classification is decided after further analysis. In general, the villages included in Jakarta's inner zone were those with urban characteristics; but of course a series of contiguous villages had to be included in the zone, so in many cases rural villages were included because they lay between clusters of urban villages that needed to be included in the zone. The average urban scores for villages included in Jakarta's zones were: core — 27.3; inner zone — 22.0; outer zone — 14.1. This indicates that Jakarta's inner zone was indeed predominantly urban.

For the other cities, the methods used attempted to maintain as great a degree of comparability as possible between the zones for the different MURs. As will be seen below, though there are certain anomalies, the comparison of data from the core, the inner zone and the outer zone for the different MURs is a generally meaningful exercise.

In a number of the studies, it was found useful to further divide the zones into sub-zones for a number of analytical purposes: for example, to determine the range of rates of population decline and increase in districts within the core; and to see whether patterns of in-migration differed between different parts of the inner zone.

Data and Definitional Problems

Despite the project's access to the complete census data for all the cities included, there were formidable problems in using this information for comparative analysis. Some of these relate to data quality and completeness, others to lack of comparable series, due to changes in definitions or in the questions asked in the census.

Data Quality and Completeness

Examples of the first set of problems — data quality and completeness — include under-enumeration in the census, which is suspected to have been substantial in most of the cities included in the study. If the undercount was of roughly the same order of magnitude in 1990 and 2000, then although it would understate the true population for both years, it would not adversely affect estimates of change. But there is reason to believe, in the case of Jakarta at least, that the undercount was worse in 2000 than in 1990. Although the evidence for this is not totally clear, both the cuts in budget for the 2000 Census, the addition of extra questions requested by the Jakarta municipality, which increased the workload of poorly paid interviewers, and the recording of population declines in areas such as South Jakarta, where population increase might have been expected, all point to the likelihood of substantial undercount.

The chronic undercount of population for these cities is not just a matter of residents being missed by census enumerators, but it also relates to the procedures for deciding on where a person temporarily residing in a particular locality should be recorded. For example, if somebody from Central Java has been living in a Jakarta household for less than six months, the census enumerator is supposed to ask whether that person intends to return to the usual place of residence, and if the answer is yes, they are supposed to be enumerated at the usual place of residence, not in Jakarta.[2] Similar modified *de jure* procedures are supposed to be followed by census takers in Thailand and the Philippines. In all such cases, the substantial movement to the city on a seasonal or temporary basis results in the recorded population being less than the *de facto* population of the city at the time of the census.[3]

As discussed later in the book, there may have been as many as two million persons not included in the HCMC 1999 census count, because those without permanent registration and residential permits are not included in the HCMC population. Similarly, there are problems with the large "floating population" in Shanghai.

For HCMC, unfortunately data on characteristics of the population by communes, though they were collected in 1989, are no longer available for analysis, so it was not possible to analyse the dynamics of change by zones over time, but only the differentials by zones in 1999. Even the analysis of population change in the zones over time is affected by this problem; the population figures for the zones in 1989 are subject to a degree of uncertainty, because the zones cut across administrative boundaries, and although this is not a problem for the 1999 data because access was possible to the detailed data, some "guesswork" was involved in calculating the basic population data for some areas in 1989.

For Shanghai, another issue of data completeness arose. Because access to data has to be arranged at the province level, it was only possible to have access to data for the Shanghai municipality itself (which has the standing of a province in the Chinese administrative hierarchy). This did not prove to be a major problem, because the Shanghai municipality is very extensive, and includes almost all areas that might lay claim to being part of the zones surrounding Shanghai. However, it is possible that access to appropriate data from the adjoining Jiangsu province would have indicated that a population of a million or two from that province could appropriately have been added to Shanghai's outer zone, and possibly a relatively small number would have been added to the inner zone, which abuts the Jiangsu border for a short distance in two areas.

Another problem for the analysis is large numbers classified as "unstated" in answer to various census questions. This is a particular problem in the Philippines census, and unfortunately introduces a large element of uncertainty into comparisons of the educational qualifications of migrants compared to non-migrants in Manila. In 2000, educational attainment is not stated for 30 per cent of migrants in Manila's core, and for 20 per cent in the inner zone. Data on usual occupation, kind of business and place of work suffered from only moderate levels of missing data in 1990, but 24 to 26 per cent in 2000. Happily, the unstated category is less of a problem for the other cities, though it is quite high for employment by industry in Jakarta in 2000 (see the notes to Table 11.11 in Chapter 11).

Limited Data on Employment

Analysis for almost all the cities was adversely affected by a decision to collect less labour force data in the 2000 than in the 1990 population census, or changes in questions asked about employment between the two censuses, or changes in definitions of occupation. In Taipei, the 2000 census did not ask anything about the occupation, industry or employment status of employed persons, and in Jakarta occupation was not asked, the argument in both cases being that such information could be obtained from the labour force survey in more detail than the census was able to provide. While this is true, the problem is that the labour force survey data is not available for the smaller geographic areas, and is therefore not available for the kind of analysis by zones that is undertaken in the present study.

For Bangkok, occupational definitions changed between the 1990 and 2000 censuses, although fortunately the industrial classification did not. For Manila, whereas changes in definitions had prevented analysis of occupational change between 1980 and 1990 (see Jones, Tsay and Bajracharya 2000), between 1990 and 2000 this was not a problem, as definitions used in 1990 remained unchanged.

Difficulties in Studying Migration

A major emphasis of this study is on measuring the flows of migration to and between the zones of the MURs, assessing their importance in the overall process of population change and studying the characteristics of migrants as compared to non-migrants. Through such measurement and analysis, the role of migration in altering the human resources of cities and regions and in meeting the changing labour needs of their economy can be assessed.

However, data issues again emerged in relation to the measurement of migration flows. The problem is on two levels. First, there is the underlying problem, already mentioned, that because of the definitions employed in the census, many short-term migrants are not counted as living in the cities or MURs at all. A further problem, however, was that in the cases of Bangkok, Shanghai and Taipei, it is not possible to measure migration flows between the zones precisely, because place of residence five years previously is only available at the city/prefecture level (Taipei), the provincial level (1990) or the county level (2000) for Shanghai, or the province (*changwat*) level (Bangkok). As the boundaries of the zones cut across these administrative boundaries, it is not possible to know precisely how many people moved across the boundaries of the zones we have identified. In the case of Bangkok, it was considered appropriate to apply ratios of the populations of sections of *changwats* included in the different zones to get a rough allocation of migrants.

We have been frank in highlighting the data problems faced in the analysis for the six MURs included in this study. These data problems are indeed serious, and limit the amount of comparative analysis that is possible between the six MURs, or over time for any given MUR. At the same time, the reader should not conclude that the study is fatally flawed by these problems. A great deal of useful analysis is still possible, and access to the detailed data for the six MURs provided a unique opportunity to conduct analysis never before possible.

Comparative Findings

Historical Growth of the Six Cities

The backdrop to the history of these six cities over the past century has been the massive population growth in the countries in which they are situated. For example, over the twentieth century, Indonesian population grew from 40.1 million to 205 million over the century, a fivefold increase, Thailand from about 6 million to 62.8 million, a tenfold increase, and the Philippines from 7.6 million (1903) to 75.6 million, also a tenfold increase. On these grounds alone, one would expect the major city to have grown very rapidly, and that is indeed what happened.

It is not, however, a simple story of the growth of the metropolis mirroring the growth of the country's population. Rather, there were factors making for an increasing concentration of economic activity, and hence of population, in these cities, resulting in their growth multiple exceeding by far the national population growth multiple. Thus Manila's population grew 52-fold over the century (using Metro Manila for the 2000 population; or 85-fold if the inner zone population is added), well above the tenfold increase for the Philippines population, and Jakarta grew 48-fold (using the DKI population for 2000; or 103-fold if the inner zone is added), again well above the fivefold increase in the Indonesian population.[4] There were also historical factors leading to spurts of growth in particular periods, and in general, to particularly rapid growth over the period from the 1960s onwards in the case of the four non-Communist cities.

Graphs of population growth of the six cities are presented in Figure 3.1. Except in the case of Shanghai, it was not until the period following World War Two that the explosive growth of these cities took place. Only in Shanghai did the population exceed one million at any time before World War Two. Shanghai was out on its own, with a population approaching four million in the 1930s. Following World War Two, the growth paths of these cities resembled each other in some ways, but their periods of most rapid growth differed, as a result of historical circumstances (for example, the fight for independence in the cases of Jakarta and HCMC) and differing economic strategies adopted by their governments, particularly in the cases of Shanghai and HCMC. Shanghai stagnated through the 1960s and 1970s, when the Chinese government policy was to "strictly control the growth of large cities", but a new era of rapid development began with the reform policies of the late 1970s.[5] By the 1990s, remarkable growth was occurring, and Shanghai, to add to its credentials as China's premier manufacturing centre, was rivalling Hong Kong as the key commercial centre of the region.

Bangkok, Manila and Jakarta were all growing rapidly over the 1960s, 1970s and 1980s, a growth fuelled by rapid economic development in the countries of which they were the primate cities (in the cases of Thailand and Indonesia; less so in the Philippines), rapid population growth nationally and economic development strategies fostering (in effect if not in design) concentration of key economic activities in the metropolis. In Figure 3.1, it is difficult to trace the precise path of population growth for these metropolises,

Figure 3.1 Population Growth in the MURs since 1865

Population (millions)

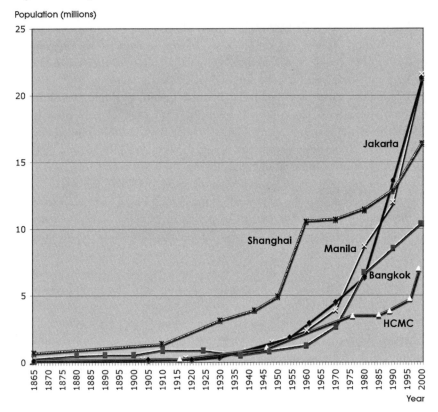

Source: Prepared by the author from a range of data on historical populations of these cities, and from 1990 and 2000 ceasus data for the MURs.

because of the gradual spill-over of population into areas outside the official metropolitan area. To include these areas in early years would be unrealistic, as they were still mainly rural at that time. But to suddenly include them at some point in time results in an unrealistic jump in population at that point.

In HCMC, the impact of the American war was to swell the population with refugees and others up to 1975. After unification, deliberate policies to prevent large cities from growing, and stagnant economic conditions, led to a decade without growth, followed by a resumption of growth with the *Doi Moi* policies from 1986, and the market-oriented reform in 1989, which accelerated growth through the 1990s. In both Shanghai and HCMC, then, severe ideologically-based restrictions inhibited growth until the 1980s (Shanghai) and the 1990s (HCMC), with the result that these cities had a good deal of "catching up" to do. This helps explain their very rapid economic growth in recent times.

Growth of the MURs over the 1990s

Table 3.1 gives the basic information on area, size and population growth rates for the MURs included in the study. As can be seen, the populations of the cores in 2000 ranged from 2.6 million in Taipei and 3.2 million in HCMC to only slightly under ten million in Manila and Shanghai. These figures can be seen as a "minimal" estimate of the metropolitan population of each of the cities. At the other end of the scale, a "maximal" estimate would be the figures including the inner and outer zones; these figures range from five million in HCMC to over 20 million in both Manila and Jakarta. But since the outer zone includes areas that are still truly rural, the figure that reflects more accurately the extent of the urbanised area of the cities and their surrounds is the figure for the core plus the inner zone. This ranges as follows (in '000):

Ho Chi Minh City 4,281 (but subject to a large undercount, as already noted)
Taipei 7,547
Bangkok 8,256
Shanghai 13,226
Manila 16,245
Jakarta 17,782

Figure 3.2 shows the areas included in the core and the inner and outer zones for each of the six cities included in the study. It uses the same scale for each MUR. In most cases, most of the inner zone lies within 30 kilometres of the centre of the city, and most of the outer zone lies within 50 kilometres of the city centre. However, there are considerable extensions of the inner zones beyond a 30-kilometre radius, in particular along key transportation routes, as evident in the cases of Jakarta and, even more clearly, Manila. In Jakarta, the development of these transportation routes reflects the existence of subsidiary urban nodes in Tangerang, Bogor and Bekasi, which in turn have grown rapidly once linked to Jakarta by expressways. In Manila, the development of the north and south superhighways reflected both the direction for the most efficient expansion of the city, as well as providing needed linkages with other parts of Luzon.

Figure 3.2 Zones of the Six MURs

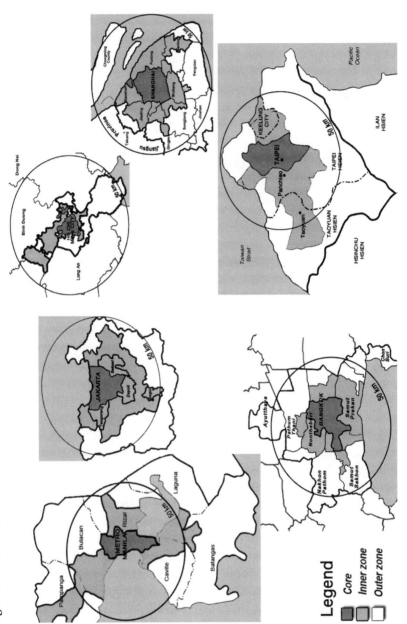

Legend

Core

Inner zone

Outer zone

Source: The author.

Actually, the total area of Manila's MUR is considerably larger than that of any of the other MURs, mainly because of the very large area included in its outer zone, as the result of choosing to delimit this zone according to provincial boundaries. This highlights the fact that the figures presented above for the core plus the inner zone are the most appropriate for reflecting the population of the heavily built-up area of the megacity.[6]

The areas of the cores are comparable, except for HCMC and Taipei, in both of which the core is considerably smaller. This appears to reflect reality, as these are by far the smallest of the six cities. Their inner zones are also, in reality, smaller than those of any of the other MURs.

In both the core and the inner zone, population density is lowest in Bangkok. One possible interpretation of this is that the boundaries for both core and inner zone in Bangkok were set somewhat wider than they might ideally have been for comparison with these zones for the other cities. However, the fact is that almost irrespective of where the zones were set, Bangkok's population density would have showed up as lower than densities in the other cities. Bangkok and its MUR is simply not as densely populated as the other cities in the study. The second lowest density in the core is found in Taipei, but the Taipei figures need to be interpreted carefully. Alone among the cities included in this study, Taipei's core contains steep, forested land with very low population density. This means that the real population density in the settled parts of the core is much higher than the average figure for the core shown in Table 3.1.

The core in HCMC was the most densely populated of all, suggesting that for comparison with the other cities, it might have been better to include some additional areas in the core. However, the inner zone of HCMC, which again is the smallest in area of any of the MURs studied, is not especially densely populated compared with the other MURs. Again, then, this reflects the fact that HCMC is not as large a city as the others included in the study, although the evidence that a very substantial population was missed by the census in HCMC complicates this assessment.

The final column of Table 3.1 shows growth rates for the zones of the six cities and for the MUR as a whole. The typical pattern is for the growth rate in the inner zone to exceed by a considerable margin the growth rates in the core or the outer zone. This pattern is found in Jakarta, Bangkok, Manila and Shanghai. However, patterns in HCMC and Taipei are different. In HCMC, the growth rate in the core is by far the most rapid, and in Taipei, the growth rate in the outer zone is the most rapid.

Table 3.1 Basic Data on the Asian Mega-Urban Regions, 1990 and 2000

	Area (km²)	Population		Density (per km²)		Annual Population Growth Rate (1990–2000)
		1990	2000	1990	2000	
JAKARTA						
Core	662	8,223	8,347	12,421	12,610	0.2
Inner zone	2,374	5,434	9,435	2,289	3,975	5.7
Outer zone	3,139	3,442	3,407	1,097	1,085	−0.1
Total	6,175	17,098	21,190	2,769	3,432	2.1
Indonesia						1.5
BANGKOK						
Core	876	5,445	5,876	6,215	6,709	0.8
Inner zone	1,907	1,596	2,380	837	1,248	4.1
Outer zone	4,465	1,593	2,163	348	472	3.1
Total	7,248	8,634	10,419	1,172	1,414	1.9
Thailand						1.4
MANILA						
Core	633	7,907	9,880	12,551	15,642	2.3
Inner zone	3,105	4,183	6,365	1,345	2,047	4.3
Outer zone	8,323	3,819	5,368	461	648	3.5
Total	12,061	15,909	21,613	1,324	1,641	3.1
Philippines						2.1
HO CHI MINH						
Core	170	2,320	3,203	13,647	18,841	3.8
Inner zone	617	904	1,078	1,465	1,747	1.9
Outer zone	1,308	700	756	535	578	0.8
Total	2,095	3,924	5,037	1,873	2,404	2.8
Vietnam						1.7
SHANGHAI						
Core	605	8,027	9,934	13,267	16,415	2.1
Inner zone	1,753	2,207	3,292	1,259	1,871	4.0
Outer zone	3,944	3,108	3,182	788	808	0.2
Total	6,302	13,342	16,408	2,117	2,603	2.0
Mainland China*						1.1
TAIPEI						
Core	272	2,730	2,624	10,047	9,655	−0.4
Inner zone	890	3,993	4,923	4,486	5,532	1.9
Outer zone	2,516	733	995	291	395	2.6
Total	3,678	7,456	8,542	2,027	2,322	1.3
Taiwan						0.9

Notes: Rates of increase for Shanghai have been adjusted for the fact that the inter-censal interval was not exactly 10 years.
HCMC populations are for 1989 and 1999.
*Excluding Hong Kong, Macao, and Taiwan.
Source: Analysis of 1990 and 2000 Population Census data for this project.

Particular interest attaches to the rate of population growth in the core, because in most cases this is defined to include the official metropolitan area. In some cases, this rate of increase is quite slow — indeed, it is negative in Taipei, close to zero in Jakarta, and well under one per cent per annum in Bangkok. However, it remains quite high in Manila, HCMC and Shanghai, in each of which it is above the rate of population increase for the country as a whole.

Within the core (whose area, it must be remembered, is very large in most of the cities — over 600 square kilometres in four of them), population growth rates varied considerably, with a tendency for a significant redistribution from the overcrowded central urban districts to the outer part of the core. In the cases of both Shanghai and Manila, the population of the core as a whole increased by over two per cent per annum over the 1990s. But in Shanghai, the populations of some central districts in the core dropped significantly over the period: by 36 per cent in the three central districts of the core. In Manila, only one of the constituent municipalities of the core (Pasay City) declined slightly in population over the decade, but another (San Juan) had a smaller population in 2000 than in 1980. In Jakarta and Taipei, where there was no growth or negative growth in the core as a whole, similar major population declines were registered for some of the more crowded districts.

The population growth rate of the inner zone is above the national population growth rate in all cases, and for Jakarta, Bangkok, Manila and Shanghai, well above it and also well above the rate of population increase in their other zones.

The outer zone growth rates are more variable. In Jakarta and Shanghai, there was no population growth at all in this zone, and in HCMC only slow growth. Low fertility probably helped explain the lack of increase in Shanghai, and the lure of the core and the inner zone for migrants from the outer zone was no doubt a major factor in all three cases. But then the outer zone population growth rates were quite rapid in Bangkok, Manila and Taipei. In Bangkok and Manila, this appears to reflect the rapid industrial development in parts of the outer zone, as well as, in the case of Manila, continuing high rates of natural increase of population. Taipei appears to be a special case in that Taipei's core is very small, and as a result its inner zone probably reflects the slow growth characteristics of the core more than is the case in the other MURs. Hence, alone among the six MURs, Taipei's outer zone has the most rapid population increase of any of its zones.

It is important to stress that with the exceptions of Shanghai and HCMC, the overall impact of adding the population of the inner and outer

zones to that of the core to assess population growth in the MUR as a whole
is to raise the rate of growth above that of the core alone.

This raises another question. To what extent has the growth of the
MURs over the 1990s been simply a growth of the zones outside the core,
leaving the core to hold a decreasing share of the MUR population? This is
examined in Table 3.2. The picture differs greatly between the four MURs
of Jakarta, Bangkok, Manila and Taipei, and the two "late comers" to end-
of-century mega-urban growth, Shanghai and HCMC. In the first group,
by far the largest part of population growth over the 1990s occurred in the
non-core zones (indeed all of it in the cases of Jakarta and Taipei), and the
share of population living in the core declined. By contrast, in Shanghai, the
core's share of population barely changed over the 1990s, and in HCMC, it
actually increased.

**Table 3.2   Non-core Regions of the MUR: Share of MUR Population in 1990 and
2000 and Share of MUR Population Growth, 1990–2000**

	Jakarta	Bangkok	Manila	HCMC	Shanghai	Taipei
% outside core 1990	51.9	36.9	50.3	40.9	39.8	63.4
% growth outside core 1990–2000	97.0	75.9	65.4	20.7	37.8	109.8
% outside core 2000	60.6	43.6	54.3	36.4	39.5	69.3

Source: Analysis of 1990 and 2000 Population Census data for this project.

MUR Population Growth in the Context of National Population Trends

The share of the MURs in national populations varies enormously, ranging
from 1.3 per cent in the case of Shanghai to 28.6 per cent for Manila and
39.1 per cent for Taipei (see Table 3.3). The share is held down in the case of
Shanghai and Jakarta by the presence of other large cities in these large and
populous countries,[7] and in the case of HCMC by the strange shape of the
country, almost guaranteeing that one large city would emerge in the north
and one in the south. The share of the MUR's population in the national
population, though impressively large in the cases of Manila and Bangkok,
is far exceeded by their share in the national economy, as already mentioned
in Chapter 2.

The growth rate of the MUR is in every case above that of the national
population, and in most cases well above it. This is an important finding. All

of these MURs are increasing their share of the national population (see Table 3.3), contrary to the conclusions reached by some observers who have used the population of the officially defined metropolitan area to conclude that many megacities have passed their period of rapid growth[8] and are holding a declining share of national populations.

As shown in Table 3.4, when the population of the core plus the inner zone is used to give the best reflection of the population of the actual built-up area of the MUR, the higher growth compared to that of the national population is even more apparent in the cases of Jakarta, HCMC and Shanghai than when the total MUR population is used. In Manila and Taipei, though, it makes little difference whether the outer zone is included on not, and in the case of Bangkok, exclusion of the outer zone reduces the growth rate of the remaining MUR.

Table 3.3   Share of the MURs in National Populations

	Jakarta	Bangkok	Manila	HCMC	Shanghai	Taipei
1990	9.4	15.8	26.1	5.9	1.2	37.5
2000	10.0	16.6	28.6	6.4	1.3	39.1

Source: Analysis of 1990 and 2000 Population Census data for this project.

Table 3.4   Population Growth Rate in the MUR Compared to Country (Region) and Urban Area

	Population – core plus inner zone		Growth rate (av. ann. – %)			
City	1990	2000	Core plus Inner Zone	Total Mega Urban Region	Country or Region	Urban*
Jakarta	13,657	17,782	2.7	2.1	1.5	4.2
Bangkok	7,041	8,256	1.6	1.9	1.4	2.5
Manila	12,090	16,245	3.0	3.1	2.1	2.5
HCMC	3,224	4,281	3.0	2.8	1.7	4.1
Shanghai	10,234	13,226	2.5	2.0	1.1	4.3
Taipei	6,723	7,547	1.2	1.3	0.9	

Note: * Including non-urban parts of the MUR.
Source: Analysis of 1990 and 2000 Population Census data for this project.

The key point is that, whether the more or less restrictive definition of a MUR is used, the growth rate of the six MURs studied exceeded that of the national population over the 1990–2000 period. This is convincing proof that the process of concentration of their countries' populations into these MURs had *not* ended during this decade, as some have argued.

Whether the MURs increased their share of their countries' *urban* population over the decade of the 1990s is another question altogether. In Indonesia, Thailand, China and Vietnam, irrespective of which set of data is used for the Jakarta, Bangkok, Shanghai and HCMC MUR — the core plus the inner zone or the core plus the two zones — the growth of their population was slower than that of the country's total urban population. The following conclusions therefore emerge:

- The Mega-urban regions continued to increase their share of their country's or region's population over the decade 1990–2000.
- Except for Manila, they did not, however, grow as rapidly as the urban population as a whole, and therefore held a declining share of the urban population.

The clarity of this conclusion is somewhat clouded by uncertainty over just how much the uncounted population living in these MURs grew over the period. The fact that the uncounted population is substantial in many of these cities would not greatly affect the conclusion about relative growth rates as long as the degree of undercounting remained much the same in 2000 as in 1990. However, if its share increased, or indeed declined, over the period, and at the same time grew less or more rapidly in the other urban centres, this could modify the conclusion that the MUR populations grew less rapidly than the countries' urban population as a whole. Even so, the consistency of the finding that the MURs' growth was below that of the urban population as a whole in every case except Manila lends a degree of credence to the finding.

One important implication of the generally faster growth in other urban areas than in the MUR in countries such as Thailand and Indonesia is that rural-urban migrants must have diversified their destination areas over the course of the 1990s. No longer were the MURs as dominant a migration destination as previously. Certainly, one factor in their slower growth was their very low fertility rates, which lowered their potential for natural increase, but other urban areas also had relatively low fertility rates, so this factor is unlikely to have been the dominant one.

Contribution of Migration to Population Growth

An important issue is the extent to which the population growth in these MURs, and in their component zones, was the result of natural increase (i.e. the net outcome of births and deaths to their population) and of net migration (i.e. the net outcome of in-migration and out-migration). There are various ways of examining this issue, the main ones being:

- Calculation of crude birth rates and death rates and hence rate of natural increase in the zones over the intercensal period, and deriving net migration as the difference between this rate and the population growth rate.
- Utilising census data on place of residence five years ago to determine how many of the present population of the MUR and its zones are in-migrants, and similarly data for the rest of the country to determine how many of the present population in the rest of the country are out-migrants from the MUR.
- Using "census survival ratio" techniques to compare the actual population aged 10+ at the end of the period with the expected survivors of the original population, by age and sex, and assume that the difference results from migration. This technique requires the utilisation of survival rates based on life tables corresponding to the mortality levels observed in the MUR. [It also requires estimates of migrants among those aged five to nine at the end of the period.]

In most of the MURs, there is a problem in using the second technique, because the definition of migration did not correspond to the geographic units used to delimit the zones in the study. The third technique can be used as long as there is complete information about the population by age and sex in each of the zones in both 1990 and 2000. However, deciding on the appropriate survival rates to use can be problematic, because of wide differences in mortality rates between the core and inner and outer zones, in some cases. The most striking example is Jakarta, where the expectation of life at birth in 2000 varied by 12 to 13 years between the core and the outer zone: for females, from 74.0 in the core, to 68.8 in the inner zone, to 61.1 in the outer zone. The equivalent value for all Indonesia was 67.3. In the case of Jakarta, both the first and third technique were used, and in all the other MURs, the third technique.

The results indicate the widely different role of migration in the growth of population in the different zones (see Table 3.5). In general, there is a

Table 3.5   Contribution of Net Migration to Population Change, 1990–2000 (%)

	Jakarta	Bangkok	Manila	HCMC	Shanghai	Taipei
Core	negative	3	19	n.a.	111.4	negative
Inner zone	60.9	71	54	n.a.	94.7	31.9
Outer zone	negative	62	42	n.a.	62.4	40.7
Mega-Urban region	16.2	52	38	46.3	104.4	n.a.

Source: Analysis of 1990 and 2000 Population Census data for this project.

close association between the rate of population growth and the percentage contribution of migration to this growth, with migration playing a major role in the more rapidly growing cities and zones.[9] Thus, for example, it is clear that the inner zone of Jakarta gained a large share of its population growth through migration, whereas both the core and the outer zone were *losing* population through migration. Both the inner and outer zones of Bangkok gained population massively through migration, whereas migration had almost no impact on population growth in the core, implying that in-migration and out-migration almost balanced out for the core. Manila was like a modified version of Bangkok, with migration contributing around half of the growth of both inner and outer zones, but much less for the core. The core of Taipei lost population through migration, whereas both the inner and outer zones gained through migration.

But important as the particular patterns of migration are, the implications of Table 3.5 go far beyond this, and have to do with the capacity of different MURs to maintain or increase their populations through natural increase. The wide range in the fertility rates presented in the previous chapter (Table 2.1) implied that some of the cities would be better able to do this than others. The enormous difference in the role of natural increase in the growth of the different cities is evident in the comparison between Manila and Shanghai. The growth rates of their core and inner zone were almost identical over the 1990–2000 period (see Table 3.1), and yet the contribution of migration to this growth differed dramatically. In the case of Manila, the continuing relatively high fertility rates in Metro Manila and the inner zone were sufficient to sustain considerable population growth, and the relative contribution of migration was modest (though as high as 54 per cent in the case of the inner zone).

By contrast, more or less the entire population increase in the core and inner zone of Shanghai resulted from in-migration. Fertility there had sunk so low that it was no longer able to generate any growth of population, even though the age-sex structure had been made more favourable to population growth through the in-migration of people in the peak childbearing ages. Most importantly, the Shanghai MUR *as a whole* no longer has the capacity to maintain its population through natural increase, so low has its fertility rate fallen. Taipei and Bangkok are likely to be the next of the MURs studied to follow suit, because their fertility rates are now very low. Further growth in the population of these MURs will be totally dependant on a net inflow of migrants. Whether migrants will continue to come in large enough numbers to maintain positive growth rates of population will depend mainly on the attractiveness of employment prospects in these MURs.

Conclusion

Even with full access to the 1990 and 2000 rounds of the population census for the various MURs, this study faced formidable data and definitional problems in seeking to compare the six MURs. Nevertheless, the exercise was well worthwhile, as it provided the first opportunity for such an intensive study of the dynamics of change of six major Asian mega-urban regions. To the extent possible, the delineation of the core, inner zone and outer zone in each MUR followed comparable procedures, so that comparisons of characteristics of the zones had meaning. Even so, difficult decisions had to be made in deciding on the boundaries of the zones. For example, Bangkok's population density in all three zones is lower than for the other MURs, with the exception of Taipei's outer zone, reflecting the reality that Bangkok is a less densely populated MUR than the others. Yet a case could be made for including an even wider area in Bangkok's outer zone. Similarly, for HCMC, the argument could be made that parts of Long An province should be included in the outer zone.

The twentieth century was a period of massive growth for all these MURs, a growth concentrated in the last few decades of the century. This growth is continuing, but may not do so for much longer, given the very low fertility reached in some of these countries and the emergence of alternative growth centres, especially associated with increased regional autonomy in Indonesia and the Philippines. Over the 1990s, the MURs continued to increase their share of the national populations, but held a declining share of urban populations.

The typical pattern was for the growth rate of the inner zone to exceed by a considerable margin the growth rates in the core and the outer zone. Only in HCMC and Taipei were patterns different. Within the cores — the heart of these extensive MURs — considerable population redistribution occurred from overcrowded central districts to outer parts of the core. Major population declines were registered for some of the more crowded central districts.

As might be expected, migration played a major role in population growth in the cities and zones where population growth was faster, though higher fertility in Manila meant that natural increase played a greater role in its growth. A considerable part of the population growth in the inner zones (except in Shanghai and HCMC) consisted of people moving out from the core, as well as substantial migration from other parts of the country. Overall, roughly half of the recent migrants to the MUR from other parts of the country went to the core, and the other half went to the zones, most of them to the inner zone. Most of these migrants were young, in the 15–34 age groups.

The following six chapters will present the specifics of MUR dynamics in more detail for each city, elaborating as well on the characteristics of migrants, the change in educational levels of the populations of the MURs, and the changes in employment structure.

Notes

1. For Manila, the zonal classification adopted by Jones *et al.*, 2000 was continued, thus allowing comparison, where necessary, with data for 1980. The inner zone in that study included cities and municipalities with population density >750 per sq. km. in 1990 and which were contiguous to Metro Manila or to other inner zone localities.

2. Similarly, the enumerator at that usual place of residence in Central Java is supposed to enquire about usual members of the household who are temporarily absent, and if they are reported to be intending to return, they are supposed to be enumerated there in Central Java.

3. In the case of Thailand's census, although anyone who had their usual place of residence in Bangkok for at least six months prior to the census should theoretically be included in the Bangkok population, there is a tendency for respondents to state their place of usual residence as their place of household registration. Surveys conducted in the 1990s showed that about a third of people living in the province of Bangkok (Bangkok Metropolitan Administration) had their household registration in other provinces (personal communication from Philip Guest).

4. These multiples are somewhat exaggerated, because the turn-of-the-century population is that living within the boundaries of the city at that time, and does not include any somewhat-urbanised populations living within the present

area of the city, such as in Jatinegara in the case of Jakarta or Caloocan or Pasay in the case of Manila.

5. Shanghai's population growth figures over the 1950s have been smoothed in Figure 3.1, because in 1959 a major expansion of area took place (from 654 sq. km. in 1958 to 5,910 sq. km. in 1959), resulting in a rise in population from 7.5 million in 1958 to 10.3 million in 1959. Note also that Shanghai's population figures in Figure 3.1 are not consistent with those from the 1990 and 2000 censuses, because for a long time series, only the residents with household registration in Shanghai are covered.

6. Actually, it is noteworthy that the population density in Manila's outer zone, despite its greater area than the outer zones in the other MURs, is higher than in three of the other MURs. Before inferring that Manila's MUR is not "over-bounded", though, it should be noted that population density overall in the Philippines is higher than in the other countries, and the density in the outer zone is not greatly above that for the country as a whole.

7. It is a typical feature of very large and populous countries that one city is unable to dominate their urban hierarchy (Jones and Visaria 1997: 6–8).

8. The U.N. study, *World Urbanisation Prospects* (U.N. 2002), revised every two years, assesses growth rates of major urban agglomerations, but using the official metropolitan areas (equivalent in most cases to the "core" in our study). This study indicates that growth rates of most of these metropolitan areas are slowing, and are now mostly quite low. As this U.N. study is the only comparative study of the world's urban areas, its findings are used by many writers on urbanisation trends and prospects.

9. There can, of course, be a considerable range in the share of migration at any given growth rate, because of differences in levels of fertility and mortality, and in the age structures resulting from past patterns of population change.

4

Bangkok — Globalising the City of Angels

Jarunun Sutiprapa, Preeya Mithranon, Paranee Watana and Chanpen Taesrikul

Background

Bangkok assumed its current role as Thailand's capital city in 1782 after earlier relocation of the capital from Sukhothai in the North down the Chao Phraya River to Ayutthaya. Called *Krung Thep*, "City of Angels", Bangkok rapidly became the centre of political power, the economy, culture and education for the Thai Kingdom. Strategically located where the Chao Phraya River enters the Gulf of Thailand, it lies between the Central Plains to the north and the extension of Thailand to the Southeast and the South, giving it a degree of centrality for the entire nation enjoyed by few other cities in Asia. This has led to its development as one of the world's foremost primate cities. In 2000 its population constituted one-third of Thailand's urban population, and its size was around 30–40 times that of the second largest city.

Bangkok's increasing dominance occurs in a national context of historically low levels and rates of urbanisation.[1] Even with the opening of the Thai economy to world trade following the Bowring Treaty of 1855, with its economy rooted in rural production of rice and all rice exports passing through Bangkok port, while Bangkok continued to increase its share of the urban population, cities and towns elsewhere stayed modest in size, dampening the overall level of urbanisation. In the 1960s and 1970s as light industry began in Bangkok, it experienced its first major waves of massive migration from rural regions of the country, particularly the poorer areas of the northeast. In the

1970s rates of urbanisation accelerated, with the share of population living in cities jumping from 21 to 27 per cent during the decade.

By 2000, census data showed that about one-third (31.0 per cent) of Thailand's population lived in urban areas.[2] Thailand was now experiencing rapid transition to an urban society that continues to focus on the expansion of Bangkok. This chapter examines the dynamics of growth and change in the Bangkok mega-urban region (Bangkok MUR) over the 1990–2000 period, using a zonal approach to give a new perspective on the growth dynamics. While migrants are attracted to the city from all over the country, within the Bangkok MUR the zonal approach reveals cross flows of people, with lower income groups mostly settling in the core while the emerging middle class has been rapidly suburbanising. Areas once thought to be remote from the city centre are now also being incorporated into Bangkok's daily urban field of interaction.

Methodology

Understanding the structural and morphological dynamics of the Bangkok MUR over time requires a definition that captures it as a nodal region (urban agglomeration) of flows and interaction rather than as an administrative unit with fixed boundaries. As with the other Asian MURs included in this study, this required the delineation of zones based on criteria other than purely administrative ones. Over the last three decades of rapid expansion, provinces surrounding Bangkok urbanised rapidly, and planning for the rapidly expanding metropolis required attention to trends in these provinces as well as in Bangkok proper. Thus in the 1990s, planners utilised two broader administrative agglomerations: the Bangkok Metropolitan Region (BMR — Bangkok plus the five contiguous provinces of Nonthaburi, Pathum Thani, Samut Prakan, Nakhon Pathom, and Samut Sakhon), and the Extended Bangkok Metropolitan Region (EBMR — BMR plus the three provinces of Ayuthaya, Chonburi and Chachoengsao).

While one convenient way of demarcating the three zones (core, inner and outer zones) used in the present study would have been to consider Bangkok as the core, the five contiguous provinces as the inner zone and the other three provinces as the outer zone, this possibility was rejected because the administrative boundaries did not appropriately reflect the degree to which different areas met the population density and agricultural employment criteria used in this study to define core, inner and outer zones (i.e. district level population density and proportion of employment in agriculture, both in 2000) (see Table 4.1). Thus even parts of Bangkok proper were placed in the inner zone (and a small part in the outer zone) rather than in the core; substantial parts of Pathum Thani, Samut Sakhon and Nakhon Pathom were placed in the outer zone rather than in the inner zone; and most of Chachoengsao, Chonburi and Ayutthaya were excluded even from the outer zone. By following this method of delineating the Bangkok MUR, we have ensured that the core and inner zones, in particular, are comparable with those defined for the other MURs (Jakarta, Manila, HCMC, Taipei and Shanghai).

Thus most, but not all, of Bangkok plus part of Nonthaburi comprises the core; the inner zone includes the remainder of Bangkok and greater or smaller sections of the surrounding BMR provinces which have become increasingly urbanised; and the outer zone includes the peri-urban areas of BMR and EBMR where urbanisation is reaching into rural areas. It is important to note, however, that substantial parts of one of the BMR provinces (Nakhon Pathom) and of each of the EBMR provinces are excluded from the MUR altogether, because they have relatively low population density and a substantial proportion of employment in agriculture.[3]

Table 4.1   Criteria Used in the Study

	Population Density (Person per km²)	**Employment in Agriculture (%)**
Core	≥ 3,000	≤ 2
Inner Zone	1,000–3,000	2–4
Outer Zone	200–1,000	4–20

Source: The authors.

Though it was crucial for the purposes of the study that the zones be delineated in this way, there is one disadvantage, namely that data on industrialisation and other data not available from the Population Census are frequently available only for the BMR and EBMR.

Data Source

Data from the Population and Housing Censuses of 1990 and 2000 conducted by the National Statistical Office were utilised both in demarcating the Bangkok MUR and for analysis of population movement, employment and education within and among the zones of the MUR. In these Censuses, both of which were conducted between 1–30 April, face to face interviews were used for data collection. Individuals were counted at their usual places of residence, including those away from home no longer than 3 months and temporary residents (less than 3 months) who did not have other living places. Students were counted at their usual place of residence. To study characteristics of the zones, we used sample data of 9 provinces in the Central region: Bangkok, Nonthaburi, Samut Prakan, Pathum Thani, Samut Sakhon, Nakhon Pathom, Ayutthaya, Chonburi and Chachoengsao. The sample was 20 per cent of total households.

Data Limitations

The Censuses have two limitations: (1) in both Censuses, *place of origin of migrants* can be identified only at the provincial level. (2) *Comparison of occupations* between the two Censuses is not possible because of different definitions used. In the 1990 Census, classification of occupation was based on the ILO International Standard Classification of Occupation, 1958 (ISCO-58), while the 2000 Census used the ILO International Standard Classification of Occupation, 1988 (ISCO-88).

Assumptions

In defining the zones using district level information, some provinces were divided between two zones, or in one case, between three zones. Because the origin of migrants was only available at the provincial level, in order to estimate the net migration in each zone, we had to subtract internal migration that occurred within the zone. As data on origin of migrants at district level are needed for this purpose, it was assumed that the distribution pattern of origin of migrants in each district is similar to the population distribution in that district. Using this assumption, net migration at district level could be estimated and aggregated to estimate net migration for each of the three zones. This adjusted net migration estimate was then applied in the three zones to the data about education, age, sex, employment, work status, industry, and occupation, based on the original pattern of both Censuses.

The Economy of Bangkok and EBMR

Economic statistics for the Bangkok MUR, which would require building up from district level data, are not available. Data for Bangkok and EBMR can, however, serve as the context for assessing MUR data from the population censuses. In the case of manufacturing and services, Bangkok and EBMR contribute a staggeringly high proportion of Thailand's total output. In manufacturing, in 2000 Bangkok and EBMR contributed 34.7 per cent and 69.8 per cent of the total product, respectively (Table 4.2). Yet the degree of concentration of manufacturing in Bangkok and EBMR had declined over the 1990s as manufacturing has expanded to peri-urban areas beyond their boundaries in the east to the Eastern Seaboard (ESB) and in the north to Ayutthaya (which is in the EBMR) and to surrounding areas, resulting in an increase in the Central Region's share of manufacturing from 7.7 per cent to 19.2 per cent between 1990–2000. Much of this increasing share can be attributed to the expansion of the Bangkok MUR.

In the case of services, in 2000 Bangkok and EBMR accounted for 43.3 per cent and 55.8 per cent of Thailand's total production, respectively. As with manufacturing, shares accruing to Bangkok, EBMR and even the Central Region are exceptionally high but are also shown to have moderately declined from 1990–2000. GRP per capita of EBMR in 1990 was baht 100,773 (US$1 = 25.6 Thai Baht). This was 8.3, 5.6 and 4.1 times higher than those of the Northeast, the North and the South, respectively. In 2000, GRP per capita of EBMR was baht 122,557 (US$1 = 40.2 Thai Baht) or 7.6, 5.1 and 3.7 times higher than those of the above-mentioned regions.

Table 4.2   Per capita Gross Regional Product and Economic Production in Thailand, 1990 and 2000 (at constant 1988 prices)

	GRP per capita (Bt.)		Manufacturing Production (%)		Service Production (%)	
	1990	2000	1990	2000	1990	2000
Bangkok	126,601	137,902	46.4	34.7	49.0	43.3
Bangkok and Vicinity	112,380	124,631	74.0	56.2	54.1	49.0
EBMR (includes BKK & Vicinity)	100,778	122,557	83.4	69.8	56.2	55.8
Central (excludes EBMR)	28,965	55,399	7.7	19.2	9.2	8.3
North	18,037	23,804	2.7	3.9	12.4	10.7
North-east	12,048	16,045	3.9	5.1	12.6	14.0
South	24,372	32,784	2.3	2.1	9.4	11.2
Whole Kingdom	34,839	48,159	100.0	100.0	100.0	100.0

Source: Economic Outlook, NESDB, 2003.

Whether this reflects the impacts of the 1997–98 economic collapse of the Thai economy, which mostly affected Bangkok, or a longer-term trend toward a more regionally dispersed pattern of non-agricultural development is not yet clear.[4] What the data of this study does show, however, is that the Bangkok MUR's share of national population has continued to increase, implying that its actual share of the national economy has also been increasing.

Population Change in Bangkok MUR and EBMR

The Bangkok MUR (Figure 4.1), while its population grew more rapidly than that of Thailand as a whole over the 1990–2000 period, showed sharply different trends by zone. The core grew by only 0.4 per cent per annum, compared with 4.1 per cent in the inner zone and 3.1 per cent in the outer zone. The total MUR population grew by 1.6 million over the period, to reach almost ten and a half million, and the population density increased from 1,172 persons/square kilometre in 1990 to 1,414 persons/square kilometre in 2000.

Figure 4.1 Core, Inner and Outer Zones of the Bangkok MUR, 2000

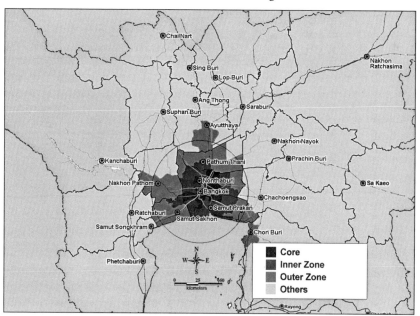

Source: Map prepared by the authors.

Table 4.3 Population and Growth Rate, Bangkok MUR and EBMR, 1990 and 2000

Population	1990 ('000)	2000 ('000)	Av. Annual Growth Rate (%)	% in Each Zone
WHOLE KINGDOM	54,549	60,916	1.1	
MUR	8,832	10,423	1.7	
Core	5,646	5,878	0.4	
Inner zone	1,594	2,381	4.1	
Outer zone	1,592	2,164	3.1	
EBMR	10,694	12,563	1.6	
– Bangkok	5,882	6,355	0.8	87% core; 11% inner; 2% outer
– Vicinity	2,707	3,804	3.4	41% core; 54% inner; 5% outer
– Nonthaburi	575	817	3.5	19% inner; 74% outer
– Pathum Thani	412	678	5.0	92% inner; 8% outer
– Samut Prakan	770	1,028	2.9	68% outer
– Nakhon Pathom	630	815	2.6	33% inner; 67% outer
– Samut Sakhon	321	466	3.7	30% outer
– Ayutthaya	701	727	0.4	24% outer
– Chonburi	851	1,041	2.0	12% outer
– Chachoengsao	552	635	1.4	

Source: Population and Housing Censuses 1990 and 2000, NSO.

Table 4.4 New Buildings Constructed in EBMR, 1995 and 2000

Province		Residential Buildings	Commercial Buildings	Apartment/ Condos	Industrial, Service & Others	Total
Bangkok	1995	32,141	4,490	2,804	357	39,792
	2000	12,719	1,348	47	91	14,205
Nakhon Pathom	1995	1,810	1,913	34	191	3,948
	2000	3,804	293	5	161	4,263
Samut Sakhon	1995	265	86	4	54	409
	2000	1,206	148	15	247	1,616
Pathum Thani	1995	8,185	2,671	87	119	11,062
	2000	4,216	217	35	110	4,578
Nonthaburi	1995	35,997	1,962	999	314	39,272
	2000	4,089	188	8	109	4,394
Samut Prakan	1995	812	244	20	61	1,137
	2000	2,585	356	18	129	3,088
Ayutthaya	1995	2,065	105	4	12	2,186
	2000	1,359	55	21	25	1,460
Chonburi	1995	5,313	1,320	195	241	7,069
	2000	8,137	1,526	4	178	9,845
Chachoengsao	1995	761	233	1	11	1,006
	2000	2,266	96	5	54	2,421

Source: Construction Statistics, NSO.

It should be noted that the zones as we have defined them highlight the differences in growth rates between Bangkok and its surrounding zones more sharply than do the Bangkok, BMR and EBMR classifications. Our more narrowly defined core grew by only 0.4 per cent, compared with 0.8 per cent for Bangkok; the inner zone grew by 4.1 per cent per annum compared with 3.4 per cent in the "vicinity" provinces of the BMR.

Pathum Thani had the highest growth rate of 5.0 per cent among provinces in the Bangkok vicinity, followed by Samut Sakhon and Nonthaburi (Table 4.3). Growth rates in these provinces were high because of two main factors. Firstly, residential areas expanded rapidly, especially in Pathum Thani and Nonthaburi. Data from the Construction Statistics in 2000 (Table 4.4) show that Nonthaburi and Pathum Thani had very large numbers of new residential buildings in 1995, though the number had fallen off sharply by 2000.

Secondly, the number of factories in Samut Sakhon, Samut Prakan and Nakhon Pathom increased dramatically (Table 4.5), as a result of the policy to decentralise investment. For example, there were 6,258 factories in Samut Prakan in 2000 compared to 2,982 in 1994.

Table 4.5   Factories in EBMR, 1994 and 1999

	1994 (31 Dec. 1994)	1999 (31 Dec. 1999)	Changes	
			Number	Per cent
Bangkok	19,492	18,142	−1,350	−6.9
Nakhon Pathom	1,131	2,392	1,261	111.5
Samut Sakhon	153	3,060	2,907	1,900.0
Pathum Thani	838	1,749	911	108.7
Nonthaburi	708	1,593	885	125.0
Samut Prakan	2,982	6,258	3,276	109.9
Ayutthaya	470	1,131	661	140.6
Chonburi	1,494	2,049	555	37.1
Chachoengsao	549	1,077	528	96.2

Source: Department of Industrial Works and Office of Industrial Economics, Ministry of Industry.

Transportation Development and the Expansion of the Bangkok MUR

When Bangkok was established as capital city, the Chao Phraya River and its lateral canals were the major network linking Bangkok with its surrounding regional cities, such as Samut Prakarn, Samut Sakhon, Nakhon Pathom, Nonthaburi, Pathum Thani and the former capital, Ayutthaya. The Chao Phraya River already had a number of natural and artificial canals along both sides of the river. Many of the artificial ones were dug as early as the Ayutthaya period (before 1767) and some in the Thonburi period (1767–82). The Chao Phraya River and canals were crucial elements of Bangkok. Apart from being used for protection against enemy assault, major transport routes, and major sources of fresh water and food, they were also used to open lands for settlement and as boundaries for land use zoning (Kasemsri and Phonpipat 1972: 165). However, the canal building period ended with the reign of King Rama V (1869–1910), after which no new canal was dug in Bangkok.

The Chao Phraya River and canals shaped Bangkok's spatial pattern. Traditionally, Bangkok's urban form was spread along the banks of the canals. The pattern was one of long narrow lots each with canal frontage, dwellings and temples, and community centres facing canals, while remaining rearward portions of lands were utilised for agricultural purposes. Places where canals intersected were naturally large communities. The influence of canals on Bangkok's spatial development started to lessen in the reign of King Rama VII (1925–35), led by the opening of Phra Ram 6 Bridge, the first bridge to cross the Chao Praya River joining Bangkok to Thonburi in 1926. Since then, construction of bridges, major roads and expressways has become the main determinant of Bangkok's spatial pattern.

Bangkok MUR's Development Corridors

Since the 1960s (the First National Plan), the building of roads has markedly changed Bangkok MUR's urban form, with rapid urbanisation of rice fields away from the canals. Urban development has expanded along a limited number of highways (see Figure 4.2); namely: (i) the corridor to the north — Highway 1, Highway 31 (Wibhawadi Rangsit Road and Uttrapimuk a.k.a. Don Muang tollway) and Highway 32, (ii) the corridor to the east — Highway 3 (Sukumwit Road) and Highway 34 (Bangna-Trad Road), (iii) the corridor to the west and south-west — Highway 4 (Phetkasem Road) and Highway 35 (Thonburi-Pak Tho Road).

Bangkok MUR has a limited number of corridors because the road development agencies tend to avoid conflicts with the public over land acquisition and high land costs. Thus, road development has a tendency to reinforce (through widening or double decking) existing corridors with a goal

Figure 4.2 Bangkok Region — Major High Systems and Rail Networks

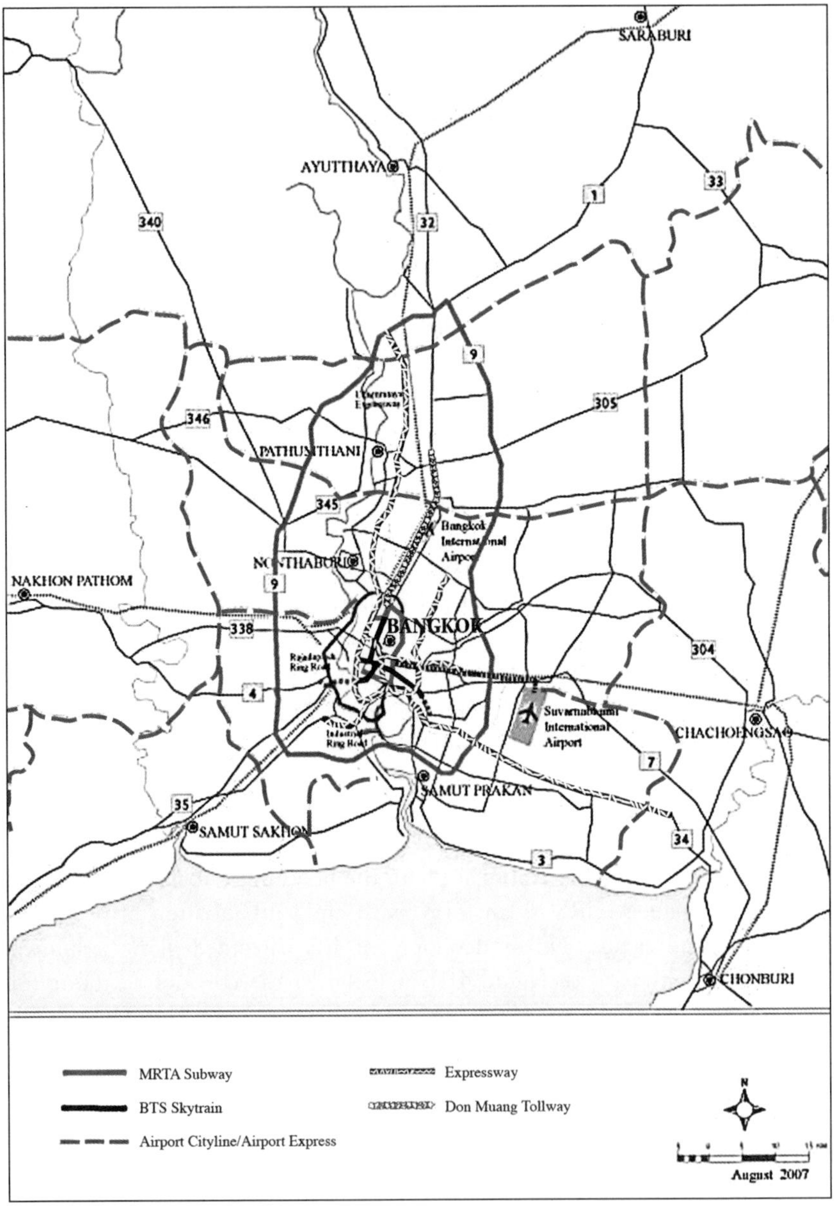

Source: Map prepared by the authors.

of moving vehicles, rather than following an urban planning perspective to serve new areas.

In terms of demographic and economic growth, the main development corridors over the last two decades have been to the north of the core city serving the existing Bangkok International Airport at Don Muang, along with Rangsit, Ayutthaya and Saraburi; and to the east/south-east along the corridor to Chonburi, Pattaya, Rayong serving the Eastern Seaboard (ESB) and in the future, the Suvarnabhumi Airport. Both corridors have been induced by industrial growth and tourism development in Ayutthaya and the Eastern Seaboard (ESB) area, the fastest growing sub-regions of Thailand. Development to the west and south-west tended to be slower before the 1980s, mostly due to the physical barrier of the Chao Phraya River. The western corridor picked up growth momentum as a result of construction of many bridges over the Chao Phraya River during the 1980s–90s.

Bangkok MUR Roadways: Inadequate Spacing and Lacking Hierarchy

The core of the Bangkok MUR developed along a general grid network of canals and roads, with many of the canals later converted to roadways. In the inner zone, the flat terrain and network of canals have resulted in arterials located generally along a grid framework. The major roadways in the outer zone have been developed somewhat in the form of a radial–circumferential network. In the core, between Sathon, Witthayu, Rama I and Krung Kasem Roads the major grid roadway network has a typical spacing of about 0.5 kilometre, which provides adequate accessibility. The space between major roadways increases greatly in the inner zone and outer zone with arterials that are more than 2.0 kilometre apart, or about 4 to 8 times the desirable spacing (Brothers 2003: 3), resulting in more than 30 superblocks totally or largely lacking in distributor roads.

The coarse road network of Bangkok MUR, without proper road hierarchy and lacking in distributor roads, coupled with inadequate land use controls, has generated ribbon development on a massive scale, leaving behind large areas of sparsely developed land. This marked the beginning of the superblock mode of major road/land development, a pattern which has continued to the present. Such development is expensive to service and impedes the flow of traffic. The ribbon development pattern of Bangkok MUR extends up to 40 kilometres from the core. As the urban areas expand, and more main roads are built in the outer suburbs, more superblocks are being created. With a few exceptions, the internal roads in these superblocks, built by private developers, follow the same inefficient pattern as before.

The spatial hierarchy of roads in Bangkok MUR consists of a concentric series of ring roads superimposed upon the upgraded radial roads, with local traffic being carried on the roughly rectangular grid of 200 major (arterial and secondary) urban roads. The Inner Ring Road (Rajadapisek Road) is completed and in operation. The Kanjanapisek Outer Ring Road (Highway #9) is scheduled to be fully completed in 2008. The newly completed Industrial Ring Road, which includes a giant bridge over the Chao Phraya River, now serves as a truck route linking two major industrial areas, namely Phra Pradaeng and Puchao Saming Prai with Klong Toei Port. The Industrial Ring Road will link with the Kanjanapisek Outer Ring Road (Highway #9) so that trucks from all over the country can go to Klong Toei Port and the two industrial areas without having to go through the city. With this series of ring roads, the regional roadway network of Bangkok MUR will be less Bangkok-centred because it will provide bypass opportunities and better access to Bangkok's expressway system.

Bangkok's Morphology

Development in the Bangkok MUR continues to follow the pattern of specialisation in terms of function among zones. The core is the centre of higher-order services, including the knowledge industry characterised by financial services, education, health and cultural activities, coupled with the public administrative functions and traditional economic activities such as wholesale and retail trading centres. It is also the zone in which global services in finance, consumer retailing and tourism concentrate and have been expanding tremendously since the late 1980s.

Manufacturing within the Bangkok MUR has become increasingly specialised and has continually expanded into inner and outer zones. For example, large multinational industrial plants and tourist attractions are found along the north and east/south-east corridors, Highway 32 to Ayutthaya and Highway 34 (Bangna-Trad Road); heavy industry is centred near Map Ta Phut and Laem Chabang ports in the Eastern Seaboard that has been developed as Bangkok's new world port area. The western corridor is dominated by medium to small industrial plants.

Changes in the spatial distribution of economic activities are paralleled by changes in the spatial structure of the MUR. The decade of the 1990s witnessed a dramatic shift in its morphology associated with Thailand's opening to global finance capital and the expansion of an affluent middle class oriented toward consumption of global consumer commodities. Both of these dimensions of globalisation resulted in unprecedented investments in urban land development in the form of very tall buildings, shopping centres, and massive expansion of suburban housing (Douglass and Boonchuen 2006). Figure 4.3 shows the new landscape of the MUR core zone. High-rise buildings, almost all of which were constructed from the mid-1980s to the finance crisis of 1997, spread across the core but are still interspersed with slum settlements, as can be seen in the foreground.

Figure 4.3   The New Urban Skyline of Bangkok, 2002

Source: M. Douglass.

Figure 4.4 gives a striking example of the urban turmoil of economic boom and crisis of the 1990s. Located in the Pratunam area of the urban core it shows a newly completed skyscraper overlooking a slum along one of Bangkok's remaining but highly polluted canals. In the background is a land development project that had gone bankrupt with the financial and economic crash that occurred throughout East and Southeast Asia in 1997–98. As of 2002 Bangkok remained dotted with 203 uncompleted tall buildings and several hundred thousand unsold houses (Herron 2001; Douglass and Boonchuen 2006).

As a new layer to the built environment, the new spatial dynamics transforming the MUR core into a centre of global business, tourism and

Figure 4.4. Skyscraper Overlooks Slum and Bankrupt Land Development Project, 2002

Source: M. Douglass.

consumption necessarily encountered the older layer of Bangkok as a royal city and political centre for all of Thailand. As shown in Figures 4.5 and 4.6, attempts have been made to allow these old and new landscapes to co-exist, although with mixed results. Figure 4.5 shows how the advent of the automobile city had by the 1990s resulted in a "Los Angeles" syndrome of building more and more elevated highways that, in the area shown, wind around Victory Monument, which was erected in 1941 to commemorate a military victory over the French in Laos and Cambodia. Although the monument remains, its visual impact and thus symbolic meaning for the city and nation is significantly marginalised. In contrast, Figure 4.6 shows how the continuing strength of Buddhism in Thailand results in the refurbishment of a Buddhist stupa next to newly constructed high-rise buildings.

Bangkok, once known as the "Venice of the East", has lost most of its canals to urban roads, and those that remain are heavily polluted. Nonetheless, as traffic congestion has led to gridlock on major roads, intrepid commuters,

Figure 4.5   Elevated Highways Surround Victory Monument

Source: M. Douglass.

Figure 4.6   Temple Being Refurbished Amidst Modern Buildings (2002)

Source: M. Douglass.

Figure 4.7   Water Taxis Ply the Few Remaining Canals in the Core

Source: M. Douglass.

Figure 4.8   The Temple Serves as Transport Node, Community Centre and Place of Worship in the Outer Zone (2002)

Source: M. Douglass.

Figure 4.9   Vernacular Housing, Outer Zone (2002)

Source: M. Douglass.

protected by plastic sheets against the spray of polluted water, use fast water taxis as a daily form of transportation even in the urban core (Figure 4.7). In other zones, particularly the outer zone in low-lying areas and near the Chao Phraya River, still a major artery for the MUR's economy, settlements along canals prevail (Figure 4.8).

In the outer zone as well, vernacular architecture composed of houses and shops built locally and often by the residents themselves also prevail (Figure 4.9). Yet, spurred by heavy traffic congestion, rising land prices and dislocation due to high-rise commercial building construction in the urban core, from the late 1980s Bangkok, as with all the other MURs of East and Southeast Asia, began to witness the construction of massive new towns with gated middle class housing constructed by global consortia of architects, land developers and financial institutions that have reached into the inner zone and can be expected to continue to spread outwardly along with major highway development.

Figure 4.10 shows in the distance the US$1 billion Muang Thong Thani privately built new city in the inner zone that went bankrupt in 1997 with the finance crisis just as it was nearly completed. Though it has remained a ghost town ten years later, other developments are now underway that

Figure 4.10   The US$1 billion New Town, Muang Thong Thani, Inner Zone (2002)

Source: M. Douglass.

over time will likely spread gated housing estates for the urban middle class into the inner and outer zones. As other chapters in this book readily show, such suburban developments are already well underway in Jakarta, Manila, Shanghai, and Ho Chi Minh City.

In more detail, the expansion of the Don Muang Airport during the 1980s, coupled with good north-south arterials ignited an explosion of growth northward from the city centre. Along the northern corridor, Uttrapimuk/ Don Muang Tollway, an upper-deck along the Highway 31 has been extended beyond the Don Muang airport to Rangsit together with the construction of the Udornrataya Expressway (Pak Kred–Bang Pa In). Considerable foreign direct investment has located in the Bang Pa-In area of Ayutthaya Province, particularly in autos, auto parts, appliances, electronics, etc. High value manufacturing plants, especially in electronics are attracted to the cleaner air and higher amenity of Ayutthaya, partly due to its strategic location at the intersection of the Kanjanapisek Outer Ring Road (Highway 9) and the Udornrataya Expressway.

In the same period the emphasis on the Eastern Seaboard (ESB) has encouraged a new corridor of development in an eastward direction, toward Bang Plee and beyond. Thus, road transportation along the eastern corridor is rapidly being upgraded with the opening of Highway 7 (Bangkok–Chonburi) and the Burapawithi Expressway (Bangna–Bangpakong), the upper-decked Expressway along the Highway 34 (Bangna–Trad Road).

The government of Thailand has begun to build a much needed mass transit system to ease traffic congestion and better manage the expansion of Bangkok well into the inner and outer zones. In 1999 the Skytrain was opened (Figure 4.11) along a limited number of major corridors in the core zone along two lines covering a total of 14 kilometres in the heart of the city. In 2004 the first part of a major subway system was inaugurated, putting Bangkok ahead of Jakarta, Manila and HCMC in coming to terms with the need for alternatives to the automobile.

Figure 4.11   The Skytrain Opens in 1999

Source: M. Douglass.

Population Structure in Bangkok MUR

Changes in population structure in the study areas over the 1990–2000 period are revealing. In 2000 (Figure 4.12) low fertility had resulted in a very low proportion of young population, particularly in the core. The pyramid in the inner zone showed a significant change. In 2000, population in working ages had increased dramatically as a result of employment expansion in this zone, while older persons slightly increased. The outer zone trend was similar, except that the proportion of young population in 2000 rose compared with that in 1990. However, in the core, the population structure changed only slightly over the decade, except for an increase in the proportion aged 70 years and over. The shape of population pyramids in the three zones was different from the overall population structure of Thailand. The proportion of population in the younger age groups was quite small, reflecting the very low total fertility rate in Bangkok (1.2 in 2000, the lowest in the country), and low rates in the inner and outer zones as well.

Migration

In interpreting the migration data presented below, it is necessary to keep in mind that many short-term or seasonal migrants to Bangkok are not recorded as migrants to Bangkok in the Census, because they are not intending to remain in Bangkok, and even some longer-term migrants may not be recorded if their place of registration remains outside Bangkok. The characteristics of such migrants could differ from that of recorded migrants in systematic ways — for example, they may tend to be poorer and with lower levels of education. Unfortunately, there is no reliable information about the number or characteristics of such *de facto* migrants who are not recorded in the Census.

Migration status of the population in the core, inner zone and outer zone in 1990 and 2000 is shown in Table 4.6. The largest migratory movement into Bangkok MUR originated from outside, especially from the Northeast (about 38 per cent in 1990 and 34 per cent in 2000). But in 2000, this was almost matched by the proportion of migrants moving between zones within BMUR; these increased their share of total migrants living in the MUR by 7 percentage points, from 25 per cent in 1990 to 32 per cent in 2000. The dominance of migrants from the Northeast was greatest in the core, where Northeastern migrants were 45 and 41 per cent of the total in 1990 and 2000, respectively. This reflects the well-known pattern of both seasonal and longer-term migration of northeasterners to Bangkok for work

Figure 4.12 Population Age Structures for Three Zones, 1990 and 2000

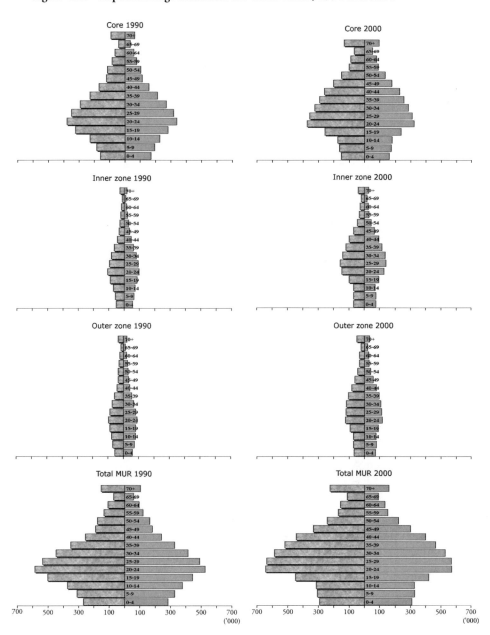

Source: Population and Housing Censuses 1990 and 2000, NSO.

Table 4.6 Migration Status of Population in BMUR by Zone, 1990 and 2000

Place of Origin	1990				2000			
	Total	Core	Inner Zone	Outer Zone	Total	Core	Inner Zone	Outer Zone
Population ('000)	**8,634**	**5,445**	**1,596**	**1,593**	**10,419**	**5,876**	**2,380**	**2,163**
%	**100.0**	**100.00**	**100.00**	**100.00**	**100.00**	**100.00**	**100.00**	**100.00**
Non Migrant	88.2	88.6	84.4	90.7	88.6	92.2	83.1	84.6
Migrant 5+	11.8	11.4	15.6	9.3	11.5	7.8	16.9	15.4
Migrants 5+ ('000)	1,016	619	249	148	1,193	458	402	333
%	**100.0**	**100.0**	**100.0**	**100.0**	**100.0**	**100.0**	**100.0**	**100.0**
Bangkok	10.2	0.4	28.4	20.7	16.7	0.7	28.4	24.4
Nonthaburi	1.9	1.4	3.5	1.5	3.0	3.3	3.2	2.1
Samut Prakan	1.9	1.8	1.6	2.9	2.3	3.1	1.1	2.5
Pathumthani	1.4	1.1	1.9	1.9	1.7	1.8	1.7	1.6
Samut Sakhon	0.9	0.7	1.2	1.2	1.0	0.9	1.1	1.0
Nakhon Pathom	2.0	1.6	1.5	4.3	1.8	1.7	1.7	1.9
Ayutthaya	2.5	2.6	1.9	3.5	1.9	1.8	1.3	2.7
Chonburi	2.1	1.7	1.1	5.8	2.4	1.5	1.4	4.8
Chachoengsao	1.5	1.2	1.2	3.2	1.0	1.0	10.8	1.4
EBMR Provinces	24.5	12.5	43.0	44.9	31.7	15.9	40.8	42.3
Central	15.9	16.4	12.7	18.9	13.3	14.6	10.8	14.6
North	13.7	15.7	10.7	10.5	13.5	15.5	11.8	12.8
Northeast	38.0	44.7	30.6	22.7	33.7	40.9	31.9	26.1
South	7.3	9.9	3.8	2.5	6.4	11.5	3.4	3.0
Foreign Country	0.6	0.8	0.2	0.5	1.5	1.6	1.5	1.2

Source: Compiled from Population and Housing Censuses 1990 and 2000, NSO.

in construction, services, etc. By contrast, migration into the inner zone originated mainly from other parts of the BMUR (43 per cent in 1990 and 41 per cent in 2000). Over two-thirds of this came from Bangkok itself: 28.4 per cent both in 1990 and 2000. The pattern was also similar for the outer zone.

Migration Distribution

The pattern of migration flows in the Bangkok MUR changed between 1990 and 2000 (Table 4.6). In 1990, 61 per cent of the 1.0 million migrants resided in the core. By contrast, of the 1.2 million migrants in 2000, only 38 per cent resided in the core, whereas the shares of the inner zone and outer zone had increased to 34 per cent and 28 per cent respectively. The changing pattern reflected the depolarisation of Bangkok, and the attraction of the emerging peri-urban areas in the inner and outer zones.

In both Censuses, migrants were highly concentrated in the age groups 15–24 and, to a lesser extent, 25–34 (Table 4.7). In 1990, 67 per cent of migrants aged 15–24 had moved to the core, 20 per cent to the inner zone and the rest to the outer zone. In 2000, only 45 per cent of these young migrants had moved to the core, whereas increasing proportions of 30 per cent had moved to the inner zone and 25 per cent to the outer zone. These flows were also similar to those of the 25–34 age group.

Table 4.7 Percentage Distribution of Migrants by Zone for Each Age Group, 1990 and 2000

	1990				2000			
	Total ('000)	Core	Inner Zone	Outer Zone	Total ('000)	Core	Inner Zone	Outer Zone
Migrants	1,016	619	249	148	1,193	458	402	333
0–4								
5–14	114	54.5	28.7	16.8	97	32.1	35.9	32.0
15–24	467	67.3	19.8	12.9	384	44.9	29.7	25.4
25–34	267	57.0	27.1	15.9	396	36.2	35.8	28.0
35–44	93	53.3	30.4	16.3	189	34.7	35.7	29.6
45–59	47	50.8	32.5	16.7	86	35.5	34.6	29.9
60+	25	54.4	36.9	14.7	39	34.5	35.9	29.6

Source: Compiled from Population and Housing Censuses 1990 and 2000, NSO.

Table 4.8 shows the proportion of the population in each age group who are migrants, by zone. It confirms the high prevalence of migrants in the 15–24 and 25–34 age groups, for both males and females and in both years. It is also noticeable that in 2000, migrants' share of the age group 35–44 in the inner and outer zones increased considerably. This confirms the depolarisation effect in Bangkok, with many families shifting from the core to the inner and outer zones. Even where this shift was to housing estates in the zones while continuing to work in the core, the shift of families out from the core stimulated economic activities and urban development in the inner and outer zones, including building of educational institutions, fuelling peri-urbanisation in these zones.

Though the patterns were quite similar for males and females, the proportion of age group 15–24 who were migrants was higher for females than for males in all zones except the outer zone in 2000 (Table 4.8). However, in age group 25–34, the proportion of migrants was higher for males than

Table 4.8 Percentage of Migrants in Each Age Group and Sex, by Zone, 1990 and 2000

	Males			Females		
	Core	Inner Zone	Outer Zone	Core	Inner Zone	Outer Zone
1990						
5–14	7.2	13.0	6.7	8.6	14.2	6.7
15–24	29.6	32.0	19.5	35.0	36.6	23.3
25–34	15.2	27.9	17.6	12.9	23.9	14.4
35–44	7.4	16.3	9.5	6.2	12.9	6.6
45–59	4.0	9.7	4.7	3.8	8.9	3.7
60+	3.8	7.6	2.8	4.1	7.6	2.8
All ages	12.4	18.5	10.4	13.2	18.4	10.1
2000						
5–14	4.5	13.4	11.2	5.0	13.4	11.5
15–24	16.6	31.2	30.6	17.8	34.7	30.5
25–34	13.3	34.8	34.4	12.1	31.5	29.8
35–44	7.4	20.0	20.4	6.1	16.8	15.6
45–59	4.1	11.8	10.8	3.4	10.4	9.6
60+	2.7	8.5	6.5	2.5	9.1	6.2
All ages	8.6	20.6	19.1	8.3	20.1	17.4

Source: Compiled from Household Socio–Economic Surveys 1990 and 2000, NSO.

for females in all three zones. The distribution pattern of male and female migrants was similar in both 1990 and 2000. Concentration of migrants was greatest in the age group 15–24 followed by age group 25–34, and was greatest in the inner zone, followed by the outer zone for both years and both genders. But whereas the migrant proportion of the core's population fell substantially between 1990 and 2000, the proportion rose slightly in the inner zone and rose sharply in the outer zone.

Migration has a complex relationship with poverty. Poverty may be a root cause of migration; certainly, people move because they want to improve their economic condition. In most areas migration appears, on balance, to bring an improved probability of survival and often an alleviation of poverty. Migrants normally have high participation in the labour force, and are absorbed into a variety of occupations in formal and informal sectors. The poverty data calculated from NSO's Household Socio-Economic Survey (Table 4.9) indicates that poverty (defined as percentage of people below the poverty line) in EBMR decreased from 3.7 per cent in 1990 to 0.8 per cent in 2000 and also decreased in other regions. It is possible, however, that the extent of poverty in Bangkok MUR is understated because of the tendency of the census to exclude from the Bangkok population short-term migrants, many of whom may be living in difficult circumstances. These are counted as residents of the home province where they are registered.

Characteristics of Economically Active and Non-active Persons

The population aged 15 years and over in the Bangkok MUR in 2000 was 8 million, up by 1.2 million from its 1990 figure. More than half — 4.6 million — lived in the core. Data from Table 4.10 show that employment increased by almost a quarter from 1990 to 2000, but much faster in the inner and outer zones than in the core. Labour force participation rates were also lowest in the core. Male employment in the core grew only slightly, by 6.2 per cent, over the decade.

Labour force participation rates fell slightly between 1990 and 2000, a fairly sharp fall for males offsetting a slight rise for females. The main reason was a decline in participation rates at ages 15–24 in all zones and for both sexes, as a result of higher proportions staying on longer in school (Table 4.11). However, older persons had higher rates in 2000 than in 1990, particularly for males. Females aged 45–59 had lower rates of participation than their male counterparts. Many stopped working before approaching the retirement age. Their participation rate was lowest in the core. However, in

Table 4.9 Poverty in Thailand, 1990 and 2000

	1990			2000		
	% of Poor	No. of Poor ('000)	Poverty Line/ Person/Month	% of Poor	No. of Poor ('000)	Poverty Line/ Person/Month
EBMR	3.7	417	630	0.8	109	1,024
Central (excl. EBMR)	24.5	1,939	523	7.0	557	873
North	23.2	2,548	498	12.2	1,372	777
North-east	43.1	8,322	477	28.1	5,927	864
South	27.6	2,070	518	11.1	922	841
Whole Country	27.2	15,296	522	14.2	8,887	882

Source: Compiled from Household Socio-Economic Surveys 1990 and 2000, NSO.

Table 4.10   Employment Change by Sex and Zone, 1990 and 2000

Zone		1990 ('000)	2000 ('000)	Increase ('000)	% Increase	% Economically Active, Aged 15+	
						1990	2000
Core	Total	2,456	2,767	312	12.7	64.7	63.1
	Male	1,370	1,456	86	6.2	75.5	70.5
	Female	1,085	1,312	226	20.9	55.0	56.7
Inner Zone	Total	799	1,189	390	48.9	70.9	68.3
	Male	431	636	205	47.5	80.0	74.9
	Female	368	553	186	50.5	62.5	62.3
Outer Zone	Total	818	1,062	244	29.8	74.8	67.7
	Male	426	545	119	27.9	81.9	72.1
	Female	392	517	125	31.8	68.2	63.7
Bangkok MUR	Total	4,073	5,018	946	23.2	67.7	65.2
	Male	2,228	2,637	409	18.4	77.5	71.9
	Female	1,845	2,382	537	29.1	58.8	59.3

Source: Population and Housing Censuses 1990 and 2000, NSO.

the outer zone, women still had high labour force participation rates as their work was likely to be in agriculture and they could continue working as long as they wanted.

As shown in Table 4.12, unemployment rates were higher in 2000 than in 1990 (6.6 per cent compared with 4.2 per cent, in the MUR as a whole). The highest unemployment rate in 2000 was in the inner zone — 7.4 per cent — where a large number of firms and industries were located. Women had a higher unemployment rate, 7.8 per cent, while the rate for men was 6.2 per cent. This appears to be because in the economic crisis (the after-effects of which were still being felt in 2000), women were retrenched from work in larger numbers than men and could not find jobs. When we investigated all 9 provinces selected in this study, the employment trends looked alike except for Ayutthaya, Chachoengsao and Chonburi. Employment in these three provinces increased because they were in the outer zone where the economic crisis had less effect. Moreover, industrial estates in these provinces and the Eastern Seaboard were able to absorb laid off workers from the core and inner zones.

Noticeably, persons who were not in the labour force concentrated in the core. Nearly 40 per cent of them were studying in educational institutions in 2000. Bangkok remained a key educational centre, with a large number of

Table 4.11 Labour Force Participation Rates by Age Group, Sex and Zone, 1990 and 2000

Zone		1990						2000					
		Total	15–24	25–34	35–44	45–59	60+	Total	15–24	25–34	35–44	45–59	60+
BMUR	Total	69.2	60.9	84.0	82.3	70.7	26.7	70.6	51.8	87.4	85.7	75.2	32.5
	Male	79.1	62.6	94.6	96.4	88.9	35.4	77.7	52.0	92.8	95.3	89.6	40.3
	Female	60.3	59.4	73.9	69.0	53.8	19.9	64.4	51.6	82.4	77.1	62.3	26.5
Core	Total	66.3	55.3	82.6	80.5	67.9	22.5	67.4	45.4	86.0	84.2	73.7	29.0
	Male	77.1	56.7	94.2	96.4	88.9	31.6	67.4	45.5	91.8	95.0	89.6	37.1
	Female	56.5	54.1	71.6	65.7	48.8	15.5	60.8	45.4	80.9	74.8	59.7	22.8
Inner Zone	Total	73.4	68.6	85.8	84.0	71.7	32.1	74.3	59.3	88.6	86.7	75.0	34.0
	Male	82.6	71.1	95.9	96.6	87.9	39.8	81.4	59.7	94.6	95.9	88.8	41.3
	Female	64.6	66.3	76.2	72.1	56.1	26.1	67.8	58.9	83.1	77.7	61.9	28.2
Outer Zone	Total	75.4	73.2	87.1	86.8	78.4	33.5	75.6	61.2	89.6	88.9	80.4	40.9
	Male	82.5	74.7	94.7	96.1	89.8	41.7	80.5	60.9	93.3	95.2	90.6	48.1
	Female	68.9	71.8	79.9	78.1	67.9	26.8	71.0	61.5	86.2	82.9	71.0	35.2

Source: Population and Housing Censuses 1990 and 2000, NSO.

Table 4.12 Population by Labour Force Status and Sex, 1990 and 2000

	1990				2000			
	Total	Core	Inner Zone	Outer Zone	Total	Core	Inner Zone	Outer Zone
Total Pop 15+	(6,343)	(4,012)	(1,166)	(1,164)	(7,990)	(4,625)	(1,796)	(1,568)
Employed	64.2	61.2	68.5	70.3	62.8	59.8	66.2	67.7
Unemployed	4.2	4.5	4.1	3.4	6.6	6.5	7.3	6.0
Waiting for farm season	0.3	0.0	0.1	1.5	0.3	0.2	0.3	0.6
Not in Labour force	31.2	34.3	27.3	24.8	30.3	33.5	26.2	25.7
Housework	*35.3*	*34.8*	*38.1*	*34.8*	*26.3*	*26.1*	*28.9*	*23.8*
Studying	*34.8*	*38.2*	*29.9*	*24.3*	*37.2*	*39.0*	*34.2*	*33.9*
Too young/old	*22.5*	*20.2*	*24.3*	*30.9*	*24.2*	*23.7*	*24.5*	*26.0*
Priest, nun etc.	*1.5*	*1.1*	*1.9*	*2.9*	*1.2*	*0.9*	*1.4*	*2.3*
Sick/disabled	*2.0*	*1.7*	*2.4*	*3.1*	*1.9*	*1.6*	*2.3*	*2.5*
Others	*3.9*	*3.9*	*3.4*	*4.0*	*8.2*	*8.1*	*7.6*	*9.2*
Unemployment rate	5.8	6.6	5.3	4.1	7.0	7.2	7.4	5.9

Source: Population and Housing Census 1990 and 2000, NSO.

good quality educational institutions. Those engaged in housework declined from 35 per cent in 1990 to 26 per cent in 2000. Their proportion was highest in the inner zone, where the non-working wives of factory workers would have been concentrated.

Change in Educational Attainment

As a result of provision of education to a higher proportion of the Thai population during the last 10 years, the proportion of the population aged 15 years and over in 2000 with none or less than primary education had fallen as compared to that in 1990 (Figure 4.13). Those residing in the outer zone had lower education than in other zones. As expected, a higher proportion of those residing in the core had completed upper secondary and tertiary education (26 per cent and 21 per cent, respectively in 2000) than those living in the inner and outer zones. At the tertiary level, those living in the outer zone had a low proportion of only 8.7 per cent, as the educational institutions were fewer than in the other zones and employment opportunities there were narrower. Nevertheless, this proportion had doubled since 1990.

The population in Bangkok MUR had higher education than in other regions of Thailand. They then had better opportunity to find jobs and could earn higher income. The good quality educational institutions in the Bangkok MUR were able to respond to the demand. The differences in education between Bangkok MUR and other regions reflects the disparity of educational investment among these areas.

It is not uncommon for migrants to have higher education than non-migrants. There seems to be a clear association between the level of completed education and the propensity to migrate (Todaro 1976: 27), as those with more education tend to move to areas of greater economic opportunity. In the current study, migrants in all zones had higher proportions than non-migrants in the middle levels of education, whereas non-migrants had higher proportions at the extremes of "none or less than completed primary", and tertiary education (Figure 4.14).

Focusing for a moment on the educational attainment of the young working-age population aged 15–34 years (Figure 4.15), we find that the proportion with none or less than completed primary education was much lower than for the total population aged 15+. This is not surprising in light of the expansion of education in more recent times. The most noticeable difference between migrants and non-migrants in this age group is the much

Figure 4.13 Number and Percentage of Population 15 Years and Above by Educational Attainment and Zone, 1990 and 2000

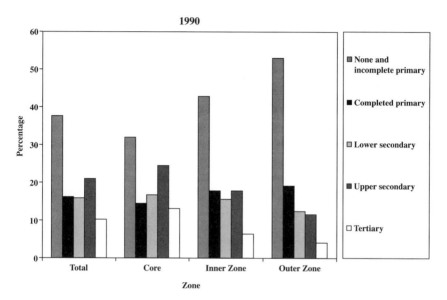

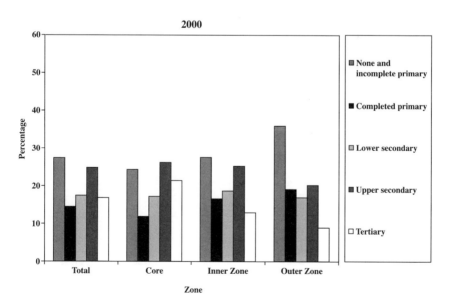

Source: Population and Housing Censuses 1990 and 2000, NSO.

Figure 4.14   Percentage of Population 15 Years and Above by Migration Status, Educational Attainment and Zone, 1990 and 2000

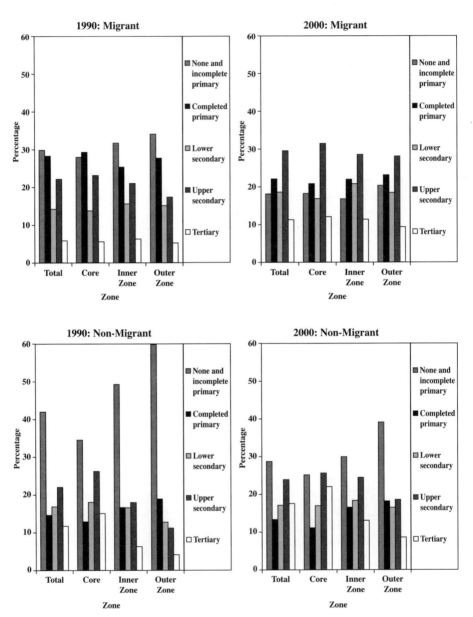

Source: Population and Housing Censuses 1990 and 2000, NSO.

lower proportion of migrants who have tertiary education. Both migrants and non-migrants had high labour force participation rates. For those aged 15–24 with all levels of education for both years, the relationship was U-shaped: the poorly educated had higher participation rates than those who completed lower and upper secondary education, while those who completed tertiary education had high rates again: exceeding 90 per cent, whether migrants or non-migrants. Migrants aged 15–24 with little education had a rate of 75.0 per cent while comparable non-migrants had only 57.2 per cent. This suggests that these migrants were poor people from rural areas who were pushed to move to find jobs in urban areas. Another interesting group were workers aged 60 years and over. They had higher participation rates in 2000 than in 1990 except those who completed tertiary education. This suggests that they could not stop working even after the retiring age, but had to struggle to survive.

Change of Employment in Various Industries

During the past 10 years, there has been a striking decline in the proportion of employment in primary industry in the inner and outer zones, as their economies have become increasingly integrated into that of the megacity, transport facilities for commuting to work in Bangkok have improved, and agricultural land has been converted to residential, commercial and industrial purposes. The proportion of workers engaged in agriculture in 2000 in the MUR as a whole was about 5.9 per cent, which was nearly half of that in 1990 (Table 4.13). In the inner zone, agriculture's share dropped from 13 per cent in 1990 to 5.5 per cent over the same period.

The employment share of the construction industry also declined between 1990 and 2000, no doubt reflecting the effects of the economic crisis, which led to the virtual cessation of construction of new apartments, offices and factories in the 1997–2000 period. The shares of trade and services increased. Manufacturing's share declined slightly in the MUR as a whole, but more importantly, the proportion of manufacturing employment in the core, already much lower than in the inner zone in 1990, declined further by 2000. In that year, manufacturing provided only 18 per cent of employment in the core, but 38 per cent in the inner zone. Trade and service sectors had similar shares of employment in both 1990 and 2000, with the core being the main focus. As a variety of professionals are concentrated in the core, service firms are often located near suppliers and professional collaborators, especially when the service involves a form of joint production (National Research Council 2003: 55). Workers in the financial sector are still concentrated in the core.

Figure 4.15 Percentage of Population 15–34 Years by Migration Status, Educational Attainment and Zone, 1990 and 2000

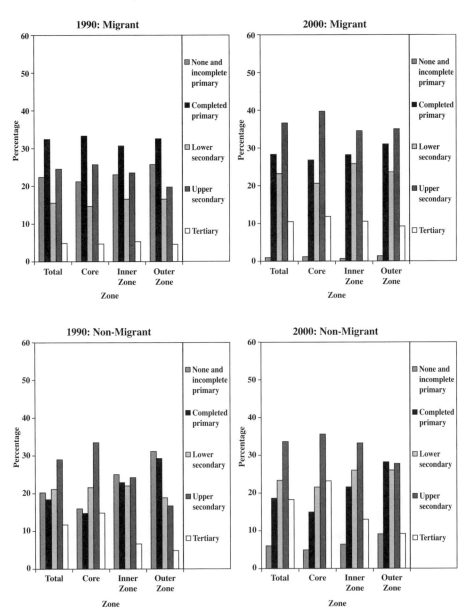

Source: Population and Housing Censuses 1990 and 2000, NSO.

Turning to employment patterns of migrants and non-migrants in 2000, in the outer zone, migrants were significantly less likely than non-migrants to work in the agricultural sector: 2.9 per cent compared with 21.5 per cent. Most of these non-migrants would have been working in agriculture without changing their occupation for a long period. Many of them may be owners of land they cultivated. In the MUR as a whole, about 40 per cent of total migrant workers engaged in manufacturing, a considerably higher proportion than non-migrants (23 per cent). Offsetting this, migrants were somewhat less strongly concentrated in trade and services than were non-migrants.

Change in Occupational Structure

In 2000, the highest proportion of employed persons (30 per cent) worked as production process and related workers (Table 4.14). These occupations made up an even higher proportion of all employment in inner and outer zones, where manufacturing industry was expanding. Sales and services, and professional and technical were the next most prominent occupations, employing 28 and 18 per cent, respectively. Sales occupations were somewhat more prominent in the core than in the other zones, whereas professional and technical workers (along with legislators and managerial and clerical workers) were much more heavily concentrated in the core than in the other zones.

Unfortunately, comparison between 1990 and 2000 is not possible as the definitions used in two Censuses were different. For example, in the 1990 Census, employed persons who were managers in the service sector were classified in the category of sales and services but in the 2000 Census they were put in the category of legislators and managerial. However, workers in production process and sales and service sectors were also the main occupations in 1990. The distribution of employed persons in these two occupations in each zone was similar to that of 2000.

Change in Work Status

Half of employed persons aged 15 years and over were private employees in both years and the proportion was highest in the inner zone, which was consistent with the employment by industry and occupation. The proportion working in the government sector and government enterprises decreased slightly in 2000. The sharpest drop was in the proportion working as unpaid family workers, which declined from 11.5 per cent in 1990 to 8.4 per cent in 2000. Those residing in the core and the inner zone probably shifted into the

Table 4.13 Percentage of Employed Persons by Industry and Zone, 1990 and 2000

Industry	1990				2000			
	BMUR	Core	Inner Zone	Outer Zone	BMUR	Core	Inner Zone	Outer Zone
Total								
Agriculture, fishing and mining	10.0	1.7	13.1	31.4	5.9	0.9	5.5	18.3
Manufacturing	27.8	25.1	38.7	25.1	25.4	17.8	38.0	30.6
Electricity	1.1	1.1	1.2	0.6	0.7	0.7	0.9	0.5
Construction	5.8	6.3	5.6	4.5	3.8	3.8	4.0	3.7
Wholesale and retail trade	18.1	21.8	12.6	12.4	23.0	26.7	19.2	18.1
Services	35.0	41.8	26.0	24.6	41.2	50.1	32.4	28.8
Unknown	2.2	2.2	2.8	1.4	–	–	–	–
Total	100.0	100.0	100.0	100.0	100.0	100.0	100.0	100.0
	(4,188)	(2,508)	(824)	(856)	(5,489)	(2,972)	(1,314)	(1,203)
Non-Migrants								
Agriculture, fishing and mining	11.4	1.7	16.2	34.9	6.4	0.9	6.5	21.5
Manufacturing	24.8	23.0	34.7	21.6	23.2	16.9	35.3	27.4
Electricity	1.1	1.3	1.3	0.6	0.7	0.7	1.0	0.6
Construction	4.9	5.3	4.8	4.1	3.7	3.6	3.9	3.5
Wholesale and retail trade	19.4	23.6	13.4	12.9	23.7	27.2	19.7	18.4
Services	36.2	42.8	26.9	24.7	42.3	50.7	33.8	28.6
Unknown	2.2	2.3	2.7	1.4	–	–	–	–
Total	100.0	100.0	100.0	100.0	100.0	100.0	100.0	100.0
	(3,460)	(2,092)	(633)	(736)	(4,755)	(2,699)	(1,064)	(992)

Table 4.13 (Continued)

Industry	1990				2000			
	BMUR	Core	Inner Zone	Outer Zone	BMUR	Core	Inner Zone	Outer Zone
Migrants								
Agriculture, fishing and mining	3.2	1.6	2.6	9.5	1.6	1.0	1.2	3.0
Manufacturing	41.7	35.7	51.7	46.5	39.7	25.9	49.7	45.9
Electricity	0.7	0.5	1.1	0.8	0.5	0.3	0.7	0.4
Construction	9.9	11.6	8.4	6.7	4.7	5.4	4.2	4.4
Wholesale and retail trade	11.7	13.1	9.7	9.8	18.5	21.2	17.0	16.9
Services	30.8	35.9	23.4	25.4	35	46.2	27.2	29.4
Unknown	2.0	1.8	3.1	1.3	–	–	–	–
Total	100.0	100.0	100.0	100.0	100.0	100.0	100.0	100.0
	(727)	(415)	(192)	(120)	(734)	(274)	(249)	(211)

Source: Population and Housing Censuses 1990 and 2000, NSO.

Table 4.14 Percentage of Employed Persons by Occupation and Zone, 1990 and 2000

Occupation	1990				2000			
	Total	Core	Inner Zone	Outer Zone	Total	Core	Inner Zone	Outer Zone
Professional and technical	7.2	8.8	5.3	4.2	18.0	22.5	15.0	9.5
Legislators and managerial	5.8	7.7	3.4	2.4	9.4	11.1	7.8	6.6
Clerical	11.0	13.7	9.7	4.4	9.0	11.0	7.8	5.0
Sales and services	27.4	32.8	19.3	19.3	27.5	29.5	23.5	26.9
Farming (skilled agriculture and fishery)	9.8	1.6	13.8	30.4	4.3	0.6	4.3	13.8
Production (craft, plant, elementary)	32.0	27.9	42.0	34.6	29.8	22.3	40.5	37.2
Armed forces	–	–	–	–	2.1	3.0	1.0	1.1
Miners, quarrymen, well drillers and related workers	0.0	0.0	0.0	0.0	–	–	–	–
Transport equipment operators and related workers	5.9	6.6	5.5	4.3	–	–	–	–
Workers not classified by occupation or unknown	0.9	1.0	1.1	0.4	–	–	–	–
Total	100.0	100.0	100.0	100.0	100.0	100.0	100.0	100.0
	(4,074)	(2,456)	(800)	(819)	(5,018)	(2,767)	(1,189)	(1,062)

Note: The 1990 and 2000 figures in this table cannot be compared, because of the difference of definition between the two Censuses. A one week reference period was used to measure employment.
Source: Population and Housing Census 1990 and 2000, NSO.

own account worker and private employee categories. Those concentrated in the outer zone who formerly worked mostly in agriculture also moved to work as private employees and to join the producer cooperatives. The proportion of employers or own account workers increased slightly in all zones (from 21 to 23 per cent). Probably many of them were workers retrenched from industries when the crisis occurred, who tried to survive by working as self-employed. Many became employers in the aftermath of the crisis as a result of the implementation of the Miyazawa Plan that focused on creating new entrepreneurs. Interestingly, the increase in the proportion of employers or own account workers was observed for migrants as well.

Living Conditions in Bangkok MUR

There is some concern about migrants' living conditions and the need for public investment to provide better services. Migrants came to Bangkok MUR mostly for work. Many were poor, and as it was difficult for them to find good housing conditions in the city, many ended up in slums and squatter settlements. In order to calculate roughly whether overall living conditions of migrants' households improved or deteriorated over the 1990s, some information on housing from the 1990 and 2000 censuses was utilised. Housing data are divided into 6 variables, namely (i) living quarters, (ii) cooking fuel, (iii) toilet facilities, (iv) drinking water, (v) water supply, and (vi) durable household appliance. Details of the calculations are in Appendix 1.

Most migrant heads of household are concentrated in the medium living condition category for both years. But it appears that in 2000, the living condition of migrant heads was better than in 1990, as the proportion in

Table 4.15   Living Conditions of Migrant Heads of Household by Zone, 1990 and 2000

	1990			2000		
	Low	Medium	High	Low	Medium	High
Bangkok MUR	**8.4**	**80.2**	**11.4**	**5.2**	**71.4**	**23.4**
Core	10.4	75.6	14.0	2.9	64.3	32.7
Inner Zone	5.4	86.1	8.5	4.6	76.5	18.8
Outer Zone	7.0	85.6	7.3	8.8	75.8	15.3

Note: Calculated from original data adjusted by using migration assumption in this study.
Source: Population and Housing Censuses 1990 and 2000, NSO.

the low and medium categories decreased and in the high category increased (Table 4.15). Turning now to consideration of the different zones, in the core, those having a low living condition dramatically declined from 10.4 per cent in 1990 to 2.9 per cent in 2000. A large proportion of migrant heads had moderate living conditions in both years. Their types of housing, public utility uses, cooking arrangement and daily living were much the same as for Thais in the country as a whole in 1990 (NSO 2002: 12).

Living conditions of employed male and female migrant heads were similar to the overall Bangkok MUR pattern. Noticeably, in the core, the proportion living in poor conditions drastically declined in 2000 but in the outer zone it increased slightly. Examining the data by educational levels of migrant heads, the proportion with low living conditions was inversely correlated with educational level for both years in all zones (Table 4.16). Migrant heads with completed primary education had better living conditions in 2000 than in 1990; the proportion with low living levels halved — from 12.1 per cent to 5.6 per cent during the 10 year period. In the core, the upgrading of the living conditions of this group was even more dramatic, with the proportion in the low category decreasing from 15.4 per cent to 3.3 per cent. However, in the outer zone, the proportion of primary educated household heads living in low living conditions rose over the period. By 2000, living conditions for migrant households were better in the core than in the other zones at every educational level, which was not the case in 1990.

Expected Future Growth Trends of Bangkok MUR

By the year 2010, population densities in the core of Bangkok are expected to increase, partly as the result of recently completed and planned developments of the mass transit system. The rail system is now the focus of Government policy to ease Bangkok's traffic congestion, promote more efficient use of energy, and reduce levels of air pollution.

The 20 kilometre initial phrase of MRTA Subway (Metropolitan Rapid Transit Authority Subway a.k.a. the Blue Line), which will cater for 40,000 riders per hour, became fully operational in August 2004. This subway links Hua Lamphong, Klong Toei, Makkasan, Huai Kwang, Sukhumwit, Lad Prao, Rajadapisek, Chatuchak, and Bang Sue. Future southern and northern extensions will run from Bang Wa to Hua Lamphong and from Bang Sue to Phra Nangklao bridge in Nonthaburi.

Four extensions are also planned to the currently operating 23 kilometre Silom and Sukhumvit Lines of BTS Skytrain (Bangkok Transit System a.k.a.

Table 4.16   Living Conditions of Migrant Heads of Household in Bangkok MUR by Educational Level and Zone, 1990 and 2000

	1990			2000		
	Low	Medium	High	Low	Medium	High
BMUR	**8.4**	**80.2**	**11.4**	**5.2**	**71.4**	**23.4**
Primary	12.1	77.7	10.2	5.6	73.1	21.3
Secondary	5.8	80.6	13.6	5.0	70.4	24.6
Tertiary	3.8	85.1	11.1	4.4	69.2	26.4
CORE	**10.4**	**75.6**	**14.0**	**2.9**	**64.3**	**32.7**
Primary	15.4	71.9	12.7	3.3	64.3	32.4
Secondary	6.6	78.1	15.3	2.7	64.3	33.1
Tertiary	1.7	83.1	15.2	3.4	64.8	31.9
INNER ZONE	**5.4**	**86.1**	**8.5**	**4.6**	**76.5**	**18.8**
Primary	7.1	85.6	7.4	4.9	78.6	16.5
Secondary	2.8	86.6	10.6	4.7	75.9	19.4
Tertiary	5.1	86.4	8.5	3.2	70.1	26.7
OUTER ZONE	**7.0**	**85.6**	**7.3**	**8.8**	**75.8**	**15.3**
Primary	7.6	86.4	6.0	8.7	76.8	14.6
Secondary	6.3	84.3	9.3	9.1	74.7	16.3
Tertiary	3.1	82.1	14.8	8.6	77.6	13.8

Note: Calculated from original data adjusted by using migration assumption in this study.
Source: Population and Housing Censuses 1990 and 2000, NSO.

the Green Line), to cater for 50,000 riders per hour. These extensions will double the current length of the Skytrain lines. However, the BTS's extensions are still pending official confirmation and more studies related to the plan's viability. Recently, the Government also approved the SRT (State Railway of Thailand) plan to build Suvarnabhumi Airport Express (25 kilometre Makkasan–Suvarnabhumi Airport) and Suvarnabhumi Airport City Line (28 kilometre Phya Thai–Makkasan–Suvarnabhumi Airport) a.k.a. the Red Line, which will cater to 60,000 riders per hour. The Government is working towards an integrated mass transit system for Bangkok, especially when it comes to fare collection. Integration will ensure a successful public transport policy and this will ensure the maximum ridership for the entire system.

As a result of the superblock mode of road/land development already mentioned, there is a need for more links in the road network, which would break up these superblocks into blocks of normal size. The BMA (Bangkok Metropolitan Administration) has prepared to infill 34 superblocks in the inner zone with 316 "missing links" between 2006 and 2026 (Arkarn and Theedin Weekly 2004: 67–71).

The development of the Mass Transit System over the next ten years will be the most important factor affecting Bangkok MUR's spatial structure since roads replaced canals as the dominant transportation mode earlier in the century. It will be an important stimulant to higher density and limitation of settlement sprawl. The private sector is developing plans to capitalize on the expected increases in land values, and the effects are already seen in higher density development near proposed major stations in the core of Bangkok MUR, e.g. at Siam Square, Makkasan, Huai Kwang and Rangsit. The Mass Transit System and the infilled superblocks will densify the core and the inner zone by increasing efficient movement of people in these areas. It will also be feasible to develop efficient subcentres with the extension of the Mass Transit System into the vast, lower density inner zone along Kanjanapisek Outer Ring Road (BMA and MIT 1996: 129–31). These centres would contain approximately one-quarter million people each and would serve to shape Bangkok MUR's outer zone.

In terms of spatial development within the Bangkok MUR, despite developments in the core that are likely to lead to higher density, more than two-thirds of population growth in the MUR is expected to occur outside the core. The development trend is toward the eastern/south-eastern corridor in terms of population and economic growth, while the northern corridor's growth is slowing relative to both its past growth rates and the eastern corridor growth rates. Rapid growth is driven by (i) the Suvarnabhumi Airport and (ii) the Eastern Seaboard (ESB).

The Suvarnabhumi Airport, Thailand's new International Airport, is located approximately 25 kilometre east of central Bangkok on a 32 square kilometre site at Nong Ngu Hao. It will be built in four phases over a 30-year period. By 2006, when the first phase opened, the Suvarnabhumi Airport was capable of handling 45 million passengers and 3 million tones of freight per year. Additional phases have been planned which will expand the ultimate capacity to 100 million passengers and 6.5 million tones of freight per year. As elsewhere in the world, an aviation complex such as Suvarnabhumi Airport will be the core for communities numbering in the millions in the Bangkok MUR. The Airport will have business zones to its east and west, and will be an economic base for the suburban centres of Lat Krabang, Minburi and Nongchok. These areas will be the new economic zones of the Bangkok MUR because of their proximity to the Airport and moderate land price. Apart from airport servicing activities, these aviation complexes will attract (i) knowledge industries in which easy access to air travel is essential and (ii) time responsive manufacturing, which is dependent on access to aviation services. Airfreight tonnage will grow even faster than passenger movements in international aviation over the next decade (Kaothien and Webster 1995).

Impact studies indicate that the new international airport will generate incremental population growth of approximately 676,000 people, over 30 years, about 350,000 of whom are expected to be in the proximity of the airport (NESDB *et al.* 2003: 5–30, 8–10). Thus the Suvarnabhumi Airport will be the strongest force reemphasising urban growth to the east, and contributing to a slowing of development along the northern and western corridors. As proposed in the Bangkok Plan (BMA *et al.* 1996: 6–11), Lat Krabang Sub Centre is being planned by BMA and JICA to structure rapid urban growth that will occur in that area. Implementation of this Sub Centre should commence as soon as possible, because otherwise the opportunity will be lost and haphazard development will ensue.

There are critical issues related to developments of the areas around Suvarnabhumi Airport that should be dealt with as soon as possible or else the opportunity will turn into the country's most chaotic and biggest blunder. First, the flood problem must be solved. The environs of the new airport are only 0.5–1 metre above mean sea level, with an average annual rate of land subsidence of 0.7 cm, and the airport and related future development will decrease floodwater retention capacity of the area. Second, a high caliber development agency must be set up for the special development area, to take over the present fragmented planning and administrative structure.

The challenge of flooding is one that affects the entire Bangkok MUR, as the area is the floodplain of the Chao Phraya River. It is anticipated that the construction of Suvarnabhumi Airport, which reduces the floodwater retention area and the construction of dykes along both side of the Chao Phraya River from Nakhon Sawan down to Bangkok during the last decade will make Bangkok MUR more prone to flooding than ever. BMA and related agencies are seriously considering a plan to construct a diversion canal east of Bangkok MUR from Bang Sai to the Gulf of Thailand as one of the flood mitigation measures for Bangkok MUR. Unless these measures are commenced immediately, floods will certainly cause serious disasters to Bangkok MUR.

Conclusion

Patterns of migration in the Bangkok MUR totally changed between 1990 and 2000. In 1990, more than 60 per cent of migrants moved to the core whereas in 2000, only one-third of migrants moved to the core, followed by the inner zone and the outer zone. As evident in Table 3.1, the most dynamic zone of Bangkok MUR is the inner zone, followed by the outer zone. Population in the core grew by only 0.4 per cent annually, well below the total growth rate. The inner and the outer zones grew much faster, by about 4.1 per cent and 3.1 per cent annually. This reflects the depolarisation tendencies in Bangkok.

The characteristics of migrants at both Census dates were consistent with those postulated by Lee (1966: 56–7) — (i) the education of migrants in both Censuses is lower than that of the non-migrants in places of destination and better than that of the non-migrants in places of origin; and (ii) most migrants were in the age group 15–34. There are no significant gender differences for migrants in education, age and population distribution.

Labour force participation rates for females were high in all three zones, as they were in Thailand as a whole. Many older people still worked after reaching retirement age, particularly in the outer zone where agriculture remained important. During this 10-year period, the employment structure did not change dramatically. Those working in the trade and service sectors were over-represented in the core, while manufacturing concentrated in the inner and outer zones. As expected, a high proportion of migrants worked as private employees. Average living conditions of migrant heads of household changed for the better between 1990 and 2000. The great majority were concentrated in the medium living conditions category.

Our analysis shows that development in the Bangkok MUR has changed migration and employment patterns, and raised the living conditions of large numbers of people, who have better access to services and resources than in other regions. The extension of the city to surrounding areas appears to have benefited their populations, although need for better provision of infrastructure in surrounding areas remains a major concern. Despite the efforts of the government to develop other regions, Bangkok MUR has grown more than these regions. Bangkok MUR remains one of the world's most dominant primate cities, and this may not be good for Thailand. Achieving more effective regional development is a key challenge for Thailand.

It is anticipated that an incremental population growth of approximately 4.2 million people will occur in the Bangkok MUR over the next 20 years. However, as outlined in this chapter, we can foresee various problems arising from the geographical features of the growth areas and the incoherent management systems. In spite of these challenges, Bangkok MUR has a fairly bright future, if it relies on the strength of the private sector, the emerging strength of civil society and the openness and creativity of Thai society that should enable it to tackle the foreseen challenges effectively.

Appendix I

Calculation of Living Conditions

1. Score for these variables were set as follows:
    (i)   Living quarter
          3 = Concrete or bricks or wood; and concrete or bricks
          2 = Permanent materials
          1 = Non-permanent materials
    (ii) Cooking fuel
          3 = Gas or electricity
          2 = Charcoal or kerosine
          1 = Wood
    (iii) Toilet facility
          3 = Flush
          2 = Pit and others
          1 = None
    (iv) Drinking water
          3 = Piped water, inside household or bottled drinking
          2 = Piped water, outside household, public well, private well, rainwater
          1 = River, canal, stream, waterfall
    (v)   Water supply
          3 = Piped water, inside household
          2 = Piped water, outside household, public well, private well, rainwater
          1 = River, canal, stream, waterfall
    (vi) Durable household appliances
          4 = Car, local farm truck
          3 = Motorcycle, washing machine, vacuum cleaner, video-tape
          2 = Bicycle, refrigerator, sewing machine, colour-television
          1 = Electric rice cooker, black and white television
          0 = Electric fan, electric iron, radio

2. After summing the scores of durable household appliances, the scores obtained have been regrouped as follows, for each household:

    0–6 = 0   22–29 = 3
    7–14 = 1   30–39 = 4
    15–21 = 2   40+   = 5

3. Means and standard deviations have been calculated and used to classify the combined variables into 3 categories of living conditions: low, medium and high.

Notes

1. This is partly because of a restrictive definition of urban places (Jones 2004: 115–7).
2. Compensating for underbounded cities, Warr and Sarntisart (2003) estimate that Thailand's actual urbanisation level was 38.0 per cent in 2000.
3. The population density of the EBMR was only 627 persons/ square kilometre in 2000, far lower than those of any of the other MURs included in this comparative study (see Table 3.1). Clearly, it would have been quite inappropriate to use the EMBR as an approximation for the Bangkok MUR in this study.
4. GRDP data is notoriously difficult to estimate, and income generated in a province or region does not mean it is received by that province or region. Transfers of income produced in provincial branch plants to corporate headquarters in Bangkok, for example, would possibly show a trend of increasing rather than decreasing concentrations of income and wealth in Bangkok. Provincial cities are growing, however, and the data confirms that Thailand's urban transition is a national, not just a Bangkok, process.

5

Jakarta — Dynamics of Change and Livability

Si Gde Made Mamas and Rizky Komalasari

Background

Since the end of World War Two and Indonesian independence in 1945, the Jakarta metropolis has experienced a turbulent history characterised by periods of very rapid expansion and transformations in its built and natural environment. Each period is marked by a shift in Indonesia's position in the world economy. Up to the early 1970s Indonesia remained an agrarian society. The driving forces of Jakarta's expansion consisted principally of primary product exports, particularly cash crops from the outer islands that had started in colonial times, timber and oil. The adoption of import-substitution industrialisation policies created a small national industrial base that centred on Jakarta, but this city's growth during this period was largely directed toward a low-income urban service sector. Studies during these years talked of "urban involution" and poverty sharing as a major dynamic of rural-urban migration (McGee 1978). Jakarta grew, but it grew around poverty and the expansion of slums with pockets of elite settlements and commerce in Glodok, Menteng and the early suburban new towns such as Kebayoran Baru and later Pondok Indah. In the eastern, western, and northern parts of Jakarta along the coast near the harbour of Tanjung Priok, the city also developed rapidly but in a more haphazard way, with sharply increasing population densities and growth of slums, especially along the railroads, rivers and canals.

President Suharto's New Order government established in 1965 was officially premised on the ideology of development, but it was not until the formation of OPEC in 1973 that the financial capacity to institutionalise a broad planning technocracy and implement major development programmes became possible. With the bounty from oil exports — 80 per cent of the national budget came from oil concessions — three "revolutions" were initiated: education, transportation and the green revolution. All three promoted ever-increasing migration to cities, notably Jakarta. For the first time the younger generation was literate,[1] which enhanced the appeal of urban life and employment. Transportation improvements dramatically increased access to Jakarta, making temporary as well as long-term migration to cities much easier. As the green revolution progressed, the shedding of labour from agriculture became pronounced through mechanisation and social changes in harvesting, resulting in more people looking for non-agricultural employment in cities (Douglass 1997). Added to this was the expansion of an urban middle class that was able to support fledgling car assembly and consumer durables sectors of production and the employment that came with it, almost all of which was located in Jakarta.

Up to the mid-1980s Indonesia remained under a strong import-substitution industrialisation regime. But with prices for primary product exports falling, oil supplies predicted to steadily diminish, and other issues clouding the future of the economy, a basic policy shift toward export-oriented industrialisation occurred.[2] At the same time, Indonesia was emerging as a "newly industrialising country". Thus, from the mid-1980s onward, Jakarta became a site for global consumerism in the form of shopping malls, global franchise food outlets that serviced not only the urban core but also increasingly a suburbanising middle class choosing to live in large-scale new towns locating in the inner zone of what was to be called Jabodetabek, the mega-urban region of Jakarta (JMUR).

This layering of export-oriented production with new forms of global consumption and finance directed toward middle-class suburban housing, new towns, commercial buildings, and consumer shopping centres made the 1990s the most intensive decade of growth and expansion of Jakarta in its history. During this decade JMUR increased by more than an average of 400,000 people per year to reach 21.2 million in population in 2000. Interestingly, the population of DKI Jakarta, the core administrative unit of JMUR, which had increased rapidly in population over the three decades from 1960 to 1990, barely increased in population size over the next decade, reaching just 8.3 million in 2000 (Badan Pusat Statistik 2000a).[3] In contrast, during the 1990s the peri-urban areas (the inner zone of this study) experienced exceptionally high population growth rates of around six per cent annually.

This chapter focuses on the 1990–2000 decade to explore JMUR's population growth and change, particularly with regard to underlying factors and their effects on the population characteristics. This metropolitan region, now frequently referred to as Jabodetabek, covers DKI Jakarta, the regencies (*kabupaten*) of Bogor, the municipality (*kotamadya*) of Bogor, the municipality of Depok, and the regencies of Tangerang and Bekasi (see Figure 5.1). The dynamics of population change are analysed by decomposing the rate of population growth into two parts — the rate of natural increase and the rate of net migration — to assess which of these factors is more dominant and to study trends and zonal variations (Mamas *et al.* 2001). The pattern of in-migration is another key topic that focuses on zonal differences, reasons for migrating, and patterns of commuting between surrounding areas of Jakarta and the centre of the city. Attention is also given to changes in educational level and employment structure, especially with regard to the differences between migrants and non-migrants. Finally, the findings from the demographic analysis are further assessed in terms of the quality of the environment in JMUR.

Methodology

The demographic analysis at the heart of this research is based on data from the 1990 Population Census, 1995 Intercensal Population Survey (Supas), and the 2000 Population Census. In addition, data is used from other sources, such as the 2001 Migration Survey, conducted by the Jakarta Statistical Board Office and the 2000 Population Survey conducted as part of the 2000 population census activities. The availability of detailed data for 1990, 1995 and 2000 enables the analysis to be conducted for two periods: 1990–95 and 1995–2000. This is fortunate because there was a sharp discontinuity during this decade. The economic crisis that began in 1997 had a devastating effect on Indonesia's economy, and particularly that of Jakarta (Sumarto *et al.* 1998). The 1990–95 analysis therefore relates to the pre-crisis period, whereas the 1995-2000 analysis includes the end of the pre-crisis period as well as the worst of the crisis period (1998).

The delineation of JMUR into three zones, namely core, inner zone, and outer zone, and their subdivisions is an essential step in the present study. For the JMUR case, the village was used as the basic unit, with each scored according to the criteria set forth in Chapter 3 and then aggregated into core, inner and outer zones (Mamas *et al.* 2001). To allow for more detailed analysis, each zone is further divided into sub-zones as follows (Figure 5.1):

I. Core, Jakarta metropolitan area consists of five municipalities:
    1.1. South Jakarta
    1.2. East Jakarta
    1.3. Central Jakarta
    1.4. West Jakarta
    1.5. North Jakarta

II. Inner Zone
    2.1. Bogor (part), including municipality of Depok
    2.2. Bekasi (part)
    2.3. Tangerang (part)

III. Outer Zone
    3.1. Bogor (part)
    3.2. Bekasi (part)
    3.3. Tangerang (part)

Figure 5.1   Zones in the Jakarta MUR

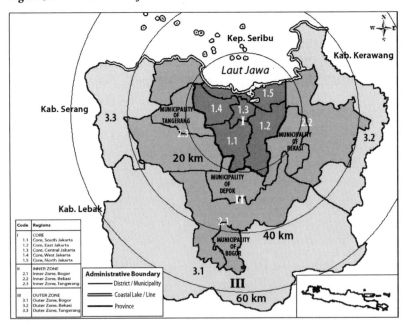

Source: The authors.

Population Size, Density and Level of Urbanisation

Table 5.1 shows residential population and density of JMUR by zone and sub-zone in 1990, 1995, and 2000. The highest population density was in the core: 12,421 per square kilometre in 1990, 13,766 in 1995, and then it declined to 12,610 per square kilometre in 2000, as the result of a decline in the population living in the core between 1995 and 2000. The inner zone shows the second highest population density in the JMUR, followed by the outer zone. Unlike the situation in the core, in the inner zone the population of each sub-zone increased sharply from 1990 to 2000. Figure 5.2 presents the population distribution in JMUR by zone. The core, and the municipalities of Bogor in the south, Tangerang in the west, and Bekasi in the east show high population density.

According to the criteria used by the Central Statistical Board to measure urbanisation, the core was 100 per cent urban, while the proportion of the

Figure 5.2 Population Distribution in the Jakarta MUR

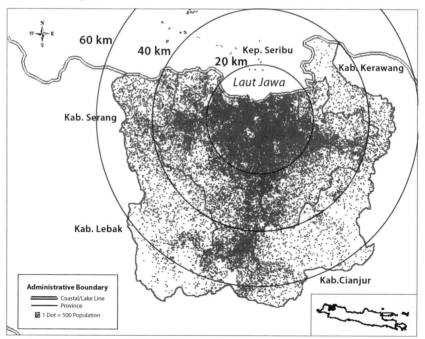

Source: The authors, based on data from Badan Pusat Statistik.

Table 5.1   Jakarta MUR: Population Density per Square Kilometre by Zone, 1990, 1995 and 2000

Regions/Sub-Regions		Area (km²)	Population			Density		
			1990	1995	2000	1990	1995	2000
I. Core	1.1. South Jakarta	145.7	2 028 477	2 041 025	1 784 044	13 920	14 006	12 243
	1.2. East Jakarta	187.7	2 008 500	2 383 394	2 347 917	10 699	12 696	12 507
	1.3. Central Jakarta	48.3	1 160 212	978 894	874 595	24 041	20 284	18 123
	1.4. West Jakarta	126.2	1 671 585	2 146 824	1 904 191	13 251	17 018	15 094
	1.5. North Jakarta	154.1	1 353 741	1 562 515	1 436 336	8 785	10 140	9 321
	Total Core	**662.0**	**8 222 515**	**9 112 652**	**8 347 083**	**12 421**	**13 766**	**12 610**
II. Inner Zone	2.1. Bogor	1020.3	2 280 288	2 484 582	3 577 717	2 235	2 435	3 507
	2.2. Bekasi	606.1	1 421 484	2 137 200	2 709 815	2 345	3 526	4 471
	2.3. Tangerang	747.4	1 731 897	2 654 353	3 147 912	2 317	3 551	4 212
	Total Inner Zone	**2373.8**	**5 433 669**	**7 276 135**	**9 435 444**	**2 289**	**3 065**	**3 975**
III. Outer Zone	3.1. Bogor	2164.2	1 726 270	2 215 727	1 825 331	798	1 024	843
	3.2. Bekasi	437.9	682 908	620 176	622 481	1 560	1 416	1 422
	3.3. Tangerang	536.8	1 033 091	934 965	959 370	1 924	1 742	1 787
	Total Outer Zone	**3138.9**	**3 442 269**	**3 770 868**	**3 407 182**	**1 097**	**1 201**	**1 085**
All Regions		**6174.6**	**17 098 453**	**20 159 655**	**21 189 709**	**2 769**	**3 265**	**3 432**

Source: Computed using data from 1990 and 2000 Population Censuses and 1995 Intercensal Survey.

inner zone's population living in urban areas rose from 79.2 per cent in 1990 to 90.5 per cent in 2000, and the outer zone increased from 16.5 per cent to 35.3 per cent urban. For the entire MUR, the proportion of the population living in urban areas rose from 76.6 per cent to 85.4 per cent over the period.

Method of Estimating Mortality, Fertility and Migration

Net migration and natural increase determine population growth. For policy and planning, understanding the relative effect of net migration on population growth, compared to the effect of natural increase (the difference between births and deaths) is important. This cannot be estimated using vital registration data, because accurate data on mortality, fertility and migration are not available in Indonesia, due to deficiencies in the vital registration system. For that reason, mortality and fertility are estimated for the period 1990–95 (Period I) based on the data from Supas 1995 and for the period 1995–2000 (Period II) based on the data from the 2000 Population Census.[4] Two basic questions on migration were asked in the population censuses and surveys: place of birth to estimate life time migration, and place of residence five years ago to estimate recent migration. Analysis of migration patterns in this paper is mainly concerned with recent migration for the 1990–95 period, estimated from Supas 1995, and the 1995–2000 period, from the 2000 Population Census.[5]

Dynamics of Population Change

Annual Rate of Population Growth

Table 5.2 shows the rate of population growth of JMUR by zone (core, inner zone, and outer zone), and sub-zone. There were extraordinarily wide differences in growth rates, both between zones and within zones over time. The population growth of the core and all its sub-zones during Period II was negative. By contrast, the rate of growth of the inner zone was extremely high: 6.0 per cent during Period I, declining to 5.3 per cent during Period II. The rate of growth of its sub-zones, however, also declined from the first to the second period, except for the inner zone section of Bogor (Code 2.1), which increased from 1.7 per cent to 7.6 per cent. The sharp increase in population growth in inner zone Bogor (Code 2.1) and a decline of population growth in outer zone Bogor (Code 3.1) was due to the annexation of some parts of the district of Bogor to the area of Bogor municipality.

Table 5.2 Jakarta MUR: Population and Annual Rate of Population Growth by Zone/Sub-zone, 1990–95 and 1995–2000

Zone/Sub-zone		Population			Annual Rate of Population Growth (%)	
		1990	1995	2000	Period I (1990–95)	Period II (1995–2000)
I. Core	1.1. South Jakarta	2 028 477	2 041 025	1 784 044	0.12	-2.66
	1.2. East Jakarta	2 008 500	2 383 394	2 347 917	3.48	-0.30
	1.3. Central Jakarta	1 160 212	978 894	874 595	-3.34	-2.23
	1.4. West Jakarta	1 671 585	2 146 824	1 904 191	5.13	-2.37
	1.5. North Jakarta	1 353 741	1 562 515	1 436 336	2.91	-1.67
	Total Core	**8 222 515**	**9 112 652**	**8 347 083**	**2.08**	**-1.74**
II. Inner Zone	2.1. Bogor	2 280 288	2 484 582	3 577 717	1.73	7.56
	2.2. Bekasi	1 421 484	2 137 200	2 709 815	8.50	4.86
	2.3. Tangerang	1 731 897	2 654 353	3 147 912	8.91	3.47
	Total Inner Zone	**5 433 669**	**7 276 135**	**9 435 444**	**6.01**	**5.33**
III. Outer Zone	3.1. Bogor	1 726 270	2 215 727	1 825 331	5.12	-3.80
	3.2. Bekasi	682 908	620 176	622 481	-1.91	0.07
	3.3. Tangerang	1 033 091	934 965	959 370	-1.98	0.52
	Total Outer Zone	**3 442 269**	**3 770 868**	**3 407 182**	**1.84**	**-2.01**
All Zones		**17 098 453**	**20 159 655**	**21 189 709**	**3.35**	**1.00**

Source: Computed using data from the 1990 and 2000 Population Censuses and the 1995 Intercensal Survey.

Among the zones in JMUR, the outer zone showed the lowest rate of population growth, 1.8 per cent during Period I and –2.0 per cent during Period II. The outer zone of Bogor during Period I showed much higher growth (5.1 per cent) than other sub-zones of the outer zone, but the growth went into reverse (–3.8 per cent) during Period II. Besides the annexation of areas of the district of Bogor to Bogor municipality mentioned above, out migration may have played a part in the decline. Most parts of this area are mountainous, and many bungalows, housing complexes, cottage industries, and shops were built along the main road from Jakarta to Bandung without much control by the government for many years. As a result, the population density and rate of population growth were increasing. However, starting in 1995 a new regulation on development of Puncak areas has been in put into affect, through strict control on the construction of buildings along the road in the mountainous areas.

Rate of Natural Increase (RNI) and Rate of Net Migration (RNM)

Both fertility and mortality rates declined in JMUR during 1990–2000, though the extent of decline varied among zones. Generally, both the fertility and mortality rate showed a clear pattern of gradation from the core to the outer zone, rising outwards from the core. This situation directly affected the trend and variation of the annual rate of natural increase by zones as shown in Table 5.3. Analysis of results of the 2000 population census (Badan Pusat Statistik 2001) shows that natural increase was more affected by the level of fertility than of mortality, hence the trend and spatial differences in natural increase generally followed the pattern of fertility. The spatial variation in rate of natural increase was relatively small and its change between Period I and II was not significant, except for the outer zone, where it declined from 22.8 to 18.8 per 1,000 population.

Unlike the zonal pattern of RNI, the RNM fluctuated in a wide range and was negative in many sub-areas, indicating that more people migrated out than migrated in during the period under study (Table 5.3). Other important findings are as follows:

1. During Period I and Period II, the RNM for each sub-area of the core was larger than RNI, except for South Jakarta (Code 1.1), East Jakarta (Code 1.2), and North Jakarta (Code 1.5) during Period I. It was hypothesised, as mentioned earlier, that the low rate of population growth of Jakarta in 1990–2000 was caused by spillover of the population to other, especially neighbouring, zones. Relatively

Table 5.3 Jakarta MUR: Total Fertility Rate (TFR), Crude Birth Rate (CBR), Crude Death Rate (CDR), Annual Rates of Natural Increase (RNI), and Rates of Net Migration (RNM) per 1,000 Population by Zone/Sub-zone, 1990–95 and 1995–2000

Zone/Sub-zone		Period I (1990–95)					Period II (1995–2000)				
		TFR	CBR	CDR	RNI	RNM	TFR	CBR	CDR	RNI	RNM
I. Core	1.1. South Jakarta	1.76	19.3	3.7	15.5	–14.3	1.80	18.9	3.4	15.6	–44.4
	1.2. East Jakarta	2.00	20.6	3.6	17.0	14.4	1.94	20.1	3.2	16.9	–19.9
	1.3. Central Jakarta	1.62	18.5	4.8	13.7	–50.7	1.53	18.00	4.0	14.0	–37.8
	1.4. West Jakarta	1.93	20.2	4.6	15.6	28.6	1.77	19.3	3.6	15.8	–41.2
	1.5. North Jakarta	2.17	21.5	4.2	17.3	9.4	1.64	18.6	3.1	15.5	–33.0
	Total Core	1.92	20.2	4.1	16.1	3.5	1.78	19.4	3.4	16.0	–34.1
II. Inner Zone	2.1. Bogor	2.42	22.9	7.0	15.9	0.5	2.56	23.7	6.6	17.1	44.0
	2.2. Bekasi	3.81	30.6	5.7	24.9	42.0	2.42	22.9	5.1	17.8	24.4
	2.3. Tangerang	2.78	24.9	5.5	19.5	50.0	2.46	23.1	5.3	17.8	13.5
	Total Inner Zone	2.93	25.8	6.1	19.7	30.8	2.49	23.3	5.7	17.6	28.2
III. Outer Zone	3.1. Bogor	4.72	35.7	11.8	23.9	20.3	3.82	30.7	11.5	19.2	–62.0
	3.2. Bekasi	3.46	28.7	9.9	18.8	–39.0	2.47	23.2	6.3	16.9	–16.1
	3.3. Tangerang	4.10	32.3	9.0	23.3	–44.3	3.12	26.8	7.2	19.6	–14.5
	Total Outer Zone	4.34	33.6	10.8	22.8	–5.4	3.35	28.1	9.3	18.8	–40.2
All Zones		2.66	24.3	6.1	18.2	6.1	2.31	22.3	5.4	16.9	–7.4

Source: Computed using data from the 1990 and 2000 Population Censuses and the 1995 Intercensal Survey.

large (and negative) numbers of net migrants during Period II lend support to the hypothesis. Rapid commercial development in many parts of Jakarta (core) in 1990–2000, the increasing price of land, air and water pollution, and traffic jams were among the strong push factors causing the population to move out from the city. In many instances, whole villages (*kelurahan*) had to be abolished for the construction of new buildings and the population of those villages was relocated to suburban areas outside the city.

2. The situation of the inner zone was quite different from that of the core. First, the rate of population growth of the sub-areas within the zone, during Period I and Period II, was much higher than in the core (see Table 5.2). Second, as in the core, the RNM of each sub-zone was much larger than the RNI, except for inner zone Bogor (Code 2.1) during Period I (see Table 5.3), meaning that migration was dominant in determining the variations of the rate of population growth by zones. The in-migrants to these sub-zonal areas came from the core, outer zone, neighbouring provinces of West Java and Banten, and other parts of the country. The origin and destination of migrants will be discussed in another section below.

3. During Period I, the RNM in the sub-zones of the outer zone was negative, except for outer zone Bogor (Code 3.1), reflecting out-migration from these zones to the inner zone, the core, and to other nearby cities like Bandung, Sukabumi, and Cianjur. Just as in the core and inner zone, the RNM was the dominant factor affecting the variations of rate of population growth, except for outer zone Bogor during Period I, and Bekasi and Tangerang during Period II.

In summary, the rate of population growth of the Jakarta MUR and each of its zones (core, inner zone, and outer zone) declined between Period I and Period II. The growth of all sub-zones within the core and the zones declined, except for Central Jakarta, inner zone Bogor, outer zone Bekasi, and outer zone Tangerang. The rate of population growth of the zones and sub-zones varied significantly. The highest growth was the 74 per cent increase over the decade in the inner zone; in striking contrast, the combined population of the core and outer zone was *smaller* in 2000 than it had been in 1990, although this decline might have been converted into a small absolute increase but for the annexation of part of the Bogor outer zone into the Bogor municipality, already mentioned. The effect of net migration — in-migration to the inner zone and out-migration from the core and the outer zone — was more

Figure 5.3   Ecological Zones and Population Density, Jabodetabek 2000

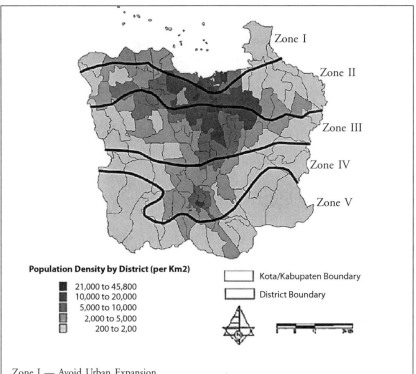

Zone I
Zone II
Zone III
Zone IV
Zone V

Population Density by District (per Km2)

- 21,000 to 45,800
- 10,000 to 20,000
- 5,000 to 10,000
- 2,000 to 5,000
- 200 to 2,00

Kota/Kabupaten Boundary

District Boundary

Zone I — Avoid Urban Expansion
- low-lying coastal zone, bad drainage, poor soil-bearing capacity for buildings
- best suited for agriculture and fishponds

Zone II — Agricultural Intensification, Limited Urban Expansion
- low-lying coastal zone, bad drainage, subject to flooding, groundwater easily polluted, poor soil-bearing capacity for buildings and high land subsidence risk
- excellent for irrigated rice growing

Zone III — Major Urban Development and Agriculture Intensification
- higher land rising from coastal plains, good drainage, groundwater is fresh and leaching soils limit water pollution
- reasonable soil-bearing capacity for buildings

Zone IV — Limited Urban Development and Agricultural Intensification
- steeper slopes, good natural drainage, limited groundwater and no deep acquifers, low flood risk, more rainfall supports agriculture
- reasonable soil-bearing capacity for buildings

Zone V — Upland Forest, Recreation and Conservation; Avoid Agriculture Intensification/ Diversification
- steep mountainous zone with limited vegetation and rapid runoff, agriculture limited to complex terrace construction and subject to erosion if deforested
- natural forest land

Source: (1) for ecological zones: Douglass 1991; (2) density: 2000 Population Census.

dominant than the rate of natural increase in determining population trends in these zones.

The Spatial Pattern of Jakarta's Growth

Having established the population growth trends in the zones of the Jakarta MUR and the role of natural increase and migration, the discussion will now move briefly to the broader explanations for the directions of Jakarta's growth — touching on planning aspects, broader economic forces and the linkages between morphological change and trends in socio-economic inequality. As shown in Figure 5.3 (which uses a set of zones based on ecological characteristics, not the zones used in the rest of the chapter), planning for Jakarta's development has long recognised that zone three is the most environmentally suitable for further expansion of the metropolis, covering as it does gently sloping areas, well drained and suitable for infrastructure development. This zone has indeed seen massive expansion of the metropolis

Figure 5.4   New Housing Estates Developed During the 1990s

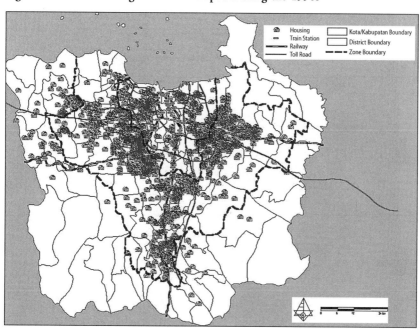

Source: Data from Badan Pusat Statistik.

along the axis from Tangerang to Bekasi and beyond to Cikarang. However, at the same time, developments have been taking place in environmentally more fragile areas in the coastal zone and inland into steeply sloping areas beyond Bogor.

Accelerated industrialisation from the late 1980s, and the opening of Indonesia's finance and banking systems to global deposits and investments contributed to boom conditions through to the mid-1990s. The logic of overcrowding in the core and rising land prices drove industry and housing to seek cheaper sites outside the core (see Figures 5.4 and 5.5). At the same time, particularly since the economic collapse beginning in 1997, insecurity, crime and the potential for uncontrolled riots so evident in May 1998 have driven the middle class to seek refuge in safer developments in the inner zone. All these factors are related to the massive growth of integrated housing and commercial developments in areas such as Serpong, Ciputat, Sawangan, Pondok Gede, Depok and Cibubur: developments with evocative names such as "Kota Wisata", "Bumi Serpong Damai", "LIPPO Karawaci" and "Kota Mandiri Internasional". Most of these housing estates (most of which provide

Figure 5.5   Large and Medium Industrial Establishments per Kecematan, 2000

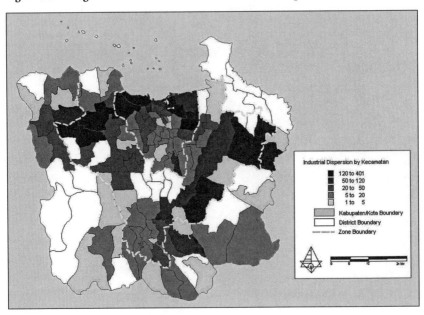

Source: Data from Badan Pusat Statistik.

limited employment opportunities locally) rely on the existing toll roads to ferry their residents to jobs in the core. The toll roads link Jakarta with Tangerang and beyond in the west, Bekasi and beyond in the east and Bogor in the south. An outer ring road is yet to be completed.

The move to the inner zone has clear benefits for industry and for the "weekend lifestyle" of residents. It does not come cost-free, however. Jakarta's lack of more than an embryonic commuter rail system (Figure 5.6) and the artificially low price of gasoline, supported by government subsidies, have meant a heavy reliance on bus transportation and on private motor vehicles. Neither surface streets nor toll roads can cope at rush hours with the volume of traffic entering and leaving. From 6.30 a.m. to after 9 a.m., entrances to freeways are subject to lengthy delays, and in the evening, from 5.30 p.m. to beyond 8 p.m. massive build-up of traffic occurs at exits from these freeways, lengthening the journey to and from work for the more than a million commuters from the suburbs adjacent to them. Insufficient capacity on the secondary roads serving the main arterial network is exacerbated by inefficient use of curb space, poor parking controls, unregulated bus stopping, mixed vehicle types, spilling of sidewalk trade onto the roads and undisciplined driver behaviour (Figure 5.7). The claims of many of the developers that their housing estates are only "half an hour" or "45 minutes" from downtown Jakarta ring hollow at peak hours when residents of these estates and of so

Figure 5.6   Jakarta's Commuter Trains are Heavily Overcrowded

Source: G. Jones.

Figure 5.7   Traffic
on Senin Raya with
Make-shift Shops
Pushing into the Road

Source: M. Douglass.

many others located "half an hour" from downtown inch simultaneously towards the packed toll roads.

All of these problems were exacerbated by the economic and political crises of 1997–98. Even several years later, major infrastructure improvements remained unfinished (Figure 5.8). While the economic downturn resulted in a fiscal crisis, the political turmoil shifted attention away from urban management to political contestations that continued beyond the economic crisis.

Both in the core and in the inner zone, housing for the poor remains a major problem. Developers prefer to build middle-class housing rather than low cost flats with poor yields, and the poor are the last people that the middle class moving out from the core want to be associated with. Indeed, aside from the security measures adopted to screen those entering and leaving, many of the large housing-commercial developments in the inner zone are geographically almost inaccessible to the poor because of location and lack of

Figure 5.8   Unfinished Highways (2003) Following 1997–98 Economic Crisis

Source: M. Douglass.

public transportation, and inaccessible in other ways because of the "American suburban" lifestyle promoted in such estates and the lack of goods and services affordable by the poor. Thus in many of the large housing developments, residents are effectively protected from both the sight of the poor and the danger they pose.

Pattern of In-migration

To analyse the pattern of migration for sub-zones or zones (core, inner zone, and outer zone), we define recent migrants as population who lived in the sub-zone or zone during the enumeration, but lived in other places five years ago. For example, for sub-zonal analysis, a person living in and enumerated in North Jakarta (Code 1.5), but living in Central Jakarta (Code 1.3) five years ago, would be regarded as an in-migrant to North Jakarta from Central Jakarta, although both Central Jakarta and North Jakarta are parts of the core. Similarly, for zonal analysis, a person enumerated in the core but living in the inner zone five years ago would be counted as a recent in-migrant to the core from the inner zone. However, those who moved from one sub-zone to another within the zone (see Figure 5.1) would not be counted as an in-migrant to the zone. Thus, by this definition we cannot obtain in-migrants to a zone by summing up the in-migrants to each sub-zone.

In-migrants to the Core

Among the sub-zones within the core, Central Jakarta shows the lowest percentage of recent in-migrants, for both 1990–95 and 1995–2000 periods: 7.4 per cent and 8.3 per cent respectively. The highest percentage was recorded in East Jakarta, 11.2 per cent in each period (see Table 5.4). We have mentioned earlier that the low rate of population growth of these zones during 1995–2000 was due to the high out-migration to surrounding areas and other places, probably soon after the economic crisis started in 1997. Although all sub-zones within the core showed negative rates of population growth during 1995–2000 (see Table 5.3), they still had some power to attract migrants, but the number moving in was less than the number who moved out. Gradual economic improvement and increasing job opportunities might be among factors that caused people to move back to Jakarta.

In the meantime, although construction of multi storied apartments, shopping malls, and office buildings almost ceased in the core with the economic and political crises of 1998 (though they would be back in full force by about 2002), continuing housing estate development was still attracting people to come to East Jakarta and West Jakarta, which show a relatively high percentage of in-migrants. These zones are located on the main road corridor from east to west, along the north coast of West Java, linking Cirebon in the east through Jakarta to Serang and Cilegon in the west. Many in-migrants to West Jakarta were probably working in nearby industrial areas of the inner zone parts of Tangerang. Similarly, many in-migrants to East Jakarta may be working in close by industrial areas of inner zone Bekasi.

Compared to East Jakarta and West Jakarta, the percentage of migrants to South Jakarta was relatively lower. These areas, e.g. Kebayoran Baru and Pondok Indah, are mostly residential areas for the middle and upper social classes. Industrial estates are not permitted to be built here. Recently, however, these areas, especially Kebayoran Baru, have changed their function from residential places to trade centres that attract in-migrants seeking jobs in services, trade, etc. Several multi-stories hotels, shopping malls and recreation places were built during the 1980s and 1990s in strategic places and later the areas were expanded to the south, along the transportation corridor to Cinere, Depok, and Bogor.

North Jakarta covers wide areas along the north coast of Jakarta where the largest harbour in Indonesia, Tanjung Priok, is located. The percentage of recent migrants for the 1995–2000 period was 10.7 per cent, almost the same as the percentages for East Jakarta (11.2 per cent) and West Jakarta (also 11.2 per cent). Like other coastal cities in Indonesia, the population is heterogeneous, consisting of ethnic groups from the Outer Islands, such as

Table 5.4   Jakarta MUR: Percentage of Population who were Recent Migrants by Zone/Sub-zone, 1990, 1995 and 2000

Zone/Sub-zone		1990	1995	2000
I. Core	1.1. South Jakarta	10.1	7.9	9.7
	1.2. East Jakarta	9.4	11.2	11.2
	1.3. Central Jakarta	7.8	7.4	8.3
	1.4. West Jakarta	10.6	8.9	11.2
	1.5. North Jakarta	11.4	6.9	10.7
	Total Core *	**7.4**	**6.3**	**8.4**
II. Inner Zone	2.1. Bogor	11.1	9.3	14.0
	2.2. Bekasi	9.7	12.9	18.5
	2.3. Tangerang	15.6	15.6	18.5
	Total Inner Zone *	**4.3**	**10.0**	**16.1**
III. Outer Zone	3.1. Bogor	1.5	2.4	5.5
	3.2. Bekasi	0.6	5.6	9.5
	3.3. Tangerang	4.3	3.0	9.4
	Total Outer Zone *	**1.2**	**2.9**	**7.1**
All Zones *		**5.2**	**5.7**	**6.4**

Note: * In-migrants to this zone are not the summation of in-migrants to each zone/sub-zone.
Source: Computed using data from the 1990 and 2000 Population Censuses and the 1995 Intercensal Survey.

Bugis from South Sulawesi, Batak from North Sumatra, Banjar from South Kalimantan, Ambonese from Maluku, Chinese etc.

In-migrants to the Inner Zone

The inner zone consists of three parts: in the south as parts of *Kabupaten* Bogor and its capital Municipality of Bogor and Municipality of Depok; in the east as parts of *Kabupaten* Bekasi and its capital Municipality of Bekasi; in the west as parts of *Kabupaten* Tangerang and its capital Municipality of Tangerang (see Figure 5.1). Bekasi and Tangerang have witnessed the development of industrial estates, and more are planned in the future. Textile industries in Tangerang and car industries in Bekasi and Kerawang, for example, have attracted many workers from other parts of Java and other islands. In the western inner zone, several large housing estates have developed during the past ten years, including transportation networks within the new city and a toll road to Jakarta and other cities. For example, the construction of Lippo City (5,000 hectares), Bumi Serpong Damai (6,000 hectares), and Alam Sutra (700 hectares) are not only limited to housing and multi-storied apartments, but also schools, universities, shopping malls, hospitals and recreation places. These areas are growing rapidly, and they will become large satellite cities of Jakarta in the future.

The development of southern inner zone Bogor was rather different, being related mainly to the development of housing estates and recreation areas along the transportation corridor from Jakarta to mountainous areas in Puncak, Cianjur and Bandung. Like the development in the western inner zone, several medium and large housing estates, including city facilities, have developed in this zone: for example, Kota Legenda (2,000 hectares), Lido Lakes Resort (1,700 hectares), and Bukit Jonggol Asri (30,000 hectares) along the alternative road corridor from Jakarta to Cianjur and Bandung. The construction of a number of housing estates was cancelled or postponed due to the economic crisis starting in 1997, but later as the economic situation gradually improved their construction continued. The University of Indonesia was re-located from the core to the southern inner zone of Depok. Also, the Bogor Institute of Agriculture, which was formerly located in the Municipality of Bogor, has moved out from the city, but it is still located in the area of the inner zone. Undoubtedly, the relocation of these universities has significantly affected the growth of areas around the campus — for example, the construction of transportation, housing for the students and lecturers, shopping centres and other facilities.

In-migrants to the Outer Zone

The percentage of recent in-migrants to the outer zone was much lower than to the inner zone and the core: 2.9 per cent for the 1990–95 period and 7.1 per cent for 1995–2000. This zone mainly consists of agricultural areas, rice fields, and rubber plantations, and the percentage of the population working in the agriculture sector remains much higher than in the inner zone. However, it is being affected by the urbanising developments associated with its proximity to Jakarta: construction of housing estates, shopping centres, etc. Each of the three sub-zones of the outer zone has large developments that attract people from outside. For example, the southern outer zone of Bogor has the Puncak area and Kota Cileungsi (2,000 hectares); the eastern outer zone of Bekasi has Lippo Cikarang, and the western outer zone of Tangerang has Gading Serpong (1,500 hectares). These newly developed cities will grow outward — in the case of those to the west, along the new toll roads and railroads to Serang, Cilegon and resort areas on the west coast of Java.

The Origin of In-migrants

In analysing places of origin of the in-migrants, analysis will be restricted to migrants to the core, inner zone and outer zones, without differentiating their sub-zones, based on the data from the 2000 Population Census. It is hypothesised that before the economic crisis started in 1997, the in-migration rate to Jakarta (core), as the centre of political as well as economic activities, was relatively high and increasing. As the economy slowed, large numbers moved out to other parts of the country. When the situation improved, in the early 2000s, the in-migrants to Jakarta gradually increased, but not much of this increase was recorded by the Census, which was held in 2000. In-migration to the core, inner zone, and outer zone over the 1995–2000 period by place of origin, estimated based on the results of the 2000 Population Census, is presented in Table 5.5.

Several Key Points Are Worth Noting:

1. In-migrants to the core numbered 702,202 persons, consisting of those originating from the inner zone (10.5 per cent), outer zone (1.9 per cent), and the remainder (87.6 per cent) from other provinces throughout Indonesia, but notably Central Java (34.9 per cent), and West Java (17.3 per cent). The core (Jakarta), the capital of Indonesia, clearly has specific pull factors for people from other parts of the country.

According to an urbanisation survey in 1995, 92 per cent of migrants to Jakarta moved directly there from their places of origin (Badan Pusat Statistik 1997). We might have expected West Java and Banten provinces, which have a common border with Jakarta, to have more in-migrants to Jakarta than Central Java, whose closest border is more than 200 kilometres away to the east of Jakarta, but the facts show otherwise. Migrants from West Java and Banten, though, outnumber migrants from Central Java in JMUR's inner and outer zones, and probably also favour large cities and towns like Bandung, Cirebon, and Cilegon as alternative destinations.

2.   Among zones within JMUR, the inner zone received the most in-migrants, 1.5 million during 1995–2000. Just over half a million (34.1 per cent) originated from the core and 371,000 (24.4 per cent) from the outer zone. These figures support the hypothesis that "spillover" migration from the core contributes much of the migration to the inner zone. Importantly, in-migrants to the inner zone from the core had distinctive characteristics; 66 per cent of them graduated from senior high school or higher education (compared to only 27 per cent of those who moved there from the outer zone) and 69 per cent worked in the service sector (special tabulation, not shown in Table 5.5). Other major areas of origin of in-migrants were Central Java (11.9 per cent) and West Java (15.5 per cent). But even when combined, migrants from these two major provinces are fewer than those who come as "spillover" migrants from the core.

3.   In-migrants to the outer zone (242,848 persons) were far fewer than to the other zones in JMUR. They consisted of in-migrants from the core (15.3 per cent), from the inner zone (37.0 per cent) and the remainder (47.7 per cent) from other provinces, including from West Java (19.1 per cent) and Central Java (12.4 per cent). Parts of the outer zone that are tending to become places of residence of migrants are along the highway from Jakarta to Bandung via the mountainous areas of Puncak and Cianjur, along the west highway corridor to Cilegon, and along the east highway corridor to Kerawang and Cirebon.

In summary, the rapid physical development and the increasing land price in the core were push factors that led to increasing migratory movement from the centre of the city to the periphery. There continues to be some in-migration to the core, dominated by Central Javanese, but the numbers moving in were less than those who moved out. In-migrants to the inner

Table 5.5   Jakarta MUR: Recent Migrants in Each Zone of Residence by Place of Origin, 1995–2000

Place of Origin	Core Absolute Number	Core %	Inner Zone Absolute Number	Inner Zone %	Outer Zone Absolute Number	Outer Zone %
I. Core	–	–	519 271	34.1	37 100	15.3
II. Inner Zone	74 018	10.5	–	–	89 969	37.0
III. Outer Zone	13 206	1.9	370 788	24.4	–	–
Sub-total	**87 224**	**12.4**	**890 059**	**58.5**	**127 069**	**52.3**
Banten (Excluding Tangerang)	25 552	3.6	28 496	1.9	7 724	3.2
West Java (Excluding Bogor and Bekasi)	121 567	17.3	235 189	15.5	46 385	19.1
Central Java	245 270	34.9	181 753	11.9	30 095	12.4
Yogyakarta	16 149	2.3	20 337	1.3	5 206	2.1
East Java	63 485	9.0	52 805	3.5	7 169	3.0
North Sumatra	27 363	3.9	27 080	1.8	4 098	1.7
West Sumatra	20 035	2.9	15 816	1.0	1 939	0.8
South Sumatra	11 346	1.6	14 974	1.0	2 183	0.9
Lampung	16 937	2.4	20 160	1.3	3 024	1.2
Other Provinces of Sumatra	18 062	2.6	13 390	0.9	3 092	1.3
Kalimantan	10 788	1.5	6 580	0.4	725	0.3
Sulawesi	15 150	2.2	4 868	0.3	857	0.4
Other Provinces	23 274	3.3	10 362	0.7	3 282	1.4
Sub-total (excluding Core, Inner Zone and Outer Zone)	**614 978**	**87.6**	**631 810**	**41.5**	**115 779**	**47.7**
All Zones	**702 202**	**100.0**	**1 521 869**	**100.0**	**242 848**	**100.0**

Source: Computed using data from the 2000 Population Census.

zone were much more numerous than those moving to the core and outer zone. They came from the core and outer zone, as well as from West Java and Central Java.

Reasons for Migration

A study made by the Jakarta Statistical Office (Badan Pusat Statistik DKI Jakarta 2001) shows that employment and other related activities are the main reason why people migrate to Jakarta's core, accounting for 62 per cent of all reasons. Employment related activities include promotion to higher working status, looking for a better job and higher salary, better working situations, etc. The second reason is accompanying husband or wife and other members of the family (27 per cent). Surprisingly, only 6 per cent of all such migrants were seeking higher education, a much lower proportion than for migrants to other large cities like Bandung (17 per cent) and Ujung Pandang (63 per cent) (see Badan Pusat Statistik 1997: 23). Since the level of education is highly correlated with employment status, we will further explore the trend and zonal variations in educational level of in-migrants to JMUR in comparison with non-migrants by zones in a later section of the chapter.

The age structure of migrants to the different zones also provides hints about the reasons for migrating. Table 5.6 shows that migrants to the core are much more heavily concentrated in the 15–24 year age group than migrants to the inner zone, a much higher proportion of whom are adults aged 35 and above and children, reflecting the importance of family migration into the inner zone from the core as well as from other parts of Indonesia.

Commuters between Zones and the Core

Another important aspect of the survey conducted by the Jakarta Statistical Office concerns commuting between areas around Jakarta (districts/*kabupaten* of Bogor, Depok, Bekasi, and Tangerang) and the Jakarta metropolitan area — in other words, from parts of the inner and outer zones to the core. The population of Jakarta metropolitan area was recorded on a *de jure* basis in the 2000 Population Census as 8,347,083 persons. This could be considered as the "night time" population, since they lived and slept in their own housing unit in Jakarta during the enumeration of the census. The average daily number of commuters aged five years and over was 1,017,339 persons (Badan Pusat Statistik DKI Jakarta 2001: 95), consisting of 813,653 males and 203,686 females. Among them, 23.9 per cent originated from

Table 5.6   Jakarta MUR: Percentage of Migrants by Zone and Age, 1990 and 2000

Zone/ Year		Age					Total	
		5–14	15–24	25–34	35–44	45+	%	Absolute Number
I. Core	1990	10.1	53.1	24.3	6.8	5.6	100.0	816,425
	2000	7.5	48.4	30.1	8.6	5.4	100.0	702,202
II. Inner	1990	21.2	31.3	27.4	12.1	8.1	100.0	660,803
Zone	2000	17.2	29.7	28.5	14.0	10.6	100.0	1,521,869
III. Outer	1990	17.5	46.2	20.3	8.2	7.8	100.0	73,397
Zone	2000	21.0	29.4	24.5	12.6	12.5	100.0	242,848
All Zones	1990	15.2	43.5	25.4	9.1	6.8	100.0	1,550,625
	2000	14.8	35.0	28.6	12.3	9.3	100.0	2,466,919

Source: Computed using data from the 1990 and 2000 Population Censuses and the 1995 Intercensal Survey.

Bogor (including Depok), 28.5 per cent from Bekasi, and 47.6 per cent from Tangerang.

If these commuters are added to the "night time" population, the total "day time" population of Jakarta would be at least 9,364,422 persons. We have to note here that the commuters recorded in the survey excluded those who come from areas beyond Bogor, Bekasi, and Tangerang, such as Bandung, Cianjur, Sukabumi, Cilegon, Kerawang, and Cirebon, so if we add these in, the daytime population would probably be closer to 9.5 million persons. We do not know what proportion of the commuters are people who had previously moved from the core to live in the inner and outer zones.

The educational level of commuters was significantly higher than that of non-migrants in the core. Just over 70 per cent of commuters graduated from senior high school and higher education compared to 49 per cent among non-migrants and 39 per cent among in-migrants, reflecting the higher social status and better jobs, on average, of the commuters. Among the employed commuters, 84 per cent were employees, compared to 72 per cent for non-migrants; self-employed persons were 11 per cent, compared to 21 per cent for non-migrants (Badan Pusat Statistik DKI Jakarta 2001).

Commuters travel to Jakarta from satellite cities in the east like Bekasi and Lippo Village, in the west like Bumi Serpong Damai, Alam Sutera,

and Tangerang, and in the south like Bogor and Kota Legenda. During the
rush hour in the morning and in the evening, public transportation is very
crowded. On the average, about 50 per cent of the commuters spent between
one to two hours getting to the place of work, with a distance of about
50 kilometres. Among the commuters, 12.6 per cent go to their place of
work by train, 49.5 per cent by public bus, 34.8 per cent by private and
government cars and the rest by other means of transportation, including *ojek*
(private motorcycles that serve as public transportation). Jakarta is probably
the largest city in the world that has no subway or elevated railroad system.
The transportation network between the core and the zones is not only far
behind the cities of developed nations but also, more relevantly, far behind
two of the developing country cities included in this book — Bangkok and
Shanghai. It is clearly insufficient for the transportation of more than one
million commuters per day. Construction of a new double track rail road
between Jakarta and Serang as well as a subway between Kebayoran Baru
and Kota (down town) are planned in the near future, and work began in
2005 on construction of two monorail lines along densely trafficked routes,

Figure 5.9   Haphazard Transformations of Peri-Urban Inner Zone

Source: G. Jones.

but it will be years before they can be completed and assist in relieving the traffic congestion.

The population growth of the inner zone will continue in the near future, probably at an accelerated pace, as the industrial estates and housing estates have already been re-located there. Its development is, however, chaotic. Industries locate next to farms, gated communities appear without nearby urban functions, and, with little provision for housing lower income populations, there is potential for proliferation of new slum areas (Figure 5.9). In the meantime, the transformation of the JMUR core from its past of small shops, open markets and low building heights toward a global metropolis of mega-malls, world business centres, and super highways moving to inner

Figure 5.10   JMURs New Skyline Emerging from the Mid-1980s

Source: M. Douglass.

Figure 5.11   Shopping Centres and Super-highways Re-organise Urban Space

Source: M. Douglass.

and outer zones is moving the city from one focused on neighbourhoods and community life to one of flows and functions (Figures 5.10 and 5.11). With these functions and government departments still preferring to locate in the core, the number of commuters will obviously increase in the near future and require major improvements in the transportation system.

Educational Changes and Differences between the Core and the Zones

We have pointed out above that the main reason for population to migrate is for employment and related activities. The kind of employment is highly correlated with the level of education. The increasing level of education has undoubtedly become one of the important factors motivating people to migrate from one place to another. Those who have a good educational background have a wider range of options for jobs and destinations. A study on the growth of six large cities in Indonesia (Badan Pusat Statistik 1997) concludes that generally in-migrants to the cities had a better educational level than their non-migrant populations, except in some parts of urban areas such as major construction and industrial zones.

Analysis of the population census data (Badan Pusat Statistik 2000a) reveals that the educational attainment of population in all parts of Indonesia has increased significantly and the variation by zones has narrowed compared to the situation two decades ago. Furthermore, although urban population always shows a better educational attainment than rural population, and males are more educated than women in all parts of Indonesia, the gap has narrowed, especially at younger ages (Badan Pusat Statistik 2000a). Changes in the educational pattern in JMUR could be expected to be consistent with the changes in other urban agglomerations of the country.

The percentage of JMUR population by educational attainment, migration status, and zones, in 1990–2000, is presented in Table 5.7. Rapid economic development and attention to expanding educational opportunities during the 1990s had clearly affected the educational pattern in JMUR as follows:

There was a significant improvement in educational attainment between 1990 and 2000. The percentage never attending school and not completed elementary school, both for migrants and non-migrants in the core and zones, declined. This was associated with an increase in the percentage who graduated from each level of education, except for migrants and non-migrants who graduated from primary school in the core and for migrants who graduated from secondary school in the inner zone and outer zones.

Table 5.7 Jakarta MUR: Percentage of Population by Level of Education, Migration Status and Age: 1990, 1995 and 2000

Zones/Years		Lower Secondary School and Below				Senior High School and Over			
		Migrants		Non-Migrants		Migrants		Non-Migrants	
		15–24	25–44	15–24	25–44	15–24	25–44	15–24	25–44
I. Core	1990	73.2	58.7	68.1	59.5	26.8	41.3	31.9	40.5
	1995	70.7	51.4	59.6	51.8	29.3	48.6	40.4	48.2
	2000	65.8	48.3	52.9	44.0	34.2	51.7	47.1	56.0
II. Inner Zone	1990	63.4	44.8	83.4	80.2	36.6	55.2	16.6	19.8
	1995	63.1	61.7	74.8	64.5	36.9	38.3	25.2	35.5
	2000	58.3	43.0	66.3	57.3	41.7	57.0	33.7	42.7
III. Outer Zone	1990	59.9	67.7	94.2	95.0	40.1	32.3	5.8	5.0
	1995	65.7	66.6	93.5	93.9	34.3	33.4	6.5	6.1
	2000	59.6	59.8	87.1	86.0	40.4	40.2	12.9	14.0
All Zones	1990	69.5	52.3	77.7	72.2	30.5	47.7	22.3	27.8
	1995	66.9	58.3	70.8	62.9	33.1	41.7	29.2	37.1
	2000	61.4	45.9	63.8	55.4	38.6	54.1	36.2	44.6

Source: Computed using data from the 1990 and 2000 Population Censuses and the 1995 Intercensal Survey.

Educational attainment levels are highest in the city core, and decrease with distance from the core. However, when education is classified by migration status, a different picture is obtained. For example, the percentage of migrants aged 15–24 years who had graduated from senior high school and higher education in the inner zone in 2000 was 42 per cent — higher than in the core (34 per cent) and the outer zone (40 per cent). The rapid development of large housing estates in the inner zone, with good employment opportunities for the better-educated, both there and by commuting to the core, might be the main reason why highly educated in-migrants came to this zone, both from the core and from all parts of Indonesia.

For the JMUR as a whole, migrants on average had higher educational attainment than non-migrants. We need to note that the educational attainment of migrants recorded in the population census was at the time of enumeration, not at the time when they left their place of origin. To the extent that migrants continued their education in their place of destination, their current educational level would be higher than at the time they migrated. In any case, Table 5.7 shows that the percentages of migrants in the core, inner zones, and outer zones, who had no formal education (no school and not completed primary school) were consistently lower than for non-migrants, with correspondingly higher proportion of migrants with secondary school education and above, except for those who graduated from senior high school and higher education in the core. Out migration of many highly educated people from the core to the inner and outer zones might have caused these differences.

Employment Changes and Differences between the Core and Zones

Migrants are heavily concentrated in the young adult ages and these are the age groups in which the Labour Force Participation Rate (LFPR) has shown the greatest change (Badan Pusat Statistik 2000a). Therefore, in analysing the LFPR differences between migrants and non-migrants in the core and zones, as well as examining the differences for the labour force as a whole, we will also present data for those aged 15–24 years.

Table 5.8 shows that generally the LFPR in both the core and zones increased between 1990 and 2000, very substantially in the case of non-migrant females. The LFPR of migrants was always higher than for non-migrants, for both males and females, in all zones. For example the LFPR of male migrants aged 15–24 years in the core in 2000 was 84 per cent,

Table 5.8   Jakarta MUR: Labour Force Participation Rates (per cent) by Zone, Sex, Age and Migration Status: 1990, 1995 and 2000

Zone/Year		Males 15–24 Migrant	Males 15–24 Non-Migrant	Males 10 + Migrant	Males 10 + Non-Migrant	Females 15–24 Migrant	Females 15–24 Non-Migrant	Females 10 + Migrant	Females 10 + Non-Migrant
I. Core	1990	81.8	44.7	84.1	64.8	67.0	32.1	58.4	26.0
	1995	83.7	45.7	87.6	66.0	65.9	37.1	57.8	27.4
	2000	83.9	49.2	88.5	72.7	73.0	41.2	64.8	37.7
II. Inner Zone	1990	63.5	57.3	74.7	66.6	50.6	27.4	36.9	21.4
	1995	95.5	58.8	91.9	69.9	48.6	33.6	41.0	26.1
	2000	67.4	50.0	78.6	70.4	57.4	41.0	48.0	38.4
III. Outer Zone	1990	80.9	62.3	79.2	69.4	80.1	20.7	59.1	18.2
	1995	91.5	68.2	91.9	68.7	67.2	41.7	44.1	26.7
	2000	67.9	54.4	76.7	69.6	61.7	41.1	48.4	37.9
All Zones	1990	75.6	51.8	79.8	66.2	63.1	28.5	50.3	23.0
	1995	91.4	54.8	92.3	68.0	61.5	36.7	50.8	27.0
	2000	81.4	50.6	85.5	71.6		71.7	53.4	38.0

Source: Computed using data in the 1990 and 2000 Population Censuses and the 1995 Intercensal Survey.

compared to 49 per cent for non-migrants in the same age group. For female migrants in the same age group, the LFPR was 73 per cent compared to 41 per cent for non-migrants. We have pointed out above that generally migrants in JMUR had a better level of education than non-migrants. The main reason why migrants had higher LFPR than non-migrants might have been that migrants moved to JMUR with the main objective of getting a better job and improving their living condition, not to study.

Changes in the Employment Pattern by Industry

Table 5.9 shows the percentage of employment by major industrial groups, for migrants and non-migrants in 1990 and 2000. Agriculture (A) group consists of agriculture, forestry, hunting and fishing; manufacturing (M) group consists of manufacturing, mining, electricity, gas and water, and construction; service (S) group consists of service, trade, transportation, finance, and others. Rapid economic growth (until 1997), and the demographic and educational changes during the 1980s and 1990s lay behind the changes in the structure of employment by industries. The share of agriculture was far lower than that of the other industrial groups, and showed a declining trend between 1990 and 2000. In the inner zone, it declined from 9 per cent in 1990 to 5.5 per cent in 2000, in the outer zone from 37 per cent to 25 per cent during the same period, and for the JMUR as a whole, from 10 per cent to 7 per cent.

The decrease in the percentage of the M sector group in the core, from 27 per cent in 1990 to 22 per cent in 2000, might have been partly due to the economic crisis (Firman 1999) and the relocation of industries from the core to inner and outer zones (Tangerang and Bekasi). As a result, the share of the M sector in the inner zone increased from 32 per cent in 1990 to 36 per cent in 2000, and in the outer zone from 22 per cent to 29 per cent during the same period. The percentage of the S sector was not only highest in the core, but it also rose from 72 per cent in 1990 to 77 per cent in 2000. Two sub-groups, namely, trade and services (community and private services) provide the bulk of sector employment.

As discussed earlier, the population growth of the core and outer zone were much affected by net out migration, and the inner zone by net in migration. Generally, in-migrants had a higher level of education than non-migrants. There are clearly causal relations in both directions between migration patterns and the employment distribution by industry. Table 5.9 shows that the percentage of migrants engaged in the A sector was much smaller than that of non-migrants in both 1990 and 2000. Migrants were also less concentrated in the S sector than non-migrants, except for those who lived in the inner zone in 1990. By contrast, the percentage of migrants engaged in M sector industries was larger than non-migrants in the core, the zones and in JMUR. Many factors affect the pattern of employment by industry, not only the level of education but also ethnic background, wage (salary), the working environment, security in old age, etc. At present, it is hard to analyse which of these factors were dominant and how they inter-related with each other, due to the scarcity of such data by small area in JMUR.

Table 5.9 Jakarta MUR: Percentage of Employed Person Aged 15 Years and Above by Regions, Main Industry and Migration Status, 1990 and 2000

Regions	Main Industry	Migrants		Non-Migrants		Migrants + Non-Migrants	
		1990	2000	1990	2000	1990	2000
I. Core	A	0.5	1.0	1.2	1.3	1.1	1.3
	M	29.7	27.3	26.7	21.3	27.2	22.1
	S	69.8	71.8	72.1	77.3	71.7	76.6
	Total	100.0	100.0	100.0	100.0	100.0	100.0
II. Inner Zone	A	1.2	4.0	10.5	6.0	8.9	5.6
	M	34.7	39.1	31.1	35.5	31.8	36.2
	S	64.0	56.9	58.3	58.5	59.3	58.2
	Total	100.0	100.0	100.0	100.0	100.0	100.0
III. Outer Zone	A	7.9	14.4	38.2	27.4	36.9	26.1
	M	62.9	44.9	20.6	27.0	22.4	28.7
	S	29.2	40.7	41.2	45.7	40.7	45.2
	Total	100.0	100.0	100.0	100.0	100.0	100.0
All Regions	A	1.2	3.9	11.5	7.4	9.9	6.8
	M	33.2	35.6	26.7	28.1	27.7	29.3
	S	65.7	60.4	61.8	64.5	62.4	63.9
	Total	100.0	100.0	100.0	100.0	100.0	100.0

Notes: A = sector include agriculture, foresty, hunting and fishing
M = sector include manufacturing, mining, electricity and water, and construction
S = sector include trade, transportation, finance, service and others
Source: Computed using data in the 1990 and 2000 Population Censuses.

Changes in the Employment Pattern by Occupation

Occupational data were not collected in the 2000 Population Census, hence we could not study the change of the employment pattern during the past ten years (1990–2000). However, based on the data from the 1990 Population Census and Supas 1995, Badan Pusat Statistik (2000b) has analysed the trend and variation of occupation in the core, inner zone, and outer zone over the 1990–95 period. Moving outward from the core to the inner and outer zone, there was a clear rise in the share of agricultural workers and a fall in share of professional, managerial and clerical workers, and service workers. The share of production workers was highest in the inner zone. In 1990, their percentage was almost the same in the core as in the outer zone, but in 1995, their percentage in the outer zone was significantly higher than in the core.

There were substantial differences in occupational structure by sex. In the core, professional, clerical and sales occupations were a more important component of female than of male employment, while the opposite was true for production occupations. In the inner zone, these male-female differentials continue to hold. As for male and female occupational patterns by migration status, in the core and inner zone, the only notable difference for males was that non-migrants were more likely to be in professional, managerial and clerical occupations. Differences between migrants and non-migrants were more marked in the case of females. In the core and the inner zone, female non-migrants were more concentrated in professional, managerial, clerical and sales occupations than migrants; in the core, female migrants were much more heavily concentrated in services. The greater concentration of migrants in services probably reflects in particular the domination of domestic services by migrants, and the concentration of non-migrants in sales probably reflects the local knowledge needed to gain a foothold in many petty trade and selling activities.

The Environment in Jabodetabek (JMUR) — The Water Crisis

Jabodetabek's ecology is under great stress from its accelerated population and economic growth and accompanying changes in the built environment and urban morphology. Air pollution is rated among the worst in the world (*World Resources* 1996/97), with vehicular emissions being its main source (Bappeda DKI Jakarta 2001). The lead level in Jakarta has exceeded the maximum suggested by the World Health Organisation (WHO) and has clearly affected the health condition of the population, especially children (Safrudin 2001).

With automobile and other vehicles using fossil fuels continuing to increase at rates much faster than population growth, and no mass transit system expected to be in place for many years to come, air pollution in JMUR is also likely to increase still more. From 1990 to 1998 the number of motor vehicles in Jakarta nearly doubled from 1.6 to 3 million, consuming almost 2 million tons of fossil fuels in the latter year (Bapedal DKI Jakarta 2000). In contrast, public transportation accounted for less than three per cent of total vehicles.

Issues surrounding the supply and quality of water in JMUR exemplify the deterioration of the region's ecological basis for supporting increasing population and human activities. Five large rivers are part of the city sewage system in Jakarta, namely Ciliwung River, Cipinang, Mookervart, Grogol, and Cakung River. In general, water quality in these rivers is deteriorating — based on two indicators: biochemical oxygen demand (BOD) and chemical oxygen demand (COD).[6] The water quality in downstream sections of these rivers is worsening as pollutants concentration from industrial, household, and agricultural wastes accumulate along the river flow.

The rivers in Bekasi are also polluted, especially the Cikedokan, Bojong, and Cikarang Rivers. These rivers have excessively high ammoniac concentration that is causing great losses. Fish are dying from river pollution, and since the rivers have been functioning for irrigation, the paddy quality is deteriorating, especially in Desa Setia Mekar (Suara Pembaruan 2002a). The same condition has occurred in parts of North Bekasi (Kompas 2002). In addition, 500,000 shrimps from a five hectares dyke in Desa Pantai Hurip Jaya were found dead and floating (Suara Pembaruan 2002b).

Demand for clean water is outpacing supply, and urban-industrial uses add to water pollution, loss of underground water supplies, land subsidence, and difficulty for government to keep pace with growing infrastructure and management needs.

Most of the water quality problems have resulted from inappropriate use of water bodies, with little consideration of the need to sustain water quality. Most industries in Jabodetabek have not implemented sufficient treatment plans.[7] Since the waste volume and characteristics have reached levels that exceed the carrying capacity of the water bodies, other beneficial uses of water in lower stream watershed areas are threatened. Thus, application of proper strategies to substantially change watershed management is of the utmost importance.

The low coverage of water supply service is also related to lack of infrastructure. The water supply companies operating through government contracts in Jakarta can only supply clean water for 48 per cent of the total population, resulting in large numbers of unserved urban inhabitants and also decreased revenues for water providers (Kompas 2003).

Industries in Jakarta have been relying heavily on groundwater for their activities, with a capacity of 33 billion cubic metres per year and an annual increase of around 1.5 billion cubic metres per year (ibid.). The excessive groundwater extraction has caused many problems. A recent study in Jabotabek has shown that the level of groundwater has decreased 0.03–2.95 centimetres per year. Water quality has also worsened, as shown by the spread of salty groundwater around 3–11 kilometres per year from the coastline (Direktorat Geologi Tata Lingkungan 1997/98). The decreased level of groundwater has been followed by land subsidence, resulting in North Jakarta becoming increasingly more susceptible to flooding.[8] Every year floods submerge at least 40 per cent of the total area in Jakarta (Media Indonesia 2003a). The worst flood crisis was in 2002, when the flood submerged around 80 per cent of all *kelurahan* in Jakarta and caused up to 1.5 million of Jakarta's inhabitants a great deal of suffering, claiming 77 lives, bringing water borne diseases such as diarrhea, skin disease, and respiratory infections to 141,477 persons and damageing 50,237 houses and 529 schools (Badan Pusat Statistik DKI Jakarta 2002).[9]

The factors identified as the source of worsening floods in Jakarta vary across the zones. Depletion of ground water is the major cause in the northern core zone. This is compounded in this area by the conversion of wet land and mangroves into housing area without developing sufficient infrastructure to control and prevent the risk of flooding. Some 80–90 per cent of the 1,144 hectares of wet land in North Jakarta have been converted into impervious land, causing routine flooding for most areas. The floods do not come only during the rainy season, but also during the dry season, when the sea tide is high. Plans for further reclamation of the north coast of Jakarta, for construction of residential areas and industrial estates, have been opposed by environmental experts, on the grounds that it will cause serious flooding in most parts of Jakarta.

Settlement over the region's acquifer is a principal issue in the inner zone. In the outer zone toward the high mountains through the Puncak pass, deforestation and siting of new housing on hillsides are the major concerns. This latter area — Bopuncur — has changed from a water catchment area into one of luxurious houses and villas (Figure 5.12).

Figure 5.12   Kota Air (Water City) in the Uplands toward Puncak (Outer Zone)

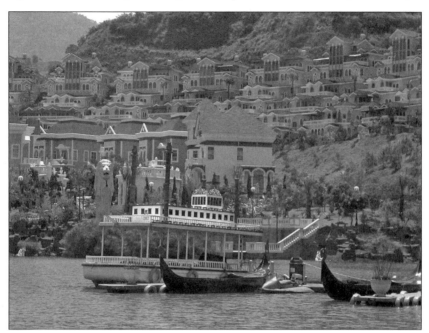

Source: M. Douglass.

To solve the many problems related to water supply and quality, the government has planned to construct a new canal in the eastern part of Jakarta, more water gates to distribute excess water when rainfall begins and water levels in the rivers reach a high level, and other infrastructure. There is no fixed timetable for the initiation and completion of this project. Meanwhile, the floods continue to hit Jakarta and its surrounding cities. The lack of coordination between local governments of Jakarta and Bopuncur, as catchment area, has exacerbated the flooding, as have inappropriate urban development and planning (Media Indonesia 2003c).

The human consequences of poor urban environmental quality are readily apparent. For JMUR, respiratory infections related to air pollution are widespread, with as many as 300,000 cases reported in 1999 (Badan Pengendalian Dampak Lingkungan 2000). Another 53,000 people were treated for skin diseases and diarrhoea, mostly resulting from poor water quality, the same year. The World Bank (2003) estimates that in 2002 respiratory inflammations accounted for 12.6 per cent of all mortality in

Jakarta, more than double the rate for all Indonesia. Solid waste dispersion is a growing threat to the quality of water, air, and land resources. Poor solid waste management contributes about 30 per cent of the local waterway Biochemical Oxygen Demand (BOD) loading and is the largest source of particulate air pollution in urban areas. It is a major contributor to water-borne diseases, respiratory ailments, and localised flooding.

The government has responded in many ways to these dire conditions. Environmental watchdog agencies have been established, clean river programmes have shown some successes, and other programmes such as the Kampung Improvement Programme are credited with upgrading environmental infrastructure of lower income communities. In the context of the scale of construction and expansion of population in JMUR in recent years, however, such efforts continue to lag behind in addressing root causes of JMURs environmental stress.

Summary and Conclusion

Jakarta MUR's annual rate of population growth slowed between 1990 and 2000, but it varied sharply by zones (core, inner zone, and outer zone). During the 1990–95 period the rate of natural increase had played a more important role than net migration in determining the annual rate of population growth, but in the 1995–2000 period migration came to the fore. Net out migration played a more dominant role than natural increase in the core and outer zone during 1995–2000, as did net in-migration in the inner zone. Of all in-migrants to the inner zone, 34.1 per cent originated from the core, 24.4 per cent from the outer zone, and the rest (41.5 per cent) from other provinces. This evidence supports the "spill over" hypothesis mentioned earlier.

The population of Jakarta metropolitan area (core) officially recorded on a *de jure* basis in the 2000 Population Census was 8.3 million persons, which may be regarded as the night time population. If we add to this number the number of commuters (1 million) who travel daily between peripheral areas and Jakarta, we would get a total of 9.3 million persons who may be regarded as the day time population of Jakarta, which would rise to about 9.5 million if we include the commuters who live in the areas beyond Jabodetabek. The educational level of commuters was much higher than that of in-migrants to the core.

There is a clear gradation in educational levels, which decrease outwards from the core. The educational level of males is higher than that of females, but the gap has been decreasing, notably for the young population (Badan

Pusat Statistik 1997). Generally, the Labour Force Participation Rate (LFPR) of in-migrants in the core, inner zone and outer zone was higher than for non-migrants. This may have been partly due to migrants having a better educational background than non-migrants (except in the core), giving them a better chance of finding jobs. As for the employment structure, the S sector has the highest percentage of total employment in the core and zones, followed by the M sector, and the A sector (agriculture) now lags far behind. The percentage of the M sector in the core is declining, since no more large manufacturing industries are permitted to be built there, and several existing industries were reallocated to the inner and outer zones. As a result, the percentage of those working in manufacturing industry in the inner and outer zone increased significantly between 1990 and 2000. The S sector has the highest, and generally increasing, share of employment in all zones, but it is most dominant in the core, where it provides more than three quarters of all employment.

Based on the present findings and results of surveys conducted by the Jakarta Office of the Central Statistics Board in 2001, and the future plan of DKI Jakarta, we can make a tentative forecast of the physical development and demographic change in JMUR over the next ten years, as follows:

Fertility and mortality rates are already low in the core and the inner zone, and they might not decline much more, hence the overall effect of natural increase on the rate of population growth will not change very much. In the outer zone, there is still potential for further declines in both fertility and mortality. The inner zone may continue to grow rapidly and net out-migration from the core may continue, but probably at a slower pace. Much planned construction in the core that was postponed during the economic crisis, including the construction of multi-storied apartments and office buildings in the "golden triangle" of Jalan Sudirman, the Kota area, Pantai Indah Kapuk, etc., has now gradually resumed. Land reclamation along the north coast of Jakarta is being planned, mainly for residential areas for the middle and upper social classes. During the construction period, a large number of construction workers from other provinces will undoubtedly be required. When the new residential areas are completed, there will be an increasing number of in-migrants to Jakarta's core, and net out migration from the core is likely to be reduced.

The master plans for the construction of residential and industrial estates in the inner and outer zones were better designed compared to Jakarta (the core). The Jakarta city master plan was formerly made by the Dutch to accommodate a population of about 500,000, on the north coast of Jakarta, close to the old harbour of Sunda Kelapa. For many years, the city has grown almost uncontrolled, as indicated by the unsystematic pattern of road construction. Despite the upgrading of the basic toll road and rail infrastructure, Jakarta MUR's traffic problems have not been solved, because the annual rate of growth of vehicles has been much faster than the growth of roads. We can infer from this trend that traffic congestion in the near future will continue to worsen.

The locations of most new residential estates in the inner zone and outer zone were well selected, and the construction of housing, drainage system, and road network within the estates well planned. However, the access roads from the housing estates to Jakarta and other cities, which actually were not all the responsibility of the housing developers, were frequently poorly constructed and caused traffic congestion. This situation could be exacerbated in the future, as the construction of residential areas still continues apace, especially in the inner zone. Many residential areas in the zones will become medium or even large satellite cities of Jakarta in a relatively short time. In the meantime, the population of Jakarta (the core) might start to increase again if in-migration starts to pick up as a result of the construction of luxurious multi-story apartments in many parts of Jakarta and residential developments on the reclamation areas along the coast of Jakarta and in other parts where under-developed land still remains.

Notes

1. The 1971 Indonesian Population Census showed literacy of 76 per cent at ages 15–29, compared with only 53 per cent for those aged 30–39. By 1980, literacy at ages 15–29 had reached 85 per cent.

2. This shift to export-oriented industrialisation was further spurred by the revaluation of the Japanese yen in 1985, which made exports from Japan uncompetitive in labour-intensive sectors and resulted in a massive shift of these segments of production from Japan to East and Southeast Asia. Transnational shoe makers and garment industries began to locate in Jakarta as well.

3. The annual *rate* of population growth steadily decreased from 4.5 per cent (1961–71) to 3.9 per cent (1971–80) to 2.4 per cent (1980–90), and then decreased sharply to 0.2 per cent (1990–2000). The growth of Jakarta's population in the early periods clearly had a large net in-migration component. By 2000 the population density of this area reached approximately 12,000 per square kilometre. Researchers are still disputing the extremely low rate of growth between 1990 and 2000, which might have two different explanations: spillover through heavy out-migration to surrounding areas or under-enumeration in the 2000 Population Census (Badan Pusat Statistik 2000a).

4. Mortality rates were estimated based on the data of the average number of children ever born and still living per women and the age structure of population, using Sullivan's method (1972). Life Tables for each zone and sub-zone were selected from the Life Table Models (Coale and Demeny 1966) that fit the mortality level of each zone. Then, using the mortality function of the selected Life Table and sex-age structure, we computed the total number of deaths and average annual Crude Death Rate (CDR) for Period I and Period II. Total Fertility Rate (TFR) was estimated using Rele's method (Rele 1967), which was then converted into the Crude Birth Rate (CBR) (see Table 5.3).

5. Rates of Net Migration (RNM) for 1990–95 and 1995–2000 were obtained through the application of the balancing equation, using the data on total population by age and sex from the 1990 Population Census, 1995 Supas, 2000 Population Census, and fertility and mortality rates for the same period (Badan Pusat Statistik 2000b). For comparison purposes, in-migrants for JMUR were also computed using forward projection, based on the age structure of the population. The results are close to the number of migrants estimated using balancing equation method. For example, net migrants for the core, inner zone, and outer zone in 1995–2000, estimated using forward projection were –31.1, +34.6, and –35.4 per 1,000 population respectively, compared to –34.1, +28.3, –40.3 respectively, estimated using the balancing equation.

6. BOD = Biochemical Oxygen Demand, which is oxygen needed for oxidising organic matter by microorganism; COD = Chemical Oxygen Demand, which is oxygen needed for oxidising organic matter by chemical reaction.

7. Based on a study by the Environmental Impact Management Agency (Bapedal), only 81 out of 535 factories discharge acceptable waste water quality; 136 factories emit poor quality; and 318 factories remain unable to process the waste water and generate polluting waste water (Bapedal 2000).

8. During the 1979–91 period, North Jakarta subsided 24.5–34 cm/year. West Jakarta subsided 8.3 cm/year, East Jakarta 4.3–4.5 cm/year, and Central Jakarta 2.3–3.0 cm/year (Pemda DKI, 1994). The elevation of this part of JMUR is now even lower than the sea level during the high tide season (Media Indonesia 2003b).

9. Locations that routinely suffer from severe floods are kelurahan Bidaracina, Pejaten Timur, Peta Mampang, Bukit Duri, Cipinang Besar Selatan and Kampung Melayu, which all are located in the coastal rivers area (Badan Pusat Statistik DKI Jakarta 2002).

6

The Manila MUR:
Continuing Magnet for Migrants

Rachel H. Racelis and Paula Monina G. Collado

In the context of the six mega-cities covered in this book, the Manila mega-urban region (MUR) is comparable to Bangkok in terms of dominance of the nation's administrative, financial, industrial, commercial and education sector. Its core, Metro-Manila, has easily maintained a tenfold multiple of the population of each of the Philippines' next two largest cities, Davao and Cebu, each of which hold about one million population. If we take Manila's entire mega-urban region which includes the six surrounding provinces, then Metro Manila's population is doubled, and the entire MUR contains one quarter of the Philippine population.

This chapter begins with a detailed background of the Manila MUR and its components. The discussions on the history of the core or Metro Manila, and the major factors that contributed to the development of the inner zone provide the context for interpreting results of the census data analysis presented later in the chapter. The 1990 and 2000 Censuses of Population and Housing are used to study the following in each MUR zone: population size and change; migration patterns; and population and migrant characteristics. Similarities and/or differences are examined across two basic dimensions — across zones and across time periods.

Background on the Manila Mega-Urban Region (MUR)

Composition

The Manila MUR is defined to include seven major administrative units, the National Capital Region or Metro Manila and the provinces of Pampanga,

Bulacan, Rizal, Cavite, Laguna and Batangas. Each administrative unit, in turn, consists of cities and municipalities as sub-units. All of Metro Manila comprises the core while portions of the six provinces comprise the inner and outer zones. As described in an earlier chapter, the composition of the inner and outer zones were determined based on an assessment of the 1990 population densities of cities and municipalities in the six provinces. Jones, Tsay and Bhajracharya (2000) set the criteria in an earlier paper. Basically, the inner zone includes cities and municipalities with population density >750 per square kilometre in 1990 and which were contiguous to Metro Manila or to other inner zone localities. The remaining areas constitute the outer zone.

Geographically, Metro Manila is located at the centre of the MUR (see Figure 3.2). Metro Manila is bounded by Pampanga and Bulacan on the north, Rizal on the East, Cavite, Laguna and Batangas on the south and Manila Bay on the west. Bulacan, Rizal, Laguna and Cavite are contiguous to Metro Manila. The inner zone radiates from the core in three directions: northwest, through Bulacan and Pampanga; eastward through Rizal; and southeast through Cavite, Laguna and Batangas.

The core, Metro Manila, is the largest urban agglomeration in the country with a population of 9.9 million in 2000, about 13 per cent of

Table 6.1   Metro-Manila and Other Large Urban Areas in the Philippines, 1970–2000

Area/Indicator	1970	1980	1990	2000
Population (million)				
Philippines	36.5	48.1	60.7	76.5
Metro-Manila	4.0	5.9	7.9	9.9
Percentage of Metro-Manila to total Philippine population	11.0	12.3	13.0	12.9
Percentage of specific city to Metro-Manila population:				
Davao	9.8	10.3	10.8	11.6
Cebu/Mandaue	10.1	10.2	10.0	9.9
Zamboanga	5.0	5.8	5.6	6.1
Cagayan de Oro	3.2	3.8	4.3	4.7
Bacolod	4.7	4.4	4.6	4.3
General Santos	1.8	2.5	3.2	4.2

Source: National Statistical Coordination Board, 2003.

total Philippine population (Table 6.1). Its population more than doubled in the last 30 years. Davao and Cebu, the next two largest urban areas in the Philippines, each have only one-tenth the population of Metro Manila. The combined population of the next six largest cities is about 40 per cent of Metro Manila's population.

The six provinces in the Manila MUR are among the ten largest provinces in the Philippines, each with population size exceeding 1.6 million in 2000. Bulacan is the largest among the six with a population of 2.2 million. Except for Batangas, the MUR provinces are also among those that have proportions of urban population exceeding the nationwide proportion of 48 per cent. In 2000, only about 8 per cent of Batangas' population was in the inner zone. But 80 per cent of Rizal's population, and about 60 per cent of the populations of Pampanga, Bulacan, Cavite and Laguna, were in the inner zone.

The Core: From Maynilad to Metro Manila

The development of the core was basically driven by economic and legal forces. It emerged from the pre-colonial settlement Maynilad and developed in three stages: as Intramuros during the Spanish regime; the incorporated City of Manila from the early 1900s to the 1960s; and the Greater Manila or Metropolitan Manila Area from the 1970s to the present. Metro Manila, as most other urban areas, started from a "mother" city that had expanded over time through the gradual accretion of surrounding territories as these became functionally integrated with the mother city. In the case of Manila the scope of the territory at each stage of expansion was legally established. The growth of the core over time in terms of the land area had progressed as follows (in square kilometres): Intramuros 1.2; City of Manila 25; and Metro Manila 617 (Serote 1991; National Statistical Coordination Board 2003).

Maynilad was endowed with two locational advantages for trading purposes: access to Laguna de Bay and inland settlements; and access to Manila Bay and to foreign trade. It was already a hub for exchange of commodities with local tribes and foreign traders, particularly from China, even before the arrival of the Spaniards (Reed 1967). Spanish settlements and fortresses were established in Cebu, Iloilo and Manila starting in 1565, and the City of Manila formally founded in 1571. It was then confined to Intramuros (meaning "within walls") and was a walled city only 1.2 square kilometres in area. Within this tiny enclosure most of the institutions of Spanish colonial administration, both civil and ecclesiastical, were established

(Serote 1991). Manila became the colonial capital and the centre not only of state and church but also of economic activities. Its excellent harbour facilities as well as its location adjacent to the "rice basket" of Central Luzon made it the undisputed choice for the headquarters of the new colony (Phelan 1959). Manila, as in pre-colonial times, continued to be the archipelago's centre for insular commerce and international maritime trade.

As the city became more prosperous, growth also occurred in the suburbs and towns around Intramuros. Commercial, manufacturing and other economic activities supporting Intramuros were located in the suburban areas. With the official opening of the City of Manila to American and European vessels in the 1790s, economic activities in the suburbs expanded to the export-import business, and to processing and manufacturing of materials for export like cigars and Manila hemp. Residential areas were likewise expanding in the suburbs to accommodate increasing numbers of Spaniards wanting to live outside of the walled city, the Filipino wage earners engaged in non-farming activities, and the Chinese traders.

Spanish rule ended and the American regime began in 1898. In 1903, Intramuros and 12 surrounding towns were incorporated by government Act No. 183 to become the expanded City of Manila (Reyes 1998).[1] At this time, the City of Manila had a population of 190 thousand and 876 manufacturing firms. Manila remained the capital city of the country throughout the American colonial period, and after the Philippines gained independence in 1945. It continued to be the preferred location of manufacturing establishments up to the mid-1950s. But by the late 1950s manufacturing firms started to drift out and locate in municipalities adjacent to Manila such as Mandaluyong, San Juan, Pandacan and Caloocan — and even further out in Taguig and Paranaque. Luna (1964) attributes this shift in location preference to four factors that were making the City of Manila increasingly undesirable: (1) inadequate space for expansion; (2) traffic congestion; (3) increasing cost of land; and (4) restricted operation of noxious industries. Along with industrial growth, population growth similarly spread to these neighbouring municipalities by the 1960s as more residential areas were developed.

The continuing growth of Manila and the surrounding cities and municipalities eventually brought common urban problems such as inadequate transportation infrastructure and traffic congestion (Figure 6.1), lack of potable water, unsanitary disposal of waste, lack of proper drainage and sewerage system, and seasonal flooding. The failure to address these problems during the postwar period was attributed, in part, to piecemeal and uncoordinated solutions employed by local governments, and to jurisdictional disputes over

Figure 6.1   Manila Metro Rail Transit System (MRT) Built Along the Middle of the Notoriously Jammed EDSA in the Late 1990s

Source: G. Jones.

responsibility for the delivery of services (Mercado n.d.) The need for a legal entity that encompassed the entire Metro Manila area was finally recognised. Presidential Decree 824 was issued in 1975, after obtaining approval from Metro Manila residents to create a new administrative structure. The decree legally constituted the City of Manila and 16 cities and municipalities surrounding Manila as the National Capital Region (NCR). In 1995, Republic Act 7924 reaffirmed the composition of the NCR or Metro Manila and created a governing body, the Metropolitan Manila Development Authority.

The economic, service provision and governmental activities indicators presented in Table 6.2 depict the dominant role of Metro Manila in Philippine society today. While 13 per cent of the country's population reside in Metro Manila, it accounts for disproportionate shares of the gross domestic product and value added in manufacturing: 36 per cent and 43 per cent, respectively. About one-third of government employees are to be found there. Similarly, Metro Manila accounts for more than double its share of higher education and hospital care services provision. If these indicators in Table 6.2 are used by the average Filipino as the gauge for availability of jobs and services, then it is not surprising that Metro Manila continues to be a magnet for migrants (Figure 6.2).

The Inner Zone

Among the many factors that may have contributed to the emergence and growth of the MUR inner zone towns, the succeeding discussion focuses on the following four: (1) population resettlement; (2) transportation development; (3) the tightening of the housing situation in Metro Manila; and (4) national industrialisation policies.

Population Resettlement

The urban core of municipalities (poblaciones) and cities of the Philippines had mostly resulted from a Spanish colonial government policy — the resettlement and consolidation of population in selected sites. Prior to colonisation, the Philippine social structure was described as "a conglomeration of tiny, independent principalities" (Noone 1986). Given the highly dispersed population and the small number of Spanish priests, who led the colonisation process, the method used in Mexico and Peru was applied in the Philippines,

Table 6.2 Metro-Manila Indicators, 2002

Indicators	Percentage
Economic Activity	
Percentage of Metro-Manila GRDP to national GDP	36%
Percentage of Metro-Manila gross value addition (GVA) to national GVA for manufacturing	43%
Percentage of Metro-Manila revenues to total national revenues earned from domestic trade freighting	40%
Services	
Percentage of higher education level students attending schools located in Metro-Manila	28%
Percentage of national total hospital bed capacity attributable to Metro-Manila hospitals	32%
Government	
Percentage of the 1.4 million total government workers located in Metro-Manila	32%

Source: National Statistical Coordination Board, 2003 and <www.doh.gov.ph>.

Figure 6.2   Makati, Wealthy Financial and Commercial Centre in Manila's Core

Source: G. Jones.

beginning in the 1580s. Filipinos were "congregated" or "reduced", to use the official terminology, into compact villages. These villages were to vary in size between 2,400 to 5,000 people, numbers which the Spanish officials regarded as suitable for efficient civil and religious administration (Phelan 1959).

Successful examples of resettlement were found around Laguna de Bay and in the provinces of Central Luzon. The six MUR provinces are among these success areas. It is said that the population in these provinces was "more compactly settled" than peoples of other regions because they were more subject to the Hispanic influences radiating from Manila (Phelan 1959). Examples of inner zone municipalities founded through Spanish resettlement and the dates founded include: Antipolo (1632) and Morong (1586) in Rizal; Apalit (1641) in Pampanga; and Baliuag (1733) in Bulacan (Coseteng 1972).

Transportation Development

The importance of water transportation in pre-colonial Philippines is reflected in the riverside and coastal location of traditional settlements. Small trails connected lowland settlements but these were rendered impassable during the rainy seasons. The Spaniards did not change the structure of transportation until the 1830s, and the rivers, Laguna de Bay and seas continued to be the main means of transportation particularly to and from Manila for over two centuries (Reed 1967). Horse-drawn vehicles were operated only within Manila and large towns. Many inner zone towns were already connected to Manila in Spanish times through water transportation.

Between 1830 and 1898, a system of roads was established connecting the heavily populated provinces of Luzon and Manila (Reed 1967). These included routes that crossed the MUR provinces as follows (Corpuz 1999):

1. From Manila through Bulacan and Pampanga and then on to northern Luzon — either on to Central Luzon and Ilocos, or on to Nueva Ecija and Cagayan; and
2. From Manila to the southeast of Luzon across Laguna and Batangas, and then on to Bicol.

Still, overland transportation remained difficult because in the rainy season bridges were frequently washed out and many roads reduced to mud.

In 1875, the Spanish government initiated plans for a railroad system in the Philippines. In the initial plans three railroad lines were proposed, but only a portion of the first line, Manila to Dagupan, completed in 1892, was built under the Spanish regime. The second and third lines as well as remaining parts of the first line were built during the American rule. The first and third lines, referred to as the Main Line North and Main Line South, ran through the length of the north and south portions of the inner zone, respectively. Additional lines constructed during the American regime, the Antipolo, Marikina and Cavite Lines, also went through the inner zone (Corpuz 1999).

Up to 1930, the MRC operated profitably. Then in the 1930s coal prices soared and effects of the worldwide depression continued to be felt. Furthermore, successive road developments by the Americans led to the rise of serious competition from trucks and buses that were encroaching further into railroad territory and traffic. The MRC started operating at a loss in 1934. Unprofitable lines such as the Antipolo, Marikina and Cavite Lines were abandoned. MRC operation halted altogether during World War Two. The North Line resumed operation after the war but had to gradually cut down on service in the 1960s and 1970s. Operation of the line had practically ceased by the 1980s as truck and bus services to northern Luzon became more convenient and inexpensive. Today only Main Line South and commuter service from Manila to Carmona, Cavite are in operation.

Corpuz (1999) made two noteworthy observations about overland transportation development in Luzon from the Spanish times. First, the railroad system was basically juxtaposed on the crude road network constructed during the Spanish colonial period. And second, the railroads formed the trunk of an insular transportation system that, in turn, became the basis of the modern network of highways. The overall layout of the railroad system was carefully worked out to satisfy the Spanish colonial government's objective to connect the capital city to the largest and most productive agricultural areas of Luzon. This objective has obviously remained as a guide in the development of two major highways emanating from Metro Manila, the North and South Luzon Expressways, for these have similar routes (at least within the MUR area) as the north and south railroad lines. These two highways, like the railroad lines, therefore also run through the length of the north and south portions of the inner zone.

Thus, all major transportation infrastructures for land travel developed in the MUR provinces over the last century traversed the inner zone. This partly explains the increasing attractiveness of the zone to migrants as shown later in the chapter.

Housing Development

The tight housing situation in Metro Manila is a result of intense competition for its fixed land resources. With the increasing demand for prime land for commercial, financial and trading purposes, the least productive and profit-generating among urban land uses, namely housing for the middle income group and the urban poor, is fast disappearing (Santiago 1996.) The high cost of land, which continues to increase, remains the major factor putting land and housing located in Metro Manila beyond the reach of middle and low income groups.

Thus, government financed low-cost housing projects and relocation sites for urban informal settlers have been placed in reasonably accessible sites outside of Metro Manila such as Rizal and Cavite. Private residential development for low and medium cost housing have similarly focused their efforts in the periphery of Metro Manila and in the MUR provinces, particularly Rizal, Cavite and Laguna (Figures 6.3 and 6.4). Of course, key to the selection of sites is easy access to Metro Manila.

Figure 6.3 Outer Zone "Greenfields" Housing Development, Manila MUR

Source: G. Jones.

Figure 6.4 *In situ* Growth of Housing in Manila MUR's Inner Zone

Source: G. Jones.

National Industrialisation Policies

Metro Manila had long been the preferred location particularly of manufacturing establishments, as evidenced by the indicator of gross value added or GVA for manufacturing presented in Table 6.2. The adoption of the import-substitution policy in the 1950s intensified the attractiveness of Metro Manila, which had all the locational advantages for the production of import substitutes including easy access to airports and seaports, access to import licensing offices and foreign exchange, and availability of skilled labour and ancillary services (Llorito 2003).

By the 1970s, Philippine economic policy turned towards addressing the regional imbalance in economic development. One policy adopted by the Philippine government was industrial dispersal and this was explicitly incorporated for the first time in a national development plan, the 1978–82 Philippine Medium Term Development Plan. The policy was supposed to result in two related outcomes: to bring industrial growth to the less-developed regions of the country; and, at the same time, to direct the location of industries away from Metro Manila. The implementing strategies for industrial dispersal are detailed in a number of laws (Republic Acts and Executive Orders) and national programmes incorporated in the national development plans.

The industrial dispersal policy has been implemented using three strategies or methods: investment incentives; industrial estates or centres; and outright ban on locating in Metro Manila. Two sets of investment incentives (and disincentives) were established: first, denial of fiscal perks (e.g. tax exemptions) to firms locating in Metro Manila; and, second, provision of maximum fiscal and other concessions to firms locating outside of Metro Manila. Industrial estates, economic zones and regional industrial centres were approved and established in areas targeted to attract industries. A short-lived Presidential directive (undated but presumed to be in the 1970s) banned the entry or expansion of industries within 50 kilometres radius of the centre of Manila (Santiago 1996). The first two strategies are still being implemented. The "50 kilometre radius ban" however was in force only for a very brief period due to the many technical, administrative and political problems it generated.

Whether firms were responding to the policies mentioned or to some other factors such as improved infrastructure, availability of land and better transportation system, they had increasingly chosen to locate in the MUR provinces. The location of new industries as well as the relocation of existing ones were in three directions from Metro-Manila — to the north (Bulacan and Pampanga), to the south (Cavite, Laguna and Batangas) and to a lesser extent to the east (Rizal) — along the major transport routes (Santiago 1996). The various sites chosen by privately developed industrial estates or economic zones that are registered with the Philippine Economic Zone Authority (PEZA) also indicate the same preference. A total of 171 industrial estates were registered at PEZA as of the end of 2003 (<www.peza.gov.ph>). Nearly half of this total, 72, are located in the six MUR provinces. Furthermore, all industrial estates in Laguna and Pampanga, and more than half of those in Cavite, are located in the inner zone.

A study of Board of Investments (BOI) registered investments from 1987–2002 conducted by Llorito (2003) analysed the change or shift in investment location choice. Results of the study for the entire Philippines indicate a gradual southern push of investments away from Metro Manila. And an analysis of Luzon investments (which accounted for 80 per cent of total BOI-approved investments) showed a gradual outward spread or dispersion of investments away from Metro Manila and towards the surrounding provinces including the six MUR provinces.

Data Limitations

One of the aims of this book is to provide comparative analysis of employment change in the six MURs. For Manila, this is problematic because the Census of Population and Housing is not meant to generate labour force or employment data.[2] The Census asks only three questions related to economic activities: usual occupation; kind of business or industry; and place of work. Usual occupation includes two broad analytical categories, gainful and non-gainful, the latter including students, housekeepers and retired.

While individuals reporting non-gainful occupations can be classified as being "not in the labour force" and "not employed", the labour force and employment status of those reporting gainful occupations cannot be determined. Based on the NSO definition, the labour force includes persons who are employed and persons who are out of work but are seeking work. Following this definition, two pieces of information not recorded in the Census are needed to establish the labour force status of an individual: employment status; and if unemployed, whether seeking work.[3] Thus, the analysis of economic activity in the MUR zones is undertaken based only on the structure implied by the reported usual gainful occupation and industry classification, irrespective of labour force or employment status.

The extent of missing data for the reference population, population 15 years old or older, in the 1990 and 2000 Censuses needs to be noted.

The percentage with missing data ranged from one to eight per cent for the variables "residence five years ago" and "educational attainment". The extent of missing data for usual occupation, kind of business and place of work was moderate (between 6 to 16 per cent) in 1990, but relatively high (between 24 to 26 per cent) in 2000.

Population Change

Population Size, Structure, and Sources of Change

The Philippine population in 2000 was 76.5 million (Table 6.3). Annual population growth for the country between 1990 and 2000 was 2.3 per cent, far exceeding the growth rate for Southeast Asia of 1.5 per cent. The Philippines has one of the highest birth rates in the ASEAN. The crude birth rate of 27 per 1000 population in 2000 is second only to Cambodia and Lao PDR's (National Statistical Coordination Board, 2003). The Philippine mortality situation (crude death rate of 7 per 1,000 population), however, is comparable to those of other ASEAN countries.

The Manila MUR population in 2000 was well over one quarter of the Philippine population (Table 6.3). Average annual population growth in the MUR between 1990 and 2000 was 3.1 per cent, exceeding the national growth rate. About one-half of the region's population is in the core and

Table 6.3   Size and Distribution of MUR Population by Zone, 1990 and 2000

Area	1990	2000
Population (million)		
Philippines	60.7	76.5
Manila MUR	15.9	21.7
Percentage of Manila MUR to Total Philippine Population	26.2	28.4
Distribution of MUR Population by Zone (per cent):		
Core	49.8	45.8
Inner Zone	26.2	29.4
Outer Zone	23.9	24.8
All Areas	100.0	100.0

Source: 1990 and 2000 Census of Population Housing, National Statistical Coordination Board.

about one-quarter each in the inner and outer zones. The annual growth rates in the period 1990–2000 were 2.1, 4.2 and 3.4 per cent in the core, inner zone and outer zone, respectively. Between 1990 and 2000, the population share of the core is observed to have declined significantly as a result of its slower annual population growth.

The age-sex structures of the population in the inner and outer zones are generally similar (Table 6.4). The core's population structure, on the other hand, differs from the structure of the two other zones in two respects. First, it has more females than males, with sex ratios of 93 in 1990 and 95 in 2000.[4] Inner and outer zone sex ratios are each about 100. Second, the core

Table 6.4 **Population Distribution by Age and Sex Group: By Zone, 1990 and 2000**

Age Group	Core		Inner Zone		Outer Zone	
	Male	Female	Male	Female	Male	Female
1990						
Population (million)	3.8	4.1	2.1	2.1	1.9	1.9
Distribution (per cent):						
0–14	35.3	31.8	38.2	36.1	39.1	37.6
15–24	20.8	23.8	20.5	21.1	20.8	20.6
25–34	19.1	19.6	16.6	17.1	15.4	15.2
35–44	12.4	11.7	11.9	11.6	10.7	10.6
45–64	10.4	10.3	10.3	10.7	10.6	11.6
65 or older	2.1	2.7	2.6	3.5	3.3	4.5
All Ages	100.0	100.0	100.0	100.0	100.0	100.0
2000						
Population (million)	4.8	5.0	3.2	3.2	2.7	2.7
Distribution (per cent):						
0–14	33.4	30.8	35.6	33.7	36.4	35.1
15–24	19.7	21.7	19.2	20.2	19.6	19.8
25–34	18.6	18.6	16.9	17.2	16.2	16.1
35–44	13.4	13.1	13.2	12.9	12.4	11.9
45–64	12.5	12.5	12.3	12.4	12.1	12.6
65 or older	2.4	3.3	2.6	3.7	3.3	4.6
All Ages	100.0	100.0	100.0	100.0	100.0	100.0

Source: 1990 and 2000 Census of Population Housing, National Statistical Coordination Board.

has a higher proportion of the population in the young working age 15–34 years, though this age-structure difference between the core and the other zones diminished between 1990 and 2000.

Data in Table 6.5 provides some explanation for these differences. The inner zone, which experienced the highest population growth rate, had the highest proportion of population growth attributable to net migration. Conversely, the core, which experienced the lowest population growth rate, had the lowest proportion of net migration relative to population growth.

Looking into age and sex composition effects, net migration to the core basically constituted additions to the population in the age group 15–29, 55 per cent of whom are females, small additions to the very young age group (children accompanying migrating parents) and deductions from all other age groups. Net migration to the inner and outer zones, on the other hand, constituted additions to the population in all age groups with only slightly more females than males.

Net Migration in Metro Manila Cities and Municipalities

The data in Table 6.5 leave the impression that migration into Metro Manila has slowed down. An examination of net migration estimated for each city and municipality of Metro Manila shows that this is true for only some localities. There are municipalities that continue to experience positive net migration, some even as high as in the inner zone.

Table 6.6 presents population size change and estimated net migration (1990–2000) for each of the 17 cities and municipalities of Metro Manila. Localities are arranged in descending order according to the percentage of net migration relative to the absolute value of population size change.[5] Nine localities have positive net migration. In the top four, the percentages of net migration to population change are as high as in the inner zone. Eight localities have negative net migration. The bottom three — San Juan, Pasay City and the City of Manila — experienced reductions in *total* population between 1990 and 2000. Natural increase was obviously not sufficient to compensate for the high out-migration from these places.

The net migration pattern observed in Table 6.6 may be explained by the locality's history and location relative to the City of Manila. Manila, the oldest settlement, has one of the highest population densities in the country (over 60 thousand per square kilometre since 1980). The other eight localities with negative net migration are in the central part of Metro Manila, surrounding the City of Manila. Being adjacent to Manila, these localities became the

Table 6.5 Net Migration by Age and Sex Group: By Zone, 1990 and 2000

Age Group	Core		Inner Zone		Outer Zone	
	Male	Female	Male	Female	Male	Female
Net migration all ages	130,526	139,881	441,816	503,450	244,766	277,920
10–14	–41,740	–22,909	54,450	61,009	44,607	45,667
15–29	268,773	330,480	187,928	225,793	82,797	89,649
30–64	–66,642	–147,286	197,899	200,339	110,969	123,637
65 or older	–29,864	–20,404	1,539	16,310	6,393	18,967
Net Migration (both sexes)	270,408		945,266		522,686	
Total population change	1,984,168		2,181,458		1,549,231	
Net migration as per cent of total population change	14		43		34	

Source: 1990 and 2000 Census of Population Housing, National Statistics Office for population data by sex/age group and National Statistical Coordination Board, 2003 for cohort survival rates.

Table 6.6   Population Size, Change and Estimated Net Migration: Metro-Manila, 1990–2000

City/ Municipality	Population (thousand) 1990	Population (thousand) 2000	Population Change (thousand) 1990–2000	Net Migration 1990–2000 Estimated Number (thousand)	Net Migration 1990–2000 As Per Cent of the Absolute Value of Population Change
Taguig	266	465	200	101	51
Las Pinas	297	473	176	85	49
Paranaque	307	450	142	63	44
Kalookan	762	1,178	416	177	43
Muntinlupa	270	379	109	42	39
Valenzuela	340	486	147	54	37
Quezon City	1,663	2,173	510	133	26
Marikina	309	391	82	14	17
Malabon	280	339	59	0	–0.1
Navotas	187	230	43	–2	–5
Pasig	427	505	78	–10	–12
Mandaluyong	246	278	32	–11	–34
Pateros	51	57	6	–4	–59
Makati	451	471	21	–43	–209
San Juan	126	118	–8	–19	–234
Pasay	367	355	–12	–65	–549
Manila	1,588	1,581	–7	–224	–3140

Notes: Estimates include only population 10 years old or older.
Source: 1990 and 2000 Census of Population Housing, National Statistics Office and National Statistical Coordination Board, 2003 for cohort survival rates.

immediate recipients of "spillover" population from Manila. The population densities in all but three of these central Metro Manila municipalities already exceeded 20 thousand per square kilometre in 1990. Historically, the eight localities with positive net migration are considered the newer settlements of Metro Manila. These are located on the north and south ends of Metro Manila, contiguous to the inner zone. The population densities in these newer settlements, except for one, were all below 20 thousand per square kilometre, even in the year 2000. All these results together indicate a negative relationship between the 1990–2000 net migration and 1990 population density in the cities and municipalities of Metro Manila — that is, high population density in 1990 implies low (or even negative) net migration in the succeeding decade. This result implies that the Metro Manila or core area needs to be broken up further in order to properly analyse the relationship between population density and net migration.

The low overall net migration for the entire Metro Manila area for 1990–2000 is a result of the averageing (of net migration) across almost equal numbers of localities that had negative and those that had positive net migration. The older central part of Metro Manila is already a net out-migration area, but the more recently settled outer parts of Metro Manila continue to be net gainers from migration.

Migrant Residents: Numbers, Place of Origin, Sex and Age

For purposes of the migration analysis presented in this section, the categories for place of migrant destination are defined to be the zones of the MUR, which are the core, the inner zone and the outer zone. The categories for places of migrant origin, on the other hand, are defined as follows: the MUR zones: core, inner zone, and outer zone; other Luzon; Visayas; Mindanao; and foreign countries. A migrant resident (of a particular zone) is defined as an individual who was residing in the indicated zone during the census-taking and reported a different place of residence five years ago.

The group of migrants covered in the analysis is limited to those who were residing in the MUR in 1990 and in 2000. And since the migration status of the population under five years old cannot be defined using the criterion set, the analysis is limited further to the population five years old and older. This section focuses on examining the place of origin, age and sex composition of migrants in each zone. The migrants' educational background and economic activities are discussed in later sections.

Consistent with results of the net migration analysis, the inner zone had the highest proportion of migrants among its resident population in 1990 and 2000 (Table 6.8). The core had the second highest proportion in 1990 but became the lowest in 2000. The proportion of migrants in the outer zone population, on the other hand, increased from 1990 to 2000. Thus, the core and the outer zone switched places in the rankings.

In terms of absolute numbers of resident migrants in 2000, there were an estimated 435 thousand in the core, 480 thousand in the inner zone, and 351 thousand in the outer zone. The core obviously continues to attract comparable numbers of migrants to the inner zone and outer zones. But the difference is that out-migration is very high in the core and low in the inner and outer zones, as implied by the net migration results presented previously.

That is, even with near equal numbers of migrants moving into each of the three zones, the core achieves only a small net gain, while the inner and outer zones achieve a much greater increase.

Place of Origin

Three sets of observations stand out from an examination of the migrants' places of origin by MUR zone destination in Table 6.7. The migrants into the core are predominantly from two regions outside of the MUR, the rest of Luzon and the Visayas, which together contributed 75 per cent of all migrants in 1990 and 60 per cent in 2000. There is significantly less movement from the other MUR zones into the core. Migration into the core from outside of the MUR is a well-established pattern. These long-distance moves into Metro Manila are generally made for work and for schooling reasons. The small proportion of core migrants coming from the inner zone and outer zones may be explained by the fact that these areas are now within commuting distance as a result of the modern highways. Residents of the inner and outer zones do not have to live in the core to work and to attend school in the core. An examination in a later section

Table 6.7 Migrant Residents (5 Years Old and Above) By Place of Origin: By Zone, 1990 and 2000

	Residence in 1990			Residence in 2000		
Residence 5 Years Ago	Core	Inner Zone	Outer Zone	Core	Inner Zone	Outer Zone
Total population (million)	7.9	4.2	3.8	9.9	6.4	5.4
Migrants as per cent of total population	7.1	9.5	4.2	4.4	7.5	6.5
Migrant place of origin (per cent):						
Core	–	54.7	34.2	–	55.7	47.8
Inner Zone	9.1	–	16.4	12.3	–	19.9
Outer Zone	5.6	6.8	–	6.9	7.7	–
Rest of Luzon	42.7	23.1	35.0	33.9	18.1	17.1
Visayas	32.8	11.3	10.7	25.7	8.9	5.3
Mindanao	8.4	3.6	3.4	14.2	4.9	3.5
Foreign country	1.4	0.5	0.4	7.0	4.6	6.4
All places	100.0	100.0	100.0	100.0	100.0	100.0

Source: 1990 and 2000 Census of Population Housing, National Statistics Office.

of commuting-to-work data shows significant numbers commuting from the inner and outer zones to the core.

More than half of inner zone migrants are from the core. The proportion of outer zone migrants coming from the core has increased from 34 per cent in 1990 to 48 per cent in 2000. These patterns may be attributed to two developments that have made the inner and outer zones more attractive compared to the core. The first is the rising number of residential developments with easy access to major transportation links to the core. And the second is improved economic opportunities as a result of increased industrial activities in the inner and outer zones.

The significance of foreign countries as a source of migrants has increased in all the zones in 2000. Migrants who lived in a foreign country five years ago may be classified into two types: overseas contract workers (OCWs); and "other" migrants such as retirees settling in the Philippines. OCWs comprised 25 per cent in 1990 and 55 per cent in 2000 of all migrants who reported to have come from abroad, reflecting a nation-wide increase in the number of returning OCWs. In 1990 and 2000 about half of non-OCW migrants were 40 years old or older, a group much older than the general population of the zones. This possibly reflected increased retirement migration of Filipinos who previously lived abroad and of foreign nationals.

In Table 6.7, the percentage distributions were re-computed (results not shown) across rows to determine the preferred zone destinations of MUR migrants by specific place of origin.[6] These calculations revealed a decline between 1990 and 2000 in the preference for the core as a destination for migrants from all origins. Percentages moving to the core declined from 74 per cent in 1990 to 54 per cent in 2000 among migrants from non-MUR areas, from 66 per cent to 43 per cent among migrants from the inner zone, and from 54 per cent to 44 per cent among migrants from the outer zone. On the other hand, the preference for the inner zone as migration destination has increased. For example, the percentage that moved to the inner zone increased from 46 per cent in 1990 to 56 per cent in 2000 among migrants from the outer zone.

There is one exception to the increasing attraction of the inner zone: migrants from the core. Of these, the percentage moving to the inner zone declined from 80 per cent in 1990 to 60 per cent in 2000. This change reflects an increasing preference for the outer zone as migration destination among core out-migrants.

In terms of volume, the top three origin-to-destination flows in 1990 were rest-of-Luzon to the core, the core to the inner zone and the Visayas to the core. In 2000, the three heaviest flows were core to the inner zone, core to the outer zone and rest-of-Luzon to the core.

Age and Sex Composition

The percentages presented in Tables 6.8 and 6.9 indicate how significant migrants are in specific sex and age population groups. Results in Table 6.8 show that in all zones the percentage of migrants is higher among females than males. The predominance of females among migrants is reflected in sex ratios that fall below 100 in all zones. But the lowest sex ratio is for core migrants, no doubt reflecting the importance of female-dominated occupations, including sales, services (especially domestic help) and clerical, in available employment in the core (as shown in a later section.) The perceived work opportunities in these occupations have made the core an attractive destination choice for female migrants.

Consistent with net migration findings, migrants account for larger proportions among the male and female 15–34 year olds compared to other sex-age groups in the core (Table 6.9). In the inner and outer zones migrants comprise significant proportions in a wider age range, i.e. 15–44 years old. The sex and age profile of migrants in each zone generally remained the same between 1990 and 2000.

Table 6.8 Migrant Residents (5 Years Old and Above) By Sex: By Zone, 1990 and 2000

	1990			2000		
Population	Core	Inner Zone	Outer Zone	Core	Inner Zone	Outer Zone
Population 5 or older (million)	7.9	4.2	3.8	9.9	6.4	5.4
Male	3.8	2.1	1.9	4.9	3.2	2.7
Female	4.1	2.1	1.9	5.0	3.2	2.7
Percent migrants						
Total zone population 5+	7.1	9.5	4.2	4.4	7.5	6.5
Male	6.2	9.0	4.0	3.9	7.2	6.3
Female	8.0	9.9	4.4	4.9	7.9	6.7
Sex ratios						
Total zone population 5+	92	100	99	97	100	100
Migrant population	72	91	91	78	91	94

Source: 1990 and 2000 Census of Population Housing, National Statistics Office.

Table 6.9 Percentage Migrants By Age and Sex Group: By Zone, 1990 and 2000

Age Group	Male			Female		
	Core	Inner Zone	Outer Zone	Core	Inner Zone	Outer Zone
1990						
5–14	4.0	8.0	3.4	4.5	7.8	3.6
15–24	9.0	9.2	4.1	14.0	13.1	6.1
25–34	8.2	12.5	6.3	9.0	13.2	6.7
35–44	5.2	9.7	4.5	4.9	8.6	3.6
45–64	3.5	6.2	2.4	3.9	6.3	2.3
65 or older	3.2	4.4	1.5	3.9	4.6	1.7
All Ages	6.2	9.0	4.0	8.0	9.9	4.4
2000						
5–14	2.1	5.6	5.3	2.6	5.6	5.6
15–24	6.4	7.2	6.1	9.4	10.7	7.8
25–34	5.2	10.0	8.6	5.6	10.5	9.4
35–44	3.1	8.2	7.7	3.1	7.3	7.0
45–64	2.2	5.6	4.9	2.3	5.3	4.6
65 or older	1.6	4.0	2.9	2.2	4.3	3.0
All Ages	3.9	7.2	6.3	4.9	7.9	6.7

Source: 1990 and 2000 Census of Population Housing, National Statistics Office.

Tables 6.10 and 6.11 present age and sex profile indicators computed for each migration stream into the MUR. A migration stream consists of migrants coming from a specific place of origin (residence five years ago) and who moved to a specific destination (residence during census-taking). In Tables 6.10 and 6.11 the number of categories for origin or previous residence has been reduced to four — core, inner zone, outer zone and non-MUR. The categories for destination or current residence remain the same, i.e. the three MUR zones. Entries in the tables that are in parenthesis are indicators computed for non-migrant residents of each zone.

A number of patterns for the relative age of migrants by migration stream emerge from Table 6.10. Among all migration streams into the MUR, the stream that started from non-MUR areas and moved to the core has the highest proportion in the young working age group. The migrant streams from non-MUR areas to any MUR zone destination have the highest proportion in the young working age group compared to other streams that moved towards the same destination. For example, of the migration streams

Table 6.10   Percentage of Migrants Aged 15–24 By Migration Stream: Manila MUR, 1990 and 2000

Place of Origin (Residence 5 Years Ago)	Place of Destination of 1990 Migrants			Place of Destination of 2000 Migrants		
	Core	Inner Zone	Outer Zone	Core	Inner Zone	Outer Zone
Core	(32)	31	31	(29)	24	25
Inner Zone	37	(33)	33	34	(30)	30
Outer Zone	47	37	(33)	47	38	(30)
Non-MUR Areas	50	45	43	54	50	47

Notes:
1. Figures in parenthesis are percentages for non-migrant residents.
2. Migrants aged 15 or older were used as reference in the computations.
Source: 1990 and 2000 Census of Population Housing, National Statistics Office.

into the outer zone in 1990, those originating from non-MUR areas had 43 per cent in the young age group compared to 33 per cent and 31 per cent for those originating from the inner and outer zones.

Migration streams moving inwards or in the direction of the core (e.g., non-MUR to outer zone, outer zone to inner zone, inner zone to core) have higher proportions in the young age groups compared to non-migrants.

Table 6.11   Sex Ratio By Migration Stream: Manila MUR, 1990 and 2000

Place of Origin (Residence 5 Years Ago)	Place of Destination of 1990 Migrants (Residence in 1990)			Place of Destination of 2000 Migrants (Residence in 2000)		
	Core	Inner Zone	Outer Zone	Core	Inner Zone	Outer Zone
Core	(92)	92	96	(96)	92	100
Inner Zone	85	(96)	92	82	(96)	100
Outer Zone	75	82	(100)	78	82	(100)
Non-MUR Areas	64	75	85	69	69	82

Notes:
1. Figures in parenthesis are percentages for non-migrant residents.
2. Migrants aged 15 or older were used as reference in the computations.
Source: 1990 and 2000 Census of Population Housing, National Statistics Office.

Migration streams moving outward or away from the core (e.g., core to inner zone, inner zone to outer zone) have proportions in the young groups similar to or lower than those of non-migrants.

An examination of the sex ratios in Table 6.11 shows three discernable patterns parallel to those found in Table 6.10. Migration streams from non-MUR areas to any MUR zone are predominantly female, as indicated by sex ratios below 100. The sex ratio is lowest for the non-MUR-to-core migration stream. Migration streams moving inward or in the direction of the core are predominantly female, with sex ratios generally below non-migrant sex ratios. Migration streams moving outward or away from the core have sex ratios similar to non-migrant sex ratios.

Education

The analysis of the education profile of the MUR's population applies to the population 15 years old or older. Table 6.12 presents a comparison of the education profile of population by zone, Table 6.13 the proportion of migrants in population subgroups classified by educational category and Table 6.14 the education profile of migrants by migration stream.

Table 6.12 shows that residents in the core are better educated compared to those in the inner zone, and in turn inner zone residents are better educated compared to those in the outer zone. The proportion with secondary education

Table 6.12   Population 15 Years Old and Above By Educational Attainment: By Zone, 1990 and 2000

	1990			2000		
Education Level Completed	Core	Inner Zone	Outer Zone	Core	Inner Zone	Outer Zone
No grade completed	0.6	1.5	3.0	0.4	0.8	1.5
Elementary	19.1	34.1	43.4	15.6	24.3	32.8
Secondary	40.0	37.5	32.6	42.9	41.6	39.3
Post secondary	4.7	3.7	3.2	8.0	7.2	6.3
Incomplete and completed college	35.6	23.2	17.8	33.1	26.1	20.1
All Levels	100.0	100.0	100.0	100.0	100.0	100.0

Notes:
1. Population 15 years old and older was used as reference in the table above.
2. Educational attainment was not reported in 2% and 3% of the data in 1990 and 2000, respectively.
Source: 1990 and 2000 Census of Population Housing, National Statistics Office.

was almost the same across zones in 2000. The sharp contrast between the core and the zones was at the lowest and highest levels of education. The proportion reporting at most elementary education rose from 19 per cent in the core to 34 per cent and 43 per cent in inner and outer zones, respectively. At the highest levels of education, about one in every three completed at least some college in the core and this proportion was lower in the inner zone and much lower in the outer zone in both years. The concentration of highly educated population in the core is consistent with two of its characteristics. First, it is the centre for higher education in the country and therefore a major producer of college graduates. Second, as shown in the next section, the economic activities in the core require highly educated labour.

In Table 6.13, the proportion of migrants in a particular education group can be considered high when it exceeds the overall proportion of migrants in the zone population. Migrants in the core are spread out relatively evenly across the educational categories but slightly more are in the lower categories. This may partly be a result of the annual influx of high school graduates who are coming from the province to attend college in Manila. Migrants in the inner and outer zones, on the other hand, are over-represented in the higher educated categories.

Table 6.14 shows that the overall education profile observed in Table 6.12 is reinforced by selectivity (by educational background) among migrants

Table 6.13   Percentage Migrants by Completed Education Category: By Zone, 1990 and 2000

	1990			2000		
Education Level Completed	**Core**	**Inner Zone**	**Outer Zone**	**Core**	**Inner Zone**	**Outer Zone**
No grade completed	6.7	5.1	2.1	3.4	3.8	2.7
Elementary	10.2	7.5	3.7	5.1	5.1	4.5
Secondary	8.6	10.7	5.3	5.5	8.2	8.0
Post secondary	7.9	11.9	5.8	5.1	11.3	8.8
Incomplete and completed college	6.3	13.0	5.1	4.2	10.0	8.2
All zone population 15 or older	8.0	10.0	4.5	5.0	8.2	6.9

Notes:
1.   Population 15 years old and older was used as reference in the table above.
2.   Educational attainment was not reported in 2% and 3% of the data in 1990 and 2000, respectively.

Source: 1990 and 2000 Census of Population Housing, National Statistics Office.

Table 6.14   Percentage of Migrants with At Least Some College Education by Migration Stream: Manila MUR, 1990 and 2000

Place of Origin (Residence 5 Years Ago)	Place of Destination of 1990 Migrants (Residence in 1990)			Place of Destination of 2000 Migrants (Residence in 2000)		
	Core	Inner Zone	Outer Zone	Core	Inner Zone	Outer Zone
Core	(35)	38	29	(32)	38	25
Inner Zone	33	(22)	22	36	(25)	25
Outer Zone	37	27	(18)	35	25	(19)
Non-MUR Areas	25	18	13	24	20	17

Notes:
1. Figures in parenthesis are percentages for non-migrant residents.
2. Migrants aged 15 or older were used as reference in the computations.
Source: 1990 and 2000 Census of Population Housing, National Statistics Office.

going to specific destinations. For example, the proportion of college educated in the migration streams originating from non-MUR areas increases as the destination gets closer to the core.

Table 6.14 furthermore shows the migration streams contributing to the patterns observed in Table 6.13. Movers into the core, particularly from the non-MUR areas (about 80 per cent of core migrants), are generally less educated than the core resident population. But movers from the core to the inner and outer zones are more educated than the residents of these zones. The core continuously receives lower educated migrants, continuously loses highly educated residents, but still manages to maintain a highly educated resident population. This situation is made possible because, as mentioned earlier, Metro Manila is itself a major producer of college graduates.

Economic Activity

Economic activity analysis is undertaken using the population 15 years old or older as reference. In 1990, roughly half this population reported a gainful occupation, but the proportion was lower in 2000, presumably because of the sharp increase in the proportion not reporting (Table 6.15). The succeeding tabulations on usual occupation, industry classification of workers, and place of work are generated based only on the subset of population that reported gainful usual occupation.

**Table 6.15   Population 15 Years Old and Above by Reported Usual Occupation:
By Zone, 1990 and 2000**

	1990			2000		
Usual Occupation	Core	Inner Zone	Outer Zone	Core	Inner Zone	Outer Zone
Population 15 or older (million)	5.3	2.6	2.4	6.7	4.2	3.1
Reported gainful occupation	2.7	1.2	1.2	2.9	1.8	1.3
Reported non-gainful occupation	2.3	1.2	1.1	2.0	1.4	1.1
Not reported	0.3	0.2	0.1	1.8	1.0	0.7
Distribution by occupation group (per cent)						
Reported gainful occupation	50.6	47.1	48.0	43.3	42.2	43.2
Reported non-gainful occupation	43.2	47.1	46.2	30.1	33.2	34.0
Not reported	6.2	5.8	5.8	26.6	24.6	22.8
All categories	100.0	100.0	100.0	100.0	100.0	100.0

Notes:
1.   Population 15 years old and above was used as reference in the table above.
2.   Usual occupation was not reported for 6% and 26% of the population 15+ for
     1990 and 2000, respectively.
Source: 1990 and 2000 Census of Population Housing, National Statistics Office.

Gainful Occupation

Both in 1990 and 2000 the core had the highest proportion of office-based
workers, followed by the inner zone and then the outer zone (Table 6.16).
Trade and related workers made up the largest group in the inner zone. The
significant proportion of farmers, forestry workers and fishermen among its
gainful workers in the outer zone indicates the relatively agricultural nature
of the economy of this zone. Trade/related workers and labourers/unskilled
workers are significant groups in all the zones. Aside from the general decline
in the importance of farming and related occupations, little definite can be
said about trends, because of the larger proportion with not stated gainful
occupation in 2000.[7]

Occupations in which migrants are over-represented (data not shown)
include service workers and labourer/unskilled workers, whereas they are
under-represented among office-based workers in the core, though not in
the inner zone. The basic explanation for migrants' over-representation among
service workers and labourer/unskilled workers is that these are the easiest

Table 6.16   Population 15 Years Old and Above by Usual Gainful Occupation: By Zone, 1990 and 2000

Gainful Occupation Category	1990			2000		
	Core	Inner Zone	Outer Zone	Core	Inner Zone	Outer Zone
Managerial*	10.4	7.2	4.0	5.1	3.7	2.4
Professionals	11.1	7.5	5.8	11.8	9.4	7.0
Technicians and Associate Professionals	5.9	2.9	1.9	6.6	5.5	3.6
Clerks	9.0	7.2	5.8	8.9	6.9	5.0
Service Workers and Shop and Market Sales Workers	9.7	6.9	6.2	10.5	7.8	7.0
Farmers, Forestry Workers and Fishermen	1.2	10.3	27.6	0.9	6.4	21.5
Trade and Related Workers	18.4	24.3	18.7	16.0	22.1	18.2
Plant and Machine Operators and Assemblers	10.2	13.3	9.8	14.5	16.5	13.5
Labourers and Unskilled Workers	24.2	20.3	20.3	25.6	21.7	21.8
All Categories	100.0	100.0	100.0	100.0	100.0	100.0

Notes:
1. Population 15 years old and above, and reporting gainful usual occupation was used as reference in the table above.
2. Usual occupation was not reported in 6% and 26% of the population 15+ for 1990 and 2000, respectively.
* Officials of the government and special interest organisations, corporate executives, managers, managing proprietors and supervisors.
Source: 1990 and 2000 Census of Population Housing, National Statistics Office.

occupations to enter, even for newly arrived migrants, requiring very little or no training.

Industrial Classification of Workers

The proportion of workers in the trade and services industries is highest in the core, and progressively lower in the inner and the outer zones (Table 6.17). The reverse is true for the workers in agriculture, hunting, fishery, forestry and mining industries, with the lowest percentage in the core and highest percentage in the outer zone. The proportion of workers in the manufacturing industries is high in all zones, but highest in the inner zone since 1990. Again, this is evidence of the effect of the shift in location of manufacturing firms from Metro Manila towards the inner zone. Migrants are over-represented

Table 6.17 Population 15 Years Old and Above by Industry Category: By Zone, 1990 and 2000

Industry Occupation Category	1990			2000		
	Core	Inner Zone	Outer Zone	Core	Inner Zone	Outer Zone
Agriculture, hunting, fishery, forestry, mining and quarrying	1.8	12.8	32.7	2.4	9.1	26.2
Manufacturing	21.9	22.7	14.5	19.5	22.2	15.3
Electricity, gas and water	0.6	0.8	0.6	0.4	0.5	0.3
Construction	7.8	11.1	9.4	12.7	14.6	14.4
Wholesale, retail and repair trade	16.9	14.6	13.3	21.3	15.8	13.4
Transportation, communication, financing, real estate, community, social and personal services	51.0	38.0	29.5	43.8	37.8	30.4
All Categories	100.0	100.0	100.0	100.0	100.0	100.0

Notes:
1. Population 15 years old and above, and reporting gainful usual occupation was used as reference in the table above.
2. Kind of business or industry was not reported in 8% and 24% of the population 15+ for 1990 and 2000, respectively.
Source: 1990 and 2000 Census of Population Housing, National Statistics Office.

in the manufacturing and service-related industries in all zones, and under-represented in primary industries, except in the core, where numbers of such workers are anyway very small (data not shown).

Commuting to Work

The analysis of commuting to work is focused only on cross-zonal commuting. Most working age residents in the core work within the core, about 94 per cent in 1990 and 2000 (Table 6.18). In contrast, for inner and outer zone residents, the proportions working within their zone of residence were a little below 80 per cent in 1990 and around 83 per cent in 2000. Cross-zonal commuting to work is thus relatively high among inner and outer zone workers.

More than ten per cent of the population with gainful occupation and residing in the inner zone commute to the core for work, and about 10 per cent of those residing in the outer zone commute to the inner zone and

Table 6.18   Working Population by Place of Work: By Zone, 1990 and 2000

Place of Work	Residence in 1990			Residence in 2000		
	Core	Inner Zone	Outer Zone	Core	Inner Zone	Outer Zone
Core	93.4	16.4	9.9	94.4	11.3	6.8
Inner Zone	0.7	76.9	3.1	1.1	82.7	3.6
Outer Zone	0.2	0.7	80.8	0.3	1.1	84.0
Non-MUR Areas	5.7	5.9	6.2	4.2	4.9	5.7
All Places	100.0	100.0	100.0	100.0	100.0	100.0

Notes:
1. Population 15 years old and above, and reporting gainful usual occupation was used as reference in the table above.
2. Place of work was not reported in 6% and 26% of the population 15+ for 1990 and 2000, respectively.
Source: 1990 and 2000 Census of Population Housing, National Statistics Office.

the core to work. Many of these commuters are likely to be migrants who had moved to the inner and outer zones to avail themselves of better and affordable housing. The next table confirms this hypothesis. Table 6.19 shows that about one-half of inner zone migrants reported places of work outside

Table 6.19   Place of Work Outside of Current Residence by Migrant Status: By Zone, 1990 and 2000 (%)

Migrant Status/Sex	Residence in 1990			Residence in 2000		
	Core	Inner Zone	Outer Zone	Core	Inner Zone	Outer Zone
All Zone Population 15 or Older	6.6	23.1	19.2	5.6	17.3	16.0
Non-Migrant	6.7	21.0	18.6	5.1	14.8	13.2
Migrant	5.6	38.7	30.2	13.7	42.4	49.5

Notes:
1. Population 15 years old and above, and reporting gainful usual occupation was used as reference in the table above.
2. Place of work was not reported in 6% and 26% of the population 15+ for 1990 and 2000, respectively.
Source: 1990 and 2000 Census of Population Housing, National Statistics Office.

their current zone of residence in 2000. Obviously, these migrants did not move to their current residence to access work opportunities there since they continue to work outside of the zone. The other half of the migrants, on the other hand, may have also moved for better housing but had presumably found work as well within their new place of residence, and do not have to cross to another zone for work.

Synthesis

The 1990 and 2000 size, zonal distribution and socioeconomic characteristics of the Manila MUR population reflect the combined historical, demographic, economic and legal forces that prevailed in the MUR over the last century. From Spanish times, through American rule and to the present, Manila (and the rest of Metro Manila) has remained the country's centre for governmental, financial, manufacturing, trade and commerce, higher education and cultural activities. Thus, Metro Manila continues to be a magnet for migrants from all over the country.

The historical development of the inner zone towns was based on accessibility to Manila by way of water transportation, and later through road networks constructed to connect Manila to the more populous towns and to the major agricultural areas of Luzon. Later on, construction of railroads and modern highways was juxtaposed on the routes of the original road system. Two other developments also contributed to rapid inner zone growth: construction of low to medium cost housing and entry of manufacturing industries into the zone. With efficient means of transportation to Metro Manila and availability of affordable housing, the inner zone became an option for Metro Manila residents desirous of owning their homes and wanting to continue working in Metro Manila. Industrial firms wanting to enjoy fiscal and other benefits of doing business, and easy access to Metro Manila, would choose to locate in the inner zone.

The 1990 and 2000 Census of Population and Housing data were used to study population size, demographic structure and socioeconomic characteristics across zones and changes across time. Key findings are summarised below.

Zone Population Size and Change

- Of the MUR population, about one-half are in the core and about one-quarter each in the inner and outer zone.

- Population growth between 1990–2000 was highest in the inner zone (4.2 per cent), followed by the outer zone (3.4 per cent) and the core (2.1 per cent).
- The absolute volume of migrants into Metro Manila remains comparable to those going into the inner and outer zones, but out-migration from Metro Manila is also very high.
- Migration's net contribution to the 1990–2000 population growth was lowest for Metro Manila (18 per cent) and highest in the inner zone (53 per cent).
- An examination of individual city and municipality population change shows that in fact parts of Metro Manila — the outer and more recently settled localities — continue to experience net migration that is just as high and positive as in the inner zone (about 39 per cent of population change), while the old settlements in the central part of Metro Manila (particularly City of Manila, Pasay and San Juan) are already net out-migration areas.

Zone Population Characteristics

- The age and sex structure of the population is similar in each zone, but the core has a slightly lower sex ratio.
- The population of the core has the highest educational attainment followed by the inner zone and then the outer zone.
- Of the population 15 years or older and reporting gainful occupation:
  - the proportion in office-based occupations is highest in the core (32 per cent) and lowest in the outer zone (18 per cent)
  - the proportion working in manufacturing industries is highest in the inner zone (23 per cent) and lowest in the outer zone (15 per cent)
  - the proportion working in agriculture and other extractive industries is still high in the outer zone (about one-third)
  - about one-fifth of the working population in the inner and outer zones commute to work outside of their zone of residence

Zone Migrants

- More than 80 per cent of migrants in the core are from non-MUR areas while half of inner and outer zone migrants are from the core.
- Roughly half of migrants in the inner and outer zones are from the core.

- Migrants in all zones are generally younger and predominantly female compared to the general population of the zones.
- Migrants who come from non-MUR areas are the youngest and have the lowest sex ratios among all migrants to the MUR.
- Migrants from non-MUR areas to the core and the inner zone are less educated than the destination zone residents. In contrast, migrants from the core to the inner and outer zones are more educated than the destination zone residents.
- Migrants make up higher proportions among service workers and labourers/unskilled workers in the core, but higher proportions among workers in office-based occupations in the inner and outer zones.
- The proportion of migrants among manufacturing industry workers is the highest compared to other industry groups in all zones, but higher in the inner and outer zones compared to the core.
- Nearly half of migrants in the inner and outer zones work outside of their zones of residence, while only about 14 per cent do so among non-migrants.

Finally, what are some of the implications of these findings for: (1) moderating the population growth of Metro-Manila; (2) transportation development within the MUR, and (3) planning the location of higher education institutions?

1. *Moderating growth of Metro-Manila.* Out-migration from the core to the inner and outer zones is already taking place voluntarily, presumably in response to affordable housing opportunities and possibly to work opportunities brought by the entry of industry and commerce in the zones. That migrants may have responded to housing opportunities is indicated by the fact that about half of inner and outer zone migrants are working outside of their zones. These migrants are obviously not living in the inner and outer zones because of work opportunities, since they continue to work outside of the zone. That migrants may have also responded to economic opportunities in both the inner and outer zones is indicated by the unusually high proportion of migrants found among workers in manufacturing industries and in office-based occupations in these zones. Clearly, people move out of Metro-Manila given the right incentives. The increase in the population of Metro-Manila can thus be moderated with continuing development of residential areas and expansion of the industrial sector in the MUR provinces as well as other areas in the country. Then, even as in-migration to Metro

Manila continues from outside the MUR, there will also be continuing migration out of Metro Manila in response to better housing and work opportunities in other regions of the country.

2. *Transportation infrastructure development.* A significant proportion of inner and outer zone residents commute quite long distances to the core to work. And while people have been willing to move and reside outside of the core, a significant proportion of these movers are apparently keeping their jobs in the core, thus adding to the number of commuters to the core. If these trends persist, there will be bigger volumes of commuters from the inner and outer zones to the core for work purposes alone. The transportation system has to be continuously upgraded to handle the increasing volume and, more importantly, to maintain the ease and convenience of commuting.

3. *Education centres.* In Metro Manila, though in-migration generally consists of persons with education lower than the resident population, and out-migration is by highly educated persons, on balance it has still managed to maintain a highly educated resident population. The Metro Manila schooling system is obviously generating sufficient numbers of graduates to sustain its own needs and in addition supply other places such as the inner and outer zones with educated manpower. These results indicate that Metro-Manila continues to play its important role as a major producer of the nation's educated labour. The out-migration result also indicates that among those who were educated in Metro-Manila there are those willing to move later on (or possibly return back) to other parts of the country. Thus, specialised and higher education institutions do not necessarily have to be dispersed, but can continue to be concentrated or located in a few education centres such as Manila.

Notes

1. The 12 other Manila towns were Binondo, Tondo, Sta. Cruz, Quiapo, San Miguel, San Nicolas, Sampaloc, Sta. Ana, Malate, Ermita, Paco and Pandacan.
2. The National Statistics Office undertakes the quarterly Labour Force Survey for this purpose.
3. Employment status could have been proxied by data on place of work — a person is assumed to be employed if a place of work is reported and unemployed if none is reported. However, place of work data among the gainfully employed is missing in a proportion much higher than the unemployment rate established by the Labour Force Surveys. Place of work is therefore not a reliable proxy

for employment status. In addition, the Census did not collect information on whether unemployed persons are seeking work.

4. The sex ratio is the number of males for every 100 females in a specified population.

5. Absolute value of population size change is used as the denominator in the percentage computation in order to maintain the (positive or negative) sign of net migration.

6. Results of the new computations are not shown here since these can easily be obtained using data in Table 6.7.

7. This may, for example, have contributed to the surprising drop in percentages recorded in managerial occupations between 1990 and 2000.

7

The Mega-Urban Transformations of Ho Chi Minh City in the Era of Doi Moi Renovation

Dang Nguyen Anh

Overview

Ho Chi Minh City (HCMC), the largest city of Vietnam, is at the beginning of a phase of massive urban expansion. Population growth, which is mainly due to net immigration, is substantially underestimated by official statistics. With an actual population of probably six to eight million people (depending on the method of estimating population size), or approaching 10 per cent of the national population, the city's share of economic activities in Vietnam surpasses that of any other city or province. In 2002, HCMC had a per capita GDP of $1,524 compared to the nation's per capita GDP of $415 (Statistical Office of Ho Chi Minh City 2003).

The city itself, not including the economic activity in the surrounding provinces that also make up the HCMC metropolitan field, accounts for nearly one-fifth (19 per cent) of the national GDP, 34 per cent of the central government budget transfer to local government, 13 per cent of local expenditures, and obtains 22 per cent of the total investment dollars in Vietnam. The city accounted for 28 per cent of all foreign direct investment attracted to the country by the end of the first half of 2001. If the entire HCMC core region, including the southern provinces of Dong Nai, Binh Duong, and Ba Ria — Vung Tau (see Figure 7.1), is considered a single metropolitan region, then this region accounts for an astonishing 74 per cent of the total foreign investment in Vietnam (Cohen 2001). Of this investment, 62 per cent has gone to joint ventures and 27 per cent to fully foreign-owned enterprises; the remaining 11 per cent has gone to business cooperation and offshore investment (Dang *et al.* 2002).

Figure 7.1   Map of Ho Chi Minh City and Surrounding Provinces — Vietnam

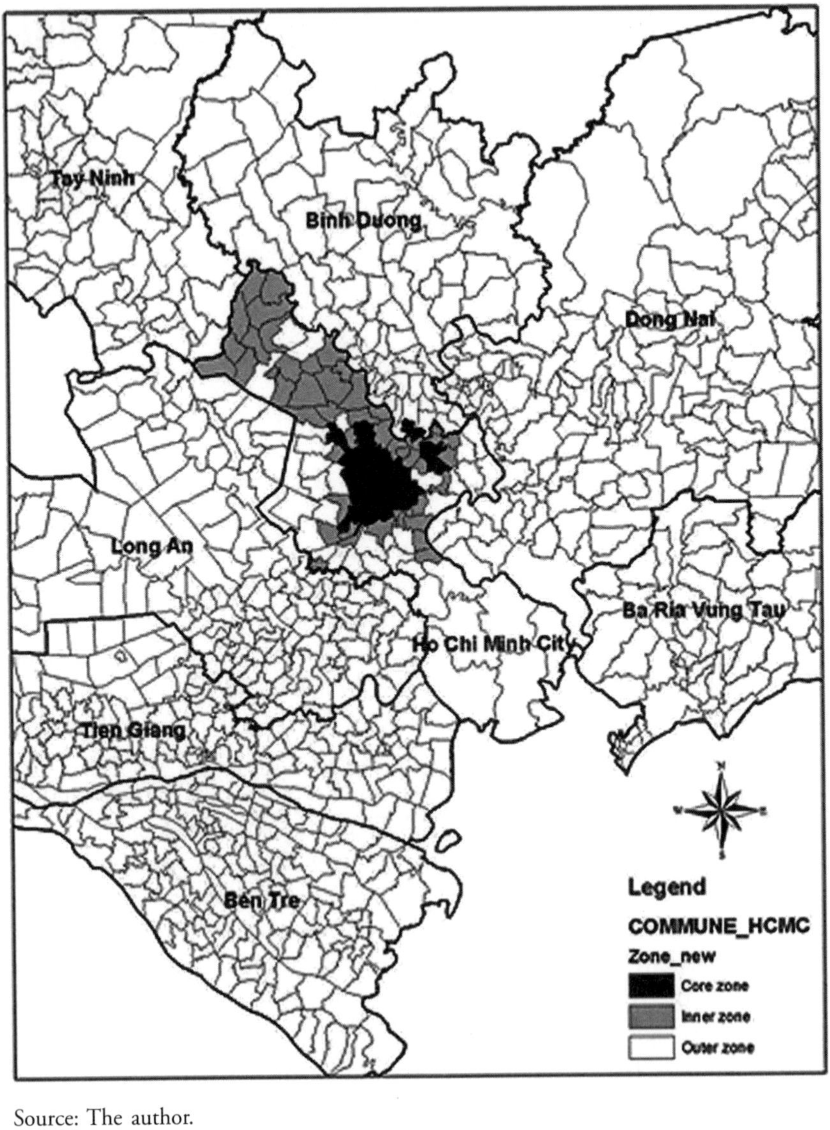

Source: The author.

The city currently consists of 17 urban districts and five rural districts. Among the 17 urban districts, ten have been established under the process of urban transformation and reclassification since 1992. The remaining seven urban districts (Districts 1, 3, 5, 10, 11, Tan Binh and Phu Nhuan) constitute inner suburban districts of the city. In particular, districts 1, 3, 5, and 10 existed from the French time and have usually been referred to as central urban districts of Saigon-Cho Lon (the former name of HCMC). The outer districts such as Binh Chanh, Thu Duc, and Binh Thanh are located surrounding the urban districts and form a third ring, to complete the extended metropolitan region (EMR) or mega-urban region (MUR).

The need for careful studies of the dynamics of growth of HCMC, its population dynamics, migration, employment, and education and the policy/ planning issues they pose has never been greater. This chapter addresses the mega-urban transformations of HCMC in a changing Vietnam as the country enters a new phase of reform and development.

Data and Method

The information presented in this chapter draws on secondary data sources. The most important one is the national population and housing census conducted in 1999 and covering all 61 provinces in Vietnam. The absence of national survey data on migration in Vietnam until now makes the census information both unique and valuable. Data for HCMC is merely a subset of the whole census data. Although the three per cent sample data can be used to estimate migration, at the provincial level like HCMC, the sample may not be representative of the total migrant population. Instead, the present analysis employs the 100 per cent data set of HCMC.

The population and housing census defines migrants as persons who have changed their place of residence (based on their *de jure* place of usual registration) within the five years preceding the census date. The census date was the 1 April 1999, and the preceding five-year period was thus that starting on 1 April 1994. Only persons aged five years or over are considered in the census analysis. International migrants, due to their negligible number, are excluded from the analysis.

The present analysis classifies migrants according to the movement among the three zones. Inter-zonal migrants are defined as those whose last place of previous residence was in a different zone from their zone of residence at the census date, whereas intra-zonal migrants' last place of previous residence was in the same zone of residence at the census date. In some cases, flows of inter-provincial migrants are estimated and defined as those whose last place of previous residence was in a different province from HCMC at the census date. The bulk of inter-provincial migration involves long distances and more or less permanent change in residence. It is usually associated with changes in work place and other labour market attributes such as income and occupational status. Needs arising from educational and training careers are also likely to lead to long distance movement. While zonal migration pertains to flows taking place within the MUR, inter-provincial migration refers to in-flows and out-flows of migrants to and from the MUR over the census interval.

Before proceeding with data analysis, some concerns must be addressed regarding the migration definition and data available for analysis, and the effect of this on estimates of the MUR's population. There are a number of limitations of the census migration data. Migrants who do not register at destination are not counted as residents; those who undertook short-term or circular movement were not considered by the census as migrants. However, micro-level studies suggest that the significance of this type of movement, both in size and in household livelihood strategies, is increasing since the implementation of *Doi Moi* (Dang 2001; UNDP 1998). As mentioned above, migrants detected by the census mainly include those who more or less permanently changed their residence. Therefore the census data underestimated the actual level of migration of Vietnam as well as HCMC. It also underestimated the total population of HCMC, though by how much is a matter of great uncertainty.

The categories of migrants that are seriously undercounted in the Census are KT3 (temporary registrants) and KT4 ("floating" migrants).[1] The Department for Agriculture and Rural Development report (2002) uses a figure of over eight million for the population of Ho Chi Minh City, claiming that there are three million people living in the city without permanent registration and residential permits (mainly KT3 and KT4). However, the exact basis for this estimate is not given, and it is possible that it is an exaggeration. It has never been officially reported by HCMC officials, or used for making plans or setting development targets, but it is widely used by the officials in discussions about population, urbanisation, migration and governance issues. The Department for Agriculture and Rural Development report also mentions the Department of Public Security's figure stating that 70,000 to 100,000 people moved unofficially into the city each year, as KT4 migrants, over the period since 1989. This would give a total of only 700,000 to one million extra uncounted residents (even if none of those unofficially entering the city moved back to their original place of residence), rather than the three million figure often cited. This may be because it does not include KT3 migrants, though it seems doubtful that there would be as many as two million of these.

In any event, what is clear is that the migrants analysed in this chapter are actually a relatively biased sample of all migrants, because they do not include those without residential permits or permanent registration, who are likely to differ from recorded migrants in terms of various characteristics. For example, it is often the groups with limited resources who engage in unregistered and short-term and circular movement. This has important implications for policy, especially relating to poverty reduction. Unfortunately, there is no satisfactory way to deal with this problem, so the reader should keep it in mind when the characteristics of migrants are discussed later in the chapter.

Another limitation of the study resulted from the difficulty of obtaining data for several provinces surrounding HCMC. Therefore, the analysis presented in this chapter adheres to the administrative boundaries of HCMC, although the MUR has in some places expanded beyond the administrative areas of the city into neighbouring provinces. In addition, because commune-level data and boundaries for the 1989 census do not exist, and also because administrative changes were made to boundaries of many communes and wards of HCMC between the 1989 and 1999 censuses, an analysis of change over the ten-year period (1989–99) is not possible. The current analysis is therefore essentially cross-sectional, focusing on the differentials across zones within the MUR by gender and migrant status rather than on changes over time.

Despite these limitations, analysis can still shed light on key aspects of HCMC MUR dynamics. We employed the criteria introduced in Chapter 3 to delineate the core, inner zone and outer zone for each of the MURs studied. Although the zonal division is not fully identical with the administrative boundaries, all the central urban districts (districts 1, 3, 5, 10, 11, Tan Binh, Tan Phu and Phu Nhuan) and some districts of the inner zone fall into the core. The inner zone includes some of the suburban districts (Go Vap, districts 2, 4, 6, 7, 8, 12) and outer districts. This is the major site for suburbanisation where land is being converted from agriculture to urban uses. In terms of population density gradations, the core blends into the inner zone. The outer zone consists of areas located in suburban districts and rural districts (Districts 9, Thu Duc, Binh Thanh, Cu Chi, Hoc Mon, Nha Be, Can Gio). Some areas of the outer zone are highly agrarian in employment and settlement patterns (see Figure 7.2). These are considered rural areas with generally low levels of public services, poor connections to road corridors and low levels of urban infrastructure development. Since many administrative districts cut across two zones, the zonal approach is valuable in showing varied dynamics even at relatively small spatial scales in such a mega-urban region as HCMC.

Figure 7.2   Agricultural Scene in the Outer Zone

Source: The author.

Historical Background, Economic Growth and Urban Development

Compared to Hanoi, Ho Chi Minh City is relatively young, dating back only 300 years. Known formerly as Saigon, it was the capital of the French protectorate of Indochina from 1862 to 1954, and of the Republic of Vietnam (formerly South Vietnam) from 1954 to 1975. Saigon was transformed from a small town into a major port city and a metropolitan centre over the period 1946–75, due to significant displacement of population from the countryside during the French-Vietminh and American wars, and the migration of one million people from the North in 1954–55. During the American War of the 1960s and 1970s, Saigon served as headquarters of the United States military operations. In July 1976, the two Vietnams were united as the Socialist Republic of Vietnam. Saigon was renamed HCMC and lost its administrative functions to the national capital city of Hanoi in northern Vietnam.

In 1975, when the country was reunified, HCMC accommodated only 3.3 million people. Over the period 1976 to 1985, its population barely increased, because of the exodus to other countries after 1975 and government-sponsored movement of approximately 840,000 people to rural areas from 1975 to September 1981 (Thrift and Forbes 1986: 155). Since the late 1980s, however, the population has increased very rapidly, reflecting largely in-migration from other provinces as HCMC achieved rapid economic growth under the economic reform policy. The population reached 4.8 million in 1996 (Department for Agriculture and Rural Development 2002). By the time of the census in 1999, it had an officially registered population of about 5.2 million with a population densely of 1,700 inhabitants per square kilometre. If unregistered population is taken into account, the population of HCMC defined by its administrative boundary was at least one million higher than this, and possibly as high as eight million people.

HCMC is located on an alluvial terrace north of the Mekong River Delta, connected to it by a string of cities and towns that extend linearly up the branches of and laterally across the Mekong and down along the coast. HCMC is not as well linked to the cities, towns and agricultural communes of the Mekong River delta as Hanoi is to those of the Red River delta. Rather, HCMC's metropolitan field extends primarily to the North into Binh Duong and East to Dong Nai provinces, although to some extent it is also expanding to the South into Long An along the national highway No.1. The orientation to the north and east is a legacy of war, influenced both by geography and contemporary market integration. First, for security reasons, only one national highway into the Mekong delta was maintained and developed during the American war (Douglass *et al.* 2002). At the same time, roads and bridges into Bien Hoa city, site of American military bases, were expanded. The centre of old Saigon, site of the Nguyen dynasty citadel, is slightly elevated and outside the area of seasonal inundation. So are the areas north, northwest, and southeast of the city centre in neighbouring Binh Duong and Dong Nai provinces.

As noted above, Saigon was the major focal point for migration during the war years and the major site of population growth and urban expansion. HCMC remains the dominant growth pole of the country. Not surprisingly, Binh Duong and Dong Nai, the two adjacent provinces, become the most important sites for the construction of industrial parks in the 1990s and have seen the most spectacular growth in industrial output, population, and productivity, led primarily by factories along their urbanised borders with HCMC. Both are also within easy reach of the port of Saigon, the region's primary link to outside markets. While the Northeastern expansion of HCMC is clear, it is difficult to intuit a longer-term direction to its industrial expansion. In addition to its service sector, the city itself is a core manufacturing area, containing tens of thousands of small factories and workshops. For example, out of a total of 238 registered and domestically owned plastic manufacturing firms in Vietnam in 1997, all but 24 were in HCMC (MPDF 1997). Moreover, in addition to these registered private and state-owned firms, there were more than 3,000 family-owned and operated plastic manufacturers within Districts 5, 6 and 11.

Equally, in the northern suburbs, there is a tendency for industry to cluster in available industrial spaces close enough to the city centre to allow access to the port of Saigon, still the main point of transfer for international trade, as well as along the Saigon, Dong Nai and Thi Vai rivers, locations that allow transfer of goods directly to port facilities without need for overland transport. The city's current development has accelerated the southward expansion. Moreover, with the Mekong Delta being a rich agricultural region with a number of key towns, the expansion of HCMC to the southwest through Long An and on to Can Tho is also already well underway. This potential is revealed in Figure 7.3 (dot map).

By almost all measures, HCMC is the major industrial, service and commercial locomotive of the Vietnamese economy. Under current national strategies and the opening of Vietnam to the world economy, it will likely absorb even larger shares of national economic resources as the urban transition continues. The city has achieved greater than national average economic growth rates for many years. Throughout the 1990s, HCMC led the country in economic growth, averaging 12 per cent per year from 1990–98 in comparison to 7 per cent for the country as a whole during the same period.[2]

The rapid growth of the HCMC economy entails an increase in the number of jobs. The number of created jobs in the four years, 1997–2000, was estimated to be about 300,000. Along with this employment growth, the unemployment rate decreased gradually from 10.3 per cent in 1997 to 6.8 per cent in 2000. This tendency is indicative of the strength of the city's labour market in absorbing manual labourers, including migrants.

In 2002, the city's service sector accounted for 54 per cent of the city's GDP, while industry and construction accounted for over 44 per cent, and agriculture was less than two per cent. Foreign firms favour investing in the industrial and hotel and tourism sectors. They come to the industrial parks to produce low value added commodities and use the low cost labour resources available while taking advantage of the locational benefits, economic acumen, and special incentives of HCMC. As of yet, however, few of these

Figure 7.3   Ho Chi Minh City Population Distribution in 1999

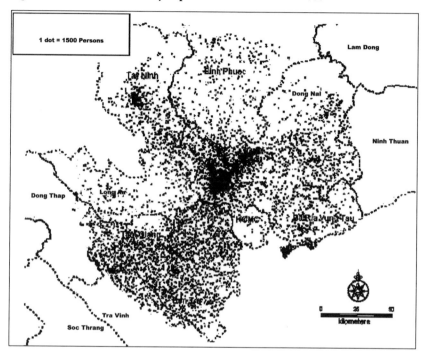

Source: The author.

activities seem to have strong employment or inter-firm multiplier effects in the economy (Douglass *et al.* 2002).

Physically, HCMC has been expanding substantially, and new districts have been established to accommodate growing population and new settlers. Private houses built by households using their own funds account for 65 per cent of all homes in HCMC. Around 70 per cent of these new houses were constructed illegally on undocumented land or without construction licenses. The rapid construction of high buildings has affected nearby residential houses and offices, some of which collapsed. This type of construction is often not in line with urban development master plans. Moreover, it generally occurs without the provision of basic infrastructure such as drainage or sewerage, which risks adding to the potential for environmental deterioration with the expansion of such housing.

By the year 1990, 33 per cent of the urban population of Vietnam lived in HCMC. This figure increased during the 1990s and reached 38.4 per cent by the year 2002 (Statistical Office of Ho Chi Minh City 2003). Together with the population of Hanoi, the population of HCMC accounted for 53 per cent of Vietnam's total urban population.

Whether successful or not in attaining a desirable pattern of expansion, the on-going economic trends reported above have clear population implications: The city's MUR will absorb increasing shares of the national population, mostly through migration, but also through extension of urban boundaries into urbanising hinterlands. As discussed in the next section, these trends in economic and urban development are reflected in the dynamics of HCMC's zones.

Dynamics of Population Changes and Patterns of Migration in Ho Chi Minh City

Population Dynamics and Zone Growth

As of 1 April 1999, the official population of HCMC (which for the purposes of this study is also the HCMC MUR) was 5,037,151 persons with 1,017,840 households. Average population density increased from 1,873 persons per square kilometre in 1990 to 2,404 persons per square kilometre in 1999, and further to 2,601 persons per square kilometre in 2002, thus intensifying pressure on the existing infrastructure and environment.

Over the ten-year inter-censal interval, the MUR's population increased at the rate of 2.8 per cent per annum due mainly to net-migration. As the level of urbanisation accelerated, the proportion of the population in agriculture declined dramatically during the 1990s (Table 7.1). Available population statistics show that the average natural growth rate of the MUR's

Table 7.1 Population of Ho Chi Minh City, 1990–2002

Year	Population	CBR (%)	CDR (%)	Agriculture (%)
1990	3,924,435	25.66	5.48	14.5
1994	4,649,387	20.35	4.96	10.9
1995	4,764,671	19.53	4.70	10.4
1996	4,880,435	18.59	4.43	9.9
1999	5,037,151	18.14	4.06	5.9
2002	5,449,217	16.72	4.0	4.8

Source: Statistical Yearbooks (Ho Chi Minh City Statistical Office 1999, 2002, 2003).

population was slightly over two per cent during the 1970s, declining to 1.7 per cent during the 1980s, and 1.5 per cent in the 1990s. By the 1999 census year, it was 1.13 per cent which is considerably lower than that of the whole country (see Department for Agriculture and Rural Development 2002).

Further analysis of population change by zone reveals the details of population growth of core, inner and outer zone in HCMC (Table 7.2). Not surprisingly, the results show that the core accounts for the smallest area of land whereas the outer zone occupies a vast area. This reflects the expansion of the City boundaries to include rural districts. However, the core area remains overcrowded and extremely densely settled. A noteworthy pattern is that the population of the core increased most during the ten years between the two censuses (3.8 per cent per year), whereas the inner zone grew at an average rate of only 1.9 per cent per year. The population of the outer zone expanded slowly by only 0.8 per cent per year. However, if the core and the inner zone are combined to represent the metropolitan population, then this metropolitan population was growing very fast in the 1990s, reflecting the effect of *Doi Moi* Renovation and policy reforms. In contrast to the other MURs under study in this book, the HCMC case seems to show an early stage of MUR formation, namely, that development still largely focuses on the core and has only just begun to enter the inner zone, with the outer zone remaining highly rural.

Table 7.2   Population Density and Growth by Three Zones: HCMC, 1989–99

Zone	Land area (km²)	Population size ('000)		Population density (per sq. km.)		Population growth rate (av. annum) 1989–99
		1989	1999	1989	1999	
Core	170	2,320	3,203	13,647	18,841	3.8
Inner	617	904	1078	1,465	1,747	1.9
Outer	1,308	700	756	535	578	0.8
Total	2,095	3,924	5,037	1,873	2,404	2.8
Bien Hoa	*155*		*471*		*3,042*	
Ben Luc	*289*		*125*		*432*	
Total (2)	*2,539*		*5,633*		*2,218*	

Note: Outer zone also includes rural areas of HCMC.
Source: 1999 Population and Housing Census.

Of course, there could be other ways of delineating the zones of HCMC. At the bottom of Table 7.2, the areas of Bien Hoa City in Dong Nai Province and Ben Luc district in Long An province have been added to see what difference it would make to include these as extensions of the MUR to the northeast and southwest respectively. It does not make a great deal of difference to the overall picture; it increases the population of the MUR by 12 per cent, and increases the proportion of the population of the MUR living in the inner and outer zones (combined) from 36 per cent to 43 per cent.

The Role of Migration in the Growth of HCMC and its Zones

During an accelerated urban transition, migration is typically one of the main factors contributing to urban population growth. Since _Doi Moi_, increased modern transportation and communication have put major cities, notably HCMC, in a position of high population interaction with other regions and rural areas. As the fertility of the city's population has been below replacement level (a TFR of 1.4), the population increase of HCMC is essentially an outcome of in-migration, which is both permanent and temporary in nature. The migrants come from all other provinces and regions of Vietnam to look for better income and economic opportunities. They furnish much of the labour to the city as well.

The movement of labour from rural areas to urban places has accompanied the onset of industrialisation in Vietnam, with the largest cities like HCMC being the recipients of the largest migration flows. Because of its special status, HCMC has experienced a faster growth rate than most other cities of Vietnam. The current income differential between the city and other parts of the country is so large (four to five times) that it acts as a powerful magnet for migrants seeking work. As a response to the booming industrial and service sector in these cities, the number of migrants coming to HCMC is the largest of anywhere in the country. For the census interval (1994–99) the net-migration rate for HCMC was reported to be +8.15 per cent, the highest of the country (General Statistical Office and UNDP 2001).[3]

HCMC is faced with growing in-migration as people expect to find jobs around the city and as firms agglomerate and create greater economies of scale among industries. In the 1980s, the main net suppliers of the City's population growth were migrants (Dang _et al._ 2002). During the 1989–98 period, a reported yearly net inflow of 73,000 migrants came to HCMC (see Hy 1999). Given that official population data does not include most of the unregistered and temporary migrants, and in view of the unofficial estimates that the population is already at the eight million mark, the metropolitan field of HCMC could readily reach 18–20 million people two decades from now.

Table 7.3 shows the distribution of population aged 5+ by sex, zone and migrant status in HCMC at the time of the 1999 census. Migrants are defined as inter-zonal migrants during the census interval. As the previous discussion highlights, about three-fourths of both migrants and non-migrants concentrated in the core zone where administrative and market activities are concentrated. There are no significant gender differences in spatial distribution of migrants in the city. At the time of the 1999 census, about 74 per cent of both migrant men and migrant women concentrated in the core zone, 18 per cent in the inner zone and 8 per cent in the outer zone of HCMC.

Migration can lead to major changes in certain characteristics of the population. In order to highlight the zonal structure of the City's adult

Table 7.3　Population Aged 5+ by Gender, Zone and Migrant Status: HCMC, 1999

Zone	Non-migrant		Migrant		Total	
	N	%	N	%	N	%
Male						
Core	1,377,214	73.9	267,893	73.2	1,645,107	73.8
Inner	297,605	16.0	68,523	18.7	366,128	16.4
Outer	187,818	10.1	29,489	8.1	217,307	9.8
Total	1,862,637	100.0	365,905	100.0	2,228,542	100.0
Female						
Core	1,525,181	74.8	294,400	74.6	1,819,581	74.8
Inner	318,360	15.6	69,821	17.7	388,181	15.9
Outer	196,592	9.6	30,211	7.7	226,803	9.3
Total	2,040,133	100.0	394,432	100.0	2,434,565	100.0
All						
Core	2,902,395	74.4	562,293	73.9	3,464,688	74.3
Inner	615,965	15.8	138,344	18.2	754,309	16.2
Outer	384,410	9.8	59,700	7.9	444,110	9.5
Total	3,902,770	100.0	760,337	100.0	4,663,107	100.0

Source: 1999 Population and Housing Census.

population (aged 15+ and above) the data are stratified by age and migrant status. In all zones, migrants are relatively young, concentrated especially at ages 15–24. The proportion of migrants in each age group declines substantially with age. This pattern observed for HCMC is consistent with the country's overall age profile of migrants (General Statistical Office and UNDP 2001).

Table 7.4   Population Aged 15+ by Age Group, Zone and Migrant Status: HCMC, 1999

	Core		Inner		Outer		Total	
Age group	N	%	N	%	N	%	N	%
15–24								
Non-migrant	556,417	72.5	134,223	70.9	88,264	81.5	778,904	73.1
Migrant	211,118	27.5	55,062	29.1	20,007	18.5	286,187	26.9
Total	767,535	100.0	189,285	100.0	108,271	100.0	1,065,091	100.0
25–34								
Non-migrant	652,028	81.3	134,216	78.7	79,180	83.0	865,424	81.0
Migrant	150,103	18.7	36,303	21.3	16,278	17.0	202,684	19.0
Total	802,131	100.0	170,519	100.0	95,458	100.0	1,068,108	100.0
35–44								
Non-migrant	556,253	87.8	99,615	85.3	57,177	87.2	713,045	87.4
Migrant	77,499	12.2	17,198	14.7	8,404	12.8	103,101	12.6
Total	633,752	100.0	116,813	100.0	65,581	100.0	816,146	100.0
45–59								
Non-migrant	347,822	89.7	64,190	87.5	38,499	89.5	450,511	89.4
Migrant	39,858	10.3	9,137	12.5	4,515	10.5	53,510	10.6
Total	387,680	100.0	73,327	100.0	43,014	100.0	504,021	100.0
60+ and over								
Non-migrant	266,126	92.6	51,234	92.0	31,322	93.2	348,682	92.6
Migrant	21,335	7.4	4,466	8.0	2,282	6.8	28,083	7.4
Total	287,461	100.0	55,700	100.0	33,604	100.0	376,765	100.0
All								
Non-migrant	2,378,646	82.6	483,478	79.8	294,442	85.1	3,156,566	82.4
Migrant	499,913	17.4	122,166	20.2	51,486	14.9	673,565	17.6
Total	2,878,559	100.0	605,644	100.0	345,928	100.0	3,830,131	100.0

Source: 1999 Population and Housing Census.

Although non-migrants outnumbered their migrant counterparts in all zones, a large proportion of labour migrants concentrated in the inner zone where over one-fifth of the population were migrants. The results reflect the "housing and land fever" and the development of industry observed in the suburban areas of HCMC. Indeed, the inner zone gained population mainly through net-inmigration from other regions. Detailed analysis of data (not presented in Table 7.4) shows that 71 per cent of recent migrants to the inner zone came from the rest of the country, while only 29 per cent of them originated from the core and the outer zone. Despite its apparent overcrowding, the core continues to receive migrants from other regions (76 per cent) and partly from other zones (24 per cent). This reflects the concentration of market activities and services in the city's core area.

While the pattern of migration to the core seems consistent with that in the other five cities included in this book, the movement to the inner zone does not seem to reflect the large movement out from the core that is seen in the other MURs. This suggests that the core and inner zone, with their urban investment and service sector, still attract people to stay or move-in. There is not yet much systematic development of housing estates, modern sector work or social services in the outer zone that would help attract people or push them out from the core and the inner zone. The city's outer zone remains rural in nature. There is therefore a sharp contrast between HCMC and other MURs in which developing areas and social services outside the core become the main factors attracting local residents and migrants to settle in them.

A Zonal Analysis of Human Resources Development

In this section, basic aspects of human resources development are considered. The analysis focuses on employment, education and other characteristics of the HCMC population as found in the 1999 census data. The analysis focuses on migrant status to gain insights into the zonal dynamics, as HCMC has become the centre of national and local migration activities. To some extent, the gender factor provides a new dimension in human resources development. In the long run, the quality of the workforce and characteristics of human resource development will probably determine the sustainability of growth and expansion of the city.

Work and Employment

The work status of the HCMC population aged 15+ and above by zones and migration status is shown in Table 7.5. The labour force participation rate appears to follow similar patterns in favour of the inner and outer zones. The rate is fairly high across the three zones. Nonetheless, a closer examination of the unemployment rate reveals zonal differences in employment. The unemployment rate varies by zones and is highest in the outer areas and lowest in the inner zone (8.2 per cent and 6.8 per cent respectively). Farm labour surplus due to the mechanisation of agriculture in the outer zone has resulted in the higher unemployment rate in agricultural areas. The unemployment rate is considerably lower among migrants than among non-migrants (in the core, 6.2 per cent and 8 per cent respectively).

In further examining the data on the structure of the employment, three broad industrial groups can be used: agriculture, manufacturing and services. Data in Table 7.5 show the distribution of labour by industrial category by zones with respect to migrant status. The results indicate a clear and consistent pattern of work and industry in HCMC. First, the service sector is the main source of employment in the core. Manufacturing is another source of employment in the core and inner zone, especially for migrants. However, compared to non-migrants, migrants concentrated more in manufacturing work and services located in the inner and outer zones. This is where the recent establishment of larger scale industry and production in export zones have been concentrated.

As expected, a large proportion of non-migrant labour in the outer zone was found to be in agriculture (35 per cent). As mentioned above, the

Table 7.5 Work Status by Zone and Migrant Status: HCMC, 1999

	Zone			
Work status	Core	Inner	Outer	Total
Non-migrant				
Labour force participation rate	61.8	65.3	64.8	62.6
Unemployment rate	8.0	7.2	8.4	7.9
Migrant				
Labour force participation rate	60.4	68.4	71.6	62.7
Unemployment rate	6.2	5.5	7.2	6.2
All				
Labour force participation rate	61.6	65.9	65.8	62.6
Unemployment rate	7.7	6.8	8.2	7.6

Source: 1999 Population and Housing Census.

Figure 7.4   Newly-Established Factory in the Outer Zone

Source: The author.

Table 7.6   Employed Workers by Industry, Zone, and Migrant Status:
HCMC, 1999

Industry	Core	Inner	Outer	Total
Non-migrants				
Agriculture	1.2	23.5	34.9	8.1
Manufacturing	40.6	41.1	35.6	40.2
Services	58.2	35.4	29.5	51.7
Total	100.0	100.0	100.0	100.0
Migrants				
Agriculture	0.9	3.6	6.9	2.0
Manufacturing	49.0	62.9	56.8	52.4
Services	50.1	33.5	36.3	45.6
Total	100.0	100.0	100.0	100.0
All				
Agriculture	1.1	19.1	30.1	6.9
Manufacturing	42.2	46.0	39.3	42.5
Services	56.7	34.9	30.6	50.5
Total	100.0	100.0	100.0	100.0

Source: 1999 Population and Housing Census.

relatively high rate of unemployment of this group reflects the shrinking of agricultural land and the mechanization of many farming activities in the outer zone. The city region's rapid urbanisation and commercialisation will continue to exert pressure for conversion of land use and reduce the agricultural workforce of the outer zone. In the long run, many parts of the outer zone may become places of residence of migrants, such as areas along the highway 1A connecting HCMC with Mekong provinces.

Education and Technical Qualifications

Table 7.7 shows the distribution of educational attainment of the population aged 15 years and over by zone for migrants and non-migrants. Examining the data in total, the share of migrants increases markedly in the groups with higher levels of education: the proportion of migrants is three times as high among the population with higher education as among the population with incomplete primary education. This finding, though, could be heavily influenced by the undercounting of various categories of migrants, as mentioned earlier. The proportion of migrants who are highly educated is highest in the core, followed by the inner zone, with the outer zone falling far behind. This reflects the concentration of better off and long term migrants, who move permanently to resettle in HCMC, in the core and the inner zone. As with migrants, the educational level of non-migrants declines in the inner and especially the outer zones as compared with the core. Outer zone residents are engaged in agriculture-related activities located in the outer area of HCMC; many of these non-migrants are Southerners who settled in the area for years during and after the war.

The educational profile of the migrant population of the inner zone resembles that of the core more than it does that of the outer zone. This suggests a major transformation of education and general human resources development of the inner zone. The expansion of the core during the 1990s facilitated the growth of the inner zone, which has, in turn, accommodated the influx of permanent migrants originating from other provinces and moving to HCMC. Indeed, within the interval 1994–99, the highest proportion of recent in-migrants was observed in the inner zone (data not shown). The results reflect a major aspect of the urban transformation of HCMC. The inner zone has become a major attraction as the destination of choice of more or less permanent migrants from the other parts of the country, including Hanoi and other cities. Local residents and better off migrants purchase land and build second houses in the inner zone. In the future, the highly

Table 7.7   Population Aged 15+ by Highest Level of Education Completed, Zone and Migrant Status: HCMC, 1999

Educational Level	Core	Inner	Outer	Total	N	Migrants as % of all with this Level of Education
Non-migrant						
Not completed primary	14.3	20.6	30.0	16.7	528,075	
Completed primary	34.3	41.0	42.4	36.5	1,150,838	
Completed lower sec.	23.6	21.8	17.5	22.7	718,286	
Completed secondary	18.1	12.5	8.0	16.3	514,525	
Higher education	9.2	4.1	2.1	7.8	244,841	
All levels of education	100.0	100.0	100.0	100.0	3,156,566	
Migrant						
Not completed primary	7.8	9.3	15.4	8.7	58,283	9.9
Completed primary	28.3	33.6	40.5	30.2	203,375	15.0
Completed lower sec.	23.4	26.7	25.0	24.1	162,469	18.4
Completed secondary	22.3	17.9	14.2	20.9	140,659	21.5
Higher education	18.2	12.5	4.9	16.1	108,778	30.8
All levels of education	100.0	100.0	100.0	100.0	673,565	17.6
Migrant & non-migrant						
Not completed primary	13.2	18.3	27.8	15.3	586,359	
Completed primary	33.7	39.5	42.1	35.4	1,354,213	
Completed lower sec.	23.6	22.8	18.6	23.0	880,755	
Completed secondary	18.8	13.6	8.9	17.1	655,184	
Higher education	10.8	5.8	2.5	9.2	353,619	
All levels of education	100.0	100.0	100.0	100.0	3,830,131	

Source: 1999 Population and Housing Census.

educated population may move from the core to the inner zone when the core's overcrowding and conversion of land use from houses to rental offices become widespread.

Further examination of the levels of technical education and training of the HCMC workforce or employed population (Table 7.8) reveals that workers with low qualifications (without degrees or certificates) accounted for 82 per cent of the workforce. The proportion of workers without degrees or certificates is relatively higher for females than males (85 per cent and 79 per cent, respectively). The core did relatively better than the zones in this respect: 20 per cent of its employed population had technical qualifications

Table 7.8   Employed Population by Gender, Zone and Technical Qualification: HCMC, 1999

Technical Qualification	Core	Inner	Outer	Total
Male				
No certificate	76.7	85.6	90.2	79.5
Technical certificate	8.3	7.1	5.3	7.8
Vocational certificate	3.4	2.5	2.2	3.1
Undergraduate degree	1.0	0.7	0.5	0.9
Graduate degree	10.1	3.9	1.9	8.2
Post graduate degree	0.5	0.2	0.0	0.4
Total	100.0	100.0	100.0	100.0
Female				
No certificate	83.0	90.3	92.5	85.1
Technical certificate	2.3	2.4	1.9	2.3
Vocational certificate	4.8	3.9	3.5	4.5
Undergraduate degree	1.6	1.1	0.8	1.4
Graduate degree	8.1	2.3	1.2	6.5
Post graduate degree	0.2	0.1	0.0	0.2
Total	100.0	100.0	100.0	100.0
All				
No certificate	79.5	87.6	91.2	82.0
Technical certificate	5.6	5.0	3.7	5.3
Vocational certificate	4.0	3.1	2.7	3.8
Undergraduate degree	1.3	0.9	0.7	1.1
Graduate degree	9.2	3.2	1.7	7.5
Post graduate degree	0.4	0.1	0.0	0.3
Total	100.0	100.0	100.0	100.0

Source: 1999 Population and Housing Census.

compared with only 9 per cent in the inner zone. The core remains the magnet for people with higher educational attainment (at least undergraduate degree). Since many institutions of higher education locate in the core, and the modern service sector is also concentrated there, it remains the centre in which better educated and higher skilled labour settles. The proportion declines gradually when moving outwards to the inner zone. To some extent, the inner zone has attracted and drawn in the better educated from other parts of the city as well as from the rest of the country — both males and females, although especially males.

Quality of Life in Ho Chi Minh City

In this section, quality of life in HCMC will be examined. The data presented in this section is not available from the Census, and thus it cannot be stratified by zones. Rather the figures and information, mostly obtained from other studies, refer to the city as a whole.

HCMC, especially its urban core, is extremely densely settled and has the highest incidence of multiple families sharing units. The average housing area per capita is 6.3 square metres. Two-thirds of the inhabitants live in the core, which creates a density of about 19,000 persons per square-kilometre in this zone. This does not include the growing number of temporary migrants who are daily present, living and/or working in the core. The density of the core is among the highest in the world, especially given the absence of high-rise housing units.

For the poor, housing, or more specifically land for housing, is the most urgent problem in HCMC as land becomes a valuable commodity that is affordable for only a small proportion of the population. A commercialised market system searching for the highest returns on land use combined with the illegal status of much of the migration to the city leaves the poor to fend

Figure 7.5   After Heavy Rain, the City is Often Flooded

Source: The author.

for themselves. As the poor must find accommodation for themselves, the result has been the creation of illegal and unauthorised settlements. People are occupying or illegally buying and selling unused public land, such as landfill sites, graveyards, riverbanks, and space below bridges, along canals or dykes. Many parts of the city are easily flooded after heavy rain, or from high tides in the Saigon River which can last for days.

In HCMC, 60 per cent of housing is classified as semi-permanent with 48,000 slum units, and five per cent of the city's population is homeless (Drakakis-Smith and Dixon 1997). The City's Land and Housing Department estimates there are 67,000 slum units which accommodate more than 300,000 inhabitants or six per cent of the HCMC area's population (Bolay *et al.* 1997).[4] The figures do not include squatter houses which are growing rapidly in the core and inner zones (Figure 7.6). The problem is that the municipal authorities at different levels often ignore these practices. Only when land clearance is required for construction projects are the poor relocated, but even then they continue to illegally occupy land in other places located in the core and the inner zones where they work daily to earn a living. Insofar as these residents can manage to survive by paying fees or asking their relatives

Figure 7.6 Slum Backing Onto Canal, HCMC

Source: The author.

to sponsor their residential status, they are able to stay and work in the city without having any of the privileges of legal permanent residents.

The pressing demand for living space puts enormous pressure on cities to provide common or civic spaces for people. Ho Chi Minh City's parks comprise about 235 hectares and are calculated to provide only about 0.4 square metres of park space per capita, which is well below the target of 1.7 square metres per capita previously set by the municipal authority (People's Committee of Ho Chi Minh City 1999). These are far from the Western standard for metropolitan park space of 20–40 square metres per inhabitant (Douglass *et al.* 2002). While it may seem inappropriate to use the standards of less densely-settled countries to compare with Vietnam, the overcrowding of streets and open spaces in HCMC attests to the challenges for the sustainable growth of the city (Figure 7.7). Moreover, to the extent that houses are too small to accommodate anything but functional activities of the household such as cooking, eating and sleeping, open outdoor spaces become all the more important and sought after by residents. The popularity of parks from before dawn until into the night in HCMC attests to this strong demand for public spaces.

Figure 7.7   Street Scene, HCMC

Source: The author.

The major environmental problems facing HCMC include contamination by residuals of industrial processes, disposal of domestic and industrial waste, and changing consumption patterns leading to new types of environmental risks. Considering the outdated technology used by many factories, industrial zones are rarely able to manage as they are designed to do. Pollution from industrial waste thus occurs even in the city's relatively early stage of industrialisation. Industrial emission is the main source of air pollution. Industrial zones are concentrated and emerging in and around the core and inner zone. Formerly, many enterprises and plants were located away from population concentrations. Due to the expansion of the city into the outer zone and peripheries, industrial zones are now situated among densely populated areas and cause serious air pollution in neighbouring communities.[5] The most polluted places are those surrounding the Tan Binh District of the core zone. Enterprises are mixed with residential areas and thus inhabitants are threatened by more severe exposure to poor air quality.

Vehicular traffic and transportation is another major source of air pollution, especially in the core and the inner zones. Although in comparison with other MURs in Asia, the density of automobiles and large vehicles in HCMC is not high, the use of such private and public vehicles is increasing rapidly. In the late 1980s, roads in HCMC were filled with bicycles, pedicabs, and occasionally trucks or other motorised vehicles. This situation began to change in the early 1990s when the number of motorcycles on city streets began to increase and replace the number of bicycles. In 2002, the number of motorcycles was reported to be 2,500,000; for cars the number is 115,000. Vehicle emissions have become a greater source of air pollution, traffic accidents, congestion and jams.[6] The volume of motorised vehicles, especially cars, is smaller than in cities in many other countries (for example, in Bangkok). But the intensity of transport noise is about the same or sometimes even higher in daily traffic congestion that can appear at any time. Several factors contribute to this: poor lane demarcations of roads is common, urban design is becoming pedestrian unfriendly, and a need to blow the horn and change speed quickly to avoid accidents has become part of the traffic routine (Pham 1998).

Solid waste collection and management represents another crucial issue of sustainable urbanisation. With its huge population size, HCMC produces the largest amount of solid waste in Vietnam. The volume and types of wastes generated in both urban and rural areas have changed over the past decades. Vietnam — particularly its large city regions — is shifting from a low consumption, thrift based society whose products were largely derived from organic materials to a high consumption society whose products are largely inorganic materials and come from industrial processes (e.g. bottled water). Plastic bags have replaced organic materials for wrapping rice and other foodstuffs. This shift in waste generation is extremely important since it has many impacts on environmental management and related health issues, and it often leads to the breakdown of inherited waste management practices based on symbiotic rural-urban exchanges and uses of organic wastes.

Since the early 1990s, the city's system of waste management has been forced to deal with new type of wastes generated by the growth of an unevenly affluent, consumption oriented, and industrialised society. Transitions in urban lifestyles have increased waste loads, increased the need to segregate waste, and increased the need to improve waste treatment. Urban solid waste generation, which is mainly municipal solid waste, has increased rapidly, widening the gap between waste generation and collection rates. Waste collection attempts by the urban environment company have not solved the problem. The collection is only the beginning of trying to address the increasingly complex problem in properly managing the mounting amounts of solid waste. Alternative waste management systems rely on landfills, but operating landfills does not solve the problem of how to either limit or recycle waste production. Eventually they present additional problems, including overfilling, which means that the amount of waste exceeds a landfill's capacity; severe water source contamination; plagues of rats, insects and unpleasant odors.

A high rate of urbanisation and increasing urban populations will lead to substantial increases in the demand for clean water in HCMC. As the clean water supplies come from both surface water and groundwater, the current situation is moving towards a crisis point. The city's water sources are being degraded through four main sources: agricultural chemicals, spontaneously rapid urbanisation, industrial waste, and poorly managed dumpsites. While some impacts can be clearly designated as affecting urban or rural areas, many cases of water quality degradation occur across environmental settings due to flows of water above and below ground, the location of urban landfills, and the increasing need for urban areas to draw water supplies from distant sources.

The city inhabitants have been utilising river and groundwater as sources for clean water supply. Dong Nai River, for example, accounts for 90 per cent of water processed in HCMC's treatment plants (Francisco & Glover 1999). Most of the urban population is not served by sewerage systems, and alternatives such as septic tanks have not prevented the disposal of waste into urban waterways. In addition, there have been changes in consumption patterns, in terms of consumption levels and the variety of consumed products, which not only increase the volume and variety of domestic waste, but also change waste characteristics from organic to more inorganic wastes. Thus, relying on the carrying capacity of waterways to receive and safely dissolve pollutants and contaminants is no longer a sufficient solution for either the growing amount of already existing pollutants or the mounting "new types" of wastewater.

Rapid urbanisation and industrialisation, notably water intensive light industries such as textiles or chemical intensive production, can add substantially to the degradation of an already overburdened water system. Even now most of the new industries emerging in HCMC, including those financed through foreign investment, have not built adequate treatment plants. Most of the waterways are heavily polluted by human settlement waste, industrial wastewater, and solid waste dumped into the city's canals (Figure 7.6). The current conditions of these canals visibly show the health risks of environmental degradation for people living along the canal. Pesticides being washed out from agricultural areas by run-off water going into the regional water system are a major component of the dangers of using untreated water supplies. Other rural factors that worsen contamination risks to water sources include: agricultural spraying of chemicals at the wrong time, over-spraying, use of banned chemicals, improper storage of chemicals, the disposing of chemical packaging, and the washing of chemically contaminated equipment.

In summary, the expansion of the market economy, population pressure, influx of migrants, rapid urbanisation and industrialisation, inappropriate or poorly implemented policies, and lack of adequate knowledge and under-standing of the environment have brought about the heightening environmental management load and degrading quality of life currently observed in HCMC. This worsening quality of life is exacerbated by the severe deficits of environmental infrastructure and public services, which include clean water supply systems, sewerage systems, industrial wastewater treatment plants, and solid waste collection and management. The problems are affecting the well-being and the life of the city inhabitants. It is important to consider policy interventions to deal with the emergent and chronic problems to protect the livability of the city, especially for the poor whose resources and assets have been insufficient to enable them to cope with the negative consequences of the rapid and unsustainable urbanisation.

Concluding Remarks

The urban transformation now underway in HCMC reveals a city region that is at the beginning of a phase of massive urban expansion (Figure 7.8). The high concentration of population in the core indicates its current leading role in hosting urban functions, jobs, services and economic opportunities. In many aspects, the outward expansion of HCMC from the core to the outer zone appears to be less pronounced than in other Asian MURs. While HCMC's urban transformations are moving rapidly outward along a very few transportation corridors, they dissipate before the outer zone is fully entered.

Results of the zonal analysis suggest that the spatial expansion of HCMC is currently at the initial stage of urban transformation. The extent of urbanisation outward to the outer zone is still limited. With a very

Figure 7.8 A Panoramic View of Ho Chi Minh City. The Skyline has not yet Reached the Manhattan-like Dimensions of Bangkok or Shanghai

Source: The author.

high population density, the core blends into the inner zone and continues attracting people, making HCMC different from other Asian mega cities. The city's inner zone is picking up the characteristics of the core while the outer zone is affected by industrial expansion and conversion of land use under the city's planning. The outer zone will possibly achieve the characteristics of the core and inner zone in the future, depending on the nature of the reallocation of the population, infrastructure and services out of the core zone.

Besides the development of road corridors and other infrastructures and provision of adequate public services in the outer zone, the HCMC authorities will need to successfully gain control over the hidden conversion of land use in the inner and outer zones. The situation will also depend on the inflows of migrants and their contribution to the development of the MUR. Migration will continue taking place at a larger scale and in new directions, blurring the differentials in activities and level of development across the city's zones. The significant inflows of migrants from other provinces to the core and especially the inner zone indicate the attraction of education, health care and other social services, as well as urban primacy inherent in the city's development policy. Despite the overcrowding in the core, local residents find it more convenient to live and work within the inner city. It is very likely that the core and the inner zone will continue capturing the salient features of accelerated growth of HCMC for many years to come.

Since HCMC is already extremely densely populated (2,400 persons per square kilometre), it would be very difficult to maintain shared life spaces and housing for residents without strategic interventions to assist in planning its growth. The increasing densities, combined with rapidly rising land prices, gradual privatisation of public spaces, and commercial land development have reduced the per capita availability of and access of the poor to these spaces. This issue characterises the urbanisation process in HCMC today. The combination of auto and industrial pollution is imposing a serious threat to human health and quality of life in and around the city. HCMC is currently encountering many new types of environmental risks. While old risks remain serious or are becoming even worse, new risks are rapidly appearing. These new risks (e.g. traffic accidents, environmental pollution, respiratory disease due to industrial air and water pollution) will add to long-standing and well-known risks (e.g. waterborne disease due to poor sanitary system). The affluent segments of the population are perceived to benefit from development, and theoretically with their better resources, they have a greater capacity to protect themselves from most of the old and new risks. The poor and the disadvantaged suffer due to their lack of resources to cope with the perilous environment and health risks. Issues of quality of life have become critical policy challenges for the rapid expansion and unsustainable urbanisation of HCMC.

Notes

1. As rural to urban migration increasingly fuels the pace of urbanisation, the fear that the rural population will flood the major cities of Vietnam has resulted in a number of policies to restrict, both directly and indirectly, migration into the major cities. These measures are grounded in the system of household registration. Four different categories are used to classify the population as residents and non-residents of a particular geographical area. These categories are nation-wide and are also used to determine access to public and social services in that locality:

    KT1 permanent registration — non-migrant with household registration
    KT2 permanent registration — intra-district mover with household registration
    KT3 temporary registration — migrant, residing independently or with relatives, without household registration book, 6–12 months registration with extension.
    KT4 "floating" migrant, residing in guest house or temporary dwelling, without household registration book, 1–3 months or no registration.

    Many KT4 migrants might be seen as having a *de facto* registration with guest house owners, who should report to the local police. The local police should have some records of who is staying in their areas and thus in theory the KT4 migrants can be counted. In practice, however, it appears that KT4 migrant numbers are estimates only, and the actual numbers are likely to be much higher than the recorded figures.

2. Today, Ho Chi Minh City plays a dominant role in the national economy. In 2001 it accounted for 18.7 per cent of the national GDP, 35.7 per cent of the value of manufactured goods, 32.6 per cent of the value of services, 40.1 per cent the value of exports, 32.6 per cent the value of imports, and 36.5 per cent the national budget (Cohen 2001).

3. The figure for Hanoi was +4.29 per cent, indicating a higher level of market opportunities in HCMC and the rapid growth of the southern economy.

4. The figure was probably underestimated as the definition of the HCMC slums is based mainly on housing conditions, not on access to safe water, sanitary environment and basic facilities.

5. Indicators of the poor air quality of the city include dust, particularly from construction and industrial processes; sulfur dioxide (SO_x), which mainly comes from coal as one of major sources of fuel; nitrogen oxide (NO_x), carbon monoxide (CO_2), and particulates, which are generally emitted from motorised vehicle engines during the combustion processes.

6. The noise levels at main intersections in the inner zone range from 83–86 dBA during the day time, which is 13–14 dBA above the standard.

8

Taipei — Post-industrial Globalisation

Li-ling Huang[1]

Introduction

Taipei Municipality is the largest city in Taiwan. Its population is 2.6 million, and it covers an area of approximately 270 square kilometres. As the capital city, it is the centre of Taiwan's economy, politics and culture. Located in the vast basin of northern Taiwan and surrounded by mountains and rivers, the earliest components of its transportation networks were established in the late Qing Dynasty, and during the colonial period the network closely linked Taipei basin with nearby towns surrounding it. The 1960s and 1970s were critical decades for the economic development of Taiwan and the positioning of Taipei Municipality as the engine of national growth. During this period, the city gradually incorporated neighboring Keelung City, Taipei Prefecture, and Taoyuan Prefecture into its hinterland. With these areas added to Taipei Municipality, the Taipei mega-urban region (Taipei MUR) had a bustling population of 8.54 million by the end of 2000, or about 39 per cent of the country's population.

This chapter on the dynamics of the Taipei MUR is divided into four sections. First, it reviews the interaction between the economic growth and the spatial re-structuring of Taipei MUR in distinct historic phases up until the late 1980s, with a focus on the provision of transportation networks and industrial distribution. Second, it compares census data from 1990 and 2000 to analyse demographic and occupational transitions, commuting patterns and housing distribution. Third, the paper examines the livability of Taipei MUR during the decades of fast urbanisation. The development of Taipei MUR after the year 2000 is then reviewed to conclude the paper.

Taipei's Development Stages

Pre-modern Time (Eighteenth Century to 1895)

Taipei Basin is the most fertile land in the north of the island and was occupied by aboriginal Taiwanese; hence, the Han people from China's coastal provinces who started to migrate to Taiwan in the early seventeenth century did not develop it until the early eighteenth century. Settlements along the Danshuei River, the main river of Taipei basin, developed as ports through cross-strait agricultural trade.

The most critical factor in Taipei's rise was the Qing government's opening of the Danshuei and Bali ports, 30 kilometres from Taipei, in response to military pressure from Western powers. With these new ports, Taipei City started to export cash crops such as oolong tea to foreign countries, and the city was incorporated to some extent into the global capitalist economy. In 1885 the Qing government upgraded Taiwan's status as a province and started to build the Taipei city wall and gates.[2] The governor at the time, Liu Ming-Chuan, dedicated himself to the modernisation of Taiwan. His important achievements were the provisioning of electricity utilities, setting up telegraph cables across the strait, and building railways from Taipei to its sea port Danshuei. Yet the growing city was quite small. Clustered mainly in three areas — the area within the city walls, and the two port cities of Manga and Dadoucheng — the total population of Taipei was still under 50,000 in 1895.

Japanese Colonial Times (1895–1945)

Taipei's status as the cultural, economic and government centre of Taiwan was cemented in the five decades of Japanese rule. Taipei was chosen by the Japanese colonial government to be the capital of the island because of its relatively weaker political resistance, stronger merchant activities and sounder infrastructures developed in the Qing dynasty.

During the Japanese occupation, Taipei Municipality grew steadily. Its population increased to 164,329 in 1920 and doubled to reach 335,397 in 1945, the final year of colonial reign. Japanese immigrants — mainly the administrative staff of the government and military sectors — contributed considerably to Taipei's population growth. The share of the population that was Japanese rose from 9 per cent in 1896 to 28 per cent in 1920 and 32 per cent in 1945.

Figure 8.1 Taipei City and Street Map, 1914. The square in the middle is the original walled city area.

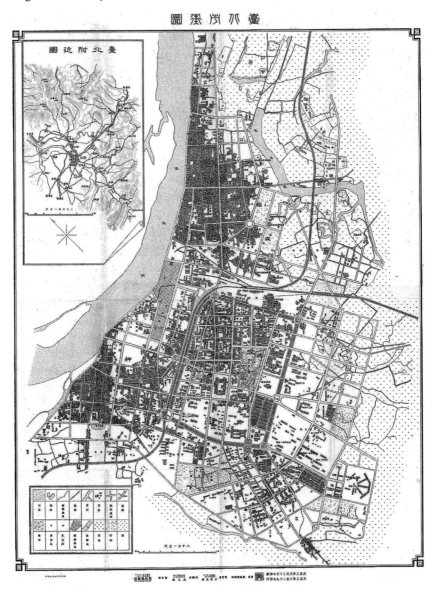

臺 北 市 街 圖

Source: Bureau of Cultural Affairs, Taipei City Government.

As in many colonial cities, the colonisers segregated themselves from the native population and had access to better urban services and infrastructure. Most Japanese lived in dormitories close to government offices located within the original walled area. The West gate area was developed into an entertainment and leisure district for the Japanese complete with restaurants and theatres, while Taiwanese people lived in the two major settlements of Manga and Dadoucheng (Figure 8.1).

Taipei was seen as a symbol of Japanese hegemonic rule and as a base to invade Southeast Asia and build its colonial empire. In accordance with such grand ambitions, large urban parks, three lines of boulevards, a newly developed grid patterned road system and administrative buildings meeting western standards were constructed in the early years of the twentieth century in the tradition of the City Beautiful Movement (a reform movement in North American architecture and urban planning). According to the city's master plan, Taipei Municipality was to accommodate a population of 300,000, and later this number was expanded to 500,000 people in 1932. The master plan also envisioned eastward expansion of the city and some light industries such as wine and paper were allocated to the suburbs in order to provide the city with consumption goods.

The completion of a railroad system was a critical factor in forming the growing metropolis. In 1898, only three years after Japanese arrival, the railroad from Taipei extended 25 kilometres northeast to Keelung. In 1901, the railway from Taipei to its annexed cities, including Manja (Wanhua), Yingge, Shulin and Taoyuan was completed, leading Taipei's development to its southwest hinterlands. Meanwhile, a new highway system connected the present Taipei Municipality and the surrounding towns of Sindian, Pinling, Shiding, Rueifang, Shuangsi, and Jinshan. Located within today's Taipei Prefecture, these mining, agricultural and fishery towns supported the early economic activities of Taipei city.

In 1908, the north-south railway that connected Keelung to Kaohsiung was completed, greatly reducing travel time along the west coast. For example, the travel time from Taipei to Tainan was shortened from nine days to just one day. The railway also led to the development of cities of varying size along its route and created the framework for Taiwan's contemporary urban development. Goods such as sugar, rice, tea, and timber were produced island wide, transported along this newly-created corridor to Taipei, and then exported to the Japan mainland through Keelung Port. The completion of this railroad on the west coast undoubtedly increased the importance of Taipei, and by centralising political, military, and cultural power, ensured its status as the primary city on the island.

Post World War II (1946 to the Late 1980s)

In 1946, with the surrender of Japan and the end of World War II (WWII), approximately 300,000 Japanese, one-third of them residing in Taipei, departed from Taiwan and the island was returned to China. The subsequent period was a tumultuous time in Taiwan's history. After the Kuomingtang (KMT, literally the Party of Nationals) lost to the Communist Party after more than two decades of civil war, Chiang Kai-shek led his troops in retreat to Taiwan. From 1949 to the early 1950s, approximately two million political refugees relocated to the island, about 300,000 of whom settled in Taipei city and more in its neighboring areas. Taipei was chosen as the provisional capital as the war between the KMT and Communists continued. The short-term plan formulated by the government was to fight back and return to China. Given that 85 per cent of the national budget was allocated to national defense, the decade of the 1950s could be summarised as a time of survival rather than development. Many of those employed in the military sector were relocated to the newly constructed military villages in the satellite towns surrounding Taipei. At the national level, the import-substitution industrialisation (ISI) mode of development was adopted. Light industries, including mechanicals, garments, and foods, were placed in the suburban areas of Taipei to provide for the domestic market and create a self-sufficient national economy.

From 1959 to 1963, as the plan to return to China gradually faded, the central government changed its national development strategies and adopted developmentalism. The national government initiated several actions to attract foreign investment, effectively shifting the economic policy from the ISI to the model of Export-Oriented Industrialisation (EOI). In the following years, many industrial zones were set up along the west coast of the island to provide incentives, including cheap land and tax exemptions. The most successful ones were the electronics and plastics factories located in Sindian, Sanchong, Banchiao, and Jhognhe, all part of Taipei Prefecture. This industrialisation greatly contributed to the surge of rural immigrants moving to the Taipei metropolitan area from the mid-1960s into the 1970s.

During this period, a policy to further escalate Taipei's function was launched by the then premier Chiang Ching-Kuo. In 1973, he announced "Ten Projects for National Construction", aiming to complete major infrastructure within the following five years to pave the way for Taiwan's industrialisation. Those projects included the Sun Yat-sen Freeway, Chiang Kai-shek (CKS) Airport, the modernising of the railways, and setting up the state enterprises of Petrochemical Industry and Ship Construction Industry.

Such projects were instrumental in Taiwan's involvement in the global economy. They also contributed to shaping the role of the island's regions. For example, the Sun Yat-sen Freeway connected the major cities on the west coast and turned the regions into production sites. Based on the infrastructure provided by the government, manufacturing industries, notably footwear, garments, electronics, plastics, and toys, developed rapidly and created the so-called "economic miracle of Taiwan". Through the rapid industrialisation decades of the 1970s and 1980s, Taipei served as Taiwan's gateway to international markets and was home to thousands of trading companies and corporate headquarters. Meanwhile, there was a high concentration of factories in Taipei Prefecture and Taoyuan Prefecture to take advantage of access to the producer services provided in Taipei Municipality.

While the 1980s was the peak of industrialisation of Taiwan, it also saw a re-direction of economic policy. By then, the export-led growth model of development had encountered as many difficulties as opportunities. On the one hand, in 1987, the US enacted Act 301 and this led to the New Taiwan Dollar appreciation of nearly 37 per cent. In addition, given growing labour costs and environmental concerns, manufacturing firms started to close down or relocate to Southeast Asian or Mainland China. The government took a series of actions to keep manufacturing industry in Taiwan, including limiting Taiwanese companies' investment to China and gradually opening opportunities for migrant workers from other countries, mostly Southeast Asian, in the labour intensive sectors in Taiwan.

On the other hand, to cope with the economic restructuring, the government chose a new strategy focused on higher value-added production in areas such as the hi-tech sector. As early as 1979 the central government had set up the Hsinchu Science-Based Industrial Park, about 75 kilometres outside of Taipei City and by the late 1980s the park had proven very successful in attracting businesses. Along with shifting economic strategies, Taipei's urban services needed to keep pace with growing demand and for the most part have done just that. This has included creating good connections with universities and research institutes and providing urban services to the rising middle class and expatriate community, such as Western schools and creature comforts. The Taipei/Hsinchu connection formed a new production corridor in north Taiwan, covering the region of Taoyuan Prefecture. Ushered in by Taipei, Taiwan's globalised economic prosperity continued from the

1960s to 1980s, resulting in nearly three decades of double digit GNP growth rate, and foreign currency reserves grew from US$20.6 billion in 1971 to $76.2 billion in 1991 (Kuo 2001).

Population Growth and the Urban Spatial Pattern 1960s–80s

From the 1960s to 1980s, the inflow of political immigrants, rural to urban migration in search of a higher standard of living, and high fertility rates led to rapid population growth in Taipei. The population of Taipei in 1950 was 503,000 and reached 704,000 in 1955. By 1967, when Taipei Municipality expanded by incorporating neighbouring districts, it was a city with over 1.2 million people. In 1974, this figure grew to 2 million and by the end of the 1980s the population reached its peak of 2.7 million.

At the same time, the population of Taipei Prefecture also leapt, reaching 2.8 million in 1987 and outnumbering the 2.6 million of Taipei Municipality. The total population of the greater Taipei Metropolitan Area exceeded one fourth of the national population, and become the core to attract governmental as well as private investment. The primacy of Taipei Metropolitan Area over other regions of this island was clear (Hsia 1990).

Based on a mixed residential and commercial land-use pattern, the Taipei metropolitan area had been transformed from a single core to a multi-core model by the late 1980s (Kuo 2001). In the 1960s high-rise office buildings first started to appear in the West Gate (Xi-men) area, formerly the area reserved for Japanese leisure and entertainment. During the 1970s and 1980s, Taipei city's centre further extended along with its high economic growth. Due to the saturated development of the west part of the city, most growth took place in the newly planned urban areas in the north and east of the city. Along the Chung-Shan North Road area, at the end close to the city centre, offices and amenities grew to serve foreign enterprises, mainly from Japan and the US; and suburbs developed at the other end of the Chung-Shan Road to house these expatriates' communities. Thus, the East District was shaped.

The transition of Taipei in this period of time could be best illustrated by the change of Chung-Shao East Road, which shifted in just one decade from rice paddies into high-rise offices, modern apartments, fashionable shopping areas and the vast open space of the Sun Yat-Sen Memorial Hall. By the mid-1980s, this area had become a symbol of modern urban life for the new middle class in the city. The commercial landscape became the dominant element of the city, in contrast with the tarnishing glamour of the old districts in the western area.

During this period, elevated roads like Huanho South Road, and the Cheinkuo and Hsinghei elevated expressways of Taipei were completed, helping to form six transportation corridors between Taipei city and its neighbouring cities including Keelung, Danshuei, Taoyuan, Sansia, Jhonghe, and Sindian (Kuo 2001).

By the end of the 1980s, what we refer to in this book as Taipei MUR was formed, including Taipei city, Keelung City, Taipei Prefecture and Taoyuan Prefecture. However, the roles of the spatial units within the MUR became quite differentiated. For example, a distinct pattern unfolded in the regional division of labour between Taipei Municipality and Taipei Prefecture. First, Taipei Prefecture served as the industrial area and hosted electronics industries and provided job opportunities for labour-intensive sectors. Second, it also accommodated the unwanted but necessary urban services for the whole Taipei metropolitan and entire northern region of Taiwan, including nuclear power stations, jails, armories, and cemeteries. As the urban periphery expanded, residences were built adjacent to them. Third, the abundant hills and coastline of Taipei Prefecture also served as popular weekend recreation destinations for Taipei citizens as the demand for mass recreation grew along with the new urban middle class. Lastly, compared to the skyrocketing price of housing in the Taipei Municipality, Taipei Prefecture provided cheaper housing, but as the better job opportunities and education resources still clustered in the Municipality, many people chose to live in the Prefecture and commuted to the Municipality for work. This in turn, increased the inter-dependency across the two administrative jurisdictions (NTUBP 1992).

From the 1990s to 2000s: The Age of Taipei Mega-Urban Region

In this research, the results of the population censuses conducted in 1990 and 2000 are used to compare changes in population growth and composition, occupation, migration, education and other dimensions taking place in the three zones of Taipei MUR. The three zones are the core, the inner ring and the outer ring.

The core is Taipei Municipality and includes the 12 districts of Beitou, Shihlin, Neihu, Jhongshan, Wanhua, Songshan, Datong, Daan, Sinyi, Nangang, Wunshan, and Jhongjheng. All residents are classified as urban. The inner ring crosses the boundaries of three cities and counties. It covers the seven wards of Keelung City (Jhongshan, Jhongjheng, Sinyi, Renai, Anle, Nuannuan and Cidu), a few more urbanised townships within Taipei Prefecture (Danshuei,

Sijhih, Shidian, Jhonghe, Yonghe, Banchiao, Tucheng, Shulin, Shingjhuang, Sanchong, Lujhou, Wugu, Taishan, and Yingge); Taoyuan City, Jhongli City, Gueishan, Bade, and Pingjhen townships of Taoyuan Prefecture.

Finally, the outer ring is the remainder of the less urbanised areas within Taipei Prefecture and Taoyuan Prefecture. In Taipei Prefecture it includes the townships of Linkou, Bali, Sanjhih, Shihmen, Jinshan, Wanli, Rueifang, Pingsi, Gongliao, Shuangsi, Pinglin, Shihding, Wulai, Shenkeng and Sansia; and in Taoyuan Prefecture it includes the townships of Dasi, Fusing, Longtan, Yangmei, Sinwu, Guanyin, Dayuan and Lujhu (see Figure 8.2).

Some data problems were encountered in the analysis. The 1990 data were much richer than those of 2000 in terms of cross classification analyses and topics covered. For example, the 1990 data included a questionnaire on residents' attitudes toward the provision of local infrastructure, which was not collected in 2000. Furthermore, since our zonal method crossed administrative

Figure 8.2 Map of Taipei MUR

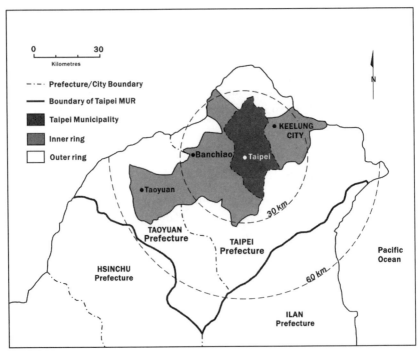

Source: The author.

boundaries, we needed to draw on the original figures of each township and then reorganise and sort them according to our zonal method. Unfortunately, not every data series in the census was reported down to the township units; therefore some compromise was needed when choosing the indicators. In the case of population, we managed to sort the data of local and foreign populations based on township; for education it was more complicated. While the 2000 census collected figures for population with college level education and above, the 1990 census data separated the population with college education from that of university level. Our solution was to extract the figures from the township level and rearrange them. However, for some important categories such as occupation, the data did not show the figures collected from the township level and so we could not match them to our zonal method. Instead we could only accept the existing format based on the administrative boundaries at the Prefecture and city level, a procedure that nevertheless still serves to shed light on the general picture of the MUR.

Population Structure, Commuting Patterns, Occupation and Education within Taipei MUR

The population of Taipei MUR increased from 7.45 million to 8.54 million between 1990 and 2000, and its share of the national population rose from 37 per cent to 39 per cent. But whereas the core experienced a slight population decrease from 2.73 to 2.62 million, the inner and outer rings underwent a rapid population increase. The population of the inner ring increased from nearly 3.99 million to 4.92 million, an increase of 23 per cent. And the population of the outer ring grew from 0.73 million to 0.99 million, an increase of 36 per cent. While the outer ring had the highest growth rate, the inner ring's gain of nearly one million made up by far the greater part of the absolute population increase for the Taipei MUR in the decade.

In 2000, the highest population density was in the core, with 9,655 people per square kilometre, followed by the inner ring at 5,532 people per square kilometre and the outer ring third with 395 people per square kilometre. The inner ring was more densely populated than those of the other five MURs included in this study, reflecting a relative "underbounding" of the core, which had the smallest area of the core of any of the MURs studied, with the exception of Ho Chi Minh City.

The change in population structure of Taipei Municipality was the result of a number of factors. Despite fertility falling to very low levels, resulting in an ageing population,[3] there was still a small net natural increase in population, of between 17,000 to 22,000 people, between 1990 and 2000. Thus net out-migration was the cause of the decline in the core's population.[4] Besides migration from the city to other areas, mainly the inner ring and outer ring, Taipei city has also witnessed a large emigration to other countries. For example, in 1996, 61,191 Taipei citizens migrated to other countries, 51 per cent of total emigration from Taiwan. Each year, the number of international emigrants slightly outnumbered that of immigrants. From 1991 to 2000, there were 230,373 emigrants versus an influx of 157,491 foreign immigrants, and this contributed substantially to the net decline of 106,733 people during that decade.

Table 8.1 Population, Area and Population Density, 1990 and 2000

Year and Component	Population	Sex Ratio	Area (km²)	Density	% change
1990					
Taiwan	19,895,725	104.31	36,006.42	552.00	
T. MUR	**7,456,866**	**103.03**	**3,678.08**	**2,027.38**	
Core	2,730,990	99.88	271.80	10,047.80	
Inner Ring	3,992,899	103.96	890.00	4,486.39	
Keelung C.	343,001	104.74	132.76	2,583.64	
Taipei P.	2,769,210	102.77	492.44	5,623.47	
Taoyuan P.	880,688	107.47	264.81	3,325.78	
Outer Ring	732,977	110.14	2,516.28	291.29	
Taipei P.	275,021	111.70	1,560.13	176.28	
Taoyuan P.	457,956	109.21	956.15	478.96	
2000					
Taiwan	21,826,796	104.28	36,006.42	606.00	8.91
T. MUR	**8,542,676**	**100.98**	**3,678.08**	**2,322.59**	**12.71**
Core	2,624,257	95.33	271.80	9,655.11	–4.07
Inner Ring	4,923,519	101.69	890.00	5,532.02	18.90
Keelung C.	387,504	104.73	132.76	2,918.86	11.48
Taipei P.	3,365,781	99.57	492.44	6,824.94	17.72
Taoyuan P.	1,170,234	107.01	264.81	4,419.20	24.74
Outer Ring	994,900	113.55	2,516.28	395.39	26.33
Taipei P.	356,301	109.51	1,560.13	228.38	22.81
Taoyuan P.	638,599	115.88	956.15	667.89	28.29

Notes: Core (Taipei Municipality), C (City), P (Prefecture)
Source: Compiled from "Population and Housing Census",Year 2000 and Year 1990, Directorate-General of Budget, Accounting and Statistics, Taipei, Executive Yuan, R.O.C. (Taiwan).

Table 8.1 also shows that the sex ratio of Taipei MUR fell slightly from 103 in 1990 to 101 per cent in 2000. Again, the patterns differ among the three zones of Taipei MUR. Both the core and inner ring witnessed a decline in the sex ratio, while the outer ring had a sharp increase. There is a major contrast between the sex ratio of the core (95) and of the outer ring (114) in 2000. This pattern is closely connected to the industrial restructuring in the MUR. As the manufacturing sector was gradually relocating outward, and the core and the inner ring were shifting significantly to the service industry, the sex ratio distribution reflected the workforce of these industries and their new location pattern, as will be further explained below.

Table 8.2 reports the migration patterns within the MUR. It indicates that from 1990 to 2000, while the percentage of non-movers in the core rose from 63 to 73 per cent and in the inner ring from 63 to 68 per cent, in the outer ring it dropped significantly from 78 to 69 per cent, indicating an increase in mobility in the outer ring, which hitherto had the least mobility.

Table 8.2 Migration Status of Population Aged 5 and Above for Zones, 1990 and 2000

| | TAIPEI MUR | | | |
| | Core | Inner Ring | Outer Ring | TAIPEI |
Year and Migration status	% Distribution by Migration Status			MUR
1990				
Non-movers	63.0	62.7	78.2	64.3
Residential movers	13.0	14.6	9.8	13.6
Movers within city/prefecture	13.6	9.8	4.9	10.7
Migrants across city/prefecture	10.4	12.9	7.1	11.4
Total	**100.0**	**100.0**	**100.0**	**100.0**
2000				
Non-movers	72.6	67.9	69.1	69.5
Residential movers	12.8	14.9	11.4	13.9
Movers within city/Prefecture	8.1·	8.6	9.0	8.5
Migrants across city/Prefecture	6.4	8.6	10.5	8.2
Total	**100.0**	**100.0**	**100.0**	**100.0**

Notes: not including migrant workers according to the regulation of Council of Labor Affairs.
Source: Compiled from "Population and Housing Census", Year 2000 and Year 1990, Directorate-General of Budget, Accounting and Statistics, Taipei, Executive Yuan, R.O.C. (Taiwan).

Note that these figures include people who simply changed their residence, some of whom moved only a short distance. But when the comparison is restricted to those who moved across a city or prefecture boundary, the same pattern holds in an even more marked form: a sharp decline in movement to the core and the inner ring, and a sharp increase in movement to the outer ring.

Based on the place of residence five years earlier, Table 8.3 reports the inter-regional flows within the Taipei MUR and between the MUR and other areas of Taiwan. From 1990 to 2000, the percentage of total migrants who moved between Taipei Municipality, Keelung City, Taipei Prefecture and Taoyuan Prefecture (in other words, within Taipei MUR) rose from 44.7 to 57.8 per cent, showing high interaction within the zones of Taipei MUR.

Table 8.3 Distribution of Migrants by Place of Residence 5 Years Ago for Zones

Place of Residence 5 years ago	TAIPEL MUR			TAIPEI MUR %
	Core %	Inner Ring %	Outer Ring %	
1990				
TAIPEI MUR	**42.6**	**46.1**	**42.7**	**44.7**
Taipei M.	–	32.4	18.9	20.5
Keelung C.	3.7	2.3	5.5	2.9
Taipei P.	32.5	6.6	14.9	16.0
Taoyuan P.	6.4	4.8	3.4	5.3
Rest of Taiwan	**50.9**	**50.4**	**52.6**	**50.7**
Foreign Countries	**6.5**	**3.5**	**4.7**	**4.6**
2000				
TAIPEI MUR	**54.2**	**57.4**	**59.7**	**57.8**
Taipei M.	–	26.7	39.8	27.5
Keelung C.	3.5	2.6	2.2	2.6
Taipei P.	44.0	22.8	12.7	22.3
Taoyuan P.	6.7	5.3	4.9	5.4
Rest of Taiwan	**34.4**	**36.2**	**35.5**	**35.5**
Foreign Countries	**11.4**	**6.4**	**4.8**	**6.7**

Notes: not including migrant workers according to the regulation of Council of Labor Affairs

M.: Municipality, C.: City, P.: Prefecture

Source: Compiled from "Population and Housing Census", Year 2000 and Year 1990, Directorate-General of Budget, Accounting and Statistics, Taipei, Executive Yuan, R.O.C. (Taiwan).

In contrast, the population flow into Taipei MUR from the rest of Taiwan became less significant than the movement within the MUR, as shown by the decline in the proportion of migrants from the rest of Taiwan from 50.7 per cent in 1990 to 35.5 per cent in 2000. An important development over the period was the pattern of interaction between the outer ring and Taipei Municipality. In 1990, 18.9 per cent of residents living in the outer ring reported their residence five years earlier as Taipei Municipality, while in 2000 this figure surged to 39.8 per cent, indicating an exodus from Taipei Municipality to the outer ring over the decade. Finally, for the general MUR area, the population residing in foreign countries five years earlier shows an increase from 4.6 per cent in 1990 to 6.7 per cent in 2000. But this migration affected Taipei Municipality (the core) most strongly, as the proportion of those who had resided in foreign countries rose from 6.5 per cent in 1990 to 11.4 per cent in 2000.

Table 8.4 further examines residential demographic patterns and activity within Taipei MUR in 2000. The population according to activity, in contrast to resident population, is defined as the population working or studying in the area, including commuters. Table 8.4 demonstrates that among the areas of Taipei MUR, Keelung City has the lowest ratio of activity to resident population, at 89.1 per cent, indicating that its population relies more on jobs or educational opportunities in other areas. In contrast, Taipei municipality holds the highest ratio at about 116 per cent. Its total population is about 2.6 million, while its activity population reaches over 3 million.

The commuting analysis from the 2000 Census revealed that among the sub-areas of Taipei MUR, Taipei Municipality and Taoyuan Prefecture were the importers of labour, while Taipei Prefecture and Keelung City were the exporters. It is clear that during the decade, the core, inner ring, and outer ring have further strengthened their intensive interaction in terms of commuting for work or education.

Table 8.5 and 8.6 report the changing patterns of employment and residence distribution within Taipei MUR. In the 1990-2000 decade, the share of the MUR population working in the core dropped from 44.2 to 37.7 per cent, while it increased from 44.3 to 48.3 per cent in the inner ring, and from 9.9 to 11.4 per cent in the outer ring. This indicates that the inner ring was the zone that provided most of the increases in jobs over the period. In addition, both the share of the population living in the inner ring but working in the outer ring, and the population living in the outer ring but working in the inner ring, saw growth in the decade (the former grew from 3.3 to 4.4 per cent and the latter grew from 16.7 to 18.2 per

Table 8.4 Commuting Population for Cities and Prefectures, 2000

| City / Prefectures | Community Population | | Population (Residence) (3) | Population (activity) (4)=(3)+(1)−(2) | % (6)=(4)/(3) |
	From other City/Prefecture (1)	To other City/Prefecture (2)			
Total Taiwan	**2,427,901**	**2,468,370**	**21,925,893**	**21,885,424**	**99.8**
Northern Taiwan	**1,318,913**	**1,193,845**	**9,663,973**	**9,789,041**	**101.3**
TAIPEI MUR	**1,156,893**	**1,053,206**	**8,398,049**	**8,501,736**	**101.2**
Taipei M.	651,597	229,063	2,590,587	3,013,121	116.3
Keelung C.	29,107	71,196	385,266	343,177	89.1
Taipei P.	315,701	626,292	3,680,163	3,369,572	91.6
Taoyuan P.	160,488	126,655	1,742,033	1,775,866	101.9
Rest of N. Taiwan	**162,020**	**140,639**	**1,265,924**	**1,287,305**	**101.7**
Hsinchu C	93,600	34,250	385,009	444,359	115.4
Hsinchu P.	59,176	74,115	439,674	424,735	96.6
Ilan P.	9,244	32,274	441,241	418,211	94.8
Central Taiwan	**466,791**	**567,326**	**5,409,702**	**5,309,167**	**98.1**
Taichung C.	224,535	91,739	979,566	1,112,362	113.6
Southern Taiwan	**632,608**	**679,067**	**6,323,036**	**6,276,577**	**99.3**
Kaohsiung M.	189,250	130,310	1,479,122	1,538,062	104.0
Eastern Taiwan	**9,589**	**28,132**	**529,182**	**510,639**	**96.5**

Notes:
1. Commuting to work or study
2. not including migrant workers according to the regulation of Council of Labor Affairs
   M.: Municipality, C.: City, P.: Prefecture
Source: Compiled from "Population and Housing Census", Year 2000 and Year 1990, Directorate-General of Budget, Accounting and Statistics, Taipei, Executive Yuan, R.O.C. (Taiwan).

Table 8.5 Place of Work by Place of Residence for the Employed (Aged 15+) in Taipei MUR in 1990

Place of Residence	Taipei MUR		Place of Work %									
			Core		Inner Ring				Outer Ring			
	No.	%	Total	Taipei	Keelung C.	Taipei P.	Taoyuan P.	Total	Total	Taipei P.	Taoyuan P.	Others
1990												
Total MUR	2777833	100	44.3	44.2	3.8	29.6	10.9	9.9	9.9	3.7	6.2	1.6
Core	1047979	100	8.0	88.9	0.5	6.6	0.9	1.5	1.5	0.9	0.6	1.6
Inner ring	1446344	100	76.0	19.1	6.7	50.9	18.4	3.3	3.3	1.3	2.0	1.6
Keelung C.	128287	100	78.3	16.2	72.2	5.3	0.8	2.9	2.9	2.6	0.3	2.6
Taipei P.	1015792	100	72.7	23.9	0.3	70.8	1.6	2.0	2.0	1.3	0.7	1.4
Taoyuan P.	302265	100	85.9	4.4	0.1	3.3	82.5	7.8	7.8	0.9	6.9	1.9
Outer ring	283510	100	16.7	6.9	1.4	6.2	9.1	74.2	74.2	25.7	48.5	2.2
Taipei P.	106655	100	18.1	12.9	3.5	12.7	1.9	67.5	67.5	66.9	0.6	1.5
Taoyuan P.	176855	100	15.8	3.3	0.1	2.3	13.4	78.3	78.3	0.7	77.5	2.6

Notes: not including migrant workers according to the regulation of Council of Labor Affairs

C.: City, P.: Prefecture

Source: Compiled from "Population and Housing Census", Year 2000 and Year 1990, Directorate-General of Budget, Accounting and Statistics, Taipei, Executive Yuan, R.O.C. (Taiwan).

Table 8.6 Place of Work by Place of Residence for the Employed (Aged 15+) in Taipei MUR in 2000

Place of Residence	Taipei MUR		Place of Work %									
			Core		Inner Ring				Outer Ring			
	No.	%	Total	Taipei	Total	Keelung C.	Taipei P.	Taoyuan P.	Total	Taipei P.	Taoyuan P.	Others
2000												
Total MUR	3920284	100	**48.3**	37.7	**11.4**	3.3	32.1	12.9	—	3.8	7.6	2.6
Core	1204382	100	**10.7**	84.5	**2.0**	0.4	9.1	1.2	—	1.0	1.0	2.8
Inner ring	2263637	100	**74.3**	18.9	**4.4**	5.1	49.4	19.8	—	1.7	2.7	2.4
Keelung C.	172224	100	**75.0**	18.6	**3.2**	63.9	10.1	1.0	—	2.5	0.7	3.2
Taipei P.	1568725	100	**71.2**	23.9	**2.7**	0.3	68.9	2.0	—	1.6	1.1	2.2
Taoyuan P.	522688	100	**83.0**	4.2	**10.0**	0.1	3.5	79.4	—	1.6	8.4	2.8
Outer ring	452265	100	**18.2**	7.2	**71.3**	1.0	7.4	9.8	—	21.6	49.7	3.3
Taipei P.	158608	100	**22.2**	14.3	**61.3**	2.6	16.1	3.5	—	59.8	1.5	2.2
Taoyuan P.	293657	100	**15.9**	3.5	**76.6**	0.1	2.7	13.1	—	0.9	75.7	4.0

Notes: not including migrant workers according to the regulation of Council of Labor Affairs
C.: City, P.: Prefecture

Source: Compiled from "Population and Housing Census", Year 2000 and Year 1990, Directorate-General of Budget, Accounting and Statistics, Taipei, Executive Yuan, R.O.C. (Taiwan).

cent). This implies that the inner ring and outer ring have strengthened their interaction, and the boundary between the inner and outer ring is gradually being blurred with the expansion of the MUR.

The economic restructuring of the Taipei MUR during the 1990–2000 period is key to the change in commuting patterns. Here because the original data set does not display the figures below the Prefecture and city level, we could not abide by the MUR zonal method, but could only show the changes at the Prefecture and City level. As Table 8.7 indicates, Taipei Municipality, Taipei Prefecture, Keelung City and Taoyuan Prefecture — all of the four administrative areas composing Taipei MUR — witnessed significant increases in the tertiary sector, i.e. commerce and services. The average share of the workforce in the primary, secondary and tertiary sectors in 1990 was 4.7, 40.3, and 55.0 per cent, respectively, compared to 1.6, 26.0 and 72.4 per cent in year 2000. The most striking increases in the share of the tertiary sector were seen in Taipei Municipality and Taipei Prefecture. In Taipei Municipality, the proportion in tertiary industry grew from 69.3

Table 8.7   Occupation of Population (Aged 15+)

MUR	Primary Sector (%)	Secondary Sector (%)	Tertiary Sector (%)	All Sectors	
Year 1990					
Taipei Municipality	1.4	29.3	69.3	100	1,047,979
Taipei Prefecture	4.3	47.2	48.5	100	1,122,449
Keelung City	3.5	33.0	63.5	100	128,287
Taoyuan Prefecture	13.1	50.2	36.7	100	479,120
Total MUR	**4.7**	**40.3**	**55.0**	**100**	
Number	130,097	1,119,404	1,528,334		2,777,835
Year 2000					
Taipei Municipality	0.5	11.0	88.5	100	1,204,382
Taipei Prefecture	1.4	29.0	69.6	100	1,727,197
Keelung City	1.1	19.5	79.4	100	172,224
Taoyuan Prefecture	3.9	43.1	53.0	100	816,345
Total MUR	**1.6**	**26.0**	**72.4**	**100**	
Number	63,964	1,019,658	2,836,526		3,920,148

Notes: not including migrant workers according to the regulation of Council of Labor Affairs.

Source: Compiled from "Population and Housing Census", Year 2000 and Year 1990, Directorate-General of Budget, Accounting and Statistics, Taipei, Executive Yuan, R.O.C. (Taiwan).

to 88.5 per cent, and in Taipei prefecture from 48.5 to 69.6 per cent. Interestingly, the occupational structure in Taipei Prefecture in 2000 was similar to that of Taipei Municipality one decade earlier. Similarly, Keelung city also witnessed a stride in tertiary industry. At the same time, Taoyuan experienced a dramatic decline in the proportion working in the primary sector (from 13.1 to 3.9 per cent), a moderate loss in the secondary sector (50.2 to 43.9 per cent), and a rapid increase in the share of the tertiary sector (36.8 to 53.0 per cent).

Not only did employment in secondary industry decline by 100,000 in Taipei MUR between 1990 and 2000, but also the distribution of this employment shifted markedly. In 1990, Taipei municipality and Keelung city between them accounted for 31.2 per cent of employment in secondary industry. By 2000, this had shrunk sharply to 16.3 per cent. Taipei prefecture's share rose slightly, from 47.3 per cent to 49.1 per cent over the same period. In contrast, the share of Taoyuan Prefecture rose from 21.4 per cent in 1990 to 34.5 per cent in 2000.

As early as 1990, all areas within Taipei MUR except Taoyuan Prefecture had already reached the point where the share of employment in the tertiary sector was higher than in secondary industry. In 2000, Taoyuan Prefecture joined the trend, with 53 per cent of its employment in the tertiary sector. The entire Taipei MUR, then, underwent a general process of de-industrialisation over the 1990s.

One prominent demographic change that took place during the decade was the increase in foreign population. Table 8.8 shows that in 1990, the foreign population was only 21,325, or about 0.3 per cent of the total MUR population, but in 2000, it had risen to 193,995 people, or about 2.3 per cent of the population. The major change was the open policy to foreign workers in 1992 and the surge of migrant spouses, mainly from Mainland China and Southeast Asia. There are some limitations in the census data in Table 8.8. Firstly, the table does not classify people according to their occupation or background, but only their nationality, so there is no way to tell migrant spouses from migrant workers. Secondly, migrant spouses who received citizenship within the decade would not be classified as foreign population. Therefore, the exact number of migrant spouses who arrived during the decade is much larger than that shown by the table; for migrant workers, in the early years, their working contract could only be valid for two years, then they have to go back to their original countries. Hence, within the decade, the actual influx of foreigners to Taipei MUR was even greater than the table indicates.

Table 8.8   The Distribution of Foreign Population

	Total Population	Alien Population	% Alien	% Japan and U.S.	% Southeast Asia	Sex Ratio of Southeast Asia Population
1990						
Core	2,760,475	16,832	0.6	0.3	0.2	100
Inner ring	348,586	3,677	0.1	*	*	90
Outer ring	4,034,968	816	0.1	*	0.1	107
Taipei MUR	**7,144,029**	**21,325**	**0.2**	**0.1**	**0.1**	**98**
2000						
Core	2,624,257	58,734	2.2	0.4	1.6	50
Inner ring	4,923,519	93,720	1.9	*	1.1	83
Outer ring	984,900	42,541	4.3	*	4.1	163
Taipei MUR	**8,532,676**	**194,995**	**2.3**	**0.2**	**1.9**	**87**

Note: *less than 0.05%.
Source: Compiled from "Population and Housing Census", Year 2000 and Year 1990, Directorate-General of Budget, Accounting and Statistics, Taipei, Executive Yuan, R.O.C. (Taiwan).

In further analysing the distribution of the foreign population in the three zones, we found that in 1990, most of the foreign population resided in the core area, i.e., Taipei city, with Japanese and Americans being the largest groups. There was a very small number of foreigners in the inner and outer ring. But in those two zones, the foreign population from Southeast Asian countries already exceeded the number of people from Japan and the US.

Apart from the sharp increase in numbers, the most dramatic change taking place by 2000 was that the foreign population from Southeast Asian countries overtook that from the US and Japan. Furthermore, out of the three zones, the core city, Taipei Municipality no longer has the biggest foreign population; this distinction has gone to the outer ring. In Taipei Municipality, the female foreign population showed a large gain and was almost double the male foreign population. This was probably mostly due to the advent of domestic helpers from abroad (Figure 8.3). The inner ring area reflects a mixed situation of growing numbers of foreign spouses and workers, with migrant workers in the industrial locations and migrant spouses residing in the peri-urban agricultural territory; while in the outer ring, figures imply a large number of foreign male workers residing in the industrial districts and

Figure 8.3   Foreign Domestic Workers, who mostly also work as caregivers, gather at the Taipei 228 Memorial Park on Sunday, while some are still on duty

Source: The author.

a relatively smaller number of foreign spouses in the coastal villages and even more depopulated agricultural areas.

Table 8.9 shows the increase in population receiving an advanced education. Between 1990 and 2000, even as the municipality's population was decreasing, the population receiving college education and above grew by 34 per cent. The college educated population of the inner and outer zones increased 2.25 and 2.41 times, respectively, in the ten-year period. During the decade, the government enforced a policy of "education revolution" which increased the numbers of people receiving advanced education by setting up more universities and colleges. Along with this government support, the urban fringe succeeded in attracting new universities or universities seeking a second campus. This was due to the relatively cheaper land and accessibility

Table 8.9   Population Aged 15+ with Higher Education*

	1990		2000		
	Number	% of Population Aged 15+	Number	% of Population Aged 15+	% Growth 1990–2000
Core (Taipei Municip.)	**656,315**	**31.5**	**881,523**	**42.0**	**134**
Keelung City	34,047	13.0	67,490	22.1	198
Taipei Prefecture	325,348	16.6	687,323	26.2	211
Taoyuan Prefecture	104,046	16.3	286,430	32.8	275
Inner Ring Total	**463,441**	**16.2**	**1,041,243**	**27.4**	**225**
Taipei Prefecture	16,514	7.9	45,565	16.6	260
Taoyuan Prefecture	40,430	11.7	91,585	20.0	227
Outer Ring Total	**56,944**	**10.3**	**137,150**	**19.7**	**241**
MUR TOTAL	**1,176,700**	**21.4**	**2,059,916**	**31.1**	**175**

Notes: *"Higher education" means junior college, college, university, and post-graduate levels of education; not including migrant workers according to the regulation of Council of Labor Affairs.
Source: Compiled from "Population and Housing Census", Year 2000 and Year 1990, Directorate-General of Budget, Accounting and Statistics, Taipei, Executive Yuan, R.O.C. (Taiwan).

to urban population and services. From the local governments' point of view, the promotion of university towns also served as a tool to bolster the local economy and real estate market.

Infrastructure Provision of Taipei MUR from the 1990s to 2000s

From 1990 to 2000 some new dynamics emerged in the MUR region. The first was the continued expansion of the transportation system. In the core, the main lines of the MRT system were completed in the 1990s (Figure 8.4). They connected Taipei Municipality to Banchiao, where the Taipei Prefecture Government resides, as well as to Taipei Municipality's satellite cities in Taipei Prefecture such as Yonghe and Jhonghe. The MRT lines not only greatly alleviated the burden of transportation within the city and across the rivers, but also regenerated the long declining West Gate area.

Figure 8.4   Taipei MRT Links up the Core and the Inner Ring of Taipei MUR

Source: The author.

The transportation web of Taipei MUR, comprising the MRT, elevated highways and outer ring roads, was mostly clustered between Taipei Municipality and the townships of Taipei Prefecture located in the southwest of the Taipei Municipality (Figures 8.5 and 8.6). For example, in Yonghe, Shingden, Chonghe and Baochiao, Dansui, the major cites in Taipei Prefecture, those commuting to Taipei Municipality for work made up more than 20 per cent of the employed population of those cities, reflecting a connection to earlier development of the Taipei basin.[5] However, a more striking development took place in the fringe of the metropolitan area. The completion of National Highway No. 3 assisted in the growth of satellite cities in the outer boundaries of the Taipei MUR. Shiji turned into a fringe city with a booming real estate industry; university and real estate development projects spawned along Sansia of Taipei Prefecture; and Long-Tan township of Taoyuan and other cities in the Hsinchu Prefecture also quickly transformed from agricultural land into newly developed towns.

The ever-growing demands for suburban recreation also turned some old fringe towns or rural countryside with beautiful scenery and natural resources originally based on an agricultural economy into tourist destinations for visitors from the metropolitan area. But along with economic benefit, tourism also brought negative impacts. For example, on weekends, people flocked to the seashore town of Danshui via the MRT and this led to issues of waste disposal as trash from the visitors began to pile up. Growing concerns over the garbage led representatives of the township to negotiate with Taipei Municipality to levy charges in order to deal with waste management.

Figure 8.5   Westbound: From Taipei City to the West Town and Taipei Prefecture

Source: The author.

Figure 8.6 Cars and Motorbikes on the Road in Banchiao of Taipei Prefecture, an Inner Zone City of MUR

Source: The author.

In the decade of the 1990s, the intensified transportation web in the inner and outer ring also enhanced urban functions and contributed to the housing boom in these zones. Within the MUR as a whole, from 1990 to 2000 housing stock in all areas other than Taipei Municipality increased at a much faster pace than the national average. There was a dramatic increase, as much as 72 per cent, in housing stock in Taoyuan Prefecture, the second highest in the country after Taichung city in the centre of Taiwan. However, the vacancy rate of the cities in the fringe of the MUR is also very high — 24 per cent in Keelung and 23 per cent in Taoyuan Prefecture — implying a spatial organisation driven by both demand and land speculation.

Economic and Spatial Restructuring of the MUR from the 1990s to 2000

The census results provide a general picture of demographic and migration changes during the decade of the 1990s. Here we would like to bring the focus back to the unseen forces of change, which mainly came from the economic dimension. As mentioned above, Taiwan's economy underwent huge restructuring after the late 1980s and a large number of firms in the traditional labour-intensive industries closed down or moved out, mostly to Mainland China or the Southeast Asian countries. On the other hand, advanced producer services and knowledge intensive manufacturing sectors became the new leading industries and attracted a new wave of foreign investment. The scale of transformation is indicated by the amount of FDI. From 1952 to 1986 (34 years), FDI in Taiwan was US$4.961 billion, but during the 1987–97 decade, it reached US$20.86 billion. Meanwhile, Taiwan's FDI to the world was US$272 million from 1952 to 1986, and it leapt to US$15 billion in the 1987–97 decade (Jou 2002).

Since the end of the 1980s, Taipei has been the industrial and commercial centre of Taiwan. In 1990, among the 500 major manufacturing companies of Taiwan, 255 companies (51 per cent) were headquartered in Taipei Municipality and among the 300 major companies in the service sector, the share is even higher at 79 per cent.

In the decade of the 1990s, Taipei made further advances toward world city status by functioning as a node for the Asia region. While most of Taiwan found difficulty in integrating into the global economy, the northern region, including Taipei MUR plus the fast growing Shinju Prefecture, became a vibrant global centre. The success was achieved by allocating the IT production to the Hsin-Chu Science Park, its outsourcing factories along the corridors and advanced producer services in Taipei Municipality. Taipei is not only the centre of Taiwan's enterprises, but also the headquarters of the multi-national companies. While the Taipei Municipality is centralising its power, its commanding territory is further dispersed, reaching over the boundary of metropolis, neighbouring counties, even across the straits to Mainland China and linking up to the Silicon Valley in California, USA. In short, Taipei's function could be identified as an "interface city" in the global economy (Chou 2005; Hsu 2005) (Figure 8.7).

A symbol for the entry of Taipei into the global economy and informational era was the development project "Hsin-Yi Planning District", the financial and logistic centre for the economic activities of Pacific Asia. Located in the eastern part of Taipei, adjacent to the Chung-Hsiao East Road, the government owned a large share of the 135 hectares in this former vast military base. In the late 1980s, as the national government aimed to transform Taiwan's economy from an industrial based to a knowledge-based economy, a strategy was adopted to develop Taiwan as a financial centre

240   *Li-ling Huang*

Figure 8.7   The Cityscape of Taipei, an Interface City

Source: The author.

in Pacific Asia. The development of the Hsin-Yi Planning District received
substantial government support; unfortunately, the development lagged from
the late 1980s to the early 1990s because private landowners were aiming for
further land speculation. In 1994, a series of measures were taken to speed up
the development, combining incentives through tax breaks and penalties for
not following codes. While the housing market in the rest of Taipei or even
Taiwan stabilised or slightly receded after the mid-1990s after the previous
overheat, the land and housing price in Hsin-Yi District almost doubled over
five years[6] (Figure 8.8).

    Several key spatial and activity elements were built into Hsin-Yi from the
late 1980s, including the relocation of the Taipei government to the Hsin-yi
district in 1994. But the present shape of Hsin-Yi was mostly forged in the
late 1990s. Besides ornate buildings that served as headquarters for local and
multi-national companies, the area also contained expensive luxury apartment
building for celebrities and CEOs in the high-tech field, symbolising the social
inequity of Taipei. It also became the biggest entertainment and consumption

Figure 8.8   Taipei Hsin-yi Planning District and Its Surrounding Area

Source: The author.

area in Taipei and included the Warner Brothers complex, department stores such as Mitsukoshi, shopping malls of New York New York, Neo 19 and the flag-ship stores of many high end goods (Jou 2005) (Figure 8.9). The most noteworthy project was Taipei 101, the world's tallest building until July 2007 (Figure 8.10).

Meanwhile, the 1990s saw the rise of the middle class and this increased the growth in the retail sector. During both 5-year periods 1986–91 and 1991–96, the revenue from commercial, including wholesale, retailing, and restaurants achieved a growth rate of over 100 per cent (Chung-Hao Real Estate Consultant Company 1999). Such growth could be attributed to the influx of FDI in the fields of supermarkets, department stores, convenience

Figure 8.9   Mitsukoshi Department Store in Hsin-Yi Planning District

Source: The author.

stores and shopping malls. After the department and convenience stores
boom in the 1980s, one element newly added in the 1990s was the big box
outlets, with sales in Taiwan already reaching NT$151.2 billion by 2000
(Wu 2005).

In 1994, to stimulate the economy by expanding domestic demand, the
Ministry of Economics targeted the rising wholesale and retailing industry.
Incentives were provided to facilitate the transformation of former industrial
sites into new spaces for retailing sectors, mostly in the form of shopping
malls and hypermarkets. The government enhanced the process by loosening
up regulations on land-use control, environment assessment and tax reviews.
By 1999, the Taipei MUR hosted 32 department stores and 32 hypermarkets
(Chung-Hao Real Estate Consultant Company 1999) and grants had been
allowed to 15 Industrial and Commercial Parks to develop more malls and
hypermarkets.[7] Tai-Mall was the first large scale shopping mall in Taiwan
built using these new policies and was opened in 1999 in Taoyuan Prefecture,
taking advantage of a location close to the exit off the San Yat-sen Freeway and

Figure 8.10   Taipei 101 Building, Formerly the Tallest Building in the World

Source: The author.

the No. 1 Provincial Road to attract customers from the Taipei metropolitan area and surrounding areas of Taoyuan.

The Livability of the Taipei MUR

By 1990, the Taipei MUR area was encountering serious problems of urban livability. In the 1990 census, residents of the MUR were asked about the most needed infrastructures or needs for improvement. They considered environmental degradation, lack of parking and parks to be the main concerns. But there were some regional variations. For citizens of Taipei Municipality, the lack of parking lots and noise pollution were the top problems, for residents of Taipei Prefecture and Taoyuan Prefecture, shortage of parks.

Taipei Municipality's infrastructure problems are rooted in the birth of an automobile city. During Taiwan's industrialisation, road development had been placed as the top agenda to facilitate the economy and build a modern city. Taipei, as the industrial and commercial centre of the island, expanded or built 410 kilometres of new roads between 1967 and 1987. At the same time, the city's provision of public transportation fell far behind the road construction and rendered Taipei a city highly reliant on private vehicles. In 1987, there were 717,000 private vehicles, including 220,000 cars and motorcycles in a population of nearly 2.7 million (Bureau of Information 1988). In addition, many vehicles are used for commuting from Taipei Prefecture to Taipei Municipality. This resulted in a huge under-provision of parking lots, especially when urban planning tended to change land intended for parking into more buildings. Air and noise pollution, road accidents and gridlock were among daily trials of commuters. It was not until the completion of major sections of the Mass Rapid Transit System (MRT) from the mid-1990s onwards that the situation was alleviated.

Meanwhile, at the peak of Taipei's growth by the end of the 1980s, the provision of housing had become problematic. Unlike Hong Kong or Singapore, the Taiwan government never adopted a de facto public housing policy and the housing market was dominated by the developers.[8] Taiwan's government saw the building and real estate industry as the engine of economic growth, and seldom adopted policies to curb the speculation in urban land. Moreover, the policy makers were allegedly deeply involved in the processes of land speculation.

Thus, Taipei's real estate prices have been on an upward trajectory since the late 1980s. Over 80 per cent of households in Taipei must spend more than one-third of their disposable income on a mortgage if they bought a housing unit between 1988 and 1993 (Chen 2005). In 1989, when people realised that as a result of land speculation, buying an apartment in Taipei Municipality would cost 30 years of household savings, a mass protest took place. But the people's appeals fell on deaf government ears, as money politics prevailed in the Executive and Legislative Yuan. Many people gave up on buying a unit in the city and resigned themselves to commuting by choosing the cheaper housing units in the satellite cities of Taipei Municipality or even marginal urban areas.

Citizens have also been heavily critical of the unruly development of the metropolitan areas. Lands reserved for environmental protection or public infrastructure were often rezoned for building development. Development of the preserved areas contributed to pollution of water sources, deforestation and landslides (Hsiao and Liu 2002). The most serious case took place in the hillside area abutting the Taipei basin. During a typhoon in August 1997, landslides in the Lincoln Community toppled buildings, leading to the death of 28 residents and injury to 24. Two employees of the Taipei Prefecture Government were sentenced for colluding with developers by issuing building permits on the dangerous hill area. The late 1980s and 1990s witnessed citizen mobilisation to protest environmental degradation. Targets included factory owners, real estate developers, and the government's failure to curb illegal activities and itself undertake improper developments.

In response to the protests from citizens about degrading urban livability, the Taipei Municipality government in 1996 initiated participatory design at the neighbourhood level to enhance the citizens' participation. Community groups could participate in planning or designing some community infrastructures and through this process, pedestrian areas, community centres, parks and squares received more attention than before (Figure 8.11). The government focused on the provision of better sidewalks and green spaces; the per capita area of green space increased from 2.3 square metres in 1987 to 4.4 square metres by the end of 2000. Thus having moved beyond the peak of its development era in the mid-1990s, the Taipei core has entered a new phase of rehabilitating or improving the environment (Huang 2005).

Although infrastructure provision in Taipei Municipality was far from satisfactory, the situation of Taipei Prefecture was even worse. Based on governmental policy to concentrate investment in the capital city, in 1991 government expenditure on each resident of Taipei Municipality was more than four times that for the residents of Taipei Prefecture. This was reflected in the relatively underdeveloped urban services of administration, medical

Figure 8.11   Long-zen Neighbourhood Park in Taipei City, Developed by Participatory Design

Source: The author.

care, and education. By the end of the 1980s, Taipei Prefecture contained more than 3 million residents and hyper population density had become a common problem for the satellite cities of Taipei. For example, Yong-He city, located across the Shin-Dien River from Taipei Municipality and connected by three bridges, has a density at 40,000 people per square kilometre, four times greater on average than Taipei. In the mid-1980s, its Shio-Lan Primary School was the world's largest, with an enrollment of 12,000 students.

From 1990 to 2000, some cities in Taipei Prefecture that had highway or freeway connection with Taipei Municipality converted from agricultural based areas into booming towns during the real estate boom that accompanied the urban expansion. Inevitably, the rapid growth led to problems of insufficient infrastructure and environmental degradation. For example, the booming town Shiji, the epitome of the edge cities of the Taipei metropolitan area, encountered regular floods in summer due to over-development.

To improve urban livability, some infrastructure projects call for collaboration across administrative boundaries. For example, although central and local governments have sped up the construction of the sewerage systems of Taipei Municipality in the past 20 years, the slow progress in Taipei Prefecture has counteracted such efforts. Household discharge and industrial waste water together have seriously polluted the rivers surrounding the Taipei metropolitan area.[9] Another example is the Fei-Tsui Reservoir, which supplies clean drinking water for the Taipei Municipality and is located in the hillside of Taipei Prefecture. Development rights and control of clean water have been major conflicts between two local governments. Unfortunately, the antagonistic nature of political parties across Taipei Prefecture, Taipei Municipality and the national government have prevented better governance of the metropolitan area.

In the more marginal areas of the MUR, such as the agricultural and industrial areas of Taoyuan Prefecture, environmental degradation went beyond merely the conventional sense of air and noise pollution. For example, Daiyuan Township suffered from constant noise pollution brought about by frequent landings at the airport; from the early 1980s, Taoyuan suffered from cadmium-contamination of rice from the chemical plants; the RCA TV plant in Taoyuan, built in 1970 and closed in 1992, was claimed to have dumped toxins into the soil and groundwater, resulting in the deaths of 216 former employees and more than 1,375 cancer cases and 102 cases of tumours.[10]

Onward from 2000

From 1999 to 2004, 8 major shopping malls opened within Taipei city. This development followed the "Six Years Plan of National Construction" announced by the national government, which sought to turn Taiwan into a logistic centre in Pacific Asia. The already discussed Hsin-Yi Planning District of Taipei, focused on the Taipei 101 building and designed to be developed into a global financial centre, soon encountered difficulties. The imperative of the global economy called for closer collaboration across the straits to make the best use of the resources on both sides, but political realities dictated otherwise. Furthermore, the emerging national fiscal crisis hindered the National Government in taking leadership of the project. The dream of the Pacific Operational Centre faded, and real estate and consumption activities took over as the main economic function of the mega project districts (Chou 2005, Jou 2005, Ching 2005).

Since 2000, the governments at the Taipei Municipality and the national level have been run by two rival political parties with increasing tensions. In the name of national balance, the national government has been avoiding investment in Taipei Municipality and instead has been reallocating the national budget to cities of southern Taiwan, where most of its loyal party supporters are located. This approach is likely to lessen the capacity of Taipei to compete with other rising cities in Asia.

But at the domestic level, the Taipei MUR continues its growth. The MRT system of the Taipei metropolitan region continues to shape the regional dynamics between Taipei Municipality and Prefecture. Currently, the three main lines and branch lines totaling 61.9 kilometres transport more than one million people per day. It has been estimated that by 2021, the MRT web would be completed with a total length of 250 kilometres and 3.6 million person/journeys per day. With high density and circle systems completed, the linkage among the major cites within Taipei Prefecture will also be enhanced.

The high speed railway, which started operation at the end of 2006, has shortened the travel time from Taipei to Kaoshiung from 4 hours to one and half hours, and turned the western plain of Taiwan into a one day living circle. The Hsinchu Prefecture area is now within a half hour commute to Taipei, further strengthening the production network of the IT industry. However, the benefits of the high speed railway to the MUR still have to be demonstrated in practice. Another promising development is the completion of Taipei Ilan Freeway in 2007. It will expand the commuting circle to Ilan Prefecture, which is 80 kilometres away from Taipei city, thus integrating it into the Taipei MUR. Because of its beautiful rural landscape, it will serve as a popular destination for weekend recreation and second homes for Taipei's people.

Conclusion

As the engine of the national economy, Taipei MUR continues its expansion. Its population increased by 12.7 per cent between 1990 and 2000, with the highest growth rate in the outer ring and largest absolute growth in the inner ring. In contrast, the population of the core, Taipei Municipality, underwent depopulation during the decade, which makes the Taipei case unique among the cases in this book.

Facing the globalisation imperative to restructure, Taipei MUR is shifting to a post-industrial society. This is evident in the dwindling size of its manufacturing sector and the huge growth in the service industry. The trend is shared by all the three zones of the MUR. Parallel with this trend is the relocation of industrial activities further outwards to the inner and outer zones, while in the core Taipei city, the tertiary sector accounts for over 88 per cent of employment. The sex ratio distribution of residents parallels the industrial pattern, with the core holding the highest ratio of female population among the three zones, and the outer ring the lowest.

Another key demographic change occasioned by the economic and social transition is the surge in foreign population, resulting from the advent of migrant workers and spouses. Within the MUR, commuting for work and education has intensified during the decade along with the expanding transportation systems and housing provision developed outwards from the core. Newly established universities in the inner and outer rings during the decade have greatly contributed to the increased population of those with advanced education beyond the core.

Although the MUR seems to be thriving in terms of economic and population growth, a bright future could be overshadowed by some recent trends. Much of Taipei's economic growth appears to be generated by consumption related to new lifestyles brought on by global franchises, while the growth of producer services appear slow, which is not a good sign for Taipei's ability to compete in the global economy. Moreover, the livability of the expanding Taipei MUR has become more and more problematic. There are huge discrepancies in infrastructure provision between zones, showing a more amenity-oriented and participatory policy in the core and a low satisfaction of basic infrastructures and problems of high pollution gravitating outwards.

The Taipei MUR is very likely to keep growing in population and expanding in its territorial reach. With the recently finished express railway project and the opening up of new highways to its northeast region, Taipei MUR is incorporating Hsinchu City and Prefecture and Ilan Prefecture into its hinterland. In this situation, the role urban governance plays among the different layers of the MUR will be even more critical for advancing the wellbeing of its increasing population.

Notes

1. The author wishes to acknowledge the substantial contribution of data for this chapter by Dr. Ching-Lung Tsay, who was originally to write the chapter but was prevented from doing so by unforseen circumstances.
2. Although Taipei was not officially designated the provincial capital until 1891, many construction projects of the city had already begun since 1885.
3. The total fertility rate of Taipei Municipality went below the replacement rate in 1977, and had been fluctuating from 1.47 to 1.31 between years of 1990 to 2000. In 2003, it further dropped to 1.08.

4. These figures were collected from tables of "Immigrants and Emigrants in Taipei", "Natural Increase and Social Increase in the population of Taipei", Taipei Statistic Book, 2004.

5. 2004, the third stage of transportation of Taiwan area, Institute of Transportation, Ministry of Transportation and Communications.

6. Annual Statistics of Land Price Indicators of Taiwan Area, 1998.

7. Ibid.

8. The total public housing stock only occupied around 5 per cent of the total housing stock. Most of this was for the teaching and military sectors; therefore it is more like a subsidy to the middle class in government service.

9. By mid-2002, only 59 per cent of Taipei was connected to the sewerage system.

10. Taipei Times 6/8/02: Ex-RCA staffers get support in the United States for poisoning charges.

9

The Resurgence of Shanghai and Its Demographic and Employment Changes in the 1990s

Yu Zhu[1]

With a total population of 16.4 million and a total area of 6,340.5 square kilometres, Shanghai is not only China's largest city, but also one of the largest urban agglomerations in the world. In a very short period of time since the 1990s, Shanghai has been experiencing the fastest development in its history. Given the fact that Shanghai was once the largest city in the Far East and its development had long been suppressed by China's urban strategy advocating "strictly control the size of large cities", such development represents the resurgence of Shanghai and the beginning of its efforts to enter the global club of world cities (Yusuf and Wu 2002), and is therefore of great significance.

Two of the major aspects of Shanghai's development in recent decades, especially since the 1990s, have been the expansion of its urbanised areas within its administrative boundary and the dispersion of its population and urban functions from the urban core to its surrounding areas; and the *in situ* transformation of the surrounding areas. These two processes, and their interaction, resemble in many aspects the transformation processes of "extended metropolitan regions (EMR)" in many Asian countries examined intensively in the literature (Ginsburg *et al.* 1991).[2] However, due to China's urban strategy and its changes mentioned earlier, the two processes of EMR development in Shanghai show some unusual characteristics, compared to other Asian cities. One of these characteristics is that while the suburbanisation

Figure 9.1   Shanghai and Its Administrative Units and Zones

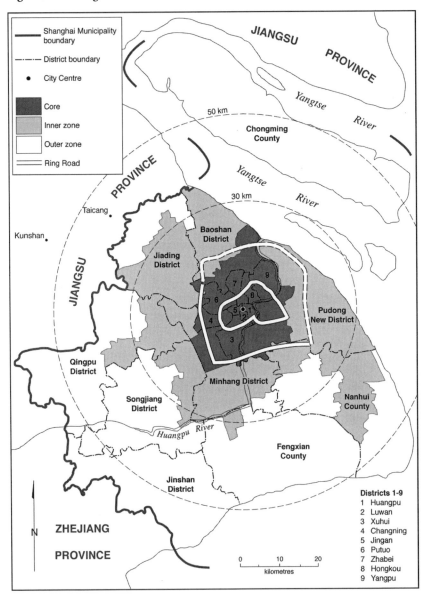

Source: The author.

process of the middle class has been observed in many developing country cities for several decades (Dick and Rimmer 1998; Potter and Lloyd-Evans 1998: 122–3), such a process in Shanghai was very limited before the 1990s. The other is that while migration to the core of Shanghai for farmers in the suburban area was strictly restricted by China's unique *Hukou* system and other relevant policies, the suburban area of Shanghai was one of China's most prominent areas for *in situ* development of rural non-agricultural activities. Thus it would be interesting to see whether and how these characteristics of Shanghai EMR have been changed by the transformation process since the 1990s, which in contrast to the earlier period has been influenced more by the forces also at work in other Asian mega-urban regions than by those unique to China.

Currently, the Shanghai municipality consists of 16 urban districts and three suburban counties (Figure 9.1). Among the 16 urban districts, seven have been newly established since the 1980s, and contain a considerable proportion of non built-up areas. These seven districts are usually referred to as "suburban districts". The suburban districts and the suburban counties are in turn divided into two groups: the inner suburban districts (including Minhang district, Baoshan district, Jiading district, and Pudong new district) and the outer suburban districts and counties surrounding these districts. The other nine districts have existed since 1949, and are usually referred to as "central urban districts".

Strictly speaking, the extended metropolitan area of Shanghai extends well beyond the above administrative areas of the Shanghai Municipality into neighbouring provinces, and it would be ideal to include all the areas of Shanghai's EMR in the analysis. However, in practice this is difficult to do, not only because there is no consensus about the scope of Shanghai EMR,[3] but also because it would be difficult to produce data needed for the analysis, which would involve several provincial level administrative units. Therefore in this chapter we confine our analysis within the administrative boundaries of Shanghai Municipality, i.e. the above 19 districts and counties. Although such an area is not complete as an EMR, this does not constitute a major problem, as the population distribution in Shanghai is much more concentrated than other cities in this project and the suburbanisation process is still limited. Besides, most dynamic processes of EMR can be reflected in this area, as it includes not only the urban core, but also the suburban areas which used to be, or still are, rural to varying degrees.

The temporal scope of the analysis in this chapter will be the period from 1 July 1990 (the date of the fourth national population census) to 1

November 2000 (the date of the fifth national population census). As with other chapters in this book, the zonal approach will be used to analyse the transformation in the 1990s in Shanghai. Using the criteria described in Chapter 3, we delineated the core, inner zone and outer zone on the basis of the township-level administrative units of the year 2000 (see Figure 9.1), and produced relevant tabulations from the 1990 and 2000 census data. The population and area figures of the three zones for the 1990 and 2000 censuses can be seen in Table 3.1 in Chapter 3. Figure 9.2 shows the spatial variation of population density in Shanghai based on the 2000 census data.

Shanghai was declared to be a treaty port in 1843, when its total population was nearly 200,000 (Hu et al. 2000: 239). From that time until the late 1940s when the communists took power, the population of Shanghai had increased tremendously with migration as the main contributor. However its area had changed only slightly. In 1949 the total area of Shanghai was 636.2 square kilometres (82.4 square kilometres built-up), essentially equivalent to the area of the core and slightly larger than the current nine central urban districts, and its population was 6.204 million in 1953 according to the first population census (Editorial Committee 1994: 2–11).

Since 1949 Shanghai has experienced a chequered development path. In the first 10 years Shanghai experienced rapid development in both area and population. Its total population increased by 5.26 million, or 7.4 per cent annually. In 1958, ten counties previously under the jurisdiction of Jiangsu Province were incorporated into Shanghai. This areal expansion largely completed the formation of the current administrative area of Shanghai Municipality, increasing the total area of the Municipality to 5,910 square kilometres (Editorial Committee 1994: 8; Hu et al. 2000: 240; Shanghai Municipal Statistics Bureau 2001).

However, since 1959 Shanghai first experienced a deceleration, and then a stagnation of population growth, partly due to the urban strategy adopted by China at the time: advocating "strictly control the size of large cities". From the first population census in 1953 to the second population census in 1964, the average annual population growth rate was as high as 5.2 per cent; but during the period between the 1964 census and the 1982 census, Shanghai's population increased from 10.82 million to 11.86 million, with an average annual growth rate of only 0.5 per cent. Shanghai's urban functions also experienced profound changes (Editorial Committee 1994: 5). Before 1949, Shanghai was a major centre of commerce and trade in the Far East, however from the 1950s until the 1980s, Shanghai's economy was increasingly dominated by manufacturing industries, with the primary, secondary, and

Figure 9.2   Population Density of Shanghai Municipality, 2000 Census

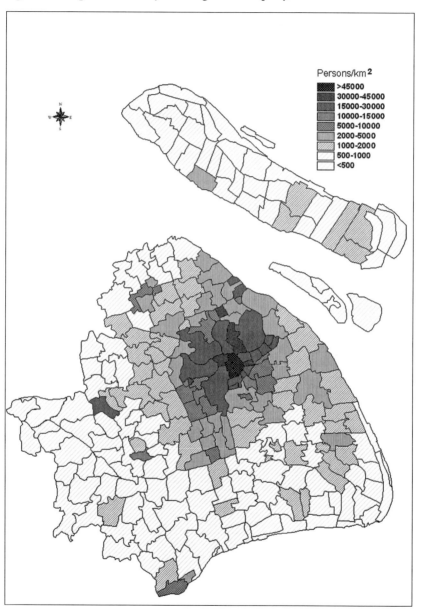

Source: The author.

tertiary industry accounting for 4.0 per cent, 77.4 per cent, and 18.6 per cent of the GDP respectively in 1978.

Although the development of manufacturing industries in Shanghai generated considerable income, a large proportion of it was transferred to other parts of China. According to one source of statistics, the net outflow of income from Shanghai to other parts of China amounted to 192.85 billion Yuan in the period 1952–79, accounting for 43.9 per cent of the national income generated in Shanghai during the same period (Hu *et al*, 2000: 246–7). This led to serious deficiency in urban infrastructure investment, and insufficient urban infrastructure in Shanghai before the 1980s. As can be seen from Table 9.1, during the whole period 1950–78, the total urban infrastructure investment in Shanghai was only six billion Yuan, less (in real terms) than the investment of any single year since 1996. Insufficient investment led to serious problems in housing, transport, environmental pollution etc.

In 1980, the per capita residential dwelling area for Shanghai's residents was only 4.4 square metres. Three generations of one family sharing one room was not an uncommon phenomenon before that time (Population Census Office of Shanghai Municipality 2001: 63). In the city centre, the per capita road area was only two square metres. In some most congested areas, 12 people squeezing into one square metre of space in the bus was a common scene at peak times, and the bus could only move at a speed as low as three to four kilometres per hour (Wang *et al*. 2000: 355–6). The per capita green space was only 0.47 square metres, and the overall proportion of green space was only 8.2 per cent in 1978 (Wang *et al*. 2000: 330).

The above urban problems in Shanghai were greatly exacerbated by over-concentration of its population and industry in the city centre, which was also partly caused by insufficient investment. Before the 1980s, Shanghai's development was largely restricted to the area already under its jurisdiction before 1949. The population growth (although slow) and the development of manufacturing industries within such a limited space made the core area of Shanghai one of the most congested urban areas in the world. In 1986, five of Shanghai's then ten central urban districts had population densities higher than 50,000 persons per square kilometre; the population density of some streets (sub-districts) was even higher than 100,000 persons per square kilometre, with the highest one reaching 198,100 persons per square kilometre (Wang *et al*. 2000: 355). In terms of the location of manufacturing enterprises, although several satellite towns had been established in the newly incorporated areas since 1958, by 1985 only 3.2 per cent of Shanghai's

Table 9.1 Urban Infrastructure Investment, Housing and Transport Changes in Shanghai, Selected Years

Year	1950 – 1978	1979	1980	1985	1990	1995	1996	1997	1998	1999	2000
Urban infrastructure investment (100 million Yuan)	60.1	6.0	9.6	23.5	47.2	273.8	378.8	412.9	531.4	501.4	449.9
Urban infrastructure investment deflated* (100 million Yuan)	60.1	5.9	8.9	18.4	21.7	58.5	74.0	78.5	101.0	93.9	82.2
Investment in residential housing (100 million Yuan)	11.7	2.2	4.2	25.2	42.9	433.8	467.0	458.2	405.0	378.8	443.9
Investment in residential housing deflated* (100 million Yuan)	11.7	2.2	4.0	19.6	19.7	92.6	91.3	87.1	77.0	71.0	81.1
Floor space of residential housing completed (10000 sq.m)			304	2,112	1,339	1,747	1,873	2,180	1,964	1,732	1,724
Length of public transport route (km)			5,231	10,138	18,593	41,563	45,840	51,220	53,901	23,007	23,260
Operating public transport vehicles (vehicle)			3,719	5,036	6,264	11,637	13,323	14,207	15,282	16,661	17,939
No. of taxi			1,813	2,033	11,298	36,991	38,554	40,977	41,183	42,056	42,943
Subways and light railway:length of routes (km)						0	15.2	20.1	20.1	20.1	62.9
Year-end length of paved roads (km)			907	1,265	1,631	3,008	3,118	3,553	4,712	5,204	6,641

Note: *To make the investment figures comparable, figures from 1979 in these columns were calculated using overall residents consumer price index provided in Shanghai Municipal Statistics Bureau (2001).
Source: Shanghai Municipal Statistics Bureau, 2001.

enterprises were located in these satellite towns (Hu *et al.* 2000: 240). In contrast, 5,793 manufacturing enterprises were located in the then 10 central urban districts at the end of 1989, accounting for 43.6 per cent of the total number of manufacturing enterprises in Shanghai; worse still, more than 80 per cent of the 5,793 enterprises were located in the core area of the central urban districts which covered only 149 square kilometres (He 1992: 97).

Shanghai's situation started to change from the late 1970s when China adopted reform and open door policies. This change has greatly accelerated since the early 1990s, bringing Shanghai into a new era of urban development. In economic terms Shanghai also experienced one of its fastest growth periods, with the annual growth rate of GDP averageing 13.0 per cent during 1991–95 and 11.4 per cent during 1996–2000, and the per capita GDP increasing from 5,910 Yuan in 1990 to 34,547 Yuan in 2000.[4] From the perspective of the zonal approach, the most important changes since then can be summarised as follows.

The first important aspect of change is economic restructuring. While the primary sector was already negligible even before the start of reform, Shanghai's GDP structure experienced a steady decline in dominance of the secondary sector and increasing importance of the tertiary sector. In 2000, tertiary industry accounted for more than half of the GDP (50.6 per cent) and primary and secondary industry accounted for 1.8 per cent and 47.6 per cent respectively. This change was faster in the 1990s than in the 1980s. In fact, the share of the secondary sector in employment increased in the 1980s due to the transfer of labour from the primary sector, but in the 1990s it started to decline again in favour of the tertiary sector, as will be seen later.

At the same time, the spatial distribution of industries has profoundly changed. Since the early 1990s, many manufacturing enterprises have been moved out of the central urban districts, especially from the 106 square kilometre area within the inner ring road. This not only made way for the location in the central areas of newly developing tertiary sector activities, such as finance, trade, commerce, housing etc, but also improved the environment of the city (Wang *et al.* 2000: 358). Shanghai's overall urban planning (2000–20) stipulates that in the area within the inner ring road, development should be focused on the tertiary sector, and only some manufacturing industries suitable for urban environment will be retained; in the area between the inner ring and outer ring roads, development should be focused on high-tech, high added value, and pollution-free industries, and in the areas outside the outer ring road, both the primary and the secondary sectors will be developed.

This kind of urban planning will further affect the spatial restructuring of Shanghai's economy.

Second, since the 1980s, especially in the 1990s, Shanghai experienced exponential growth in investment in urban housing and infrastructure projects. As can be seen from Table 9.1, the deflated figure of urban infrastructure investment in the single year of 2000 was 1.4 times that of the whole period from 1950–78, and nearly 3.8 times that of 1990; the deflated figure of investment in residential housing in the year 2000 was even 6.9 times that of the whole period from 1950–78, and 4.1 times that of 1990. These investments brought about an important change with significant spatial implications for Shanghai as a whole as well as for its zones: the expansion of Shanghai's residential areas and transport networks. As Table 9.1 shows, the completed floor space of residential housing each year has greatly increased in Shanghai since the 1980s. Shanghai's length of public transport routes and the number of buses and taxis have increased tremendously, and underground railway and light railway transport systems also emerged and are still in the process of rapid development. These have enabled large scale relocation of residents to the newly developed areas. Such large scale housing and transport development has been a major driving force for urban expansion in Shanghai. It has also been a major cause of the massive intra-Shanghai migration since the 1990s, as it has involved a great number of people resettled for and by housing development.

Thirdly, to accommodate the need for spatial expansion brought about by the above changes, Shanghai's city proper (defined administratively as the areas under the administration of districts rather than counties) was expanded rapidly, from 223 square kilometres in 1981 to 3,924 square kilometres in 1999, accounting for 62 per cent of the total area of Shanghai. Its built-up area increased from 181 square kilometres in 1984 to 550 square kilometres in 2000 (Urban Social and Economic Survey Organisation 2001). The most dramatic change brought about by such spatial expansion has been the establishment and spectacular development of Pudong New Districts. Based on a suburban county and some of the areas of three urban districts on the eastern side of Huangpu River, Pudong New District was established in 1992, occupying 523 square kilometres. Since then, Pudong district has become the major focus of Shanghai's development. In the space of less than ten years, it attracted one million migrants both from other parts of Shanghai and from further afield, and became a major new financial, commercial, and trade centre in Shanghai (Figure 9.3). It attracted US$20.92 billion in foreign direct investment in the period 1991–2000, amounting to 47 per cent of the

Figure 9.3 The Pudong Financial Core

Source: G. Jones.

total foreign direct investment in Shanghai as a whole in the same period. The dramatic development of Pudong symbolises the extension of Shanghai's development since the 1990s to a much wider space.

Fourthly, while the above changes have been mainly related to the expansion and restructuring of the core urban areas, Shanghai's development has also been shaped by another force, which is the *in situ* transformation of its suburban areas. Since the 1980s, the economic and employment structure in Shanghai's suburban areas have also experienced fundamental changes. In 1980, the proportions of local rural labour force employed in the primary, secondary, and tertiary sectors in Shanghai were 67 per cent, 26 per cent, and seven per cent respectively; by 1990, these proportions changed to 30 per cent, 52 per cent, and 18 per cent respectively (Zhu 2002: 8), indicating that the suburban areas were already industrialised in the 1980s. However, this was very much a process of "industrialisation without urbanisation", achieved mainly by the *in situ* development of township and village enterprises (TVEs).[5] Since the 1990s, the industrialisation process has been gradually transformed to an urbanisation process (Zhu 2002: 13), manifested mainly by the accelerated growth of suburban towns as a result of both the concentration trend of the suburban population and the decongestion trend of the population from the central urban districts to the suburban towns and counties (Zhu 2002: 44–9). However, Shanghai's economic structure as a whole was becoming increasingly technology- and capital-intensive, and the labour demand of TVEs, which were closely linked with industries in the central urban districts, decreased in the 1990s. This trend, together with the inflow of migrants from outside Shanghai, caused the reversed transfer of local rural labour force from the secondary to the primary sector (Zhu 2002: 21–5).

The above four aspects of urban development largely determined the growth dynamics of both Shanghai as a whole and its zones, as will be seen below.

Population Changes in the 1990s

As mentioned earlier, the total population of Shanghai was 16.41 million in the 2000 population census. Compared to its population of 13.34 million in the 1990 census, this represents an increase of 23 per cent, double the national average growth rate (11.7 per cent) for the same period, and is commensurate with Shanghai's enormous growth in general since the 1990s.[6]

Analysing in more detail the population growth dynamics of each zone, the population of the inner zone grew the fastest, increasing almost 50 per cent during the ten years. By contrast, the population of the core grew by only 23.8 per cent, and the population of the outer zone stagnated, growing by only 2.4 per cent. The proportion of the population in the inner zone increased significantly, from 16.5 per cent to 20.1 per cent, largely at the expense of the proportion of the population in the outer zone, which dropped from 23.3 per cent to 19.4 per cent.

The rapid inner zone growth seems to mirror the situation in many other Asian countries, especially Bangkok, Jakarta, and Manila (see Table 3.1), which already exhibited such a pattern in the 1980s (Jones *et al.* 2000). However, it is noticeable that if the inner and outer zones are taken together as the periphery in relation to the core, then Shanghai's core was growing faster than the periphery as a whole during the 1990s (21.8 per cent) (Figure 9.4). This reflects the fact that although Shanghai's development has already expanded to the inner part of its periphery, unlike some Asian mega-cities, which have already experienced the slowing down of the development in the urban core (Jones *et al.* 2000, see also Table 3.1 of Chapter 3), Shanghai's urban core still maintained strong growth dynamics in the 1990s, probably due to its late start in development.

It is important to note that within the urban core, there was a significant redistribution of the population from the overcrowded central urban districts to the outer part of the core. One indication of this is that the population of the three districts (Huangpu District, Luwan District and Jingan District), which are located at the centre of the core without a border with the inner zone, dropped from 1.90 million in the 1990 census to 1.21 million in the 2000 census; their proportion of the total population of the central urban districts decreased from 25.7 per cent to 17.4 per cent. This led to the reduction of the average population density for the three districts from 73,466 persons per square kilometre to 46,725 persons per square kilometre, and considerably improved the living environment of the residents.

Unfortunately, due to the administrative changes between 1990 and 2000, we are not able to make more detailed comparison between the population distribution of the 1990 census and that of the 2000 census to show the trend of population redistribution from the centre to the outer part within the core; however, some existing research results may be worth mentioning for a better understanding of this trend. According to the Population Research

Figure 9.4   Crowded Housing and Emerging High Rises Bordering the Huangpu River in the Core of Shanghai

Source: G. Jones.

Institute of East China Normal University, during the 1990–2000 period, the populations in the areas within 2.5 kilometres and between 2.5 and 5 kilometres from the central point of the city decreased by 25 per cent and 18 per cent respectively; however, the populations in the areas between 5 and 7.5 kilometres and between 7.5 and 10 kilometres from the central point of the city increased by 20 and 75 per cent (Hu 2002: 161). Research by the Population Census Office of Shanghai Municipality further suggests that in the period 1990 to 2000, the most important change in Shanghai's population distribution was that the population within the area of the inner ring road, which runs through the middle of the central urban districts and Pudong district (see Figure 9.1), considerably decreased, while the population between the inner ring road and outer ring road, which is very close to the boundary between the core and the inner zone, considerably increased (Population Census Office of Shanghai Municipality 2001). Zhang's analysis for the 1990–97 period also confirms this trend (Zhang 1999). Such a pattern of population redistribution suggests the need for more detailed sub-zonal analysis within the core.

Migration and Its Role in the Growth Dynamics of Shanghai and Its Zones

Taking Shanghai as a whole, natural population growth has played a very limited role, and migration is the main factor contributing to the above population changes. In fact, as a result of the extremely low fertility rate,[7] Shanghai's local population has experienced slightly negative growth since the early 1990s (Population Census Office of Shanghai Municipality 2001: 4), and migration has played a role in offsetting such negative growth, especially in the core. This can be confirmed by estimating net migration using forward life table survival method and child-woman ratio method presented in Table 3.5 of Chapter 3, which shows that net migration accounted for 104.4 per cent of the increase in the total population of Shanghai as a whole. It is also noteworthy that migration plays quite different roles in different zones. Migration played a dominant role in the growth of both the core and the inner zone, accounting for 111.4 per cent and 94.7 per cent of the increase in the population of the core and the inner zone respectively, however in the outer zone, the picture is quite different, with migration contributing only 62.4 per cent of the increase in its total population. Figure 9.5 shows further that net migration was concentrated in young working age groups for Shanghai as a whole; in fact this pattern applies to the core and the inner zone as well. However, the outer zone represents a different picture, with much lower age-specific migration rates peaking in age groups 25–29 and 80+ and touching bottom in age group 15–19.

More and better understanding of the role of migration in the growth dynamics of Shanghai and its zones can be obtained by analysing the migration data of the 2000 census. Before this some issues regarding migration definitions and the limitation of the migration data need to be addressed. First, different definitions of migration were adopted in the 1990 and 2000 censuses. In the 1990 census, migrants were defined as those who were living in a different county-level place five years before the census, and either had changed their household registration to their current place of residence or

Figure 9.5   Age-specific Net Migration Rates, Shanghai, 1990–2000 Censuses

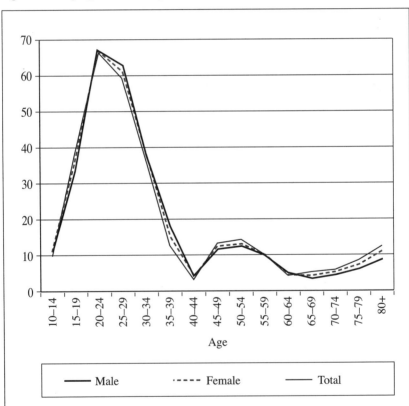

Source: Calculated by author from 1990 and 2000 census data.

left their place of household registration for more than a year; however, in the 2000 census, the above temporal and spatial criteria were changed to the township-level place and half a year respectively. Besides, in the 2000 census people younger than five years of age were also taken into account in the migration questions, while in the 1990 census this was not the case. These differences make direct comparisons of migration data from the two censuses difficult. Second, as the place of origin for migrants was only identified at the provincial level in the 1990 census and the county level at the 2000 census, it is not possible for us to define migrants as those who had crossed the boundary of one of the zones, as in the case of most other cities in this project. This makes it difficult to analyse the migration flows between the zones in Shanghai. Third, migration data are only available from the ten per cent sample population in the 2000 census (the exact sampling proportion is 9.64 per cent of the total population). We assume that the sample population is representative of the total population, and in the text, all the absolute figures derived from it will be converted to those for the total population according to the sampling proportion.

Bearing in mind these definitions and data limitations we will first examine the migration trend for Shanghai as a whole during the five year period 1 November 1995 to 30 October 2000. It can be estimated from Table 9.2 that among the 16.4 million people counted in the 2000 population census, 5.45 million[8] were migrants. Among these migrants, 2.18 million or 40 per cent of the total were from outside Shanghai. It can also be estimated from the census data of other provinces that during the same period of time, 204,710 migrants in China's other provincial-level units were from Shanghai.

Table 9.2   Number of Migrants by Zones in Shanghai, 2000

	Migrants from outside Shanghai		Migrants from within Shanghai		All Migrants		% of Each Zone's Population who are Migrants
	Number of Persons	%	Number of Persons	%	Number of Persons	%	
Total	210,089	100.0	315,438	100.0	525,527	100.0	33.2
Core	117,944	56.1	261,197	82.8	379,141	72.1	39.6
Inner zone	65,512	31.2	35,556	11.3	101,068	19.2	31.8
Outer zone	26,633	12.7	18,685	5.9	45,318	8.6	14.8

Source: 10% sample data from 2000 population census.

As mentioned earlier, we are not able to make a strict comparison of migration volumes between the 1990 and 2000 censuses; however, some general trends can be identified. First, if migration data for the 2000 census are adjusted by excluding those migrating within the county-level units, the number of migrants in Shanghai identified for the 2000 census would be 3,745,405 persons. If this number is further lowered by 32 per cent[9] to exclude those who had stayed in their destination in Shanghai for less than one year, than the number of migrants would still stand at 2,546,875 people in the five years before the 2000 census This represents an increase of 202 per cent compared to the number of migrants (843,762) in the five years before the 1990 census.[10] Both the migration from outside Shanghai and that within Shanghai increased tremendously, with the latter increasing much more (515 per cent) than the former (123 per cent).

Data from the 2000 census show that migration from outside Shanghai contributed to the population redistribution among the zones. Among the 2.18 million migrants from outside Shanghai, 56.1 per cent, 31.2 per cent, and 12.7 per cent chose the core, the inner zone and the outer zone respectively as the destination. Compared to the zonal distribution of the total population calculated from Table 3.1 of Chapter 3 (60.5 per cent in the core, 20.1 per cent in the inner zone, and 19.4 per cent in the outer zone), a much higher proportion of migrants from outside Shanghai lived in the inner zone; a lower proportion of them lived in the core, and a much lower proportion lived in the outer zone. Thus the distribution of the migrants from outside Shanghai enhanced the trend of population redistribution to the inner zone mentioned earlier.

As for the intra-Shanghai migration flows, we will restrict the analysis to identify some general trends rather than the exact direction and volumes of migration between the zones. Table 9.2 suggests that the destination of intra-Shanghai migration during the later half of the 1990s was concentrated on the core, accounting for 83 per cent of the destinations of intra-Shanghai migrants. Although we are not able to identify the origin of these migrants by zones, indirect analysis suggests that they were mostly from the core itself, and migration from outside the core was not significant. As Table 9.3 shows, 73.3 per cent of the migrants moving to destinations in the core were from the nine urban districts within the core. Among the 20.6 per cent of migrants moving from the four inner suburban districts to the core, some of them might also be from the core, as 55.9 per cent of the population in the four inner suburban districts were classified as living in the core. If we assume that among the migrants moving from the four inner suburban districts to

Table 9.3   Origin of Intra-Shanghai Migrants in the Core, Inner Zone and Outer Zone, 2000

Origin	Zone of Current Residence					
	Core		Inner Zone		Outer Zone	
	Number of Persons	%	Number of Persons	%	Number of Persons	%
Total	261,197	100.0	35,556	100.0	18,685	100.0
9 central urban districts	191,486	73.3	7,910	22.2	1,007	5.4
Four inner suburban districts	53,815	20.6	17,375	48.9	793	4.2
Outer suburban districts and counties	8,981	3.4	8,776	24.7	16,548	88.6
Unidentified*	6,915	2.6	1,495	4.2	337	1.8

Note: *Places of origin for some migrants were not identified due to miscoding.
Source: 10% sample data from 2000 population census.

the core, 55.9 per cent of them also originated from the area within the core, then it can be estimated that another 11.5 per cent of the migrants identified in the core also came from the core. Therefore, only 15.2 per cent of the intra-Shanghai migrants with the core as the destination would have come from outside the core. This might have led to some net migration to the core (i.e. more than offsetting the numbers moving out from the core), however due to the constraint of the data we are not able to confirm and quantify it.

It is noteworthy that among those migrants with the core as the destination, nearly 40 per cent went to the areas under the administration of the four suburban districts in the outer part of the core (Table 9.4). This percentage is higher than the proportion of the overall population of the core who live in these four suburban districts (30 per cent), reflecting no doubt the movement of people from more crowded to less crowded parts of the core. Calculations based on Tables 9.3 and 9.4 show further that while 1,636,369 people from Shanghai migrated to the nine central districts in the core, 1,986,369 people migrated out of these districts, suggesting a negative net migration of 350,000 for the nine central urban districts located in the middle of the core. Given the earlier review on the trend of population redistribution within the core during the 1990–2000 period, it is also very likely that within the nine central urban districts, there were significant migration flows from the centre of these districts to their outer part. All this suggests that a major migration flow in the five year period before the 2000 census was migration away from the over-crowded part of the nine central urban districts.

Judging from the distribution of destinations of intra-Shanghai migrants shown in Table 9.4, it seems that most migrants from the core only moved to the outer part of the core, and only a small proportion of them moved to the inner zone. In fact, even within Pudong new district, which experienced the most phenomenal development in the 1990s, it is the core part of this district that attracted more migrants (228,683 persons from other parts of Shanghai, with 87.4 per cent of them from the nine central districts; and 220,664 from outside Shanghai) than the inner zone part of this district, which attracted only 25,384 migrants from other parts within Shanghai, and 180,882 migrants from outside Shanghai.

An important implication of these findings is that population redistribution in Shanghai since the 1990s has been a decongestion process, and still confined within a relatively short distance from the urban centre. The real suburbanisation process has just started and is far from fully fledged. This almost certainly has to do with the fact that new residential areas are mostly located in the core, and the public transport network, especially underground railway and light railway systems, has not extended to the inner and outer zones.

Table 9.4   Destination of Intra-Shanghai Migrants in the Core, Inner Zone and Outer Zone, 2000

Destination	Core		Inner Zone		Outer Zone	
	Number of Persons	%	Number of Persons	%	Number of Persons	%
Total	261,197	100.0	35,556	100.0	18,685	100.0
Central urban districts	157,746	60.4	*	*	*	*
Four inner suburban districts	103,451	39.6	27,517	77.4	339	1.8
Outer suburban districts and counties	*	*	8,039	22.6	18,346	98.2

Note: * Not applicable.
Source: 10% sample data, 2000 population census.

Employment Changes

Looking at the employment changes in Shanghai in the period between the 1990 and 2000 censuses, the most striking fact is that the number of employed people increased very moderately by only 4.5 per cent during the ten years, well below the growth rate of the total population. Several demographic and socio-economic changes are responsible for this, and can be analysed in two aspects.

First, compared with the 1990 census, Shanghai's labour force participation rate (LFPR) decreased substantially. It was as high as 75 per cent in 1990, but only 65 per cent in 2000. This can be attributed to several factors, including the rising proportion of people aged 15 and above who had retired, were studying, staying at home for domestic work, or were not in the labour force for other unidentified reasons. Among these factors, the rising proportion of retired people — from 13.6 per cent to 19.3 per cent between the two censuses — played the biggest role. The accelerating population ageing process is partly responsible for this. If the 1990 census age structure is used as the standard, the LFPR in the 2000 census would be raised to 67 per cent; however this still represents a sharp decline from the 1990 rate. The other important trend was that among the retired people, the proportion of those who retired before normal retiring age (male 60, female 55) increased from 14 per cent in the 1990 census to 24 per cent in the 2000 census. Another important contributor was the rising proportion of young people who were studying rather than working, which increased from 5.0 per cent in 1990 to 6.9 per cent in 2000.

Second, during the period between the two censuses, Shanghai's unemployment rate increased substantially. Among people aged 15 and above, only 1.2 per cent were unemployed in the 1990 census, but this proportion increased to 6.2 per cent in the 2000 census.[11] This seems contradictory to the phenomenal urban development, fast growing economy, and the influx of the floating population in Shanghai, but as mentioned in the previous section reviewing Shanghai's development, it has much to do with the profound restructuring of the economic and employment structure in Shanghai. Many unemployed people are those laid off from the traditional industries such as textile and machinery industries.[12] They either do not want to take, or are less competitive than migrants for, many newly created jobs which are low paid, unstable, and in some cases 3D (difficult, demanding, and dangerous), as a result of an institutionally-determined high expectation of wage rate (Zuo 2000: 146-147). This leads to the situation where a large number of local people are unemployed while the influx of migrants persists, a phenomenon not uncommon in many Chinese cities.

In terms of the variation between the zones, it is the inner zone that experienced the fastest growth in employment. The number of employed people in the inner zone increased by 32.3 per cent during the period between the two censuses. Although this is still slower than the growth of the total population and that of the population age 15 and above, it contrasts sharply with the negative growth in both the core (–1.2 per cent) and the outer zone (–2.0 per cent). Correspondingly, the inner zone's share of total employment also increased, in contrast to the declining shares in both the core and the outer zone.

Changes in Industrial Structure

Unfortunately, due to changes in industrial classification between the 1990 and 2000 censuses, figures for most of the industrial categories from the two censuses cannot be compared directly for Shanghai; however, figures for broader categories, especially primary, secondary, and tertiary sectors, can still be compared.

As can be seen from Table 9.5, for Shanghai as a whole the most important change between the two censuses was the decreasing importance of the secondary (manufacturing) sector and the increasing importance of the tertiary sector. The share of the primary sector in employment was already insignificant in the 1990 census, and it remained so in the 2000 census. Analysed in more detail, it seems that the major growth area within the tertiary sector in the 1990s was industries like wholesale and retail sales, catering, services for public need, and real estate.

This contrasts to the declining importance of such industries in Taipei, Jabodetabek, and Bangkok EMR in the 1980s (Jones *et al.* 2000: 136). The share of more advanced tertiary industries, such as banking, insurance, education etc., only experienced an insignificant increase in Shanghai. Compared to the shares of finance industry in employment in Taipei (6.7 per cent), Jabodetabek (4.8 per cent), Bangkok EMR (2.4 per cent), and Manila EMR (6.2 per cent) even in 1990 (Jones *et al.* 2000: 134–5), the embryonic status of more advanced service industries such as the finance and insurance sector in Shanghai is even more evident. This suggests that Shanghai still has a long way to go in its transition from an industrial base to a service centre.

In terms of the spatial differentiation in the changes in employment structure, the three zones exhibited very different patterns. The core experienced the biggest change. Its economic structure transformed from

Table 9.5   Industrial Structure of Employment by Zones, Shanghai, 1990 and 2000 Censuses (%)

	Total	Core	Inner Zone	Outer Zone
		1990		
Total	**100.0**	**100.0**	**100.0**	**100.0**
Primary sector	**12.3**	**1.6**	**18.3**	**31.9**
Agriculture, forestry, animal husbandry, fishing and water conservancy	12.3	1.6	18.3	31.9
Secondary sector	**58.4**	**60.1**	**62.1**	**52.0**
Mining and Manufacturing	52.8	55.0	55.0	46.3
Construction	5.6	5.2	7.2	5.6
Tertiary sector	**29.3**	**38.3**	**19.6**	**16.1**
Geological survey and exploration	0.1	0.1	0.0	0.0
Transportation, postal service and communication	4.3	5.4	2.7	2.7
Trade, public catering, material supply and marketing, and storage	9.1	11.8	6.5	4.8
Finance, Insurance	0.4	0.6	0.3	0.3
Real estate, public utilities, and residential services	4.2	6.1	1.8	1.7
Health, sports, and social welfare	2.1	2.6	1.5	1.2
Education, culture, arts, broadcasting, film, and television	4.3	5.5	3.1	2.6
Scientific research and comprehensive technological services	1.2	1.9	0.5	0.1
Government agencies, political and party institutions, and social organisations	3.6	4.2	3.1	2.6
Others	0.0	0.0	0.0	0.0
		2000		
Total	**100.0**	**100.0**	**100.0**	**100.0**
Primary sector	**11.5**	**0.7**	**11.4**	**36.0**
Agriculture, forestry, animal husbandry, and fishing	11.5	0.7	11.4	36.0
Secondary sector	**45.8**	**40.9**	**59.1**	**44.4**
Mining	0.0	0.0	0.1	0.0
Manufacturing	38.3	33.9	49.1	38.3
Production and supply of electricity, gas, and water	1.0	1.1	1.0	0.8
Construction	6.4	5.8	9.0	5.3

Table 9.5 (*Continued*)

	Total	Core	Inner Zone	Outer Zone
			2000	
Tertiary sector	**42.7**	**58.4**	**29.5**	**19.6**
Geological exploration and water conservancy	0.1	0.1	0.2	0.2
Transportation, storage, postal service and communication	5.1	6.7	3.8	2.5
Wholesales, retail sales, catering	14.9	20.7	10.5	6.2
Finance, Insurance	1.3	1.9	0.7	0.5
Real estate	1.9	2.9	1.0	0.4
Service for the public needs	8.4	11.9	5.5	3.4
Health, sports, and social welfare	2.1	2.8	1.4	1.3
Education, culture, arts, broadcasting, film, and television	4.4	5.9	2.9	2.4
Scientific research and comprehensive technological services	1.2	1.9	0.4	0.2
Government agencies, political and party institutions, and social organisations	2.9	3.4	2.7	2.1
Others	0.4	0.4	0.4	0.4

Source: 2000 census data.

the domination of secondary (especially manufacturing) industry in the 1990 census to that of tertiary industry, conforming to Shanghai's overall urban planning. The inner zone was still experiencing a decline in the share of the primary sector, and the secondary sector was still dominant in the employment structure during the 1990–2000 period, although its importance slightly decreased. The share of the tertiary sector also experienced significant increase in the inner zone. For the outer zone, it is noteworthy that the share of the primary sector in employment actually increased in the 1990s, reflecting the reverse flow of labour into the agricultural industries mentioned earlier. It is also important to note that such reversal only occurred in the outer zone, where agricultural employment still occupies a relatively important position (see Figure 9.6). The share of tertiary industry in employment also increased, and the secondary sector suffered a great decline in its share of employment. The outer zone presents a rather stagnant picture, with a declining share of the total population and a declining

Figure 9.6   Agriculture Remains Important in Outer Zone Shanghai

Source: G. Jones.

volume of employment, compared with the growing inner zone and the fast changing core.

Changes in Occupational Structure

Fortunately there was no major change in occupational classification between the 1990 and 2000 censuses, and therefore the occupational structure of the 1990 and 2000 censuses can be directly compared in Table 9.6. Taking Shanghai as a whole, the biggest change was the significant decrease in the share of production workers and the increase in clerical, sales, and service workers, commensurate with the changes in industrial structure of employment during the same period analysed earlier. Surprisingly, the share of professional and technical workers and administrative and managerial workers decreased slightly during the ten years, which may be partly explained by the embryonic status of the tertiary sector mentioned earlier.

Looking at changes in occupational structure of the zones compared with that of the MUR as a whole, the core exhibited an even stronger trend of change from a production worker-dominated occupational structure

Table 9.6 Occupational Structure of Employment by Zones, Shanghai, 1990 and 2000 (%)

	Total		Core		Inner zone		Outer zone	
	1990	2000	1990	2000	1990	2000	1990	2000
Total	100.0	100.0	100.0	100.0	100.0	100.0	100.0	100.00
Professional and technical workers	13.3	12.8	17.5	17.6	8.9	8.2	7.1	6.4
Administrative and managerial workers	3.7	3.4	4.5	4.2	2.8	2.8	2.3	2.2
Clerical workers	5.8	11.8	8.1	16.8	3.2	7.7	2.3	4.5
Sales and service workers	15.2	22.4	17.8	29.0	13.7	18.3	10.4	11.5
Workers in agriculture	11.5	11.3	1.3	0.7	16.8	11.2	30.6	35.3
Production workers	50.5	38.2	50.7	31.7	54.6	51.8	47.3	40.1
Others	0.0	0.0	0.0	0.0	0.0	0.0	0.0	0.0

Source: 2000 census data.

to one with a growing importance of clerical, sales and service workers. In the inner zone, although the share of clerical, sales and service workers was increasing, the share of production workers declined only slightly, and still dominated in the 2000 census. It is also noticeable that the inner zone was still experiencing a decline in the share of workers in agriculture in the 1990s. For the outer zone, although the share of clerical, sales and service workers also increased slightly, the most important change was the increase in the share of workers in agriculture and the decreased share of production workers. The above changes in occupational structure of the zones are consistent with the changes in their industrial structure mentioned earlier.

Following Jones *et al.* (2000: 134–5), the index of dissimilarity (ID) can be calculated to summarise the changes in occupational structure over time and the difference between zones at given times. The value of the index was highest in the core (13.9), followed by the inner zone (9.2) and the outer zone (8.0). This suggests that the greatest change in occupational structure was in the core, contrasting to Bangkok and DKI Jakarta in the 1980s where the greatest change was in the inner zone, and Taipei with the greatest change in the outer zone (Jones *et al.* 2000: 135–6). Although we are not able to calculate the index for the change in industrial structure of Shanghai, the pattern of the difference between the zones is very likely similar, given the consistency of changes between the occupational and industrial sectors mentioned above. The unique patterns of structural and spatial transition in Shanghai deserve further investigation.

Changes in Educational Attainment[13]

During the period between the 1990 and 2000 censuses, the educational levels of Shanghai's population increased significantly. As can be seen from Table 9.7, while the proportion of the population aged 15 years and above who were illiterate or semi-illiterate or had only received primary school education decreased significantly, the proportions of those who had received lower secondary school, upper secondary school, and tertiary education all increased, especially the latter. It is noteworthy that 76.6 per cent of Shanghai's population aged 15 years and over had received at least lower secondary school education, and the proportion of those who had received tertiary education had reached 12.9 per cent.

Examined in more detail by zones, all three zones exhibited similar changes to that of Shanghai as a whole, however the intensity and detail of the changes, and the average levels of education achieved, are different among the three zones. Moving outwards from the core to the inner and outer zone, there is a progressive decline in literacy and educational levels. It is also noticeable that the core is still the main concentration of people having received tertiary education, and the inner zone stands out as the zone

Table 9.7   Educational Attainment of the Population Aged 15 and Above by Zones, Shanghai, 1990 and 2000 Censuses* (%)

	Total		Core		Inner zone		Outer zone	
	1990	2000	1990	2000	1990	2000	1990	2000
Total	100.0	100.0	100.0	100.0	100.0	100.0	100.0	100.0
Illiterate or semi-illiterate	13.5	8.2	9.0	5.6	16.9	9.5	23.1	15.1
Primary	18.4	15.2	13.0	9.9	25.2	20.2	28.0	26.7
Lower secondary	36.2	36.9	35.9	34.0	39.5	43.6	34.5	39.4
Upper secondary	23.9	26.8	30.4	32.6	15.1	19.9	12.6	15.3
Tertiary (less than 4 years)	4.0	6.9	5.7	9.2	1.7	4.1	1.2	2.3
Tertiary (4 years or more)	4.0	6.0	5.9	8.6	1.6	2.8	0.6	1.1

Note: *The educational attainment data in this table include all persons who have ever studied at the relevant level of education, even if they have not finished.
Source: 2000 census data.

with the highest proportion of people with lower secondary school education. In terms of the intensity of change, it is the inner zone that experienced the biggest change, followed by the outer zone and the core. This can be confirmed by the fact that the indices of dissimilarity for the three zones are 12.45, 9.25 and 8.4 respectively. If this trend of change continues, then the inner zone and outer zone, especially the former, may catch up with the educational level of the core, but this depends on whether the suburbanisation process will be expanded further to more areas in the inner and outer zones, bringing better educated and wealthy people from the inner part of Shanghai to its outer part.

Urban Livability

As already mentioned in the previous sections, urban development in Shanghai before the 1990s, especially the 1980s, was characterised by the concentration of both the population and industries in the extremely crowded urban core, lack of infrastructure investment, and the manufacturing industry-dominated economic structure. Many of the changes since the 1990s described in the previous sections have greatly changed the above situation, producing positive effects on urban livability in Shanghai.

Although data on urban livability for the core, inner zone and outer zone in Shanghai are not available, some analysis on Shanghai as a whole as well as its administrative districts may be conducted to shed light on the issue. The most noticeable improvement in Shanghai's livability since the 1980s, especially the 1990s, has been the great improvement in Shanghai's housing and transport conditions. Taking Shanghai as a whole, the per capita usable floor space in Shanghai's city proper was only 4.4 square metres in 1981, but it increased to 11.7 metres in 2000. Looking at the per capita floor space by district and county (Table 9.8), there is a clear pattern: the further the district (county) is from the urban core, the bigger the per capita floor space. This can be attributed not only to the relatively low population density and bigger farmer's houses in the suburban areas, but also to the fact that new residential development has been mostly located at the edge of the central urban districts, and the suburban districts and counties mentioned earlier.

The improvement in transport conditions has already been mentioned in an earlier section and Table 9.1. The emergence of new means of transportation, especially underground railway and light railway systems, and the increase and improvement in both the quantity and quality of roads and transport vehicles, have greatly changed the daily life of Shanghai's residents.

This is evidenced partly by the fact that the number of persons per square metre of space in the bus at peak times dropped from 12 people in the early 1980s to 5 people at the end of the twentieth century, and the speed of buses in the city centre at peak times increased markedly, from less than four to 18 kilometres per hour (Shanghai Urban Comprehensive Transport Planning Institute 2000).

Table 9.8   Housing Condition and Green Space in Shanghai by Districts, 2000

	Per Capita Floor Space of Residential Housing	Coverage Rate of Urban Green Areas*	Per Capita Public Green Areas (sq.m)*	Number of Parks*
Shanghai	24.0	22.2	4.6	117
Central urban districts				
Huangpu	10.8	9.1	0.9	4
Luwan	13.4	13.3	0.9	4
Xuhui	18.4	18.4	3.2	11
Changning	17.5	23.2	4.6	8
Jingan	13.8	12.2	0.5	3
Putuo	16.9	12.8	2.6	12
Zhabei	15.5	14.9	1.7	7
Hongkou	15.8	15.0	1.4	8
Yangpu	15.8	15.3	2.7	11
Inner suburban districts				
Pudong New District	23.6	30.2	11.0	13
Minhang	25.3	32.0	14.7	7
Baoshan	23.4	28.9	5.4	11
Jiading	31.5	30.0	10.2	5
Outer suburban districts and counties				
Jinshan	38.2	31.7	13.9	7
Songjiang	33.7	22.8	9.7	3
Qingpu	32.2	12.4	4.1	3
Nanhui	39.0			
Fengxian	34.1			
Chongming	42.6			

Note: * Data not available for counties.
Source: Shanghai Municipal Statistics Bureau, 2001.

Table 9.9   Selected Environment Indicators in Shanghai, 1996–2000

Indicators	1996	1997	1998	1999	2000
Environment quality					
Average yearly and daily indicators of airborne dust (mg/cu.m)	0.239	0.231	0.215	0.168	0.156
Average yearly and daily indicators of sulfur dioxide (mg/cu.m)	0.059	0.068	0.053	0.044	0.045
Average yearly and daily indicators of nitrogen oxide (mg/cu.m)	0.089	0.105	0.100	0.099	0.090
Up-to-standard rate of drinking water quality	89.0	83.3	92.4	93.2	96.6
Up-to-standard rate of urban surface water quality	88.9	83.3	92.9	98.2	96.3
Average indicator of urban noise (decibel)	58.8	57.1	57.8	57.2	56.6
Average indicator of main traffic line noise (decibel)	72.6	72.2	70.2	70.3	70.5
Pollution control					
Coverage rate of soot control	100	100	100	100	100
Coverage rate of up-to-standard noise control	51.9	52.0	55.9	56.0	80.7
Up-to-standard rate of industrial waste water discharge	87.4	86.6	88.2	89.9	93.2
Up-to-standard rate of automobile exhaust discharge		82.8	85.1	84.6	83.3
Rate of comprehensive utilisation of solid industrial waste	86.4	90.9	92.9	93.0	93.3
Rate of comprehensive utilisation treatment of hazardous waste	94.3	99.9	99.9	99.9	99.3
Environment Improvement					
Rate of treatment of city waste water	39.7	39.9	53.3	50.4	49.4
Rate of centralised heating	52.3	59.0	69.9	75.2	76.9
Rate of gas utilisation in the city	91.4	92.0	98.0	100	100

Source: Shanghai Municipal Statistics Bureau, 2001.

The living environment in Shanghai has also improved. Shanghai had long been troubled by various pollution problems (Ning 2001: 302–7). A notorious reminder of such problems was the offensive smells emitted from the Huangpu river, which runs through the heart of Shanghai. Although these problems still exist to different degrees, the general trend since the 1990s has been positive. As can be seen from available data for the late 1990s in Table 9.9, most indicators point in the direction of better environmental quality and pollution control. Furthermore, this development has been accompanied by increasing green space in the city. The per capita green space and the overall proportion of green space stood at 4.6 square metres and 22.2 per cent respectively by the end of 2000, which is in sharp contrast to 0.47 square metres and 8.2 per cent in 1978 mentioned earlier. It is noticeable that although green space has generally increased in Shanghai, the suburban districts (especially the inner suburban districts) are clearly more advantageous in this aspect. This may be an important factor affecting future residential movement of Shanghai residents, especially those of the emerging middle class, thus reinforcing the suburbanisation process.

Although urban livability in Shanghai has improved, some new issues have emerged since the 1990s. One is that while Shanghai's housing and transport conditions have greatly improved, this has brought about the new problem of wider population distribution and hence longer commuting times (Zhu 2002: 191–2). Furthermore, several issues relating to social stratification in the development process need more attention. The rising urban unemployment rate mentioned earlier is one such issue. Unemployed urban residents form a disadvantaged group in Shanghai. According to a survey of 195 poverty-stricken people conducted in 2001 by Shanghai Federation of Trade Unions, 60 per cent were from families with all or some members unemployed (Wang 2002). The floating population is an even bigger disadvantaged social group. While the housing conditions of local residents in Shanghai have greatly improved in the 1990s, many members of the floating population still live under crude conditions. The 2000 census showed that 20 per cent of the floating population from outside Shanghai lived in dormitories or temporary shelters on construction sites and 36 per cent of them rented private housing. These forms of housing are usually more crowded and only equipped with very simple facilities, compared with housing conditions of local people. Besides, members of the floating population are still disadvantaged in the labour market when competing with local people who are protected by various regulations giving priority to local applicants (Wang *et al.* 2000).

The floating population's problems affect other residents as well. The areas where they are concentrated are often filthy and poor in basic infrastructure, and this reduces the living quality of all residents. The influx of the floating population also causes planning problems, as it creates a considerable demand for low cost housing, and many low quality buildings not conforming to planning regulations have quickly emerged. Rising crime rate and social disorder are also major concerns of these areas. Some research suggests that the crime rate of the floating population was much higher than that of the total population in Shanghai, and half of the crimes were committed in the areas where the floating population are concentrated (Ding *et al.* 2001). Thus the spectacular urban development and great improvement in Shanghai's livability may not be equally shared by all urban areas and residents in Shanghai, and this raises a new challenge for Shanghai in the future.

Conclusions

Employing the zonal approach, the analysis in this chapter shows that as with many other Asian mega-urban regions, the inner zone is the most dynamic area in Shanghai, exhibiting the highest growth rates in terms of both population and employment, and the fastest changes in educational attainment. Such dynamism of the inner zone is driven by both the decongestion process of the urban residential and production functions from the core and *in situ* development of the rural areas in this zone, as well as in-migration from outside Shanghai. Clearly, the inner zone will be the area with the greatest potential for growth of both its population and manufacturing industries in the near future.

In contrast to the dynamic growth in the inner zone, the analysis in this chapter presents a picture of stagnation for the outer zone of Shanghai. There is still much room for further structural change from agricultural to non-agricultural employment, and great potential for population growth, in the outer zone. How such changes will unfold depends on the spread effect of the core on the one hand, and the *in situ* structural transformation and urbanisation processes of the outer zone itself, on the other hand.

One interesting finding is that compared with the experience of some other Asian mega-urban regions, the core in Shanghai seems more dynamic. In fact, in terms of industrial and occupational changes of employment, the core has been the most dynamic area in Shanghai in the 1990s. Another related fact is that although there has been a massive decongestion of the population in the over-crowded areas of the core in the 1990s, and some of the population has moved out of the core, the majority of the relocation has been confined within the core and the extent of suburbanisation in Shanghai is still limited. Such experience is different from that of many major mega-urban regions in Asia since the 1980s, and should be paid more attention.

Relating to the recent history of Shanghai's urban development reviewed earlier, the continued dynamism of the core in Shanghai in the 1990s seems to have much to do with the high concentration of Shanghai's urban functions and the dominance of manufacturing industries in the core before the 1990s, and its profound spatial and industrial restructuring since then. It also has much to do with the fact that while many other Asian cities were experiencing the "overspill" of urban development from the core, Shanghai's development was still suppressed by China's urban development strategies. Besides, the middle class, which has played an important role in the development of suburbanisation in Southeast Asian cities (Dick and Rimmer 1998), is still in the process of formation in Shanghai due to its latecomer status mentioned earlier; Shanghai municipal government adopts policies restricting the use of private cars, and the number of private cars was only 87,100 in Shanghai in 2001, compared to 624,000 in Beijing. Restriction of private car ownership may also partly explain the limited suburbanisation process of Shanghai in the 1990s.

All this suggests that the spatial expansion of Shanghai in the 1990s is just the prelude to more large scale spatial restructuring and further relocation of the population and industries out of the core. This trend, together with the faster growth of towns and further *in situ* transformation of rural areas in the periphery, especially the outer zone (Zhu 2002: 85–107), will not only maintain the growth dynamic of the inner zone, but also boost the development in the outer zone, causing more in-migration, more profound population redistribution, and employment changes in Shanghai. At the same time, the emerging social stratification and related issues are becoming more prominent. If not handled well, they may cause further suburbanisation of the middle class, the formation of more gated communities and their segregation from low income communities, especially the majority of the floating population, and the formation of slum areas. Whether Shanghai will maintain the trend of continued improvement in urban livability will not only depend on the further economic development and investment in urban infrastructure and environment, but also on the proper handling of social issues.

Notes

1. The author would like to thank the Population Census Office of Shanghai Municipality, especially Mr. Gu Yihua, Mr. Chen Wei and Ms. Xie Yan, for producing relevant tabulations for the project. He would also like to thank Mr.

Ian Heyward for drawing the map, and Mr. Shangguan Yang, Mr. Kaijin He, Ms. Meihua Wu and Ms. Yuexiang Yi for research assistance.

2. Zhou (1991: 89–112) has conceptualised some major regions in China undergoing similar processes, including Shanghai and its surrounding areas, as the "Metropolitan interlocking region".

3. For example, in Hu *et al.*'s study (2000: 237), what they term "Shanghai Metropolitan Region" includes Shanghai Municipality and two county-level municipalities in Jiangsu Province, i.e. Taicang and Kunshan municipalities; Wang *et al.* (2002), refer to the region including Shanghai Municipality, a prefecture-level municipality (Suzhou) in Jiangsu Province, and a prefecture-level municipality (Jiaxing) in Zhejiang Province, as Shanghai's "urban field".

4. One US$ is equal to about 8.28 Yuan.

5. According to the Township and Village Enterprise Act of the People's Republic of China, TVEs are those enterprises located in townships and towns (including villages under their jurisdiction), with investment mainly from rural collective economic organisations or farmers and the obligation of supporting agriculture (Tang and Kong 2000: 4).

6. The above growth rates are calculated without taking into consideration that the minimum duration of absence from the place of household registration for a migrant, who did not have the household registration of the destination, to be counted into the population of the destination, was changed from no less than a year in the 1990 census to half a year in the 2000 census. If the one-year criterion was adopted for both censuses, the growth rate for Shanghai between the 1990 and 2000 census would be 15 per cent.

7. Shanghai's TFR was already below the replacement level of 2.1 as early as 1971. In the subsequent 30 years, it further decreased to 1.29, and remarkably, to 0.68 according to the 1990 and 2000 censuses, respectively.

8. It should be noted that this figure includes those who only moved within one of the zones and therefore overestimates the amount of migration compared with other city studies defining migrants as those who had crossed the boundary of one of the zones.

9. This percentage is derived from the 2000 census result showing that 32 per cent of migrants had spent less than one year at their destination in Shanghai. The above estimated volume of migration in the 2000 census conforming to the migrant definition of the 1990 census would be somewhat lower than the actual figure, as it excludes those who migrated to the destination and changed the *Hukou* registration from the place of origin to the place of destination at the same time, and who would have been included in the volume of migration in the 1990 census (and 2000 census too).

10. The migration volume of the 1990 census may be a little underestimated compared to that of the 2000 census in the sense that those who were under five years old were not included in the migration figure in the 1990 census.

However, this is more than offset by the underestimate of the migration volume of the 2000 census mentioned in footnote 9.

11. It needs to be noted that the unemployment figure for the 1990 census might be underestimated because the existence of unemployment was still not officially recognised at that time. In fact, the official term for unemployment in the 1990 census was "waiting for employment in cities and towns".

12. For example, the number of workers employed in the textile, knitwear, and printing and dyeing industries dropped from 424,293 in the 1990 census to only 161,753 in the 2000 census.

13. Note that educational attainment is defined differently from that in other cities, as mentioned in the note of Table 9.7.

10

The Livability of Mega-Urban Regions in Southeast Asia — Bangkok, Ho Chi Minh City, Jakarta and Manila Compared

*Mike Douglass, Trung Quang Le, Cameron Kawika Lowry,
Hao Thien Nguyen, Anh Nguyen Pham, Nghi Dong Thai and
Hernani Yulinawati*

Introduction

Globalisation and urbanisation are profoundly transforming societies throughout the world. Over the past three decades in Southeast Asia, these two processes have directed population and economic shifts to a limited number of very large urban regions. In just a few decades the majority of people in Southeast Asia will be living in cities, and most of these people will reside in city regions with populations greater than ten million. This pattern of urban transition is associated with and substantially driven by the collapse of the time-space relationships transcending national boundaries — a collapse which has incorporated city regions more deeply into the global economy (Wong 1999). The resultant urban form — a vast, functionally integrated extended metropolis — has moved beyond "megacity" as defined by administrative boundaries and into the realm of "mega-urban region" (MUR), with expanded daily fields of interaction reaching as far as 50 kilometres or more from the urban core into peri-urban hinterlands (McGee and Robinson 1995).

Jakarta (Jabodetabek) in Indonesia, Manila in the Philippines, Bangkok in Thailand, and most recently Ho Chi Minh City (HCMC) in Vietnam are among the largest and most rapidly growing MURs in Southeast Asia.

In adapting to and being shaped by their globalising economic and political realities, these MURs have become centres of concentrated economic growth (Douglass 2002b; McGee 1995). However, their economic successes have been attended by undesired consequences, including growing disparity among their populations in terms of the basic conditions of urban living. Urban growth has also exerted extreme pressure on physical infrastructure such as housing, transportation systems, water supply, and sewerage and drainage systems; social services such as education, health, and recreation; and the natural environment. Moreover, the distributional aspects of economic growth and market mechanisms have favoured rich over poor in the allocation of public as well as private goods and services, especially with regard to low-income migrants who are often not recognised as being legitimate residents of cities (UNDP 2002, 2003).

The Livability of Cities

To better account for the successes and limitations of contemporary processes of globalisation and urbanisation, the discussion here focuses on the livability of cities. Drawing from a variety of concepts, this chapter proposes that a livable city has three interconnected components: lifeworlds, personal well-being, and environmental well-being. In constructing this formulation it draws from four prevailing paradigms — economic versus environmental sustainability, deep ecology, poverty and livability, and human-centred (Beatley 2000; Chertow and Esty 1997; Ekins 1986; Khan 1994; Roseland 1997; Douglass Ho, and Ooi 2002) — but also adds a relatively neglected dimension of socio-cultural lifeworlds intrinsic to the search for convivial city life.

In the economic versus environment paradigm, the quest for urban sustainability originates from the realisation that economic growth has irreversibly depleted natural resources and greatly compromised the regenerative capacity of our planet's bio-systems (Hardoy, Mitlin, and Satterthwaite 1992; Haughton and Hunter 1994; Pugh 2000; Satterthwaite 1999). Although the term "sustainability" has many possible definitions, the term came to be linked with economic growth, and in so doing elevated economic priorities over social equity issues (Edwards 1993; WCED 1987; Rogerson 2000). Noting that in Southeast Asia, rapid economic growth has been associated with severe degradation of urban environments (Douglass and Ooi 2000; Wong 1999; WRI 1996), the concern of this paradigm is in how much economic growth must be sacrificed if a certain level of environmental sustenance is to be achieved.

In contrast to the economic growth versus environmental sustainability model, the deep ecology paradigm places livability as the outcome of the long-term integrity of the natural environment, with the "rights" of nature of higher virtue than the human use of environmental resources (Dobson 2000; Tokar 1997). The model developed in this chapter draws from this paradigm by acknowledging that the integrity of the natural environment is vital to livability. However, the focus on livability necessitates a human-centred approach and an emphasis on human outcomes of environmental policies. The concept of livability put forth here accepts environmental management as both a key dimension and a guide for the expansion of cities, and thus requires orientations toward renewable energy, environmentally efficient urban form, open spaces, and other elements that seek to minimise the effects of human activities on the environment (Beatley 2000; Register 2002; Rohter 1992).

The poverty and livability paradigm adds a clear social equity and justice dimension to assessing the performance of cities (Evans 2002; Hardoy *et al.* 1992; Satterthwaite 1999). As expounded by Hardoy *et al.* (1992), development cannot be sustained unless issues of basic needs and social inequality are addressed. As with most other livability paradigms, the focus is on material welfare, including that derived from income through remunerative employment. This paradigm maintains a human-centred approach, yet does not either directly or explicitly enter into realms of cultural life.

While the literature related to livable cities covers a wide range of economic, ecological, and social priorities (Beatley 2000; Evans 2002; Girardet 1999; Hancock 1997; Register 2002; Rohter 1992; UNCHS 2002; UNESCAP 1995; WB 1996, 2000), two tendencies need to be redirected if cities are to be more human-centred and livable. First, the exclusive focus on economic growth and physical health dimensions of human life neglects psychological well-being, social relations and cultural (re-)production so vital to human existence. In other words, the lifeworlds (Habermas 1989; Madsen and Plunz 2001) or life spaces (Friedmann 2002) of cities — the spaces of associational life — are not given due consideration in current proposals for livable cities. Second, the spatial dimension of livability is also in need of more direct consideration. According to Douglass (2002b), the idea of livable cities rests on the understanding that "development as improvement in the quality of life requires a physical as well as social habitat for its realisation" (p. 59). In looking at quality of life issues with the inclusion of a spatial dimension, livability can be defined as "healthy, convivial and socially just living and working conditions in a city or region for all people, and is shaped by the conditions of their natural and built environments" (Douglass, DiGregorio, *et al.* 2002: 4-1). Harmony is sought between the natural and built environment, which includes community and civic spaces that are socially inclusive and have a substantial degree of autonomy from both the state and the market (Douglass, Ho *et al.* 2002).

In going beyond material conditions and accepting the need to explicitly consider the spatial dimensions of changes in the urban habitat, the concept of livability presented here contrasts with mainstream paradigms in three ways. First, livability is more than an environment trade-off with economic growth. It extends into other realms of urban living such as cultural vitality and personal security. Second, the management of the natural environment in the city depends greatly upon its built environment (UNCHS 2002). The relationship between the built and natural environment is a key interface in the environmental sustainability of cities, which is one of the three principal components of livability in this chapter. Third, by incorporating the concept of civic spaces, the proposed model of livability is better suited for understanding the full experience of human living — that the quality of life is a product of human relationships that are both extended and constrained by the physical, social, and natural environments of urban habitats.

As shown in Figure 10.1, the framework developed here is based on three interconnected components of livability: (1) lifeworlds, (2) personal well-being, and (3) environmental well-being. It also reflects the understanding that the achievement of livability depends on processes of governance, with good governance as both a means of realising livability and an end in itself.

Figure 10.1 Dimensions of MUR Livability

Source: Douglass and Le *et al.,* 2003.

The circular, multi-directional flow of the model also indicates that livability is not merely the sum of the attributes within each of the three components, but is more importantly the outcome of interaction among them. Further, issues of social justice — which now include rights of growing numbers of internal and international migrants, many of whom are without resident or citizenship rights — are among the complex realities of multiple publics. Likewise, the increasing presence of global forces in urban economies, politics, and cultures calls for new ways of linking the public sphere of the city with global actors. Governance, as a public policy sphere that includes government, civil society, and economic interests, is envisioned here as an inclusive process of collaboration and conflict resolution among these societal forces.

Methodology

The study's focus is on a comparison of livability among the four MURs, with special attention to zones within each — the core (urban core), inner zone (suburban), and outer zone (peri-urban) — where data permits. This study reveals that both the dynamics of urban growth and the quality of urban life vary substantially among MURs and across these zones in every MUR.

Livability indices are formulated to quantify and compare certain aspects of livability among the four MURs. Due to the lack of quantitative data for lifeworlds, however, this chapter includes indicators for only personal well-being and environmental well-being. For each indicator, raw data was converted to a numerical scale, with zero as the lowest, or least desirable, and five as the highest, or most desirable. Indicators with the lowest scores signal the need for concerted attention. Scores for each indicator are arrayed in a radiograph for visual comparison. Indicators are based on interpolations of scaled secondary data. Comparisons are only made among the four MURs, and are not based on any international comparisons or standards, which are beyond the scope of this chapter.

Intra-MUR data analysis across the three MUR zones is impeded due to scarcity of data. For this reason, the indices focus on inter-MUR trends within the core zones, except for HCMC where only aggregated inter-zone data is available. Rather than drawing definitive comparisons or conclusions, the intention here is to highlight data collection gaps, rethink current formulations of existing indicators, and place livability in a more prominent position in urban policy discussions.

Urban Lifeworlds

This section examines the modes of lifeworld spaces in the form of new towns, public space, and civic space. The existence of spaces for vibrant community association is essential for the nurturing of lifeworlds and the creation of a more tolerant, convivial society. However, urban land allocation in market systems typically fails to provide spaces that have community value outside of for-profit uses. In the current era of urban space privatisation and commodification, the provision of public and civic spaces is under duress. At the same time, government surveillance of public spaces does not provide adequate distance of civil society from the state, thus limiting the potential for open and free social interaction. Box 10.1 identifies the key sources of stress being placed on lifeworld spaces that, to varying degrees, are common to the four MURs.

New Towns and Gated Communities

Since the 1970s, new towns and gated communities have accompanied the emergence of the middle class and have become symbolic of the fragmentation of space by socioeconomic status. These suburban islands are indicative of a broader shift from society-wide collective provision of urban infrastructure by governments into new public-private partnerships favouring commodity relations and commercially profitable provision of public goods and services. Stimulated by the globalisation of finance capital reaching into Southeast Asia from the late 1980s, this shift limits the overall provision of public space as former community spaces become semi-exclusive enclaves. Such exclusive community developments are pervasive across the Bangkok, Jakarta, and Manila MURs.

Box 10.1   Sources of Stresses on Lifeworlds in Southeast Asian MURs

- Increasing stress on more traditional forms of public and civic spaces, with very limited production of such spaces. These trends result from the pressures of increasing population density, and the privatisation and commercialisation of urban land use.
- Economic polarisation leading to spatial fragmentation along socio-economic class lines, including exclusion of the poor, which is seen most clearly in the continuing trend of gated communities and new town developments.
- A paucity of cohesive policy approaches to narrow the divides among classes, to address the encroachment of private capital into civic and public spaces, and to counter the erosion of social networks that have helped to sustain marginalised populations such as the urban poor.

In recent decades, the respective MUR landscapes have all been shaped by speculative land development episodes in the form of new towns and suburban communities, often located in their inner zones. Jabodetabek's development history is representative of this trend. In the 1990s, investors bought up to 60,000 hectares, an area nearly equivalent to the city itself (65,656 hectares), to be used for golf courses, luxury housing estates, and gated communities that are typically self-contained with their own shopping malls, restaurants, schools, sports, and entertainment centres (Dharmapathni and Firman 1997). With public space limited in the inner zone, the net result of urban expansion is an increase in exclusive spaces for a few, while urban congestion and business district development in the core diminish open and public spaces for lower income groups that concentrate in this area. Bangkok, Manila, and even HCMC show similar tendencies (Douglass and Boonchuen 2003a; Douglass, DiGregorio, *et al.* 2002).

The direct and indirect impacts on lifeworlds of such exclusive and often privatised communities are, however, difficult to quantify. Governments do not routinely collect data on indicators such as the area of urban land in gated communities to allow for systematic tracking. Nevertheless, field observations readily show the striking mix between opulent gated communities and lack of public amenities in other inner zone spaces.

Public Space

Public space normally implies openness to all urban residents and visitors. In ideal democratic societies, implicit in this idea is provision of spaces for freedom of action and expression that are crucial to linking everyday lifeworlds to the public sphere of political life. When such public spaces act as the locus for free public speech and interaction among diverse populations, new ideas germinate, social capital is created, and citizen voices enter directly into the political life of the city (Douglass 2002a).

Public sidewalks are a quintessential public space. Where they exist in the core zones of the MURs they are typically lined with small shops, street stalls, and vendors. Unlike the interior of shopping malls, public sidewalks in commercial areas function as primary spaces for socializing that can allow for free expression and action and cannot be readily colonised by adjacent commercial spaces (Boonchuen 2002). Distinctive areas of the core such as the open Pahurat Market and Sukhumvit Road in Bangkok are generally bustling with activity and a broad spectrum of community members (Chandler 2000). The co-existence of so many activities taking place on sidewalks, narrow passageways, and larger roads suggests these areas are not merely transportation corridors but are equally public spaces for civil society to engage in more open-ended encounters.

Many public spaces face threats ranging from commercial conversion to colonisation by both local vendors and government. The trend of commercial conversion is of particular concern given the current respective MUR contexts. In the inner zone of Bangkok, for example, parks and playgrounds were outnumbered by entertainment spots, such as pubs, karaoke, and massage parlors, by a ratio of one to ten (Ploenpote 2003). Encroachment by households and local vendors on public sidewalks and parks is also prominent, especially in HCMC (Drummond 2000; Shannon 2001). Co-optation also often involves competing governmental priorities, as measures to address urban crowding and the lack of facilities and infrastructures displace public spaces. The demolition of the historic Mehan Garden to build a city college and commercial parking in Manila is a clear example of such developmental challenges (Baguioro 2002).

Green spaces are another type of public space frequently recognised for attenuating some of the environmental impacts associated with urbanisation and providing city residents with a sense of enjoyment (Jim and Chen 2003). For example, the 60-hectare Rizal Park in the Manila MUR has gardens, plazas, open spaces, and other amenities that make it a popular destination for both residents and visitors seeking refuge from urban congestion. These green spaces are thus important spaces for recreation and congregation (Baguioro 2002) even though they are often unevenly dispersed throughout the urban landscape and are limited in number. Figure 10.2 shows current green space availability in the MURs.

One of the most well-known assaults on public space is the shopping mall (Douglass, Ho, *et al.* 2002; Kunstler 1993). In recent years, malls have become the new face of the Southeast Asian MURs. Residents have often embraced such air-conditioned convenience as an escape from the hot open spaces of sidewalks that now must contend with automobile noise and exhaust fumes. Yet, what is not readily appreciated is the loss of lifeworld spaces when traditional open markets and sidewalks give way to malls. Though shopping malls appear to be "public", they are privately owned spaces seeking to maximise consumption while limiting all other forms of lifeworld expression. They discourage activities that diminish land rent from the use of floor space, such as free seating in open areas or spaces for people to gather without spending money (Boonchuen 2002). This is not to suggest that spaces of commerce cannot also foster associational life, but rather that such opportunities are

Figure 10.2 Green Space per Capita

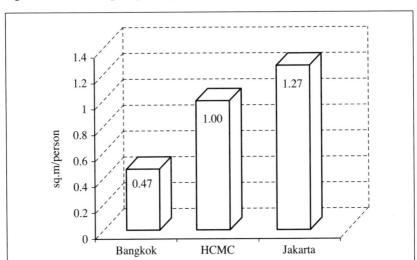

Source: Bangkok: Boonchuen, 2002; HCMC: Dang, 2003; Jakarta: Bureau Statistics Jakarta, 2002.

minimised in the design and operation of the mall, which is typically complete with surveillance cameras and hired security forces authorised by mall owners to prevent public gatherings that have no shopping purpose.

   The most subtle and telling erosion of spaces that foster lifeworld is the degree with which malls have been embraced as spaces of recreation and leisure. Many of Jabodetabek's citizens have learned to define consumption as leisure and even freedom of choice (Jellinek 2000). In some instances, malls inventively include potential lifeworld spaces, such as in Metro Manila where some malls have allowed for religious services in them. Such strategies help to explain the ubiquity of malls in Metro Manila, which has 20 large malls in addition to scores of smaller ones, as the premier gathering place of people seeking leisure activities (Connell 1999).

   That going to the mall represents "free choice" cannot, however, be taken at face value. First, Southeast Asian MURs have among the least amount of green/public space per capita of all city regions of similar size in the world. Going to the mall exists in a vacuum of alternatives. Second, governments have often assisted in demolishing traditional markets to make way for commercial centres and tourism site development (Boonchuen 2002). Third, as will be noted, the poor record of managing air pollution and drainage makes malls seem like an oasis — not for shopping per se, but for escape from tropical heat and deteriorating urban environments. Fourth, as citizen identities are shifted from social and political spheres toward consumerism through a wide variety of media intruding into daily life, public awareness of what is being lost in the city is displaced by commodity relations. For all of these reasons, the displacement of public space by commercial development is complex and cannot be reduced to simply an issue of demand. As with the city in regard to many other issues, private land development decisions are fraught with imperfections related to unequal distribution of wealth and social power and are thus open to further analysis and public discussion about socially desirable uses, particularly with regard to public spaces.

Civic Space

While the previous examples of public space are important to the functioning of society and therefore the livability of cities, the potential of such spaces is not measured simply in quantity and distribution, but also in their civic character. These public spaces, along with other private establishments that allow people to meet without constant demand to spend money, are "spaces in which people of different origins and walks of life can co-mingle without overt control by government, commercial, or other private interests or *de facto* dominance by one group over another" (Douglass, Ho, *et al.* 2002: 345). These civic spaces are inclusive spaces that allow for daily life and civic activities, and thus are the core of the associational life that is central to the ideal of social lifeworlds (Habermas 1989). For civil society to flourish, provision must be made for such spaces to be created to facilitate the association of people in a civil manner. Given that civic space often escapes critical attention, the analysis here relies on qualitative research in examining their function and nature.

Civic space, as with social institutions, is culturally defined. In Bangkok, the *wat* or temple is representative of such culture-space intertwining and is an important form of civic space that continues to be a focal point of community life. The local community typically takes on the responsibility of maintaining the temple, thereby forming an intricate relationship between community and spiritual life. Open spaces in temple compounds have generally been used by all age groups for social gatherings, festivals for young people, and playgrounds for children. They are rich in social activities, serving as civic spaces that have brought cohesiveness to traditional communities (Boonchuen 2002). The spatial and cognitive centrality of *wat* to daily life results in an alignment of community functions, including religious, cultural, social, educational, recreational, and political activities integral to civic life. Yet, widespread urban land commodification has threatened the traditional roles of temples, as spaces for associational life in temples have shrunk, been sold off, or rented as commodities (Boonchuen 2002). Nonetheless, the preservation of and reverence for temples in Bangkok attest to the continued vitality of this form of lifeworld.

While global economic pressures place traditional forms of civic spaces such as temples and traditional markets under duress, new forms of civic spaces made possible by telecommunication technologies are emerging. Habermas's (1989) concept of the bourgeois public sphere assumes face-to-face communicative relations between discussants in personalised, unmediated cyber space. As seen in the remarkable role that the internet played in the popular social movements leading to the downfall of Suharto in Indonesia, the potential of this new form of civic space is already manifest (Lim 2002).

As in the case of the internet in Indonesian cities, the most promising forms of civic space in HCMC are also in cyberspace. Scholars have asserted that "Internet cafes, coffee shops and leisure sites will undoubtedly also be key sites for the fuller development of civil society in Vietnam, with students playing an increasingly important role in initiating social and political change and taking on new forms of media and technology" (Thomas and Drummond 2003: 6). Despite the current constraints on civil society, and on the internet in particular, this avenue for civil society to form associational life is likely to continue to expand under the country's renovation (*Doi Moi*).

Although globalisation and commercialisation place greater stress on civic spaces, they may also drive popular demand for new forms of civic space — even if they take the form of insurgency. Coupled with citizens' increasing demand for participation, globally-linked flows of information contribute to the rise of civil society throughout the world, including Asia. Whether as open citizen protest at Monas, the national monument in Jakarta, unauthorised mass assembly on the public streets of HCMC (Thomas 2003), or text-message mediated political expression in Manila, such instances of citizen mobilisation are indicative of the need for routine access to civic spaces to facilitate non-violent state-civil society interaction. The demand for such sites for expression and interaction justifies a more active role by the respective MUR governments in fostering potential civic spaces and better balancing the interplay of the commercial and public sphere as they transform urban space.

Lifeworlds, in summary, the attributes of which are difficult to quantify and are often viewed as forms of consumption rather than being vital to societal well-being, economic resilience, and political reform, are rarely included in notions of livable cities. However, a focus on lifeworlds gives important insights into the livability of cities and represents a first attempt to add non-material dimensions to the concept of livability. This emphasises the need for a more active role of governments, civil society, and economic enterprises in creating convivial urban life through the creation and sustenance of inclusive life spaces in the MURs.

Personal Well-being

Differences in the quality of life within and among the MURs can be seen in terms of livelihood (absolute and relative poverty), health (health service delivery system, prevalence of diseases, and children's health-related illness), education (literacy rate, school completion, and school costs), and safety and security (child labour, child abuse, and crime). Both a general and zonal analysis has been conducted for the four MURs to provide more detailed information regarding MUR dynamics with regard to the personal well-being of residents. Box 10.2 provides a brief synopsis of the status of personal well-being in the four MURs.

Livelihood

Livelihood, defined as the means of living and the capacities, assets and activities reproducing personal and household material existence (Chambers and Conway 1992), reflects coping abilities as well as personal advancement as MURs expand and experience economic and social transformations over time. Among all issues linked to livelihood, poverty is the most striking (Cahn 2004). At the macro-level, a singularly momentous rise in poverty rates was associated with the 1997–98 economic collapse of several Pacific Asia countries, summarised as the Asian Financial Crisis. In the cases of Manila and Jabodetabek, this crisis resulted in longer term continuation of high levels of urban poverty (BPS, Bappenas, and UNDP 2001; Reyes 2002). At the micro-level, those who lack the ability or entitlements to resources (e.g., educational or technical qualifications, good physical health, and community and familial support) to adapt to changing urban conditions are more likely to become the new urban poor (Douglass, DiGregorio, *et al.* 2002; SCF 1999). This is particularly so for migrants who lack education and other human capital to advance in the city.

In most MURs, governments use poverty lines to measure absolute poverty defined by lack of access to minimum basic needs. While the concept

Box 10.2   Overview of Personal Well-being in the MURs

- Personal well-being in the Bangkok, HCMC, Jakarta, and Manila MURs is better than that of their respective countries in poverty reduction, health status, and educational attainment.   Dynamics within MURs coupled with concentration of national economic growth in these MURs underlies these achievements.
- The incidence of poverty is spatially varied within each MUR.   Different measures of poverty also yield different poverty trends.   While basic needs poverty lines principally using food (calories) as the measure show decreasing rates, other indicators that include shelter, health conditions and extreme environmental risk can yield opposite trends.   The spatial coincidence of poverty with environmentally deteriorated settlements and inadequacy of environmental services shows how caloric intake can underestimate actual conditions of impoverishment.
- Health facilities are increasingly provided by both the public and private healthcare sectors, giving residents in the MURs greater access to health services than elsewhere in the nation.   However, greater spatial access does not mean equal access when poor households struggle with unaffordable costs.
- Education for residents is also improving in every MUR as evidenced by higher literacy rates and increased school completion levels.   However, educational costs are still a burden to poorer households.
- Child safety/security is threatened by increased incidences of child labour and exploitation.   Further, crime is a serious threat to personal well-being and appears to be the worst in Thailand when compared to the other three MUR countries.
- Overall, core areas have the most to offer in terms of personal well-being while the inner zones are experiencing the most striking transformations for residents of these four MURs.   The outer zones remain mostly agricultural with a higher poverty rate, lower quality and quantity of educational and health facilities, and a majority of the child labour force.

of basic needs is open to a broad array of elements, governments invariably focus on the amount of income needed to purchase a minimum intake of calories to sustain life. Some also include an estimated amount to cover such needs as clothing and housing, but this is not common. Poverty line definitions for each country as well as for each of the zones within the MURs utilise different methods. Studies have also shown that poverty lines are typically set at the lowest possible poverty threshold level because they do not account for other variables such as household composition or cost differences among locations (NSO, NESDB, and Office of Prime Minister 1999).

With the caveat that definitions are not necessarily consistent from country to country, while poverty rates appears to be decreasing over time for the Bangkok core (NESDB 2002; UNFAO 2000) and HCMC (Nguyen 2001; Thai, Pham, Nguyen, Nguyen, and Duong 2001), it is increasing for the core areas of the Jakarta and Manila MURs. For example, the poverty rate in the core of the Manila MUR increased from 6.5 per cent in 1997 to 7.6 per cent in 2000 (NSCB 2003). Zonal information is unavailable for HCMC, but in the Jakarta and Manila MURs the core areas had the lowest rates of poverty (BPS *et al.* 2001), while in the Bangkok MUR the core had the highest rate of poverty when compared to the outer zones (Jitsuchon 2001).

A commonality among the four MURs is their lower poverty rates compared with their respective national rates. In Thailand, 14.2 per cent of the population was below the poverty line in 2000, but just 0.3 per cent of the population in Bangkok was determined by the government to be below this line (NESDB 2002). However, it should be noted that about 1.5 million people, or about one quarter of the core Bangkok population, live in slums with substandard housing and poor environmental conditions. In all countries, whereas rural poverty might be more accurately reflected by access to food, in the city poverty is associated with much higher risks in relation to environment and inadequate urban services. For example, infant mortality in the city is highly related to unsanitary environmental conditions, particularly polluted water supply typical of slums (Douglass and Ooi 2000).

The poor in each of the MURs share a number of characteristics: higher incidence of poverty among single person headed households; employment that provides inadequate income, often from only one source; economic assets that are unable to allow for self-provisioning outside of the market; inability to access health and educational services leading to under-education or no education and chronic ill-health; polluted living and working environments; and finally, the threat or experience of eviction because of illegal occupation (Firman 2002; Mac 2001; Sasaki 1998; SCF 1999; UNFPA 1996).

Health

Because of the availability and variety of health facilities in both the public and private sectors, as well as a greater concentration of high quality health services, the health status of MUR residents is better than the rest of the nation (DOH 2002; DHS 1992; HCMCPC 1996; WHO 2003). There have been significant increases in private hospitals in Bangkok and Manila in the last decades.

Zonal information for health facilities is only available for Manila and HCMC. While more hospitals and hospital beds might be expected to be found in the core of the MURs, the case of Manila shows that this is not necessarily true. The hospital bed to population ratio for the inner zone is

12.19 per 1,000 people while it is only 2.84 for the core and 0.68 in the outer zone (DOH 2002; NSCB 2003). Similarly, most health facilities are also located in the inner zone of HCMC. This suggests that growth in the inner zones for health facilities may be more dynamic than in the core and outer zone. Nonetheless, it is interesting to note that while the inner zone of the Manila MUR has a disproportionate number of hospitals and hospital beds, the core has the lowest infant mortality rate (IMR), suggesting that the presence of public health facilities might not be singularly responsible for improved health of very young children.

In fact, the availability of health services does not necessarily mean that the poor have adequate access to them. The poor of the MURs use very basic health facilities, such as the commune health stations in HCMC and the *puskesmas* in Jabodetabek, disproportionately more than other residents. Such places have inadequate health equipment and medicine, sometimes unhygienic conditions, and insufficient numbers of doctors or well-trained health staff (GSO 2001). Interestingly, while private health facilities are accessed by both the rich and the poor in HCMC, only the rich in Jabodetabek and Bangkok can afford the same. Further, HCMC and Jabodetabek residents select traditional medicines or rely on self-treatment as alternatives when they cannot afford the services provided at higher quality facilities (Mukherjee, Hardjono, and Carrierre 2002; WB 2003c).

The incidence of diseases and chronic ailments in the MURs is also of great concern, particularly those related to exposure to pollution in working and/or unsanitary living conditions that can cause illness. In Jabodetabek, respiratory diseases are correlated to the emissions from factories, transportation vehicles, and people who smoke. Other major health concerns in the MURs are diarrhea and skin diseases, which are related to poor water quality and hygiene (Bapedal DKI Jakarta 2000).

The fastest growing disease in the MURs is HIV/AIDS. With the rapidly changing migration patterns, people coming in and out of the MURs have been major agents of the transmission of HIV/AIDS, particularly for the MURs but also for the nations in general. Bangkok has seen an increase in new HIV infections among teenagers and housewives (Kanabus and Fredrikson 2003), while HCMC has witnessed an increase of HIV/AIDS incidences among pregnant women and children (*Thanh Pho HCM* 2001; Thien 2003). In Jakarta, the majority of cases appear to be drug users who share intravenous needles (Naommy 2003). The data on HIV/AIDS for Manila is inconsistent and the statistics are so limited that some have called it a miracle that HIV/AIDS has not spread more widely (Wilkinson 2002).

An important indicator in health assessment is the infant mortality rate. Advances in medical technology and knowledge as well as increased access to higher quality facilities show that over time the IMR is decreasing in each of the four MURs, with the lowest rates in the core. In 1999, the Jakarta MUR outer zone had an IMR of 49 per 1,000 live births while in the core the rate was 29 per 1,000 live births (BPS *et al.* 2001). The higher rates in the outer zone are perhaps unsurprising considering the higher poverty rates there, implying it is more difficult for individuals and families to access quality health care.

Over time, malnutrition appears to have been decreasing in each of the four MURs. However, for the Jakarta and Manila MURs, malnutrition is higher in the core than in the inner and outer zones. For example, 23.7 per cent of children in the Jabodetabek in 1998 were malnourished in the core while there were 20.5 per cent in the inner zone and 20.4 per cent in the outer zone (BPS *et al.* 2001). This is comparable to data suggesting that the poverty rates have been increasing in the cores of Jakarta and Manila over time. In the absence of zonal data for the HCMC and Bangkok MUR, malnutrition is expected to be highest for slum areas in the core and in the outer zones.

Education

As an indicator of basic education, literacy rates are high and increasing over time across the MURs. The rate is 97.8 per cent in Jakarta (BPS *et al.* 2001); 95.9 in Bangkok (NSO 2000); between 92 and 94 in HCMC (DSO 2000); and 92.4 in the Manila core in 1994 (ADB 1999). For those MURs with available zonal data, the rate is highest in the core and lowest in the outer zone. In HCMC, the rates were identical in the core and the inner zone, perhaps because of a proliferation of schools built in the inner zone from 1995–2001 (SOHCMC 2002).

Educational attainment is also seen in the number of years completed or percentage of people who have completed certain levels of schooling. While Jabodetabek and the Bangkok Metropolitan Region have seen an increase in the mean number of years of schooling over time (BPS *et al.* 2001; Jones 2003; NSO 2003), for the Manila MUR, there was a decrease from 1993 to 1998 (NSO 1993, 1998). When comparing school completion in terms of rates or mean years, more people are completing school in the core and inner zone than in the outer zone of the Bangkok, Jakarta, and Manila MURs. For example, 1999 data for Jakarta shows 9.7 and 9.2 mean years of schooling for the core and inner zones, respectively, while the mean years of schooling for the outer zone was 7.1 years (BPS *et al.* 2001). In contrast, the school completion rates for the HCMC were 71 per cent for all three zones in 1999 (DSO 2000). Therefore, despite the lower literacy rate in the HCMC outer zone, the school completion rates show that residents in this zone are not behind in terms of educational achievement.

However, despite positive results in school achievement, unmet subsistence needs threaten school attendance for poor children. As seen in the Bangkok Metropolitan Region and HCMC, the drop-out rates increase as poor households cannot afford schooling for their children and expect them to work to supplement the household income. Other reasons children drop out of school include traveling long distances from home, poor health, low quality of education, and an unwillingness to study (Bhumirat 1984; DSO 2000).

Safety/Security

Safety and security cover a number of concerns, including child labour and abuse, human trafficking, work-related accidents, crime, and other threats of violence in the city at large. The focus here is on child labour and crime, as children are consistently vulnerable to unsafe conditions in the MURs. Despite government instituted age regulations in the various MURs, children are becoming an important segment of labour for many types of industries. MURs are a major destination for many children from poor households due to readily available non-agricultural employment. They can be found working as construction site workers, restaurant or shop workers, street vendors, shoe shiners, and in jobs such as carpet weaving, gem stone cutting, and scavenging. Children are also involved in the commercial sex industry, which is intertwined with human trafficking. In Indonesia, there are around 75,000 registered sex workers though the more realistic number is between 140,000 to 230,000 sex workers (Hull, Sulistianingsih, and Jones 1998; Lim 1998). Further, about 30 per cent are under the age of 18, meaning very substantial numbers of children are involved in prostitution (Farid 2004). The conditions for employment of children are arbitrarily fixed by employers and often include long hours, lack of appropriate facilities, physical and mental abuse, and exposure to health hazards while receiving wages far below the minimum rate (Save the Children 1997; UNICEF 2000).

The child labour problem appears to be significant for all of the MURs discussed (NSO 1995; Save the Children 1997), although it is underreported in every MUR and its respective nation. For example, the National Commission for Child Protection in Indonesia reported an increase in the number of street children in Jakarta from 15,000 before the 1997 crisis to 40,000 afterwards (Dursin 2000). Qualitative information shows that concentrations of child labourers vary by occupations across the zones. In the core and inner zone, child labour exists in the form of nonagricultural work such as domestic servants, industrial/manufacturing work, as well as street children and children involved in prostitution. However, it was found that except for Bangkok, the agricultural sector, which is usually found in the outer zone, remains the largest sector in which child labour is used. This exploitation of a child's human capital creates an enduring poverty trap for future generations and exposes them to harmful situations that threaten their physical, psychological, and emotional development (Edmonds and Turk 2002). Child labour is also detrimental for the educational development of children. In Metro Manila, less than a quarter of working children had beyond three years of education (NSO 1995).

Regarding crime, data is not available for all four MURs but does exist for their respective countries. Generally, the reported crime rate for the four countries is lower compared to industrialised countries (Winslow 2004a, 2004b, 2004c, 2004d). While Table 10.1 does not include statistics for all crimes because of lack of data, it shows that Thailand has the highest reported rates of murder, aggravated assault, and rape when compared to the other three countries. Because of wide variations in underreporting of crime among countries, great care is needed in interpreting the data, which should not be taken as an indication that one city has higher rates of crime than another. For example, in Indonesia, "Women's rights activists believe that rape is seriously underreported due to the social stigma attached to victims" (Winslow 2004a: 27). However, reported numbers do show significant levels of crime in the MURs studied.

The livability indices arrayed in Figure 10.3 allow for comparisons using selected indicators of personal well-being. The graph shows that Bangkok

Table 10.1 Crime Rates per 100,000 Population — Indonesia, Philippines, Thailand and Vietnam

Indicator	Indonesia[a]	Philippines[b]	Thailand[b]	Vietnam[b]
Murder	1.0	7.9	8.5	1.1
Aggravated Assault	4.4	15.1	33.2	7.2
Rape	0.6	4.2	6.6	1.6
Robbery	5.1	8.1	1.3	1.5

Source: Winslow 2004a, 2004b, 2004c, 2004d; (a) Data from 1999; (b) Data from 2000.

has the best profile of personal well-being, followed by Jakarta, Manila, and HCMC. In addition, personal well-being in all of the MURs is better for their residents than for other residents of their respective larger national and territorial domains. MUR residents experience a better standard of living with less poverty, children's health-related issues have improved, and access to educational facilities has increased with a concomitant increase in the literacy rate.

Among the three major dimensions of livability, the findings in this section suggest that personal well-being in terms of education and health has enjoyed the most discernible improvements during the 1990–2000 decade. Literacy and general citizen health have been demonstrably improved. Security and livelihood are somewhat less unequal in progress due to impacts of global crises and the fact that they are less amenable to resolution through public services. While urban core areas tend to fare better than other zones across most indicators, this is not always the case. In some MURs where governments have been more attentive to inner and outer zones, significant improvements have been achieved.

Figure 10.3   Personal Well-being Comparison of the Four Cities

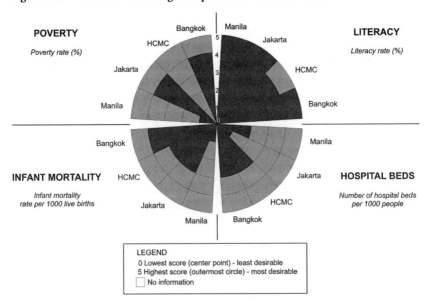

Source: Douglass and Le *et al.,* 2003.

Environmental Well-being

Intensive urbanisation has greatly jeopardised environmental quality and human life in the MURs. The human consequences of the impacts of deteriorated environment on the livability of cities are manifold. A decade ago, the World Bank estimated that in large Asian cities the costs of environmental degradation were equivalent to five to ten per cent of the urban GDP (Brandon 1994). With pollution levels increasing by 10 to 20 per cent per year — well ahead of economic growth rates — the costs have continued to mount over the past decade as the underlying factors such as energy demand and automobile ownership also continue to expand at two to five times the pace of economic growth. This study assesses five components of environmental well-being — water, air, land, solid waste, and slums — in the core, inner, and outer zones among the MURs. An overview of environmental well-being status of the four MURs is shown in Box 10.3.

Box 10.3   Overview of Environmental Well-being in the MURs

- The Bangkok, HCMC, Jakarta, and Manila MURs all face environmental degradation. The degraded urban and suburban environments appear to be reaching or surpassing their ability to absorb and dissipate the volume of pollution generated.
- While the percentage of residents with access to safe drinking water has increased, none of the MURs had consistent access to water 24 hours a day. Poor water quality and sanitation contribute to high rates of waterborne diseases.
- Air pollution from vehicle and industrial emissions are serious problems in the MURs. Particulates pollution is the major threat to the MURs' citizens. Bangkok's overall air quality, though poor, ranks ahead of the remaining three MURs.
- Land pollution poses a serious threat but is less well-researched in the MURs than other aspects of environmental management.
- Solid waste generation in the MURs has increased significantly. Poor solid and hazardous waste management is leading to land, air, and water pollution across the MURs.
- There is growing inequality regarding access to a clean environment, as the urban poor are left to find shelter and make livelihoods in the most despoiled areas, increasing their exposure to the health-endangering pollution.
- In the core, despite greater accessibility to environmental services, air and water pollution are the main threats to livability. In the inner zone, access to environmental services is limited because of the inadequate coverage of services. Land pollution sources are from industrial zone wastes as well as intensification of agriculture in inner and outer zones. The outer zone has very low coverage of urban environmental services; yet it is among the most vulnerable to natural resource loss and degradation from MUR expansion.

Water

Although water access is inadequate throughout most of the MURs studied, the core area typically has the highest rate of infrastructure-based water delivery compared to the other zones. However, the water supply infrastructure in the core is in a decrepit state in all cities, with high rates of water loss or non-revenue water. They all had very low rates of effective coverage by piped water (e.g., HCMC at 32 per cent, Manila at 32 per cent, Jakarta at 31 per cent) except for Bangkok with 72 per cent. Furthermore, none of the other MURs had consistent access to water 24 hours a day (McIntosh 2003).

Access to water was found to correlate with social status. It is generally lower for the poor than city averages reported in government and NGO figures because these marginalised people are more likely to acquire their drinking water in an unaccounted manner from independent vendors or illegal sources. A lack of water service connections encourage those who are not served to find access to water by other means, such as leaching from piped water systems, or, perhaps more often, by purchasing water at very high costs or tapping wells. The same trend is true with water quality. Acute social divisions in most areas result in higher exposure of urban poor to drinking water that is unhealthy to consume compared to the middle and upper classes (McIntosh 2003).

Within the sprawling development of the suburban inner zone, piped water is usually accessible only for those residing in newer housing estates and those living near the inner zone municipality centre. For the more destitute inner zone's residents, groundwater is the primary source of drinking water. Residents in the outer zone typically rely on groundwater, surface water, and irrigation networks. Thus, access can be problematic, as the limited availability of water proves unreliable with increased water demand stemming from new development. Some improvements have been made in recent years to increase water access through new policy interventions involving both public and private sector participation in increasing water supply. However, the potable water supply in all four MURs is continually threatened by the contamination of water bodies from untreated human excrement, municipal and industrial wastes.

Low rates of sanitary sewerage infrastructure connections are a common water quality problem across the MURs, with untreated sewerage corrupting the water supply (McIntosh 2003; WB 2003a). Concentrations of municipal solid waste dumping in the core also further reduce water quality and the ability of the water body to support life. In the inner zone, water quality is jeopardised as the clustering of newer industries conflicts with residential development. In the outer zone, where the predominant land use is agriculture, water quality is directly influenced by farming and development activities, such as runoffs from fertiliser and pesticides, and poor land husbandry or development practices.

Along with issues of water pollution is the increasing severity of seasonal flooding in all of the MURs studied. Historically, settlement patterns exist in low-lying areas of the core near large bodies of water that serve as water supply and/or transportation corridors. This has proved problematic in tropical climates as development pressures increase. In the core, intense population densities create devastating losses of properties and occasionally loss of life from flooding that is worsening due to lack of ground cover. Squatters in the core who build makeshift developments around and over drainage corridors increase the extent of flooding damage. In the upstream areas of the inner and outer zones, development activities such as deforestation, erosion, waste disposal, and impervious surface construction increase the severity of flooding problems downstream in the core.

Air

Air pollution is one of the more dramatic urban environmental issues in MURs as they are among the most heavily air polluted cities in the world. Increases in industrialisation and automobile ownership threaten the future livability of these city regions (Douglass and Ooi 2000). Air quality across MURs is difficult to compare using average values measured at specific locations, as these locations might not be representative of the whole airshed region and the methods of measurement can also vary. A reference standard is typically adopted, but more often the instrumentation and quality assurance protocol are different.

The two most serious pollutants in the MURs are total suspended particulates (TSP) and particulate matters below ten micrograms (PM_{10}) from mobile sources and sulfur dioxide (SO_2) from point sources and diesel-fueled vehicles. Carbon monoxide (CO) and nitrogen dioxide (NO_2) are two other significant mobile pollutants concentrated along the roadside. Recently, ozone (O_3) levels have also caused concern.

Among the MURs, Thailand has made remarkable progress in improving air quality over the past decade. With the exception of particulates and O_3, all pollutants now comply with Thailand's air quality standard. However, while air quality measurements and expert reports indicate Bangkok's air quality is getting better, three in four Bangkok residents view air pollution as the most significant pollution problem (WB 2002). One reason for this is the soaring rates of asthma in Bangkok, as in most cities in the world, which is thought to be highly associated with air pollution (Masoli, Fabian, Holt, and Beasely 2004).

Air quality in the remaining three MURs is much worse than Bangkok. The TSP concentration in Jakarta is between 200–300µg/m³ compared to Bangkok and Manila, which were around 100–200µg/m³ (WB 2003b). In HCMC, the average CO, NO_2, and TSP concentrations exceed national standards and are increasing (ADB 2003). In 1999, PM_{10} was the critical parametre that caused Jakarta's air quality to be classified as "unhealthy", a condition in which people were living for about 25 per cent of the year (Bapedal DKI Jakarta 2000). In Manila, 80 per cent of the population lives in areas where air quality is worse than the official Manila standards for air quality (Shah and Nagpal 1997).

Another critical air quality issue in the MURs is the phase-out of lead-based additives in gasoline. The lead phase-out, particularly in Indonesia, has been delayed by the 1997 economic crisis, which has decreased the capacity of the MURs to combat air pollution. However, while the health effects of lead exposure remain a grave concern, the future effects of carcinogenic methyl tertiary butyl ether (MTBE), which has replaced lead, may lead to other adverse effects related to increased levels of benzene and toluene in the air (Leong, Muttamara, and Laortanakul 2002).

Air quality is worst where transportation is congested and industries are located in close proximity to each other. Difficulty arises in comparing the air quality for the inner and outer zones due to lack of air monitoring equipment in those zones. Urban core air pollution is most likely worse than inner and outer zones because of the intense population density in the core. Any zone with increasing population has the potential to further degrade air quality due to the additional number of motor vehicle emissions. MURs with dense concentrations of industry operating in the core zone have greater degradation of air quality. The inner zone typically has the next highest concentration of industrial pollution as a result of the fastest rate of land conversion to new development of industrial complexes.

Land

Industrial pollution and municipal solid waste are the two common sources of land pollution. Industrial discharges and illegal dumping occur in all zones of all four MURs, contributing to a large proportion of toxic land and water pollution. Industrial wastes are hypothesised to be worst in the core and inner zones where industries are typically located. Municipal solid waste pollution is highest in the core where municipal governments are often overwhelmed with problems of collection and proper disposal (Douglass and Ooi 2000). Land pollution also occurs increasingly from chemically intensive farming in inner and outer zones of MURs.

Land subsidence is problematic in some areas in the north of Jakarta (34 cm/year), Pathumthani in Bangkok (15 cm/year), and Manila (0.65 cm/year). Unsustainable yields of groundwater extraction and the sheer pressure exerted by the weight of the city on the water table further aggravates problems of flooding.

Land conversion in the core occurs mostly as the commercial and government sectors develop derelict parcels of land or attempt to develop areas of established public and open space. In the inner and outer zones of the growing MURs this threatens the natural vitality of an area as habitats and ecosystems are diminished. Suburban sprawl often transforms agricultural land and results in numerous instances of degradation and damage, which in turn further exacerbate the extent of damage the MURs sustain in the event of natural disasters. Land conversion often results in soil erosion and sedimentation in upland inner and outer zones, with deforestation and subsidence in urban core and inner zones.

Solid Waste

Solid waste in the form of uncollected garbage piled up on the streets, burned, or thrown into water bodies is often the most visible environmental problem in MURs. Solid waste generation in the four MURs has increased significantly over the past five years with the core zones generating a tremendous amount. In 1995, Bangkok generated more solid waste than was recorded for both Jakarta and Manila combined (Figure 10.4) (UMP 1999). Although the rate of collection in Bangkok is higher (75 per cent) compared to Jakarta and Manila (both 70 per cent), its recorded total uncollected waste is also the highest among the MURs. The increase in services has not been able to keep pace with the increase in waste. Although up to 75 per cent of municipal wastes are recyclable, only approximately 10 per cent are recycled, mostly by the private sector (WB 2003a).

Due to the limited space and high price of land in the urban core, landfills are typically placed in the inner or outer zone. This leaves rural residents to bear the burden of problems associated with trash originating from the core.

Figure 10.4   Solid Waste Management in 1995

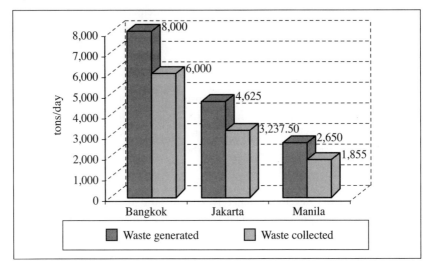

Source: UMP, 1999.

Inadequate collection and unmanaged solid and hazardous waste disposal presents a number of problems for human health and productivity. It is a major contributor to water-borne diseases, respiratory ailments, and flooding.

Slums

The existence of slums in cities not only attests to the level of economic disparity in urban areas, but also serves as a profound statement about the inability of government or the private housing market to provide for the needs of large numbers of MUR inhabitants. Attempts at slum evacuation and resettlement by municipal governments, no matter how well intended, are not adequate solutions to the construction of spontaneous housing in urban core areas where the number of slum dwellers is increasing as a result of migration of low-income workers and households (Coit 1998). As shown in Table 10.2, slum populations are substantial in each MUR. They number from over one to 2.5 million in Bangkok, Jakarta and Metro Manila. Although the numbers in HCMC are substantially lower, these are likely to be significantly underestimated due to exclusion from surveys of unauthorised migrants to the city, which may be as many as two to three million people (Chapter 7).

These urban poor are the most vulnerable to the impacts of environmental degradation. Slum dwellers are exposed to areas of high air and water pollution as well as various problems stemming from improper solid and hazardous waste management. Since most are productive members of the urban labour force, slum conditions also limit their ability to make even higher contributions to the urban economy and society. Rather than being a source of environmental degradation, lower income households are more accurately described as its victims.

While the core has the most degraded urban environment, the inner zone is experiencing rapid transformations that are also leading to undesirable environmental conditions. Outer zone residents enjoy relatively good environmental well-being, but the trend of sporadic low density development and loss of forests and natural ground cover in the outer zone threatens the livability of these areas as well. Chemical based farming and intensive animal husbandry are also increasing threats to land and water in peri-urban areas.

Table 10.2   Estimated Slum Dwellers in the MURs

City	Year	Estimated Slum Dwellers
Bangkok (a)	1990	1,260,000
HCMC (b)	1997	300,000
Jakarta (c)	2003	2,000,000
Manila (d)	2003	2,500,000

Sources: (a) <http:///www.achar.net/th_overview.htm>;
         (b) Bolay *et al.* 1997;
         (c) McCarthy 2003;
         (d) Ragragio 2003.

The data in Figure 10.5 can serve as an indicator for areas of the MURs that need improvement towards a more livable environment.

Overall, environmental well-being in the MURs is less than ideal for the basic requirements of a livable city. Residents suffer from pollution on all fronts: water, air, and land. Inadequate collection and disposal of municipal solid waste blemish city aesthetics, serve as vectors for disease and sickness, and worsen flooding problems. The persistence of poverty compounds these problems through lack of basic services and other entitlements of personal well-being. Water service coverage is also an area of immediate concern, and the increased exposure to different forms of air pollution greatly reduce the livability

Figure 10.5   Environmental Well-being Comparison of the Four Cities

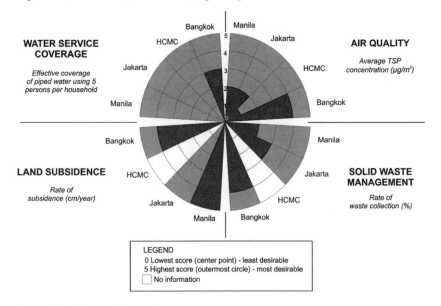

Source: Douglass and Le *et al.*, 2003.

of an urban region as incidences of environment-related illnesses amplify.

In terms of environmental well-being, Bangkok was found to be the most livable during the time period under study. Great strides to improve air quality and relatively higher effective coverage of potable water separate Bangkok from the other cities. Although Bangkok excelled in these components, much work is still needed to improve the lives of slums dwellers and solve municipal solid waste collection and disposal problems. The HCMC, Jakarta, and Manila MURs have chronic deficits that are deepening the human consequences of unhealthy and socially uneven quality of environment.

MUR Governance and Livability

Defined as the "sum of ways through which individuals and institutions (public and private) plan and manage their common affairs" (UNDP 2001: 90), governance is a process that reveals both the politics of and opportunities for enhancing MUR livability. Throughout Asia, pressures for political reform toward good governance are widespread. Common directions being pursued to affect good governance are twofold: (1) devolution of state power to enhance local autonomy and governance capacities, and (2) greater accountability of government through political reform. Attending these major drives are efforts for greater transparency, elimination of corruption, and more participatory processes of policymaking and planning (WB, ADB, and UNDP 2000).

Local Autonomy

To clarify the first direction, devolution of state power can be contrasted with deconcentration of state administration. Whereas deconcentration is functionally specific and shifts administrative duties but not policymaking authority to lower levels of government, devolution indicates an authentic shift of the locus of policy decision-making as well as administrative authority from the centre to local level. Good governance, while potentially benefiting from some forms of deconcentration, is ultimately contingent upon devolution of authority. Only when the authority of the state is nearby can citizens effectively participate in governance processes.

Until very recently, the record in most of Southeast Asia showed that decentralisation policies were principally forms of deconcentration rather than devolution. Central governments and their ministries continued to hold decision-making power and the purse strings while passing administrative duties to local levels. Fiscal decentralisation programmes have received substantial support from international development agencies (Wiest 2002), but these were modest in the 1990s and were often undertaken without devolution of decision-making powers. Table 10.3 shows that for the three countries for which there are data, the levels of national income spent by local governments were quite low at ten per cent or less compared to more than 30 per cent for Japan, North America, and Europe. Such data underscore the reality that in practice, the governments of the MURs are all very limited in capacity to accommodate the hyper-growth they have experienced over the past decade. Yet variations among MURs are significant, and recent initiatives in some countries have opened a new era of devolution of government power to cities and other local levels of governance.

Indonesia

Until 1998, Indonesia was among the most highly centralised governments in Asia. Following the overthrow of the Suharto regime that had held power for

more than three decades, the new government of Indonesia adopted a policy
of regional autonomy in May 1999. Its implementation began in 2001 with
full efforts to accelerate devolution of political authority to local levels. The
steps taken include the principle that all functions not specifically assigned
to the centre automatically belong to the locality. Central ministries are no
longer allowed to maintain independent offices in the provinces, cities, or
districts for purposes of executing central level programmes. Urban and rural
district heads are now fully autonomous. They function solely as the head of
the autonomous local government and are directly and solely responsible to
the local parliament (Buentjen 2000).

The reforms are not without their problems. A lack of transparency
continues, and corruption has in some areas shifted downward along with the

**Table 10.3   Sub-national Share of Public Expenditure and Revenues in Selected
Countries, 1990s**

Country	Year	Sub-national Share of Expenditures	Sub-national Share of Revenues	Sub-national Expenditures as Share of GDP	Sub-national Revenues as Share of GDP
Indonesia	1998	10.1	3.1	2.0	0.5
Philippines	1992	8.7	4.7	1.9	0.9
Thailand	1998	8.4	8.0	2.1	1.4

Source: Wescott and Porter, 2002.

localisation of revenue generating taxes and fees. Local capacities remain weak.
Expenditure responsibilities are vaguely defined. Regional disparities can be
expected to increase if the rich natural resource regions of the outer islands
retain revenues from their exports. Yet one year into the implementation
of the policy, the reforms continue to go forward despite constant political
turmoil (Aspinall and Fealy 2003).

Philippines

Following the adoption of a far-reaching devolution programme in the early
1990s, the Philippines has one of the most decentralised governance structures
in Asia. Between 1991 and 1994, 61 per cent of the field personnel of
concerned agencies were devolved to local governments. Regular elections
were required for local officials and legislatures. A Devolution Master Plan

(1993–98) was formulated to further implement the process. Adopting the principle of subsidiarity, which states that all powers not expressly given to a higher level of government remain with the lower level, the programme has led to more integrated and cost effective service delivery, and better focus on local priorities. Local governments have become more interested in providing investment and maintenance support for projects they themselves have formulated and implemented (Blair 2000).

As elsewhere, even with the reforms, corruption remains a public issue and a great diversity exists in the quality of leadership in local governments. Many local governments continue to severely lack the financial and human resources needed to provide services to their residents, especially the poor (ADB and EDI 1991; USAID 2004). Yet some have succeeded in developing and using the processes of participatory governance and have fared well.

Thailand

Thailand continues to have among the most highly centralised governments with limited local autonomy in terms of functions, area, staffing, funding, and decision-making. The central government spends 93 per cent of total general expenditures and collects 95 per cent of general tax revenues. About 25 per cent of municipal revenues are locally collected and retained (Wiest 2002). The central government appoints local officials, determines local salaries, and approves local budgets. Most local governments in Thailand have weak financial management, planning and service delivery, and deficient public infrastructure. These local governments generally lack adequate resources — in terms of limited revenue sources, poor mobilisation of existing revenues, and a reluctance to borrow — to deliver services effectively or to undertake needed capital projects. Local staff often lack technical capabilities or are reluctant to use all of the powers allocated to them. Lack of clarity in the assignment of expenditure responsibility further diminishes the effectiveness of service delivery. Although a National Decentralisation Act was promulgated in 1999, implementation of the Act shows continued control over budgets and decisions by central government (Blair 2000).

Vietnam

Doi Moi reform since the late 1980s has involved greater local autonomy as a matter of improving efficiency in service delivery. This has involved transferring certain ministerial units to the relevant public enterprises or local authorities. Two kinds of organisations exist in the structure of the local authorities: the People's Council and the People's Committee. The People's Council is downwardly accountable through local elections, and although without legislative authority, it is the main state power body in the locality. It acts as the official channel to disseminate policy instructions and provide legal understanding to the masses. The People's Committee functions as the executive body of the People's Council and is the administrative body in the locality, representing the superior administrative level. Upwardly accountable, its primary responsibility is organising the local people for the implementation of centrally mandated socio-economic development policies (Nguyen 1998).

Participatory Governance

Good governance gives political voice to all individuals and groups in society (UN 1999; UNCHS 2000; WB 2000). Devolution of government authority and fiscal autonomy to local governments creates the potential for active participation of urban residents in the public sphere through mechanisms for accountability, which is realised through an electoral process, transparency in the flow of information, and enforcement of the rule of law (Witoelar 2001; WB *et al.* 2000).

Figure 10.6 presents an index of voice and accountability of government that is composed of a variety of indicators including orderly change in government, free and fair elections, and representative legislature and political parties. Up to the late 1990s, the Philippines and Thailand were the only two of the four MUR countries to have positive scores (Gonzalez and Mendoza 2002).

Table 10.4 shows a similar set of scores for the four countries. It mirrors Figure 10.6 with the exception of Indonesia, which, following deep reforms noted above, has moved it into higher scores of democratic governance (Box 10.4). Vietnam, while scoring low, nonetheless has elected local administrative bodies, and electoral laws at local levels have been revised to expand the rule of law (Pham and Pham 2004). In recent years, the country has also witnessed increasing participation by the people in a public forum. A draft of the Ninth Party Congress's Political Platform was widely circulated down to the grassroots level for comments before being presented to the Party Central Committee members to debate and ratify.

A key dimension of democratic governance is transparency, which refers to public access to information about government and its inner-workings (UN 1999). Transparency is paralleled by freedom of speech and the press.

Figure 10.6   Index of "Voice" in Selection and Accountability of Government, 1997–98 (Higher index = more voice)

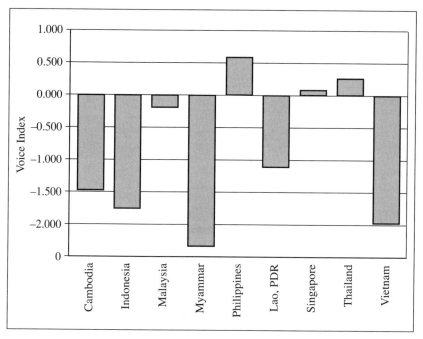

Source: Gonzalez and Mendoza, 2002.

Thailand and the Philippines have long established traditions of free press. In the case of Indonesia, post-Suharto reforms have been dramatic, with citizens enjoying greater access to information, which was exceptionally limited during most of the 1990s.

In Vietnam the media's explicit role is as the voice of the party and the masses (Thayer 1996). Although the traditional function of reporting and analysing the news exists, the Vietnamese press is primarily a medium for educating the public and filtering information, as opposed to presenting unbiased news accounts. However, the press has also more recently begun to facilitate governmental transparency through broadcasting sessions of the National Assembly, and increasing numbers of op-ed articles voicing public opinions. Such journalistic freedom has invariably spurred the desire for better investigative reporting and more journalistic freedom to report accurately. It has allowed for the dissemination of selective public documents and official information not previously published, such as reports on riots issued through

Table 10.4   Indicators of Democratic Institutions

Indicator	Thailand	Philippines	Indonesia	Vietnam
Civil and political liberties*	4.5 (47/141)	4.5 (51/141)	3.5 (73/141)	0.5 (128/141)
Democratic institution rating**	9.0 (31/141)	7.0 (50/141)	7.0 (53/141)	–7.0 (128/141)

Notes: * Units: Index ranging from 7 (high level of liberties) to 1 (low). This is the
average of both civil liberties and political liberties).
** Scale ranging from –10 (Autocratic) to +10 (Democratic).
Source: Southeast Asia, 2004.

the state controlled mass media. However, the government of Vietnam also maintains that some national economic data such as the rate of inflation can be kept as a state secret (See 2001).

Lack of transparency can also lead to political discontent. A major reason for local residents' budget dissatisfaction in Jakarta is found to be the lack of transparency (Brodjonegoro 2003). Despite the passage of the Official Information Act in Thailand in 1997, similar concerns are voiced in Bangkok (Bolongaita 2003). Corruption is another dimension of a lack of transparency. Besides the obvious implications of governance failure, corruption can undermine citizen participation by creating the perception of futility. Using a corruption perception index (CPI), the four countries under study are

Box 10.4   Direct Elections System in Indonesia

Following the fall of Suharto in 1998, Indonesians now enjoy extensive political freedoms such as the freedom to organize, form political parties, and enjoy freedom of the press. The extremely centralized authoritarian state has given way to a highly decentralized form of government. While retaining a political presence, the military no longer overshadows all other political groups. Political reformers have called for a thorough overhaul of the constitution and the electoral system to ensure that leaders are responsive and accountable to the voters. New laws have also been adopted to regulate elections to the legislature at the national and regional levels. Regional autonomy laws have vastly expanded the powers of provincial and district governments. The most important reform has been the adoption of direct presidential elections in 2004 in place of the indirect system that was mired in the backroom dealing of political parties and "money politics". The government plans to introduce direct elections of governors and district heads along the same lines as direct election of the president (ICG 2003).

perceived to be among the most corrupt of the 133 countries assessed (Table 10.5). The corruption score for Indonesia has not changed since 1995 (CPI score 1.9) although significant corruption reform is expected to decrease the score significantly in the coming years (Transparency International 2004). Since the CPI deals with perceptions of corruption rather than actual measurement, caution should be used in interpretation of the data.

Governance is a vital though problematic process in advancing efforts for livable cities. The evidence from the 1990s shows severe limitations in governance capacities and structures in the countries of the four MURs. Most urban governments had highly circumscribed decision-making powers, inadequate revenue generating possibilities, and lacked sufficiently skilled manpower to keep pace with the expansion of MURs (Alm and Bahl 1999; Laquian 1995). Such deficiencies partly explain why certain problems of livability worsened during the decade, especially in the areas of environmental management and provision of public spaces. Yet by the late 1990s, reform in governance was underway in varying degrees in each of the countries. Furthermore, MURs — especially those that are capital cities — generally enjoy much greater status and financial attention than all other local level political and administrative units. All of the four MURs studied here enjoy the equivalent of provincial or special capital region status. Although HCMC is the only MUR among the four that is not the capital city, its position as the economic engine of much of the nation also gives it a high profile in public funding. In this regard, the MURs are likely to benefit most from on-going devolution efforts. How this will bear fruit in improving cities in the future allows for more optimism than might have been the case even a decade ago.

Table 10.5   Corruption Perception Index, 2003

Country	Rank	CPI 2003 Score
Thailand	75	3.3
Philippines	97	2.5
Vietnam	105	2.4
Indonesia	122	1.9

Note: *CPI 2003 score relates to perceptions of the degree of corruption as seen by business people, academics, and risk analysts, and ranges between 10 (highly clean) and 0 (highly corrupt) in 133 countries. Source: Lambsdroff, 2004.

Conclusion

This comparative study of the four MURs of Bangkok, HCMC, Jakarta, and Manila focuses on three principal realms of livability: lifeworld, personal well-being, and environmental well-being. Where possible the analysis is further disaggregated into three concentric zones of each MUR: the urban core, inner zone, and outer zone.

In terms of lifeworld, which is the most under-researched of the three components of livability, a general decline is observed in needed public, green, and civic spaces due to growing commercialisation of land, resulting in a dampening affect on community life separate from state and economy. The trend has been part of a notable shift from public to private land uses and toward global commercial linkages over locally produced social and cultural uses of urban space. Growing economic polarisation leading to spatial separation along class lines and a further marginalisation of the poor has exacerbated this trend.

In terms of personal well-being, livability in the MURs is typically better than life in other cities of the nation. Levels of poverty are lower, and official statistics using cash equivalents of basic food (and sometimes other requirements) show them to be declining since the spike in poverty increases following the globally linked finance crisis of 1997–98. Healthcare and education facilities are more prevalent, providing greater access for those who can afford their services; and longitudinal data for education, infant mortality, and longevity show strong general improvement.

Significant areas of concern continue, however, with most related to widening economic disparities. School drop-out rates, for example, have increased in every MUR as poorer households require their children to stay out of school to help meet subsistence needs; child labour and exploitation is generally increasing; many poor households cannot afford healthcare; and poverty coincides spatially with deteriorated environmental settlements and a chronic inadequacy of environmental services.

In terms of environmental well-being, all of the MURs exhibit poor environmental quality, especially to the extent that the degradation of MUR environments appears to be surpassing government capacity to keep pace through the provision of environmental infrastructure and services. Inequalities in access to non-polluted environments are readily observable in the contrasts between slums and new housing for the more affluent. Negative health effects are compounded in lower income communities by high population density and a general neglect of environmental infrastructure and services as well as open space and disease transmission is highest among the poor. Air and water pollution remain the greatest threats to livability in the core of the MURs.

A zonal analysis of the four MURs reveals that the urban core has a pronounced richness of lifeworlds (e.g., more cultural amenities and civic engagement) and is strongest for personal well-being (e.g., lower poverty rates, higher quality health services, and increased educational facilities). However, environmental well-being is the worst as the urban core contains the most degraded environment and highest concentration of slums. As for the inner zone, it suffers the greatest difficulties for lifeworlds as suburban housing and certain policies direct land use decisions toward the construction of fragmented and enclosed neighbourhoods and shopping malls. Environmental services are also limited because of the inadequate public budgetary allocations for them. On the other hand, in terms of personal well-being, the MURs are experiencing the most exciting transformations for residents as health and educational facilities are increasingly being built in the inner zone. In the outer zone, lifeworld spaces are still mostly traditional and can be expected to rapidly transform as the MURs expand. Similarly, the outer zone offers the lowest levels of public or private investment in services to enhance personal well-being; however, the levels are still higher in this zone than for the nation as a whole. As for environmental well-being in this zone, environmental services are lowest and serious threats of deforestation and industrial pollution are a growing problem.

The MURs examined collectively show a common degree of stress on their residents' livability in the components of lifeworlds, personal well-being and environmental well-being. The intention of this chapter is to shed light on the MUR as a place for human habitation in the context of societies that have experienced rapid economic growth and success. Without diminishing the contributions that rapid economic expansion has brought to the MURs in terms of material improvements and general areas of personal attainment, this study finds that the stresses on environment — including impacts on personal health — and lifeworlds for convivial urban living have become critical. By highlighting problems of environmental well-being, personal well-being, and lifeworlds, we hope to assist in focusing greater public policy attention on these issues, leading to concerted and successful efforts for improvement.

11

Mega-Urban Region Dynamics in Comparative Perspective

Mike Douglass and Gavin Jones

Chapter 3 compared the changes in basic demographic structure of the six MURs and their zones over the decade of the 1990s. All of these MURs continued to increase their share of the national population over this period, with migration contributing substantially to this trend. In the individual MUR chapters, migration patterns were dealt with in more detail, as were changes in employment structure and in education. The purpose of the discussion in this chapter is to draw from the commonalities and differences among the MURs, with a further purpose of sketching pathways into the future. The discussion begins by comparing and contrasting the population dynamics and trends with particular reference to migration to and among the zones of each MUR.

The Contribution of Migration to MUR Dynamics

Among the most momentous transformations continuing through the 1990s to the present is the transition toward urban societies. From levels as low as 15–20 per cent urban in the 1970s, Pacific Asia countries have already surpassed or are now rapidly nearing the 50 per cent mark. During the most rapid phases of this transition, rural-urban migration is the greatest contributor to urban population growth. Although the contribution of migration tends to diminish at higher levels of urbanisation, variations at each level are significant. Also, the zones in the MURs experience very different levels of migration at any one moment in time. Regardless of the levels of urbanisation, however, all the MURs continue to increase their shares of national population.

Because in-migration is counter-balanced to a greater or lesser degree by out-migration, the proportion of in-migrants in the current population can differ widely among cities even where the contribution of net migration in overall population growth is similar. Table 11.1 makes this clear. Although the contribution of net migration to the cores of Jakarta and Taipei was actually negative (see Chapter 3), the proportion of migrants in their populations in 2000 was higher than in Manila where net migration actually made some contribution to population growth. In other words, flows of people into and out of MUR zones can remain quite high even where net migration is low or even negative in some of them.

Table 11.1 Recent Migrants* as a Percentage of Total Population by Zone, 1990 and 2000

	Jakarta	Bangkok	Manila	HCMC	Shanghai	Taipei
1990						
Core	7.4	11.4	7.1	n.a.	7.2	10.4
Inner zone	4.3	15.6	9.5	n.a.	7.4	12.9
Outer zone	1.2	9.3	4.2	n.a.	3.4	7.0
MUR	5.2	11.8	7.0	n.a.	6.3	11.4
2000						
Core	8.4	7.8	4.4	5.8	39.6 (11.9)	6.4
Inner zone	16.1	16.9	7.5	4.4	31.8 (19.9)	8.6
Outer zone	7.1	15.4	6.5	4.8**	14.8 (8.4)	10.5
MUR	6.4	11.5	5.9	4.9	33.2 (12.8)	8.2

Notes: The definition of migration in Shanghai differs from that in other cities, and includes moves within zones, though in 1990 it also excludes some moves between the zones. Two sets of figures are given for 2000. The first figure includes all moves within zones; the figure in brackets includes only those who migrated from outside Shanghai. Compared with the figures for the other cities, the first figure overstates migration, whereas the figure in brackets understates it. For further detail on the Shanghai migration definitions, see Chapter 9.

For HCMC, intra-district migrants are not included in total migrants. Intra-HCMC and inter-provincial migrants are included.

* As measured by place of residence 5 years ago.

** Includes "rural".

For Taipei, migration flows among the zones cannot be identified properly, as place of residence five years ago is available only at city/prefecture level, not at town/city level, which is needed for properly identifying flows between the zones.

Source: Analysis of census data for the individual MUR studies.

As the migration data suggest, the share of migrants in the population of the cores tended to decrease between 1990 and 2000 (Table 11.1). Trends in the inner zone have varied, with Jakarta showing a great upsurge in the proportion of migrants, but Manila and Taipei showing a decline. The share of migrants in the outer zones has increased over the period in all cases where the data are available.

Although the numbers of recent migrants as a proportion of the total population may not seem to be particularly high from the data in Table 11.1, those interpreting the data need to bear in mind that these are migrants who had come during the previous five years. If the definition of migrants is broadened to include those who had moved in over the previous 20 years, in most cases the proportion of migrants in the population would probably rise to 20 to 40 per cent of the city population. Their contribution to population growth is much greater still, because they build up the population base to which children are born, and this increases the number of local-born.

The sources of migrants to the core and the inner zone varied widely. The core of these cities has continued to attract migrants from all parts of the country, and the contribution of migrants from other parts of the MUR was quite small, except in the case of Taipei (Table 11.2). By contrast, for all of the MURs except Shanghai and HCMC a considerable part of the migration gain to the inner zone consisted of people moving out from the core —

Table 11.2   Recent Migrants to the Core by Source Area, 1990 and 2000 (%)

	Jakarta	Bangkok	Manila	HCMC	Taipei
1990					
Inner zone	10.1	12.5	9.1	n.a.	42.6
Outer zone	3.1	*	5.6	n.a.	*
Rest of country	86.8	87.5	85.3	n.a.	57.4+
Total	**100**	**100**	**100**		**100**
2000					
Inner zone	10.5	15.9	12.3	9.5	54.2
Outer zone	1.9	*	6.9	14.2	*
Rest of country	87.6	84.1	80.8	76.3	45.8+
Total	**100**	**100**	**100**	**100**	**100**

Notes: * Included in inner zone figure.
    + Includes 6.5% from foreign countries in 1990, 11.5% in 2000.
Source: Analysis of census data for the individual MUR studies.

Table 11.3   Recent Migrants to the Inner Zone by Source Area, 1990 and 2000 (%)

	Jakarta	Bangkok	Manila	HCMC	Taipei
1990					
Core	53.0	28.4	54.7		32.4
Outer zone	18.0	14.6	6.8		13.7
Rest of country	29.1	57.0	38.5		53.9+
Total	**100**	**100**	**100**		**100**
2000					
Core	34.1	28.4	55.7	17.3	26.7
Outer zone	24.4	12.4	7.7	11.6	30.7
Rest of country	41.5	59.2	36.6	71.1	42.6+
Total	**100**	**100**	**100**	**100**	**100**

Note: + Includes 3.4% from foreign countries in 1990, 6.4% in 2000.
Source: Analysis of census data for the individual MUR studies.

27 per cent in Taipei, 28 per cent in Bangkok, 34 per cent in Jakarta and 56 per cent in Manila (Table 11.3). But in addition, many people moving to the MUR from other parts of the country chose to live in the inner zone rather than the core, presumably mainly because of the availability of more affordable housing, less crowded conditions, and in some cases because the workplace was also located in the inner zone.

The more restricted movement from the core to the inner zone in the cases of Shanghai and HCMC suggest that the different economic systems, the restrictions on migration — particularly those applying until fairly recently — and their delayed start in experiencing rapid urban growth, means that there is not yet so much systematic development of inner zone housing estates that serve to attract the new urban middle class to move from the core to the inner zone as they do in the other cities. Ho Chi Minh City is in a similar situation, though upscale housing estates and the huge new town of South Saigon are appearing just at the interface between the core and inner zones.

Overall, roughly half of the recent migrants to the MUR from other parts of the country went to the core, and the other half went to the other zones, with most going to the inner zone. In the case of Manila, the distribution in 2000 was 55 per cent to the core, 27 per cent to the inner zone and 18 per cent to the outer zone. In Jakarta, the distribution was 45 per cent to the core, 46 per cent to the inner zone, and 9 per cent to the outer zone.

For Bangkok, the core received 47 per cent, the inner zone 29 per cent and the outer zone 24 per cent.

There was, then, a great deal of population redistribution going on both to and within the MURs. Migrants from other parts of the country were attracted to the metropolitan areas and their hinterlands, moving mainly to the core and the inner zone. These were mostly young migrants in the 15–34 year age range. But as well as receiving large numbers of such migrants, the cores, in many cases, were at the same time suffering a loss of an equally large number of people to the inner and outer zones. These were different kinds of migrants, more of them families and more widely spread over the age ranges.

Characteristics of Migrants and Non-migrants

From the characteristics of migrants — their age and sex, education and employment patterns — it is possible to infer something about their contribution to the city to which they have moved.

As is normally the case with migration to large cities, young people aged 15–34 are over-represented in the move. The pattern is clearly evident in the data for Shanghai (Chapter 9). In Shanghai's core, net migration rates peaked at ages 20–24. In the inner zone, the peak was broader across the age range 15–34. In the outer zone, by contrast, there was net outmigration for males at ages 15–24, and only a modest net inmigration at ages 25–34. However, turning attention from net migration to the proportion of population in different age groups who are migrants, this was much higher in age group 15–24 in Shanghai than in any other age group (Table 11.4).

In the other cities, too, the migrant proportion of the population in the core typically peaked at ages 15–24 and more broadly at 15–34, whereas in the zones the peak migration age range was typically wider — 15–34, and in many cases (for example, in Manila and Jakarta), not very much lower at ages 35–44 (see Table 11.4). In Manila MUR, patterns of female and male migration were different, with female migrants more heavily clustered in the 15–24 age group than were males. The high rates of migration in the young ages also mean that a very large share of all migrants is in these ages. For example, in Jakarta's core in 2000, 48 per cent of all migrants (and 56 per cent of female migrants) were aged 15–24.

Were the migration streams to the MURs balanced in terms of gender? This differed among the six cities (Table 11.5). In general, females predominated in the migration streams to all the MURs except Shanghai, and this female predominance was most marked in migration to the core. Manila showed

Table 11.4 Migrants as Percentage of Population by Age Group

Age Group	Jakarta	Bangkok	Manila	HCMC	Shanghai
CORE 1990					
5–14	4.6	7.3	4.2	n.a.	4.4
15–24	21.4	24.5	11.7	n.a.	28.8
25–34	12.1	12.3	8.6	n.a.	6.5
35–44	6.0	6.3	5.0	n.a.	6.2
45+	4.4	3.8	3.7	n.a.	3.2
CORE 2000					
5–14	4.1	4.5	2.3	10.6	35.9
15–24	16.8	14.7	8.0	27.5	54.7
25–34	10.8	11.2	5.4	18.7	55.7
35–44	5.2	6.3	3.1	12.2	35.8
45+	3.2	3.2	2.2	9.1	29.6
INNER ZONE 1990					
5–14	10.1	11.9	7.9	n.a.	2.6
15–24	17.8	25.6	11.2	n.a.	20.7
25–34	19.2	20.5	12.9	n.a.	8.1
35–44	13.5	12.7	9.1	n.a.	5.8
45+	8.0	7.9	5.9	n.a.	4.1
INNER ZONE 2000					
5–14	14.1	11.8	5.6	10.9	27.1
15–24	27.5	24.8	9.0	29.1	55.1
25–34	22.0	24.8	10.3	21.3	46.2
35–44	16.7	15.5	7.8	14.7	23.6
45+	13.2	9.3	5.2	10.5	13.7
OUTER ZONE 1990					
5–14	1.4	6.3	3.5	n.a.	1.8
15–24	5.5	17.6	5.1	n.a.	7.8
25–34	3.0	13.7	6.5	n.a.	4.4
35–44	1.7	7.4	4.1	n.a.	3.0
45+	1.1	3.5	2.1	n.a.	1.9
OUTER ZONE 2000					
5–14	6.2	10.2	5.4	8.4	12.9
15–24	10.4	23.4	7.0	18.5	36.9
25–34	10.1	24.2	9.0	17.1	26.9
35–44	7.5	15.2	7.4	12.8	10.1
45+	6.1	7.9	4.3	8.9	4.4

(Continued overleaf)

Table 11.4 (*Continued*)

Age Group	Jakarta	Bangkok	Manila	HCMC	Shanghai
TOTAL MUR 1990					
5–14	5.8	8.0	5.0	n.a.	3.4
15–24	17.7	23.5	10.0	n.a.	21.2
25–34	12.8	14.0	9.2	n.a.	6.3
35–44	7.6	7.7	5.9	n.a.	5.4
45+	4.8	4.5	4.0	n.a.	3.1
TOTAL MUR 2000					
5–14	9.2	7.5	4.2	10.4	29.0
15–24	17.9	18.7	8.0	26.9	52.1
25–34	15.6	17.2	7.6	19.0	47.5
35–44	10.6	10.2	5.5	12.6	28.7
45+	7.9	5.4	3.8	9.3	21.8

Note: On Shanghai, see note to Table 11.1. Unfortunately, data are not available by age for those who migrated from outside Shanghai.
Source: Analysis of census data for the individual MUR studies.

the strongest female predominance in migration to all zones, but especially to the core. The proportion of females among migrants was particularly high for those originating outside the MUR. This reflects the larger role of family migration in movement within the MUR, especially out from the core to the zones. It might also reflect the tendency toward both labour-intensive export-processing industries and low-wage urban services such as domestic helpers being dominated by women. In Jakarta, too, females were strongly predominant in migration to the core, and to a lesser extent, this was the case in Bangkok and HCMC. Sex ratios were fairly balanced among migrants to their inner and outer zones. Shanghai showed a completely different pattern to the other MURs, with males heavily predominant as migrants in all zones in 1990, but this male predominance had almost totally disappeared by 2000. This perhaps reflects the effect of policy changes in China in freeing up patterns of female migration, though changes in definitions of migrants between the two censuses may also have played a part.

The question of whether the migration streams were balanced by gender, though, needs to be examined in more detail, specifically for particular age groups. This is done in Table 11.6. Clearly, sex ratios among migrants differ widely between the different age groups. In all cities except Shanghai, there is a preponderance of females among young migrants (aged 15–24), especially in

Table 11.5   Sex Ratios of Migrants and Non-migrants in Each Zone, 1990 and 2000

	Jakarta	Bangkok	Manila	HCMC	Shanghai
TOTAL MUR 1990					
Migrants	88	91	81		191
Migrants from outside MUR	101	90	71		
Non-migrants	102	94	98		100
TOTAL MUR 2000					
Migrants	98	96	86	93	107
Migrants from outside MUR	93	95	72	91	
Non-migrants	103	91	98	92	101
CORE 1990					
Migrants	80	88	72		200
Migrants from outside MUR	100	87	64		
Non-migrants	103	93	92		102
CORE 2000					
Migrants	86	92	78	91	106
Migrants from outside MUR	84	91	69	91	
Non-migrants	104	89	96	90	103
INNER ZONE 1990					
Migrants	101	95	91		192
Migrants from outside MUR	100	96	75		
Non-migrants	100	95	96		96
INNER ZONE 2000					
Migrants	103	96	91	99	112
Migrants from outside MUR	101	97	69	94	
Non-migrants	102	94	96	94	101
OUTER ZONE 1990					
Migrants	83	97	91		149
Migrants from outside MUR	102	92	85		
Non-migrants	103	95	100		97
OUTER ZONE 2000					
Migrants	103	102	94	100	99
Migrants from outside MUR	100	101	82	89	
Non-migrants	104	93	100	96	97

Note: For Shanghai, see note to Table 11.1.

Source: Analysis of census data for the individual MUR studies.

Table 11.6   Sex Ratios of Migrants in Particular Age Groups by Zone, 1990 and 2000

MUR	1990			2000		
	Core	Inner zone	Outer zone	Core	Inner zone	Outer zone
Jakarta						
15–24	65	80	47	62	86	80
25–34	116	108	144	123	108	110
35–44	116	143	215	133	134	132
45+	92	112	131	122	123	127
Bangkok						
15–24	78	82	80	84	83	96
25–34	105	106	110	95	100	103
35–44	110	117	130	104	110	117
45+	87	96	105	97	95	96
Manila						
15–24	54	68	70	60	63	78
25–34	84	91	98	91	93	94
35–44	106	114	129	98	114	118
45+	80	91	90	93	93	91
HCMC						
15–24				94	95	98
25–34				94	103	108
35–44				91	97	91
45+				70	72	74
Shanghai						
15–24	209	158	111	102	85	69
25–34	234	219	168	111	120	104
35–44	205	213	175	115	155	138
45+	186	334	273	100	126	135

Note: sex ratio=males per 100 females.
    For Shanghai, see note to Table 11.1.
Source: Analysis of census data for the individual MUR studies.

the core. Manila is a particularly striking case. Among young migrants (aged 15–24) in 1990 there were two females for every male among recent migrants to the core, and the proportion of females, though lower, remained quite high among migrants in the inner and outer zones. By contrast, among migrants aged 25–34, the female dominance was not as great, and among migrants aged 35–44, males predominated. In 2000, these figures had changed slightly, but the general pattern of female dominance of the flow of young migrants, but a male majority at ages 35–44, remained.

Bangkok's patterns of sex ratios by age resembled those of Manila, though in a less extreme form. As in Manila, at ages 15–24, the female predominance was quite marked, except in the outer zone in 2000. The slight male predominance at ages 35–44 characterised all zones in both years. Jakarta also resembled Manila, with a very strong preponderance of females among migrants aged 15–24, but it differed from Manila and Bangkok in having a stronger predominance of males among migrants aged 25–34. HCMC, in contrast, had fairly balanced sex ratios, though with a slight female predominance at ages 15–24, but with a strong male predominance at ages 45+. In Shanghai, the picture was totally different, but this may have resulted from the different procedures in measuring migration. The female predominance in migration at ages 15–24 in the inner and especially outer zones in 2000 could reflect marriage migration within the zone, or the opportunities for factory or other work for females, or some combination of these or other factors.

Educational Changes in the Zones

Given that the MURs had become the economic powerhouses of their respective countries, the quality of their human resources needed to be maintained and increased. In 1990, there was a gradation in educational attainment of the population between the core and the zones in all of these MURs (very sharp in the cases of Jakarta and Shanghai), with the outer zone in particular displaying its much more rural characteristics through its lower levels of educational attainment (see Table 11.7). However, the population of the MURs was becoming increasingly well educated over the 1990s. The main reason for this was that the increase in enrolment ratios at all levels of education was continuing over the decade in all these countries, with the result that the educational level of the adult population — both MUR residents and migrants — was gradually increasing. Theoretically, another reason might have been that the educational level of migrants from outside the MURs was higher

Table 11.7 Educational Attainment, Population Aged 15+, 1990 and 2000

(1) Proportion completed lower secondary school and above

City	Core	Inner Zone	Outer Zone	MUR
JAKARTA				
1990	55.8	36.4	12.4	42.1
2000	71.9	58.9	26.7	59.7
BANGKOK				
1990	45.4	32.8	22.5	38.9
2000	55.6	48.9	38.6	50.6
MANILA				
1990	80.3	64.4	53.6	69.7
2000	84.0	74.9	65.7	76.8
HCMC				
2000	45.3	35.1	25.2	41.8
SHANGHAI				
1990	95.3	87.6	86.4	92.0
2000	94.7	87.1	86.3	91.6
TAIPEI				
1990	n.a.	n.a.	n.a.	n.a.
2000	n.a.	n.a.	n.a.	n.a.

(2) Proportion with tertiary education

City	Core	Inner Zone	Outer Zone	MUR
JAKARTA				
1990	6.3	3.5	0.3	4.3
2000	11.0	8.1	1.8	8.4
BANGKOK				
1990	13.0	6.3	4.1	10.2
2000	20.9	12.6	8.7	16.2
MANILA				
1990	35.6	23.2	17.8	28.1
2000	33.1	26.1	20.1	27.8

Table 11.7 (*Continued*)

(2) Proportion with tertiary education

City	Core	Inner zone	Outer zone	MUR
HCMC				
2000	17.4	11.8	8.2	15.7
SHANGHAI				
1990	11.6	3.3	1.8	8.0
2000	17.8	6.9	3.4	12.9
TAIPEI				
1990	31.5	16.2	10.3	21.4
2000	42.0	27.4	19.7	31.1

Note: The Philippines uses only one level for secondary education – so in section 1, the computation is for population with secondary education or higher. For tertiary education, includes both incomplete and completed tertiary education.

For Shanghai, the proportion with lower secondary education or higher includes those with incomplete lower secondary education, and for tertiary education, includes those with incomplete tertiary education.

Source: Analysis of census data for the individual MUR studies.

than that of the resident population in the same age groups, but this does not appear to have been the case, at least in Bangkok and Manila.

In relation to expansion of educational opportunities in the country, Thailand made particularly impressive strides in raising school enrolment ratios at the lower secondary level through the 1990s, and Indonesia made some progress as well (Jones 2003). These two countries also made progress in expanding enrolments at the upper secondary and tertiary levels. The Bangkok and Jakarta mega-urban regions, which were already ahead of the rest of their respective countries in educational levels, benefited from this expansion. The Philippines already had higher levels of education than the other countries in 1990, but made little improvement over the following decade (Herrin and Pernia 2003: 288–9). It is notable that in 1990, the proportion with tertiary education in all the zones of Manila MUR exceeded that in Taipei, but by 2000, Taipei had moved well ahead of Manila. Shanghai ranked high in proportion completed lower secondary school and above, but not so high in proportion with tertiary education.

As far as the impact of migration in raising or lowering educational levels is concerned, this tended to differ by zones. In Jakarta, young migrants

Table 11.8 Educational Attainment of Migrants from Outside the MUR Compared with MUR Resident Population, 2000 (%)

Educational Level	Jakarta		Bangkok		Manila	
	Migrants	Residents	Migrants	Residents	Migrants	Residents
ALL AGES 15+						
None or primary	39.4	52.3	46.8	49.5	21	23
Lower secondary	22.1	16.5	18.1	14.9	50*	42*
Upper secondary	31.1	24.5	26.7	20.5		
Tertiary	7.4	6.7	8.3	15.1	29	35
All levels	**100**	**100**	**100**	**100**	**100**	**100**
AGED 15–34						
None or primary	29.2	31.8	35.8	24.7	17	15
Lower secondary	26.7	24.8	22.6	23.4	53*	48*
Upper secondary	37.0	35.7	33.6	33.6		
Tertiary	7.1	7.7	8.0	18.3	30	37
All levels	**100**	**100**	**100**	**100**	**100**	

	HCMC		Shanghai	
ALL AGES 15+				
None or primary	42.0	56.5	28.2	30.0
Lower secondary	22.9	21.4	49.0	37.2
Upper secondary	19.6	15.2	12.5	24.0
Tertiary	15.5	6.9	10.3	8.7
All levels	**100**	**100**	**100**	**100**
AGED 15–34				
None or primary	33.4	42.8		7.4**
Lower secondary	26.6	29.5		41.7**
Upper secondary	21.6	18.9		40.0**
Tertiary	18.4	8.7		10.9**
All levels	100	100	100	100

Notes: For Shanghai, data include all persons who have ever studied at that level of education, even if they did not complete the level. Residents refer to those who never moved in the five years before the Census, excluding also those who moved within Shanghai.

* Philippines schooling system has only one level (4 years) for secondary education.

** For ages 15–44.

Source: Analysis of census data for the individual MUR studies.

to the core (aged 15–24 years) had lower average levels of education than non-migrants at the same ages, but migrant-non-migrant differentials at ages 25–44 were very slight. By contrast, in the inner and outer zones, migrants at all ages had much higher levels of education than non-migrants, reflecting both the low levels of education of non-migrants in these zones and the relatively high levels of education of many of the migrants, both those moving out from the core and those coming from further afield. Overall, for the Jakarta MUR, migration tended to raise the average levels of education of the population (Table 11.8), but mainly because the migrants were predominantly young, and the young have higher levels of education, on average. When the comparison is restricted to those aged 15–34, there was not much difference between the educational level of migrants and residents.

The Shanghai and Ho Chi Minh City MURs mirrored the Jakarta situation: migration tended to raise the average educational levels of the population. In the HCMC case, at least, the reason was not just that migrants tended to be younger; in the 15–34 age group as well, the average educational level of migrants was considerably above that of residents. In interpreting these figures, though, caution is advised because of the large number of migrants not included in the census figures (see discussion in Chapter 7), a substantial proportion of whom were probably poorly educated.

In Manila, as for Jakarta, movers into the core are generally less educated than the core resident population, whereas movers from the core to the zones are better educated than the residents of these zones. But migrants to the zones from outside the MUR tend to have lower education than do the residents of these zones. Therefore the net impact of migration on educational levels in the zones is dampened by these offsetting differences. Overall, for the Manila MUR as a whole, migration tended to lower the average educational attainment of the population. The same is the case in Bangkok, where the greatest contrast between migrants and longer-term residents is in terms of tertiary education. Among migrants aged 15–34, 8 per cent have tertiary education, compared with 18 per cent among longer-term residents in the same age group (Table 11.8).

Employment Changes in the Zones

Chapter 2 noted a surge in export-oriented industrialisation in Thailand, Indonesia and to a lesser extent in the Philippines in the 1980s, creating rapid increases in manufacturing employment. Vietnam and China were also joining this group of newly industrialising countries by the 1990s.

In the 1990s, however, global forces were focusing on consumer services and retail development and land development in the MURs, culminating in the financial and economic crisis of 1997 in Thailand, Indonesia, and the Philippines, among others. These trends provide the background to interpreting employment changes in the MURs in the 1990s.

Before discussing trends in specific employment sectors, it should be noted that employment recorded in the censuses is attributed to the zone of residence of labour, which is not necessarily the zone where the job is located. Increasingly, as MURs expand, substantial numbers of those living in the inner zone commute to work in the core. In the case of Jakarta, extra information collected as an adjunct to the 2000 Census indicated that more than one million people commute to Jakarta daily, travelling by train (13 per cent), bus (49 per cent), private and government cars (35 per cent) and other means (3 per cent). About 50 per cent of these commuters spend between one and two hours reaching their place of work.

Table 11.9 shows the distribution of employment by broad industrial sector in 1990 and 2000. For the A sector (primary industries), there are two consistent tendencies. Not surprisingly, the proportion of the labour force engaged in primary industries tends to increase with distance from the core. Thus in 1990 the core-inner zone-outer zone percentage of A sector employment in Bangkok was two, 13 and 31 respectively, and the Manila, Jakarta and Shanghai percentages were very similar, except that in Jakarta's and Shanghai's inner zones, the percentages were lower and higher respectively. The other consistent tendency is for the share of A sector employment in each zone to decline over time — except in the core of some cities, where the share was very tiny anyway.[1] Thus in the inner zone of Manila the A sector's share fell from 13 per cent in 1990 to 9 per cent in 2000, and in the outer zone, it fell from 33 per cent to 26 per cent. The outer zone declines were sharper in Jakarta and Bangkok, but Shanghai, surprisingly, went against the trend, showing a rise in the outer zone.

Characteristics of the M sector (basically, manufacturing and construction industries) were also quite consistent. The inner zone had a higher M sector share than the core, in all MURs, in both 1990 and 2000. The M sector's share was lower in the outer zone than in the core in all cases in 1990, but by 2000 this was not the case for Bangkok or Shanghai, and in Jakarta, Manila and HCMC, the difference was no longer very great. This seems to reflect the tendency for manufacturing industry to move out from the core, not only to the inner zone but also increasingly to the outer zone, and also for a lot of construction activity to be taking place in these zones.

Table 11.9 Distribution of Employment by Broad Industrial Sector, 1990 and 2000 (%)

	Jakarta	Bangkok	Manila	HCMC	Shanghai
CORE 1990					
A	1.1	1.6	1.8	n.a.	1.6
M	27.3	32.6	30.3	n.a.	60.1
S	71.6	65.9	67.9	n.a.	38.3
Total	100	100	100	n.a.	100
CORE 2000					
A	1.3	0.8	2.4	1.1	0.7
M	22.1	22.4	32.5	42.3	40.9
S	76.6	76.9	65.0	56.6	58.4
Total	100	100	100		100
INNER ZONE 1990					
A	8.9	13.0	12.8	n.a.	18.3
M	31.8	45.6	34.6	n.a.	62.1
S	59.3	41.5	52.6	n.a.	19.6
Total	100	100	100	n.a.	100
INNER ZONE 2000					
A	5.6	5.4	9.1	19.0	11.4
M	36.2	43.0	37.3	46.1	59.1
S	58.2	51.7	53.6	34.9	29.5
Total	100	100	100	100	100
OUTER ZONE 1990					
A	36.9	30.9	32.7	n.a.	31.9
M	22.4	30.7	24.5	n.a.	52.0
S	40.7	38.4	42.8	n.a.	16.1
Total	100	100	100	n.a.	100
OUTER ZONE 2000					
A	26.1	18.0	26.2	29.5	36.0
M	28.7	35.1	30.0	39.9	44.4
S	45.2	47.0	43.8	30.6	19.6
Total	100	100	100	100	100
TOTAL MUR 1990					
A	9.9	9.8	12.1	n.a.	12.3
M	27.8	34.9	30.1	n.a.	58.4
S	62.3	55.4	57.9	n.a.	29.3
Total	100	100	100	n.a.	100

(*Continued overleaf*)

Table 11.9 *(Continued)*

	Jakarta	Bangkok	Manila	HCMC	Shanghai
TOTAL MUR 2000					
A	6.8	5.7	10.3	6.8	11.5
M	29.3	30.0	33.3	42.7	45.8
S	63.9	64.3	56.4	50.5	42.7
Total	100	100	100	100	100

Notes:
1. A sector includes agriculture, forestry, hunting and fishing
   M sector includes manufacturing, mining, construction, and utilities
   S sector includes trade, transportation and services
2. In Manila and Jakarta, fairly large proportions giving "industry not stated" answer. (In Manila, 8% in 1990 and 24% in 2000; in Jakarta, 15% and 14% in the core in 1990 and 2000 respectively; 12% and 26% in the inner zone in 1990 and 2000 respectively; 8% and 25% in the outer zone in 1990 and 2000 respectively.) In the table above, these were pro-rated across industry groups.

Source: Analysis of census data for the individual MUR studies.

Considering now the employment structure for these MURs in their entirety, the share of the M sector showed different trends over the 1990–2000 decade. It increased slightly in Jakarta and Manila, but decreased substantially in Bangkok and Shanghai. What is clear is that earlier trends towards an ever-increasing M share (Jones, Tsay and Bajracharya 2000) have run their course, and the decline in the A sector share is reflected instead in a rise in the share of the S sector.[2] The S sector dominates employment of those living in the core — providing roughly two thirds or more of total employment in all cities except Shanghai, and in all cities except Shanghai and HCMC, it provides a substantially larger share of employment than the M sector in the inner and outer zones as well.

Occupation

Further light is shed on employment trends by Table 11.10, which shows employment trends and differentials by broad occupation group. Particular interest attaches to the group of occupations labelled PMC (professional, managerial, and clerical), which tend to increase their share of employment in economies moving into the post-industrial phase, and to absorb their better-educated workers. In 1990, the PMC occupations were much more prevalent in the core than in the inner zone, and in turn much less prevalent

Table 11.10   Distribution of Employment by Broad Occupational Group, 1990 and 2000 (%)

	Jakarta	Bangkok	Manila	HCMC	Shanghai
CORE 1990					
PMC	25.9	30.1	36.4		30.1
Sales & service	39.7	32.8	28.1		17.8
Production	33.1	34.5	34.0		50.7
Farming	1.2	2.6	1.6		1.3
Total	100	100	100		100
CORE 2000					
PMC		47.5	32.4	18.3	38.6
Sales & service		29.5	29.0		29.0
Production		22.3	37.2		31.7
Farming		0.6	1.4		0.7
Total	100	100	100	100	100
INNER ZONE 1990					
PMC	16.8	18.4	24.8		14.9
Sales & service	31.4	19.3	21.1		13.7
Production	42.5	47.5	41.7		54.6
Farming	9.0	14.9	12.3		16.8
Total	100	100	100		100
INNER ZONE 2000					
PMC		31.7	32.4	8.9	18.7
Sales & service		23.5	29.0		18.3
Production		40.6	37.2		51.8
Farming		4.3	1.4		11.2
Total		100	100	100	100
OUTER ZONE 1990					
PMC	5.1	11.0	17.5		11.7
Sales & service	24.8	19.3	18.6		10.4
Production	32.3	38.9	31.8		47.3
Farming	37.6	30.8	32.2		30.6
Total	100	100	100		100

(*Continued overleaf*)

Table 11.10   (*Continued*)

	Jakarta	Bangkok	Manila	HCMC	Shanghai
OUTER ZONE 2000					
PMC		21.1	18.0	8.1	13.1
Sales & service		26.9	19.0		11.5
Production		37.2	39.0		40.1
Farming •		13.8	23.9		35.3
Total		100	100	100	100
TOTAL MUR 1990					
PMC	19.3	24.0	28.7		22.8
Sales & service	34.5	27.5	23.9		15.2
Production	35.8	37.9	35.5		50.5
Farming	10.2	10.7	11.8		11.5
Total	100	100	100		100
TOTAL MUR 2000					
PMC		38.4	26.9	15.7	28.0
Sales & service		27.5	24.2		22.4
Production		29.7	40.2		38.2
Farming		4.3	8.7		11.3
Total		100	100	100	100

Notes: PMC=professional, managerial and clerical. No information on occupation was collected in the Indonesian Population Census for 2000. For Bangkok in 1990, a very small group of "miners and quarrymen etc." and of "not classified and unknown" were included with agriculture. A larger group of "transport equipment operators and related workers" (5.9% of all workers in the MUR) was included with production workers. For Bangkok in 2000, "armed forces" (2.1% of employment in the MUR) were included in PAC. For Manila, "miners and quarrymen etc." was included with production. For HCMC, "armed forces" (0.7% of employment in the MUR) were included in PAC.

Source: Analysis of census data for the individual MUR studies.

in the outer zone. But their share of all employment in the Bangkok and Shanghai MURs as a whole increased substantially between 1990 and 2000: in Bangkok, from 24 per cent to 38 per cent; in Shanghai, from 22 per cent to 28 per cent. These increases occurred in all zones. Manila showed a different pattern, with PMC's employment share declining in the core and the outer zone, though increasing in the inner zone. PMC's share declined overall in the Manila MUR, quite a surprising finding.[3]

Production occupations, reflecting mainly the manufacturing sector, show interesting variations between cities and zones. In 1990, these occupations had a higher share of total employment in the inner zone than elsewhere; by 2000, this remained the case, but the key trend was a sharp decline in the share of production occupations in the core, reflecting the decline of the M sector's share of employment in the core (except in Manila), shown in Table 11.10.

*   *   *

In looking at all of the population trends compared above, where population growth was faster migration has played a major role in population growth in the cities and zones, though higher fertility in Manila meant that natural increase played a greater role in its growth. A considerable part of the population growth in the inner zones (except in Shanghai and HCMC) consisted of people moving out from the core, as well as substantial migration from other parts of the country. Overall, roughly half of the recent migrants to the MURs from other parts of the country went to the core, and the other half went to the zones, mostly to the inner zone. Most of these migrants were in the 15–34 age group. The suburbanisation of the new urban middle class is reflected in the slightly older age group of migrants moving from core to inner and outer zones.

The educational attainment of the MUR populations increased quite markedly over the 1990s. The contribution of migration to the rise in educational attainment is harder to generalise. In some of the MURs it tended to raise the average educational levels, in others to lower them. Offsetting influences of migration were often observable: for example, migrants from the core to the inner zone were frequently much better educated than migrants from other parts of the country.

Structures of employment also changed with globalising forces, and population mobility was oriented to the expanding opportunities in the MURs. What emerges from the detailed comparative dynamics of migration and employment change are some interesting commonalities, but also substantial differences in aspects such as population densities and patterns of migration to the zones, implying that each mega-urban region must be considered in its own terms, even before considering the sharp differences in governance structures.

Generalised Patterns of MUR Formation and Growth

Interpreting the trends more broadly, they reveal the following tendencies covering roughly five phases of MUR formation (Table 11.11). From the perspective of population dynamics, these phases can be seen as resulting from an interplay between the urban transition, which includes rural-urban migration, and the demographic transition marked by rapidly increasing and then sharply declining natural population growth.

1. The precursor to the contemporary MUR begins in (semi-)colonial times, but its foundations are augmented when national independence produces strong "developmental states" that adopt national strategies of accelerated industrialisation. Based on import-substitution policies protecting infant industry, the result is slow industrial expansion around inefficient industries. The advent of the green revolution as a parallel policy to provide basic food for urban workers and their families leads in many instances to rapid shedding of population from rural grain producing regions with the arrival of mechanised farming. These industrial and agricultural strategies push hundreds of thousands of rural people into the MUR, which is experiencing relatively slow rates of economic growth. Urban slums proliferate, and urbanisation is seen as a process of shifting poverty from the countryside into the city. As described by McGee (1971), the overall MUR growth process was one of "urban involution", or poverty sharing, among low-income households.

2. The second phase of MUR formation — roughly from the 1960s and 1970s or, in the cases of Shanghai and HCMC following political reform in the 1980s — is the most explosive in terms of population growth. It is fuelled by the new international division of labour (Chapter 2) and accompanied by a combination of high rates of national population growth and high rates of rural-urban migration directed toward the MUR. This combination can add hundreds of thousands of new residents to the MUR every year. In most of the MURs under study, this phase lasted about one to one and a half decades. At the end of this phase, the MURs had reached or exceeded five million in population. While personal well-

being in terms of education and skill levels improve enormously and poverty is reduced during this phase, urban environmental degradation becomes severe.

3. In the third phase of expansion, the sheer size of the MURs coupled with continuing high natural population growth rates sees migration diminish as a share of total MUR population growth, especially where population growth rates remain relatively high. The MUR economy is also beginning to manifest a shift beyond labour-intensive industrialisation, turning toward a new service economy oriented toward consumerism, global management functions, and spectacular events related to tourism.

4. In the fourth phase the growth of MURs tends to slow down due to declining natural population growth rates that also lead to shrinking pools of potential migrants to the MURs. Massive rural depopulation begins. Though slower in growth, MURs expand faster than national population growth due to migration again taking a dominant role. Their shares of national population thus continue to increase, albeit at a much slower rate than in earlier phases.

5. In the fifth phase of MUR growth, population increases are no longer principally driven by rural-urban migration from with the national territory, which slows down as the demographic transition turns to below replacement fertility and the completion of the urban transition results in 75 per cent or more of the population now living in cities, with MURs accounting for very large shares of national urban populations. Intercity migration to the MURs becomes more pronounced when secondary cities begin to face deep economic crises as their labour-intensive manufacturing base shifts offshore to low-wage economies of other countries in the region, notably China in recent years. MUR economic growth turns to global business and management functions and higher levels of global consumerism. National labour shortages see MUR population growth at this point starting to be driven by immigration of workers from other Asian countries. This represents a new moment in MUR history as urban poverty and other livability issues begin to increasingly show divides along ethnic lines between a citizen population and a host of minority non-citizen populations.

Chapter 3 (Figure 3.1) has shown actual trends in the growth of selected MURs and confirms at this level the dynamics described above. There are of course key exceptions and variations to these general patterns. Some are related to population growth rate differences. The Philippines, for

Table 11.11 Phases of MUR Dynamics: Globalisation and the Demographic and Urban Transition

Phase	The National Demographic Transition	Migration and the Urban Transition	Economic sources of MUR Growth	MUR Growth Dynamics and Livability
(I) Precursor to the MUR – Developmental States/Socialist States	High natural population growth rates due to improved health and population stability	Moderate increases in rural-urban migration	Import-substitution industrialization and the green revolution	'urban involution' from rural push and limited urban industrial growth. Urban slums proliferate in core areas
(II) MUR Industrial "take-off" – NIDL	High natural population growth rates	Beginning of massive rural-MUR migration	New International Division of Labour – export-oriented industrialization	Rapid urban-industrial growth leads to rising incomes, declining poverty but great stress on the environment
(III) 5 Million plus MURs	High (but declining) natural population growth; MUR reproduces its own population	Migration still high, but natural population growth of MURs reduces share of migration in total population increases	The arrival of global retail and franchise consumerism with the rise of an urban middle class	Migration to the MUR targets the core while the MUR middle class shifts outward to new housing in inner zone suburbs.

Table 11.11 (*Continued*)

Phase	The National Demographic Transition	Migration and the Urban Transition	Economic sources of MUR Growth	MUR Growth Dynamics and Livability
(IV) Return of the Migrant City – Decline in share of mfg., growth of global services and consumption	Rapidly falling population growth rates toward below replacement	Migration still high, though declining in levels due to slowing population growth	Finance capital and investment in urban land development	(Domestic) migration becomes the only source of MUR population growth. Urban development reaches into the outer zone while overall MUR population growth tapers off.
(V) The mature Global MUR	Below replacement fertility	Large-scale immigration of foreign workers	Post-industrial-(global) services, tourism and the experience economy	Shrinking domestic labour force leads to rapid increase in foreign workers and multicultural MURs. MUR population growth slows but its share of national population continues to increase.

Source: The authors.

example, with its continuing high rates of natural population increases and high levels of migration to Manila, shows a continuing high rate of MUR growth in the 1990s, a decade during which the other MURs had already began to slow in growth due to declining fertility rates. Similarly, with its significant international community and workers already coming from abroad to fill occupations such as domestic helpers, construction workers, sex and entertainment, and low-wage factory work, Bangkok is already among the more multicultural MURs. In contrast, Taipei, a MUR that has clearly entered the fifth phase and is therefore the most likely candidate for massive influx of foreign workers (and brides), is just at the beginning of foreign communities appearing at a significant scale.

Having noted these exceptions, the combination of demographic and urban transitions nonetheless exerts very powerful influences on the formation and expansion of MURs. The research in this volume has established that at a macro-spatial scale, the outcome of these influences is a continued polarisation of national development into the MURs. This is not to say that other city regions are not growing. Many are. Yet from a national perspective the consistent findings that every MUR continues to accrue higher shares of the national population is a clear indication that their powers of agglomeration have not reached a peak.

Moreover, many of the secondary cities that are growing rapidly, such as Nakhon Ratchasima or the Eastern Seaboard to the southeast of Bangkok, are doing so because they are being drawn into the orbit of the Bangkok MUR. In the case of Nakhon Ratchasima, the gateway city to the northeast that is increasingly integrated into the northeastern industrial expansion of Bangkok MUR, its growth is now surpassing that of Chiang Mai, which was the second largest city in Thailand before Nakhon Ratchasima overtook it about a decade ago. If Taiwan represents the pattern of the future, once-rural regional towns such as Nakhon Ratchasima that are now falling into the orbit of Bangkok will eventually form a super-agglomeration, or megalopolis, that will include most of the urban population of Thailand.

As explained in Chapter 2, demographic and urbanisation processes are intertwined with global economic forces that also have a profound impact on MUR formation and expansion. The emergence of MURs from the 1960s onwards coincides with the opening of the respective countries and cities to the offshore movement of low-wage segments of global assembly and manufacturing, which for the first time began to annually bring tens of thousands of migrants from rural regions to become factory workers in the emergent MURs. Over time, new global linkages in the form of consumer

Table 11.12 Phases of MUR Growth among Zones

Phase	Core	Inner Zone	Outer Zone
I	MUR development focuses on core	Transportation networks spread outward from core	Still dominated by agriculture
II	MUR development focuses on core	Beginning of MUR expansion along corridors	Intensification of agriculture for MUR markets
III	Population in core stabilizes with net migration near zero but high rates of in and out migration	First significant suburban housing development, thickening of corridor development	Transport corridors and ribbon development of urban functions and housing.
IV	Population displaced by mega-projects (global office complexes, tall buildings	Suburbanization fill in with housing, shopping malls, pushing larger-scale industry further out	Large-scale agriculture displacement by housing, factories, new towns
V	Complex urban field with multiple centres. Differentiation among zones diminishes for daily life; higher order and global functions remain in core.		

Source: The authors.

shopping, speculative urban land development projects and finance capital each furthered the growth while transforming the structure of the MURs. These impacts are most apparent when viewed across the three zones used to analyse dynamics within each MUR (Table 11.12).

Interpreting the trends more broadly, they reveal the following tendencies covering roughly five phases in MUR formation. From the perspective of population growth, these phases can be seen as resulting from an interplay between the urban transition, which includes rural-urban migration, and the demographic transition marked by rapidly increasing and then sharply declining natural population growth:

1. In the precursor phase of MUR formation, migration from rural areas to the urban core dominates. Slum and squatter settlements fill in docklands and public land; old elite neighbourhoods continue to occupy central

locations. With the exception of some industrial development (import-substitution), inner and outer zones are still relatively untouched by migration to the MUR.

2. The second phase bringing massive rural-urban migration to fill global factory positions continues to focus on the core. Production for export linked with transnational corporation augments seaport, rail and airport Natural population increases in all zones are also high, but the intensive focus of migration on inner urban areas results in increasing population pressures on the urban core.

3. The third phase sees a spread into suburban areas as the MURs expand over the official administrative boundaries of the core municipality.

4. Three processes characterise the fourth phase: (a) the capture of the urban core by mega-projects oriented toward global connectivity and services. Jakarta's "Golden Triangle", mega-malls in central Manila, Rama III world business complex in Bangkok, skyscrapers in Taipei and eventual redevelopment of Shin Yi military base into a global core complete with Taipei 101, the world's tallest building in 2004, exemplify this pattern. (b) massive suburban housing development, complete with new towns and transportation hubs; and (c) expansion into the outer zone that displaces agriculture with housing, new towns, and industry. Some agriculture continues in the inner and outer zones, but it is small in share of MUR employment and is "urbanised" for such consumer markets as picked flowers, pick-your-own fruit orchards, golf course grass, and organic farming. Low-income settlements continue to flourish in the core as the urban middle class shifts toward the inner and outer zones and migration from rural areas continues to bring young, less wealthy and less educated populations into the core.

5. The fifth phase results in the formation of a complex urban field in which many of the distinctions among zones disappear into a matrix of interaction using multiple modes of transportation that traverse the MUR as a network rather than as a dendritic transportation tree focused only on movement into and out of the core. The core retains its role in hosting highest order national and global functions, but elements of these functions are also relocated to inner and even outer zone locations. Foreign worker populations begin to increase in all zones, with differentiation among zones in terms of occupations, some of which are associated with a particular ethnic group. With natural population growth below replacement for the entire MUR, domestic and international migration becomes the only source of its population growth.

In summarising the patterns that have been documented, it is important to note that in the decade of the 1990s under review each MUR was in a different phase or combination of phases. Taipei was the most advanced and, with plans in place for a high-speed train from Taipei to Kaohsiung, was about to enter the fifth phase of MUR morphology. Bangkok, Jakarta and Manila were traversing from the third to the fourth phases, while Ho Chi Minh City and Shanghai were experiencing the second phase of accelerated population growth still focused on the core.

In many ways, however, the belated take-off of HCMC and Shanghai has compressed elements of all phases into one. Even though core-centred development prevails in Shanghai, its population growth is totally dependent upon in-migration rather than natural increase. Shanghai has also moved into a period of urban mega-projects complete with what are probably the world's largest export processing zone (Pudong) and the world's tallest building in 2005. It has also connected its airport to the city centre by constructing Asia's first magnetic levitation train service. In this regard, Shanghai is simultaneously positioning itself as a site for low-wage global assembly and as a world city with global information and regional headquarter functions. Ho Chi Minh City has not embarked on such lavish schemes, but it, too, has suburban shopping centres and has embarked on the private sector construction of a suburban development project, Saigon South, that is planned for one million middle class residents on the outskirts of the city. Both the Shanghai and HCMC experiences are important in showing how the time-space collapse that is accelerating processes of globalisation is also compressing the morphology of MUR dynamics into shorter, overlapping time frames.

Into the Urban Future

While each MUR seems to be encountering similar forces shaping patterns of growth and change, none faces a pre-destined future. The major transitions of many types — demographic, economic, environmental, urban — that are underway appear in sufficiently varied patterns and combinations to suggest that while a number of transformations are common to the MURs, they do not amount to a single development path for all. Chapter 10 shows, for example, that in terms of livability, variations are significant even among MURs that are at a similar point in their economic and demographic transitions.

Five factors cut across these transitions to lead to significant variations in MUR dynamics. First, the cultural, social and political histories of each society are quite different. For example, Thailand, a predominantly Buddhist society that was never colonised and exists as a constitutional monarchy has a political system that has a relatively low level of intervention in urban planning and regulation, leaving the private sector to be the major source of urban land development. On the other extreme are China and Vietnam, both of which until recently instituted strong, top-down master planning and regulation for their cities. State-driven mega-projects in Shanghai such as the creation of the export-processing zone and business hub of Pudong, which is equal to the size of the core of Shanghai itself, contrast with the global mega-malls and the exclusive business and residential area of Makati, a fortified privately developed city in the heart of Manila that until the overthrow of Marcos was infamous for its glaring gaps between rich and poor (Binay 2006).

Second, in an era of political reform toward more participatory forms of government, governance is among the many defining differences guiding cities toward the future. Chapter 10 has shown the broad spectrum of governance structures among four of the MURs and their nations. It ranges from continuing authoritarian governments having low accountability to societies that have in recent years experienced fundamental political reform toward more democratic forms of governance. In all cases, however, local governments at the MUR or sub-MUR level remain weak, and this will prove to be one of the most limiting factors in the future as governments and citizens attempt to translate economic growth into more livable cities. Without greater local autonomy, these MURs will continue to be under national planning bureaus that show a marked tendency to favour national and global roles such as world city status over local livability concerns (Douglass 2006).

When combined, the different levels of democratic governance and local autonomy suggest a wide array of pathways among the MURs. These differences in state-civil society-private sector relations of power have decisive outcomes in urban form and the quality of urban life over space and among social classes and, particularly as international migration becomes a more prominent feature of MUR population dynamics, ethnic groups as well. In their transition economies, Mainland China and Vietnam are forming strong state-corporate economy linkages in urban land development, with limited participation of citizens or non-government organisations. The results are observable as mega-projects such as the Saigon South private new town development slated for one million middle class residents without a single unit of low cost housing in what is among the poorest countries in Pacific Asia. In contrast, in Taipei, citizen movements and elected local governments have built community parks and opened to the public sites that were previously exclusively reserved for political leaders (Chapter 8). In the case of Indonesia, political reform and devolution of power following the fall of the Suharto New Order Government in 1998 have created democratic governance institutions, but these are still in flux and have yet to be translated into major improvements in the built environment of cities.

Third, as explained in Chapter 2, differential impacts of global economic turbulence constitute powerful influences on the patterns and human outcomes of MUR expansion. Events such as the financial crisis and the later collapse of the "dot.com" "new economy" are likely to continue to occur in unexpected forms and with varied impacts on cities and nations. Thailand and Indonesia were much more profoundly affected by the Pacific Asia financial crisis of 1997–98, and while Thailand has substantially recovered from it with little political change, the impact on Indonesia was to bring down a long-standing authoritarian regime that has been replaced by a fledgling democracy that is still finding its way forward. These differences find their way into the city. For example, whereas Bangkok has been able to begin to build a much-needed mass transit systems with the SkyTrain and new subway, Jakarta, now a mega-urban region of 21 million people, has no such system in place and now faces ever-increasing traffic congestion and the air pollution it generates. Once a principal attraction of FDI, first in natural resource extraction and later in global assembly and manufacturing, Indonesia since 1998 has dropped to a very low level of FDI, which is not only related to its own political circumstance but also to poor infrastructure in Jakarta (Husna and Kyne 2006).

Fourth, globalisation as an acceleration of flows in a collapsing time-space equation is raising the portent of debilitating epidemics and pandemics such as SARS and Avian Flu that can quickly spread around the world in a matter of weeks. They will have disparate impacts among cities depending on, for example, patterns of inter-city linkages or even the migration patterns of birds. Natural disasters, brought to the fore by the 2005 Indian Ocean tsunami and 2006 earthquakes in Indonesia, add to the unexpected in this world region of active volcanos and earthquakes. While such disasters have occurred throughout history, what differentiates the present from the past is the speed at which an event at one location can impact another. Mega-urban regions, as nodes articulating global flows, are the most likely sites to both receive and transmit such impacts. This was revealed in the finance crisis of the late 1990s, which affected the MURs more heavily than other regions in their respective countries.

Fifth, with regard to the global economy, of special importance to the cities under discussion are the changing international patterns of competition

Table 11.13   Top 10 Destinations for FDI in Developing Asia, 1991–93 and 1998–2000: Average Annual Total Inflows (US$ billion)

Rank	Host Economy	1991–93	Rank	Host Economy	1998–2000
1	PRC	14.3	1	PRC	41.6
2	Malaysia	5.0	2	Hong Kong, China	33.8
3	Hong Kong, China	3.9	3	Singapore	11.1
4	Singapore	3.9	4	Korea	8.0
5	Thailand	2.0	5	Thailand	5.6
6	Indonesia	1.8	6	Malaysia	3.5
7	Taipei,China	1.0	7	Taipei, China	2.7
8	Philippines	0.9	8	India	2.4
9	Korea	0.8	9	Philippines	1.6
10	Kazakhstan	0.7	10	Vietnam	1.5
	Total Developing Asia	35.4		Total Developing Asia	111.6
	(% of world total)	(19.3)		(% of world total)	(10.6)

Source: UNCTAD, FDI database, available: <http://r0.unctad.org/en/subsites/dite/fdistats_files/fdistats.htm>, downloaded 15 September 2003.

within Pacific Asia. Specifically, political reforms in China leading to its wider opening to the world economy from the 1980s have begun to influence changes in economic structures of other countries in the region. Especially after the 1997–98 finance crisis in Asia, labour-intensive assembly and light industry propelling urbanisation in Southeast Asia in the 1970s and 1980s began to discernibly shift to China, leaving Southeast Asian economies and their cities to search for new foundations for economic growth and resilience. These changes are reflected in Table 11.13, which shows that China and Hong Kong increased their combined FDI totals from $18 billion in 1991–93 to $75 billion in 1998–2000, thoroughly dominating FDI in Pacific Asia by the year 2000. These trends are likely to continue into the coming decades, though conditions in China such as widespread social unrest over such issues as forced conversion of agricultural to urban land and rural unemployment are internal dimensions of development that could impact China's position in the world economy.

The main purpose of the book has been to show and explain MUR dynamics over the momentous decade of the 1990s. However, by viewing the comparative analysis of MURs as patterns related to different stages and moments of growth and development also suggests implications for the future of each. At the same time, significant variations among MURs are revealed even at the same stage of formation. As noted, Thailand seems to have politically and economically weathered the 1997–98 financial crisis, while Indonesia has remained at a lower level of economic performance and global investment than it had previously enjoyed. The Philippines is taking a quite different global path through its increasing specialisation in the export of migrant labour throughout the world — 20 per cent of the Philippine labour force is abroad — that is generating a continuing focus of national economic growth on Manila as gateway to the world. In contrast, Shanghai, and to a lesser extent, Ho Chi Minh City, are accelerating in both population and economic growth through global linkages in manufacturing and urban services. Taipei, the most advanced MUR in terms of economic transitions, has moved well beyond manufacturing and into tertiary services in its global linkages.

Projecting the evidence of the past decade into the future underscores the variations among the MURs within broader, more commonly experienced global relations and national transitions. As such, the purpose of the comparative analysis presented in this and the preceding chapters is not to predict any one MUR future but rather to reveal the ways in which global-MUR dynamics might extend into the future in variant ways. A further purpose is to link the analysis of population data with the normative questions of livability of cities (Chapter 10), including personal well-being, environmental integrity and community lifeworlds. While great strides have been made among all the MURs in such areas of personal well-being as education and health, significant variations exist among the zones of each MUR, which represents not only spatial patterns of access to education and welfare, but also spatial variations in income and occupational attainment.

When looking at other dimensions of livability such as environmental quality, the trends are more disparate. In some MURs, such as Bangkok, previous records of steep environmental degradation have apparently experienced some positive reversals. In others the environmental quality continues to worsen and represents one of the most formidable issues facing the MURs in the coming decades.

Concerning spaces of associational life — lifeworlds — evidence is not clear, particularly because data related to this sphere of livability is not routinely collected. The limited evidence suggests, however, that globalisation brings both increasing stress on community and civic spaces through new trends toward privatisation, mega-projects serving commercial rather than community interests, and a shift in government attention toward global intercity competition for investment under neoliberal policy regimes (Douglass 2007). At the same time, information technologies have allowed for global exchanges of ideas and information that foster the rise of civil society as a political force in the Pacific Asia region that has led to political reform and a greater voice of MUR residents in the making of city spaces. How these two tendencies of globalising urban landscapes and mobilising citizens to create local community spaces will play out is one of the more fascinating questions unfolding in the livability of each mega-urban region.

The evidence of the past decade and many decades before indicate that these city regions will continue to accrue both larger shares of national populations and larger shares of their national economies. As national population growth continues to slow at varying paces in the countries under review, and as MURs becoming ever more open to global flows of people as well as finance and commodities, they will also become more cosmopolitan in ethnic diversity and origins of their residents. This will in turn present new issues concerning national identity, citizenship and right to the city. The decade of the 1990s proved to be one of immense changes in the formation and livability of Pacific Asia's mega-urban regions. Events at the end of that decade — economic turbulence, political reform, epidemics and natural disasters, new technologies such as the spread of the Internet, and many others — have brought societies into the twenty-first century with a promise of new issues surrounding population dynamics that are increasingly focused on a relatively small number of mega-urban regions. As each of these MURs takes on an increasingly prominent position in the local-global organisation of space, they will be of increasing importance to national well-being. Research on the dynamics of these city regions and their outcomes for the quality of life for people residing in them will likewise be of value in national as well as MUR policymaking.

Notes

1. It is likely that the share of the A sector is somewhat overestimated, especially in the inner and outer zones, as a result of the requirement for respondents in the census to designate only one occupation. In cases where respondents have traditionally been farmers, but are now engaged in multiple activities, they are likely to continue giving agriculture as their industry, although they may earn more income from other pursuits.
2. The S sector consists of trade, transporation, finance and services industries.
3. PMC's share of employment in 2000 appeared to be much lower in HCMC than in the other MURs, both in the core and in the zones. The reason for this is not entirely clear, but may have to do with a different system for classifying occupations.

Bibliography

Abeyasekere, Susan. 1987. *Jakarta: A History*. Singapore: Oxford University Press.

Alm and Bahl. 1999. *Decentralisation in Indonesia: Prospects and Problems*. Atlanta: Georgia State University, Department of Economics.

Arkarn and Theedin Weekly. 2004. "The Master Plan to Acquire Land to Construct 316 Missing Links in 2006–2026". *Arkarn and Theedin Weekly* (14–20 February 2004): 67–71.

Asian Development Bank. 1986. *Statistical Indicators*. Manila, Philippines: Asia Development Bank.

———. 1998. *Financial Crisis in Asia*. Manila, Philippines: Asia Development Bank.

———. 2003. *Integrated Action Plan to Reduce Vehicle Emissions in Vietnam*. Manila, Philippines.

Asian Development Bank and Economic Development Institute (ADB and EDI). 1991. *The Urban Poor and Basic Infrastructure Services in Asia and the Pacific* (Vol. 1). A Regional Seminar, 22–28 January, Manila, Philippines.

Aspinall, Edward and Greg Fealy (eds.). 2003. *Local Power and Politics in Indonesia: Decentralisation and Democratization*, Singapore: Institute of Southeast Asian Studies.

Badan Pengendalian Dampak Lingkungan. 2000. Laporan Prokasih 2000 (*Prokasih* Report 2000), Jakarta: Bapedal DKI Jakarta.

Badan Pusat Statistik. 1997. *Profil Migran Masuk di Enam Kota Besar* (Profile of In-migrants in Six Large Cities). Jakarta: Badan Pusat Statistik.

———. 2000a. *Ringkasan hasil Sensus Penduduk 2000* (Summary of 2000 Population Census Reports). Unpublished report.

———. 2000b. *Pertumbuhan Penduduk dan Perubahan Karakteristik Tujuh Wilayah Aglomerasi Perkotaan di Indonesi. 1990–1995* (Population Growth and Changing Population Characteristics in Seven Urban Agglomerations in Indonesia 1990–95). Jakarta: Badan Pusat Statistik.

———. 2001. *Estimasi Fertilitas, Mortalitas dan Migrasi* (Fertility, Mortality and Migration Estimates). Jakarta: Badan Pusat Statisti.

Badan Pusat Statistik DKI Jakarta. 2001. *Migrasi Penduduk Jabotabek 2001* (Migration of the Population of Jabotabek 2001). Jakarta: Badan Pusat Statistik Propinsi DKI Jakarta.

————. 2002. *Laporan Eksekutif Pendataan Musibah Banjir DKI Jakarta* (Executive Report on Flood Disaster Documentation). Jakarta: Badan Pusat Statistik Propinsi DKI Jakarta.

Badan Pusat Statistik, State Ministry of Population/BKKBN, Ministry of Health, and Macro International. 1997. *Indonesia Demographic and Health Survey 1997,* Calverton, Maryland: Badan Pusat Statistik and MI.

Baguioro, L. 3 May 2002. "Manila Turning into a Real Concrete Jungle: As the Philippine Capital's Green Spaces and Places of Interest Dwindle at an Increasing Rate, City Conservationists Sound a Warning". *The Straits Times Interactive.* Retrieved from <http://www.ecologyasia.com/NewsArchives/May_2002/straitstimes.asia1.com. sg_story_0,1870,117553,00.html>.

Bapedal DKI Jakarta. 2000. *Neraca Kualitas Lingkungan Daerah DKI Jakarta.* Retrieved 9 November 2003 from <http://www.dki.go.id/bapedalda/Buku-II/docs/442.htm>.

BAPPEDA DKI Jakarta. 2001. *Pencemaran Udara Ibukota* (Air Pollution in the Capital City). Jakarta: Bappeda DKI Jakarta.

Beatley, Timothy. 2000. *Green urbanism: Learning from European Cities.* Washington, D.C.: Island Press.

Bello, Walden. 1997. "The End of the "Southeast Asian Miracle?" In *Focus on the Global South* (FOCUS) Bangkok. Thailand (Number 17, August). Retrieved from <http://www.focus.org>.

Bhumirat, C. 1984. "Thailand". In *UNESCO, The Drop-out Problem in Primary Education: Some Case Studies: China, India, Peninsular Malaysia, Socialist Republic of Viet Nam, Sri Lanka, Thailand.* Bangkok: UNESCO Regional Office for Education in Asia and the Pacific.

Binay, Jejomar C. 2006. "Essay by Jejomar C Binay, Mayor of the City of Makati, Philippines". Retrieved 14 Sept. 2006 from <http://www.worldmayor.com/ essays06/makati_essay.html>.

Blair, Harry. 2000. "Participation and Power at the Periphery: Democratic Local Governance in Six Countries". *World Development* 28(1): 21–40.

BMA and MIT [Bangkok Metropolitan Authority and Massachusetts Institute of Technology]. 1996. *The Bangkok Plan: A Vision for the Bangkok Metropolitan Administration Area 1995–2005.* Bangkok.

BMA and others. 1996. *Metropolitan Subcentres.* Bangkok.

Boley, Jean-Claude., Sophie Cartoux, Antonia Cunha, Thai Thi Ngoc Du, and Michel Bassand. 1997. "Sustainable Development and Urban Growth: Precarious Habitat and Water Management in Ho Chi Minh City, Vietnam". *Habitat International* 21(2): 185–98.

Bolongaita, Emil. 2003. "Southeast Asia". *Global Corruption Report 2003.* Profile Books Limited.

Boonchuen, Pornpun. 2002. "Globalisation and Urban Design". *International Development Planning Review* 24(4): 401–18.

BPS-Statistics Indonesia, Bappenas, and United Nations Development Programmeme (UNDP). 2001. *Indonesia Human Development Report 2001, Towards a New*

Consensus: Democracy and Human Development in Indonesia. BPS-Statistics Indonesia, Bappenas and UNDP.

Brandon, C. 1994. "Reversing Pollution Trends in Asia". *Finance and Development* 31(2): 21–3.

Brodjonegoro. B. 2003. *Jakarta Metropolitan Area in Decentralisation*. Paper presented at Exit Symposium on Indonesia's Decentralisation Policy: Problems and Policy Direction, 4–5 September, Jakarta, Indonesia. Retrieved 15 April 2004 from <http://icds.co.jp/sympo/pdf/S7(6)2.pdf>.

Bronger, Dirk. 1985. "Metropolitanization as a Development Problem of Third World Countries: A Contribution towards a Definition of the Concept". *Applied Geography and Development* 26: 71–97.

Brothers, Terry. 2003. "Transportation Plan, Suvarnabhumi Aerotropolis Study". Unpublished background paper, Bangkok.

Buentjen, C. 2000. *Fiscal Decentralisation in Indonesia: The Challenge of Designing Institutions*. Manila, Philippines: Asian Development Bank.

Bureau of Information. 1988. *Two Decades after the Upgrading of Taipei Municipality*. Taipei: Taipei Municipal Government.

Bureau of Statistics Jakarta. 2002. *Jakarta in Figures*. Jakarta.

Cahn, Miranda. n.d. Sustainable Livelihood Approach: Concept and Practice. Retrieved 1 November 2003 from <http://www.devnet.org.nz/conf2002/papers/Cahn_Miranda.pdf>.

Castells, Manuel. 2000. "Materials for an Exploratory Theory of the Network Society". *British Journal of Sociology* 51(1): 5–24.

Chambers and Conway. 1992. "Sustainable Rural Livelihoods: Practical Concepts for the 21st Century". In IDS *Discussion Paper No. 296*. IDS, Brighton.

Champion, Tony and Graeme Hugo. 2004. *New Forms of Urbanisation: Beyond the Urban-Rural Dichotomy*. Hants: England: Ashgate.

Chandler, Nancy. 2000. Nancy Chandler's Map of Bangkok: Alias "The Market Map and much more" (20th ed.) [Map and Index]. Bangkok, Thailand.

Chen, Yi-ling. 2005. "Provision for Collective Consumption: Housing Production under Neoliberalism". In Reginald Yin-Wang Kwok, ed., *Globalising Taipei: The Political Economy of Spatial Development*. London: Routledge.

Chertow, Marian. R. and Daniel Esty (eds.). 1997. *Thinking Ecologically: The Next Generation of Environmental Policy*. New Haven, CT: Yale University Press.

Ching, Chia-ho. 2005. "The Development of Economic Structure: Producer Services and Growth Constrains". In Reginald Yin-Wang Kwok, ed., *Globalising Taipei: The Political Economy of Spatial Development*. London: Routledge.

Chou, Tsu-lung. 2005. "The Transformation of Spatial Structure: From a Monocentric to Polycentric". In Reginald Yin-Wang Kwok, ed., *Globalising Taipei: The Political Economy of Spatial Development*. London: Routledge.

Chung-Hao Real Estate Consultant Company. 1999. "The Development of Commercial Activities in Taiwan: The Factor Analysis from 1986 to 1996". *SPACE* 120 (August): 82–92.

Clark, David. 1996. *Urban World/Global City*. London: Routledge.

Coale, Ansley. J. and Paul Demeny. 1966. *Regional Model Life Tables and Stable Populations*. New Jersey: Princeton University Press.

Cohen, Margot. 2001. "Hanoi to Ease Its Hold: Ho Chi Minh City is Set to Win Some Autonomy from the Central Government in Hanoi by Promising the Move will Attract Business and Generate more Revenues". *Far East Economic Review*, 13 September.

Coit, Katharine. 1998. "Housing Policy and Slum Upgrading in Ho Chi Minh City". *Habitat International* 2(3): 273–80.

Connell, J. 1999. "Beyond Manila: Walls, Malls and Private Spaces". *Environment and Planning* 31: 417–39.

Corpuz, Arturo G. 1999. *The Colonial Iron Horse: Railroads and Regional Development in the Philippines, 1875–1935*. Quezon City: University of the Philippines Press.

Coseteng, Alicia M.L. 1972. *Spanish Churches in the Philippines*. Quezon City: New Mercury Printing Press.

Dang, Nguyen Anh. 2001. *Migration in Vietnam: Theoretical Approaches and Evidence from a Survey*. Hanoi: Communication Publishing House.

Dang, Nguyen Anh, Le Kim Sa, Nguyen, Duc Vinh, Nguyen, Thien Hao and Nghiem, Thi Thuy. 2002. "Sustainable Urbanisation, Migration and Living Environment in Vietnam". *Population Research Series No. 304*. Tokyo: National Institute of Population and Social Security Research.

Dang, Vy. 2003. 24 June. "Gan 1 Ty Dong De Phat Trien Mang Xanh Do Thi". In VnExpress.net (Tin Nhanh Vietnam). Retrieved 28 October 2003 from <http://vnexpress.net/Vietnam/Xa-hoi/2003/06/3B9C90D1/>.

Department of City Planning, Bangkok Metropolitan Administration. 2002. "Urban Study and Planning of New Special Economic Development at Rama Project. Final Report", Bangkok.

Department of Health (DOH). 2002. *List of Licensed Hospitals*. Retrieved 20 January 2004 from <http://www.doh.gov.ph>.

Department of Statistical Office (DSO). 2000. *Population of Ho Chi Minh City: Population and Housing Census Vietnam 1999's Results*. Ho Chi Minh City, Vietnam: Statistical Publishing House.

Dharmapatni, I.A.I., and Firman, T. 1995 "Problems and Challenges of Mega-urban Regions in Indonesia". In T.G. McGee and Ira Robinson (eds.), *The Mega-urban Regions of Southeast Asia*. Vancouver, Canada: UBC Press, pp. 296–314.

Dick, Howard W. and Peter J. Rimmer. 1998. "Beyond the Third World City: The New Urban Geography of South-East Asia". *Urban Studies* 35(12): 2303–32.

Ding, Jinhong, Yang, Hongyan, Yang, Jie, Weng, Jianhong, and Zhang, Binbin. 2001. "The Characteristics of Crimes Committed by the Floating Population in Shanghai and Their Social Control (in Chinese)". *Renkou Yanjiu (Population Research)* 25 (6): 53–8.

Direktorat Geologi Tata Lingkungan. 1998. *Annual Report 1997/1998*, Direktorat Geologi Tata Lingkungan.

Division of Health Statistics (DHS). 1992. *Public Health Statistics.* Bangkok, Thailand.

Dobson, Andrew. 2000. *Green Political Thought.* New York: Routledge.

Douglass, Mike. 1991. "Planning for Environmental Sustainability in the Extended Jakarta Metropolitan Region". In Norton Ginsburg, Bruce Koppel and T.G. McGee (eds.), *The Extended Metropolis: Settlement Transition in Asia.* Honolulu: University of Hawai'i Press, pp. 239–73.

———. 1992. "Regional Inequality and Regional Policy in Developing Countries: The Case of Thailand". In NESDB, ed., *National Urban Development Policy Framework,* Area 3. Chapter 6: 153–77.

———. 1997. "Structural Change and Urbanisation in Indonesia: From the 'Old' to the 'New' International Division of Labour". In Gavin Jones and Pravin Visaria (eds.), *Urbanisation in Large Developing Countries: China, Indonesia, Brazil, and India.* Oxford: Clarendon Press, pp. 111–41.

———. 1999. "Unbundling National Identity — Global Migration and the Advent of Multicultural Societies in East Asia". *Asian Perspectives* 23(3): 79–128.

———. 2001. "Inter-City Competition and the Question of Economic Resilience — Globalisation and the Asian Crisis". In Allen J. Scott (ed.), *Global City-Regions — Trends, Theory, Policy.* Oxford: Oxford University Press, pp. 236–62.

———. 2002a. "Civic Spaces, Globalisation and Pacific Asia Cities". *International Development and Planning Review* 24(4).

———. 2002b. "From Global Competition to Cooperation for Livable Cities and Economic Resilience in Pacific Asia". *Environment and Urbanisation.* Special Issue on Globalisation and Cities 14(1): 53–68.

———. 2006. "Local City, Capital City or World City? Civil Society, the (Post-) Developmental State and the Globalisation of Urban Space in Pacific Asia". *Pacific Affairs* 78: 4 (Winter): 543–58.

———. 2007. "Civil Society for Itself and in the Public Sphere: Comparative Research on Globalisation, Cities and Civic Space in Pacific Asia". In Mike Douglass, K.C. Ho and Giok Ling Ooi (eds.), *Globalisation, the City and the Rise of Civil Society — The Social Production of Civic Spaces in Pacific Asia.* London: Routledge (forthcoming).

Douglass, Mike and Pornpun Boonchuen. 2003a. "Bangkok — Edge Cosmopolis". Paper presented at the International Studies Association Convention, 25 February–1 March, Portland, OR.

———. 2003b. "Bangkok: Intentional World City". Paper presented at the International Studies Association Convention, 25 February–1 March, Portland, OR.

Douglass, Mike, Michael Digregorio, Valuncha Pichaya, Made Brunner, Wiwik Bunjamin, Dan Foster, Scott Handler, Rizky Komalasari, and Kana Taniguchi. 2002. *Urban Transition in Vietnam.* Research report to UN-HABITAT. Department of Urban Planning, Honolulu: The University of Hawaii.

Douglass, Mike and Giok Ling Ooi. 2000. "Industrialising Cities and the Environment in Pacific Asia: Toward a Policy Framework and Agenda for Action". In David

Angel and Michael Rock (eds.), *Asia's Clean Revolution: Industry, Growth and the Environment*. Sheffield: Greenleaf, pp. 104–27.

Douglass, Mike, K.C. Ho, and Giok Ling Ooi. 2002. "Civic Spaces, Globalisation and Pacific Asia Cities". *International Development and Planning Review* 24(4): 345–61.

Douglass, Mike, T.Q. Le, C.K. Lowry, M.S. Momen, H.T. Nguyen, A.N. Pham, M.P. Rogers, L.L. Rothbam, B. Da Silva, N.D. Thai, H. Yulinawati. 2003. "Livability and Mega-Urban Region Dynamics in Southeast Asia". Department of Urban and Regional Planning, Globalization Research Center, University of Hawaii, Manoa, Unpublished.

Department for Agriculture and Rural Development. 2002. *Spontaneous Migration in Ho Chi Minh City: Situation and Solutions*. Ho Chi Minh City: Department for Agriculture and Rural Development.

Drakakkis-Smith, David, and Dixon, Chris. 1997. "Sustainable Urbanisation in Vietnam". *Geoforum* 28(1): 21–38.

Drummond, Lisa. 2000. "Street Scenes: Practices of Public and Private Space in Urban Vietnam". *Urban Studies* 37(12): 2377–91.

Dursin, Richel. 2000. "Street Children Need Government Protection Too". Retrieved 24 November 2003 from <http://www.hartford-hwp.com/archives/54b/081.html>.

Editorial Committee. 1994. *Kua Shiji De Zhongguo Renkou: Shanghai Juan (The Population of China towards the 21st Century: Shanghai Volume)*. Beijing: China Statistical Publishing House.

Edmonds, Eric and Carrie Turk. 2002. Child Labour in Transition in Vietnam. Retrieved 11 November 2003 from <http://unpan1.un.org/intradoc/groups/public/documents/apcity/unpan005947.pdf>.

Edwards, M. 1993. *Urban Sustainability*. New Zealand: Ministry for the Environment. Retrieved from <http://www.mfe.govt.nz/publications/rma/urban-sustainability-93.html>.

Ekins, Paul. (ed.) 1986. *The Living Economy: A New Economics in the Making*. New York: Routledge.

Evans, Peter (ed.). 2002. *Livable Cities? Urban Struggles for Livelihood and Sustainability*. Los Angeles: University of California Press.

Farid, M. n.d. *Sexual Abuse, Sexual Exploitation, and the Commercial Sexual Exploitation of Children (CSEC) in Indonesia*. Retrieved 3 June 2004 from <http://www.cwa.tnet.co.th/vol16-1/sexexploitation.htm>.

Firman, Tommy. 1999. "From 'Global City' to 'City of Crisis': Jakarta Metropolitan Region Under Economic Turmoil". *HABITAT* 23(4): 447–66.

————. 2002. "The Restructuring of Jakarta Metropolitan Area: A Global City in Asia". *Cities* 15(4): 229–43.

Fischer, Elizabeth. E. 2000. "Building Livable Communities for the 21st Century". *Public Roads* 63(6): 30–4.

Francisco, Herminia and David Glover. 1999. *Economy and Environment: Case Studies in Vietnam*. EEPSEA.

Freedman, Ronald, Ming-Cheng Chang, Te-Hsiung Sun. 1994. "Taiwan's transition from high fertility to below — replacement levels", *Studies in Family Planning*, 25(6): 317–31.

Friedmann, John. 1986. "The World City Hypothesis". *Development and Change* 17: 69–83.

———. 1996. *World City Futures: The Role of Urban & Regional Policies in the Asia-Pacific Region*. Chinese University of Hong Kong: Hong Kong Institute of Asia-Pacific Studies.

———. 2002. *Life Space and Economic Space: Essays in Third World Planning*. New York: Transaction.

———. 2002. *The Prospect of Cities*. Minneapolis: University of Minnesota Press.

Fröbel, Folker, Jurgen Heinrichs and Otto Kreye. 1980. *The New International Division of Labour*. Cambridge: Cambridge University Press.

General Statistical Office (GSO). 2001. *Selected Results of the 1999 Population and Housing Census*. Hanoi: Census Steering Committee.

———. 2001. *Statistical Yearbook 2000*. Hanoi, Vietnam: Statistical Publishing House.

Ginsburg, Norton, Bruce Koppel and T.G. McGee. 1991. *The Extended Metropolis: Settlement Transition in Asia*. Honolulu: University of Hawaii Press.

Girardet, Herbert. 1999. *Creating Sustainable Cities*. Devon, UK: Green Books.

Gonzalez, Eduardo.T. and Magdalena Mendoza. 2002. *Governance in Southeast Asia: Issues and Options*. Manila: Philippine Institute for Development Studies.

Graduate Institute of Building and Planning, Naitonal Taiwan University (NTUBP). 1992. *Comprehensive Planning for Taipei Prefecture*. Taipei: Graduate Institutes of Building and Planning, National Taiwan University. (In Chinese.)

Habermas, Jurgen. 1989. *The Theory of Communicative Action* (Vol. 2): *Lifeworld and System: A Critique of Functionalist Reason*. London: Beacon Press.

Hancock, T. 1997. "Healthy Sustainable Communities: Concept, Fledging Practice, and Implications for Governance". In Mark Roseland (ed.), *Eco-city Dimensions: Healthy Communities, Healthy Planet*. Gabriola Island, British Columbia, Canada: New Society Publishers, pp. 42–50.

Hardoy, Jorge, Diana Mitlin, and David Satterthwaite. 1992. *Environmental Problems in Third World Cities*. London: Earthscan.

Harvey, David. 2002. *Spaces of Hope*. Berkeley: University of California Press.

Haughton, Graham and Colin Hunter. 1994. *Sustainable Cities*. London: Jessica Kingsley.

He Xinggang. 1992. "The Development of Pudong and the Structural Optimisation of Shanghai's Urban Territory". (In Chinese.) *Dili Xuebao* (*Acta Geographica Sinica*) 47(2): 97–105.

Herrin, Alejandro N. and Ernesto M. Pernia, 2003. "Population, Human Resources and Employment". In Arsenio M. Balisacan and Hal Hill (eds.), *The Philippine Economy: Development, Policies and Challenges*. Oxford: Clarendon Press.

Herron, Scott. 2001. "Ghosts of the Past". *Bangkok Post*. 30 January.

Hirschman, Charles, Joo Ean Tan, Apichat Chamratrithirong, Philip Enest. 1994. "The path to below replacement — level fertility in Thailand", *International Family Planning Perspectives* 20(3): 82–87.

Ho Chi Minh City's People Committee. 1996. *Master Plan on Ho Chi Minh City's Socio-economic Development Towards 2010.* Ho Chi Minh City, Vietnam.

Ho Chi Minh City Statistical Office. Various Years. *Statistical Yearbook*, Ho Chi Minh City: Ho Chi Minh City Statistical Office.

Hsia, Ju-joe. 1990. "The Transformation of Regional-Spatial Structure of Taiwan in the Global Economic Restructuring". In National Policy Research Centre, ed., *The Challenge of National Planning.* Taipei: National Policy Research Centre. (In Chinese.)

Hsiao, Hsin-Huang and Hwa-Jen Liu. 2002. "Collective Action toward a Sustainable City: Citizen's Movement and Environmental Politics in Taipei". In Peter Evans, ed., *Livable Cities: Urban Struggles for Livelihood and Sustainability.* Los Angeles: University of California Press.

Hsu, Jinn-yuh. 2005. "The Evolution of Economic Based: from Industrial City, Post-industrial City to Interface City". In Reginld Yin-Wang Kwok, ed., *Globalising Taipei: The Political Economy of Spatial Development.* London: Routledge.

Hu, Qi, 2002. "The Present Situation and Rational Redistribution of Shanghai's Population and Countermeasures". In Office of the Fifth Population Census of Shanghai Municipality, Shanghai Municipal Population and Family Planning Commission, and Shanghai Municipal Statistics Bureau (eds.), *"Xianzhuang, Zhanwang Yucelue — Shanghaishi Diwuci Renkoupucha Lunwen Huibian"* (The present Situation, Prospects and strategies: A collection of Papers Based on the Fifth Population Census of Shanghai). Shanghai: Office of the Fifth Population Census of Shanghai Municipality, Shanghai Municipal Population and Family Planning Commission, and Shanghai Municipal Statistics Bureau.

Hu, Xuwei, Zhou, Yixing, and Gu, Chaolin. 2000. *Zhongguo Yanhai Chengzhen Mijidiqu Kongjian Jiju Yu Kuosan Yanjiu* (Studies on the Spatial Agglomeration and Dispersion in China's Coastal City-and-Town Concentrated Areas). Beijing: Science Press.

Huang, Li-ling. 2005. "Urban Politics and Spatial Development: the Emergence of Participatory Planning". In Reginald Yin-Wang Kwok (ed.), *Globalising Taipei: The Political Economy of Spatial Development.* London: Routledge.

Hull, T., Endang Sulistyaningsih, and Gavin Jones. 1998. *Prostitution in Indonesia: Its History and Evolution.* Jakarta, Indonesia: Pustaka Sinar Harapan.

Husna, Farida and Phelim Kyne. 2006. "Indonesia's 1Q 2006 Approved FDI Slows To $2.4B", *Dow Jones Newswires*, Retrieved 14 Sept. 2006 from <http://sg.biz.yahoo.com/060426/15/40cei.html>.

International Crisis Group (ICG). 2003. *Indonesia Backgrounder: A Guide to the 2004 Election.* (Asia Report No. 71). Jakarta/Brussels: ICG.

Japan International Cooperation Agency (JICA). 1990. *Study on Medium to Long Term Improvement/Management Plan of Road and Road Transport in Bangkok.* Bangkok.

Jellineck, L. 2000. "Kampung Culture or Consumer Culture". *Development and Change: Globalisation and the Urban Property Boom in Metro Cebu, Philippines* 34(4): 713.

Jim, C.Y. and Chen, S.S. 2003. "Comprehensive Green Space Planning Based on Landscape Ecology Principles in Compact Nanjing City, China". *Landscape and Urban Planning* 998: 1–22.

Jitsuchon, S. 2001. "What is Poverty and How to Measure it?" *TDRI Quarterly Review* 16(4): 7–11.

Jones, Gavin W. 2002. "Southeast Asian Urbanisation and the Growth of Mega-urban Regions". *Journal of Population Research* 19(2): 119–36.

———. 2003. "Strategies and Achievements in Expanding Lower Secondary Enrollments: Thailand and Indonesia". *Asian Metacentre Paper Series No. 13.* Retrieved 13 November 2002 from <http://www.populationasia.org/Publications/ResearchPaper/AMCRP13.pdf>.

———. 2004. "Urbanisation Trends in Asia: The Conceptual and Definitional Challenges". In Tony Champion and G. Hugo (eds.), *New Forms of Urbanisation: Beyond the Urban-Rural Dichotomy.* Hants, England: Ashgate.

Jones, Gavin W., Chet Boonpratuang and Chanpen Taesrikul. 1996. "Dispelling Some Myths about Urbanisation in Thailand". *Journal of Demography* 12(1): 21–36.

Jones, Gavin and Richard Leete. 2002. "Asia's Family Planning Programmes as Low Fertility in Attained". *Studies in Family Planning* 33(1): 114–26.

Jones, Gavin W., Ching-lung Tsay and Bhishna Bajracharya. 2000. "Demographic and Employment Changes in the Megacities of Southeast Asia". *Third World Planning Review* 22(2): 119–46.

Jones, Gavin W. and Pravin Visaria. 1997. *Urbanisation in Large Developing Countries: China, Indonesia, Brazil and India.* Oxford: Clarendon Press.

Jou, Sue-ching. 2005. "Domestic Politics in Urban Image Create: Xinyi as the Manhattan of Taipei". In Reginald Yin-Wang Kwok (ed.), *Globalising Taipei: The Political Economy of Spatial Development.* London: Routledge.

Kanabus, A. and Fredrikson, J. 2003. *HIV and AIDS in Thailand.* Retrieved 21 November 2003 from <http://www.avert.org/aidsthai.htm>.

Kaothien, Utis and Douglas Webster. 1995. *Bangkok: Regional Form, Economic Restructuring, and Changing Social Expectations.* Paper presented to the International Symposium on Regional Cities, 16–19 September 1995. Cambridge, Massachusetts, USA.

Kasemsri, Saengsom and Wimol Phonpipat. 1972. *History of Ratanakosin Period during King Rama I to King Rama III (B.E. 2325–2394).* Bangkok: Mitara Karn Pim.

Khan, Amir. 1994. "Interrelationships between Demographic Factors, Development and the Environment in the ESCAP Region". *Asia-Pacific Population Journal* 9(3): 37–54.

Knox, Paul. 1993. *The Restless Urban Landscape.* Englewood Cliffs: Prentice Hall.

Knox, Paul and Peter Taylor. 1995. *World Cities in a World-System.* Cambridge: Cambridge University Press.

Kompas. 2002. *Air Tercemar Limbah, Petani Terpuruk* (*Water Polluted by Waste, Farmers Suffer*). 28 June.

————. 2003. "Sutiyoso Agrees to Raise 45% Clean Water Tariff for Middle and High Income Groups". 20 March.

Kristof, Nicholas with David Anger. 1999. "How U.S. Wooed Asia to Let Cash Flow". *New York Times.* 16 February.

Kunstler, James. 1993. "Better Places". In James. Kunstler (ed.), *Geography of Nowhere* (pp. 245–75). New York: Simon and Schuster.

Kuo, Nein-Hsiung. 2001. "The Taipei Region". In Roger Simmonds and Gary Hank (eds.), *Global City Regions: Their Emerging Form.* New York: E & FN Spon.

Lambsdorff, J.G. 2004. "Corruption Perception Index 2003". In Transparency International, *Global Corruption Report 2004.* London, Sterling: Pluto Press.

Lao Dong 2001. 13 March. "Thanh Pho HCM: Da Co Hon 50 Tre Em Bi Nhiem HIV" (HCMC: There have been more than 50 children infected with HIV). Retrieved from <http://vnexpress.net/Vietnam/Xa-hoi/2001/03/3B9AEA3C/>.

Laquian, A.A. 1995. "The Governance of Mega-urban Regions". In T.G. McGee and Ira Robinson (eds.), *The Mega-urban Regions of Southeast Asia.* Vancouver, Canada: UBC Press, pp. 215–41.

Lee, Everett S. 1966. "A Theory of Migration". *Demography* 3: 47–57.

Leong, S.T., Muttamara S., and Laortanakul, P. 2002. "Influence of Benzene Emissions from Motorcycles on Bangkok Air Quality". *Atmospheric Environment* 36: 651–61.

Lim, Lin Lean. 1998. "The Economic and Social Bases of Prostitution in Southeast Asia". In Lin L. Lim (ed.), *The Sex Sector: The Economic and Social Bases of Prostitution in Southeast Asia.* Geneva, Switzerland: ILO, pp. 1–28.

Lim, Merlyna. 2002. "Cyber-civic Space in Indonesia: From Panopticon to Pandemonium?" *International Development Planning Review* 24(4): 328–400.

Llorito, David L. 2003. "Applications of Centrographic Techniques to the Analysis of Private Investments in the Philippines: Focus on Projects Registered with the Board of Investments". M.A. Thesis. Quezon City: University of the Philippines School of Urban and Regional Planning, Sept.

Luna, T.W. Jr. 1964. "Manufacturing in Greater Manila". *Philippine Geographical Journal* 8(3).

Luong, Hy V. 1999. "Ho Chi Minh City: Economic Growth, Migration and Urbanisation". Paper presented at the International Conference on Poverty Alleviation in the Process of Urbanisation in Ho Chi Minh City, Social Science Research Council and HCMC Institute of Social Sciences, Nha Trang City, 13–15 Dec.

Mac, Duong. 2001. "Poverty and Poverty Overcoming in Urbanisation: Case Study of Three Sites of Ho Chi Minh City". In Nghia T. Nguyen, Duong Mac, and Vinh Q. Nguyen (eds.), *Poverty Reduction in Urbanisation Process of Ho Chi Minh City.* Ho Chi Minh City, Vietnam: Centre for Social Sciences and Humanities, Social Sciences Publishing House.

Madsen, Peter and Richard Plunz (eds.) 2001. *Urban Lifeworld: Formation, Perception, Representation*. London: Routledge.

Mamas, Si Gde Made, Gavin W. Jones, and Toto Sastrasuanda. 2001. "Demographic Change in Indonesia's Megacities". *Third World Planning Review* 23(4): 1–20.

Masoli, M., Fabian, D., Holt, S., and Beasely, R. 2004. *The Global Burden of Asthma*. Wellington, N.Z.: Medical Research Institute of New Zealand.

Mason, Andrew. 2001. *Population Change and Economic Development in East Asia: Challenges Met. Opportunities Seized*. Stanford: Stanford University Press.

McCarthy, P. 2003. "Urban Slums Report: The Case of Jakarta, Indonesia". In *Understanding Slums: Case Studies for the Global Report on Human Settlements*. The World Bank.

McGee, T.G.1967. *The Southeast Asian City*. London: Bell.

———. 1971. *The Urbanisation Process in the Third World*. London: Bell.

———. 1991. "The Emergence of Desakota Regions in Asia: Expanding a Hypothesis". In Norton Ginsburg, Bruce Koppel and T.G. McGee (eds.), *The Extended Metropolis: Settlement Transition in Asia*. Honolulu: University of Hawaii Press.

———. (ed.). 1995. "Metrofitting the Emerging Mega-urban Regions of ASEAN: An Overview". In T.G. McGee and Ira Robinson (eds.), *The Mega-urban Regions of Southeast Asia*. Vancouver, Canada: University of British Columbia Press.

McGee, T.G. and Ira M. Robinson. 1995. *The Mega-Urban Regions of Southeast Asia*. Vancouver, Canada: University of British Columbia Press.

McIntosh, Arthur. 2003. Asian Water Supplies: Reaching the Urban Poor. Manila, Philippines: Asian Development Bank and International Water Association (IWA). Retrieved from <http://www.adb.org/Documents/Books/Asian_Water_Supplies/default.asp>.

Media Indonesia. 2003a. "Banjir adalah Hiburan" (Floods are Recreation). Friday, 14 Feb: 1.

———. 2003b. "Kapan DKI Bebas Banjir?" (When will DKI be Flood Free?). 15 Jan.

———. 2003c. "Kondisi Umum Provinsi DKI Jakarta" (General Condition of the Province of DKI Jakarta). 15 Jan.

Mekong Project Development Facility (MPDF). Informality and the Playing Field in Vietnam's Business Sector. Washington D.C.: IFC.

Mercado, Ruben G. Undated. *Megapolitan Manila: Striving Towards a Humane and World Class Megacity*. Makati: Philippine Institute for Philippine Studies.

Moriconi-Ebrard, Francois. 1993. *World Urbanisation since 1950*. Paris: Anthropos.

Mukherjee, Nilanjana, Joan Hardjono, and Elizabeth Carrierre. 2002. *People, Poverty and Livelihoods: Links for Sustainable Poverty Reduction in Indonesia*. The World Bank and Department for International Development.

Naommy, P.C. 2003. 23 December. "Schools Reluctant to Join HIV/AIDS Discussion". Jakarta Post. Retrieved 14 January 2004 from <http://www.thejakartapost.com/Archives/ArchivesDet2.asp?FileID=20031222.G02.>.

National Economic and Social Development Board (NESDB) and others. 2003. *Suvarnabhumi Aerotropolis Study*. Bangkok.

National Research Council. 2003. *Cities Transformed: Demographic Change and Its Implications in the Developing World.* Panel on Urban Population Dynamics, M.R. Montgomery, edited by R. Stren, B. Cohen, and H.E. Reed. Committee on Population, Division of Behavioural and Social Sciences and Education. Washington, DC: The National Academies Press.

National Statistical Coordination Board. 2003. *2003 Philippine Statistical Yearbook.* Makati City.

———. 2003. Annual per Capita Poverty Thresholds and Poverty Incidence, by Province: 1997 and 2000. Retrieved 15 October 2003 from <http://www.nscb.gov.ph/poverty/2000/povertyprov.asp>.

National Statistics Office (NSO). 1992. *Female and Male Heads and the Level of Household's Living.* Bangkok, Thailand.

———. 1992. *The 1990 Population and Housing Census.* Bangkok, Thailand.

———. 1993. *National Demographic Survey.* Manila, Philippines.

———. 1995. *Survey of Children* (A component of ILO's International Programme on the Elimination of Child Labour). Bangkok, Thailand.

———. 1998. *National Demographic and Household Survey.* Manila, Philippines.

———. 2000. *Report of Population and Housing Census.* Bangkok, Thailand.

———. 2002. *The 2000 Population and Housing Census.* Bangkok, Thailand.

———. 2003. *Concluding Workshop on Enhancing Social and Gender Statistics.* Asian Development Bank/United Nations Economic and Social Commission for Asia and the Pacific (ADB/UNESCAP). Concluding Workshop on Enhancing Social and Gender Statistics, 24–27 June, Bangkok, Thailand. Retrieved 21 October 2003 from <http://www.unescap.org/stat/meet/esgs2/esgs2_thailand2.pdf>.

National Statistical Office (NSO), National Economic and Social Development Board (NESDB), and Office of Prime Minister. 1999. *Concept Paper on Poverty Measurement in Thailand.* Paper prepared for Seminar on Poverty Statistics, Economic and Social Commission for Asia and the Pacific, 21–23 June, Bangkok, Thailand. Retrieved 20 November 2003 from <http://www.unescap.org/stat/meet/povstat/pov7_thi.pdf>.

New York Times. 1999. "High-Rise Ghost Town — Muang Thong Thani Rises Up Above Barren Fields on the Edge of Bangkok". 16 February.

Nguyen, Q. 2001. "Some Findings on Poverty Threshold Identification Ways". In Nghia T. Nguyen, Duong Mac, and Vinh Q. Nguyen (eds.), *Poverty Reduction in Urbanisation Process of Ho Chi Minh City.* Ho Chi Minh City, Vietnam: Centre for Social Sciences and Humanities, Social Sciences Publishing House.

Nguyen, T.T. 1998. "Government Reform for Socio-economic Development in Vietnam". *Asian Review of Public Administration* 10: 1–2.

Ning, Yuemin. 2001. "Globalisation and the Sustainable Development of Shanghai". In Fu-Chen Lo and Peter Marcotullio (eds.), *Globalisation and Sustainability of Cities in the Asia Pacific Region.* Tokyo: United Nations University Press.

Noone, Martin J. 1986. *General History of the Philippines, Part I, Volume I: The*

Discovery and Conquest of the Philippines, 1521–1581. Quezon City: R. P. Garcia Publishing.

Pemda DKI Jakarta. 1994. *Neraca Kualitas Lingkungan Hidup Daerah DKI Jakarta 1994 (Balance Sheet of Environmental Quality in DKI Jakarta 1994).* Jakarta: Pemda DKI Jakarta.

People's Committee of Ho Chi Minh City (PCHCMC). 1999. *Feasibility Study of Sai Gon River Bridge Construction.* JBIC Project Management Unit, Ho Chi Minh City.

Pham, Minh Hac. and Nghi Pham. 2004. *Value Surveys on Democracy and Market in Vietnam.* Paper presented at the Citizens democracy and markets around the Pacific Rim Conference, East West Centre, 19–20 March, Honolulu, Hawaii. Retrieved 3 April 2004 from <http://hypatia.ss.uci.edu/democ/papers/vietnam.hawaii.pdf>.

Pham, Ngoc Dang. 1998. "Urban Environment and Industrialisation in Vietnam". *Vietnamese Studies* 3(129).

Phelan, John. 1959. *The Hispanization of the Philippines: Spanish Aims and Filipino Responses, 1565–1700.* Madison: University of Wisconsin Press.

Ploenpote, A. 2003. 27 April. "Civic Amenities: Playgrounds, Parks Lacking for Children". *The Bangkok Post.*

Population Census Office of Shanghai Municipality. 2001. *Shanghai Renkou Fazhan Baogao (Shanghai's Population Development Report).* Shanghai: Office of the Fifth Population Census of Shanghai Municipality and Shanghai Municipal Statistics Bureau.

Potter, Jack M. 1976. *Thai Peasant Social Structure.* Chicago: The University of Chicago Press.

Potter, Robert B. and Sally Lloyd-Evans. 1998. *The City in the Developing World.* Harlow: Longman.

Pugh, Cedric. 2000. *Sustainable Cities in Developing Countries: Theory and Practice at the Millennium.* London: Earthscan.

Ragragio, J.M. 2003. "Urban Slums Report: The Case of Manila, Philippines". In *Understanding Slums: Case Studies for the Global Report on Human Settlements.* The World Bank.

Reed, Robert R. 1967. "Hispanic Urbanism in the Philippines: A Study of the Impact of Church and State". *University of Manila Journal of East Asiatic Studies* 11: 12–22.

Register, Richard. 2002. *Ecocities: Building Cities in Balance with Nature.* Berkeley, California: Berkeley Hills Books.

Rele, J. R. 1967. "Fertility Analysis Through Extension of Stable Population Concept". Ph.D. Dissertation. Institute of International Studies, University of California, Berkeley.

Reyes, C.M. 2002. "Movements in and out of Poverty in the Philippines". Paper presented in a conference on Assessment of Poverty Reduction Policies, organised by INSEA and IDRC under Micro Impacts of Macroeconomic Adjustment Policies (MIMAP) Project, 28–31 January, Rabat-Morocco.

Reyes, Marquesa C. L. 1998. "Spatial Structure of Manila: Genesis, Growth and Development". *Philippine Planning Journal* 24(2) and 30(1).

Rogerson, R. 2000. "Quality of Life in Europe: Towards an Urban Renaissance". In Foo, Tuan Seik, LanYuan Lim, and Wong Khei Mie Wong (eds.), *Planning for a Better Quality of Life in Cities*. Singapore: National University of Singapore, pp. 110–25.

Rohter, I. 1992. *A Green Hawai'i: Sourcebook for Development Alternatives*. Honolulu, Hawaii: Na Kane O Ka Malo Press.

Roseland, Mark (ed.). 1997. *Eco-city Dimensions: Healthy Communities, Healthy Planet*. New Haven, Connecticut: New Society.

Sachs, Jeffrey. 1999. Missing Pieces. *Far Eastern Economic Review*. 25 February.

Safrudin Ahmad. 2001. "Current Situation to Unleaded Gasoline in Indonesia". Clean Air. Regional Workshop, Fighting Urban Air Pollution, from Plan to Action, 13–14 February.

Santiago, Asteya. 1996. "Case Study of Land Management in Metro Manila". In Jeffry Stubbs and Giles Clarke (eds.), *Mega City Management in the Asia and Pacific Region, Volume One: Recommendations of the Working Groups, Theme Papers and Case Studies*. Manila: Asian Development Bank.

Sasaki, H. 1998. *Urbanisation Transition and Its Impact on Thailand*. Retrieved 2 November 2003, from <http://www.arclinghaus.net/Sandra/Arlinghaus/Courses/545/1996/sasaki.html>.

Sassen, Saskia. 1991. *The Global City: New York, London and Tokyo*. New Jersey: Princeton University Press.

————. 1998. "Losing Control? The State and the New Geography of Power". *Global Forum on Regional Development Policy*. UNCRD. Nagoya. 1–4 December.

Satterthwaite, David (ed.). 1999. *Earthscan Reader in Sustainable Cities*. London: Earthscan.

Save the Children. 1997. *Invisible Children: Child Work in Asia and the Pacific*. Bangkok, Thailand: Child Workers in Asia.

Save the Children Fund (SCF). 1999. *Poverty in Ho Chi Minh City: Results of Participatory Poverty Assessments in Three Districts*. Ho Chi Minh City, Vietnam.

See, Ch'ng K. 2001. "Government Information and Information about Governments in Southeast Asia: A new Era? An Overview". *Inspel* 35(2): 120–36.

Serote, Ernesto M. 1991. "Socio-Spatial Structure of the Colonial Third World City: The Case of Manila". *Philippine Planning Journal* 23(1): 1–14.

Shah, Jitendra and Tanvi Nagpal (eds.). 1997. *Urban Air Quality Management Strategy in Asia: Metro Manila Report*. World Bank Technical Paper No. 380.

Shanghai Municipal Statistics Bureau. 2001. *Shanghai Statistical Yearbook (2001) (CD)*. Beijing: China Statistics Press.

Shanghai Urban Comprehensive Transport Planning Institute. 2000. *Shanghai Comprehensive Transport Planning (2000–2020)*. Unpublished manuscript. Shanghai: Shanghai Urban Comprehensive Transport Planning Institute.

Shannon, Kelly. 2001. *Vietnam's Hybrid Urban Landscapes: The Dream of Western Architects/Urbanists?* Coping With Informality and Illegality in Human Settlements in Developing Cities. ESF/N-AERUS Annual Workshop 23–26 May, Leuven and Brussels.

Siam Future Development. 2002. *Bangkok Highrises*. Retrieved from <http://atlas.spaceports.com/~bkksky/ranking30-39.htm>.

Simmonds, Roger and Gary Hack. 2000. *Global City Regions: Their Emerging Forms*. London and New York: SPON Press.

Soja, Edward. 2000. *Postmetropolis: Critical Studies of Cities and Regions*. Oxford: Basil Blackwell.

Sopon, Pornchokchai. 2002. "Bangkok Housing Market's Booms and Busts. What Do We Learn?" Paper presented at the PRRES 2002. Christchurch. New Zealand. 21–23 January.

Southeast Asia: Thailand: Democracy (n.d.). Retrieved 15 April 2004 from <http://www.nationmaster.com/country/th/Democracy>.

State Railway of Thailand. 2002. "Bangkok Metropolitan Transportation Hub-Feasibility Study, Preliminary Design and Environment Impact Study", Bangkok.

Statistical Office of Ho Chi Minh City (SOHCMC). 2002. *Statistical Yearbook 2001*. Ho Chi Minh City, Vietnam: Statistical Publishing House.

———. 2003. *Statistical Yearbook Ho Chi Minh City 2002*. April. Ho Chi Minh City: SOHCMC.

Suara Pembaruan. 2002a. "Pencemaran 10 Sungai di Bekasi Mengkhawatirkan" (Pollution in 10 Rivers in Bekasi is Worrying). 23 May.

———. 2002b. "Pencemaran Penyebab Kematian Ribuan Udang" (Pollution Causes Deaths of Thousands of Shrimps). 30 July.

Sullivan, Jeremiah M. 1972. "Model for the Estimation of the Probability of Dying between Birth and Exact Ages of Early Childhood". *Population Studies* 26(1): 79–97.

Tang, Zhong, and Kong, Xiangzhi. 2000. *Zhongguo Xiangzhen Qiye Jingjixue Jiaocheng* (*A Course on the Economics of China's Township and Village Enterprises*). Beijing: Renmin University of China Press.

Thai, Thi Ngoc Du, Pham Gia Tran *et al.* 2001. Constraints Faced by the Urban Poor in Housing and Infrastructure in Can Tho and Ho Chi Minh City. The World Bank (unpublished report).

Thayer, Carlyle. 1996. *Political Developments in Vietnam: From the Sixth to Seventh National Party Congress* (Discussion Paper Series, Number 5). Australia: The Department of Political and Social Change, Research School of Pacific and Asian Studies, The Australian National University.

Thien, Phuc. 2003. 23 May. "Ngay Cang Co Nhieu Phu Nu Nhiem HIV/AIDS O Thanh Pho HCM" (More and more women are infected with HIV/AIDS in HCMC). *VnExpress.net*. Retrieved from <http://vnexpress.net/Vietnam/Suc-khoe/2003/05/3B9C8187/>.

Thomas, Mandy. 2003. "Spatiality and Political Change in Urban Vietnam". In Lisa Drummond and Mandy Thomas (eds.), *Consuming Urban Culture in Contemporary Vietnam*. New York: Routledge Curzon.

Thomas, Mandy and Lisa Drummond. 2003. "Introduction". In L.B.W. Drummond and M. Thomas (eds.), *Consuming Urban Culture in Contemporary Vietnam*. New York: Routledge Curzon.

Thrift, Nigel, and Dean Forbes. 1986. *The Price of War: Urbanisation in Vietnam 1954–1985*. London: Allen and Unwin.

Todaro, Michael. 1976. *Internal Migration in Developing Countries*. Geneva: International Labour Office.

Tokar, Brian. 1997. *Earth for Sale: Reclaiming Ecology in the Age of Corporate Greenwash*. Boston: South End Press.

Transparency International. 2004. *Global Corruption Barometer 2003*. London, Sterling: Pluto Press.

United Nations (UN). 1999. *Looking Ahead: A Common Country Assessment*. Hanoi, Vietnam: Author.

———. 2001. *World Urbanisation Prospects: The 1999 Revision*. New York: United Nations, Department of Economic and Social Affairs, Population Division.

———. 2002. *World Urbanisation Prospects: The 2001 Revision*. New York: United Nations, Department of Economic and Social Affairs, Population Division.

———. 2004. *World Urbanization Prospects: The 2003 Revision*. New York: United Nations, Department of Economic and Social Affairs, Population Division.

United Nations Centre for Human Settlements (UNCHS). 2000. *The Global Campaign for Good Urban Governance*. Retrieved 15 April 2004 from <http://www.unchs.org/campaigns/governance/campaign_overview.asp>.

———. 2002. *Report of the Ninth Conference on Urban and Regional Research "Sustainable and Livable Cities"*. Retrieved 6 October 2003 from <http://www.unece.org/env/documents/2002/hbp/sem/hbp.sem.53.2.e.pdf>.

United Nations Children's Fund (UNICEF). 2000. *Vietnam: A Situation Analysis*. Hanoi, Vietnam.

United Nations Conference on Trade and Development (UNCTAD). 1999. *World Investment Report 1998*. New York: UNCTAD.

———. 2001. *World Investment Report 2000*. New York: UNCTAD.

United Nations Development Programme (UNDP). 1998. *The Dynamics of Internal Migration in Vietnam*. UNDP Discussion Paper 1. United Nations Development Programmeme, Hanoi: UNDP.

———. 2001. *Urban Governance: The State of the World's Cities*. New York. Retrieved 6 October 2003 from <http://www.un.org/ga/istanbul+5/90pdf>.

———. 2002. *The State and Progress of Human Development*. Human development report 2000. New York.

———. 2003. *Human Development Report 2003; Millennium Development Goals: A Compact among Nations to End Human Poverty*. New York.

United Nations Economic and Social Commission for Asia and the Pacific (UNESCAP). 1995. *Healthy Cities in Asia: A Diagnostic Manual.* New York.

United Nations Food and Agriculture Organisation (UNFAO). 2000. *The State of Food Insecurity in the World.* Retrieved 4 November 2003 from <http://www.fao.org/focus/e/sofi00/img/sofirep-e.pdf>.

United Nations Population Fund (UNFPA). 1996. *State of World Population 1996: Changing Places: Population, Development and the Urban Future.* Retrieved 15 December 2003 from <http://www.unfpa.org/swp/1996>.

Urban Management Programmeme (UMP). 1999. "Solid Waste Disposal in Asia Cities". *UMP Asia News* 2: 2.

Urban Social and Economic Survey Organisation of National Bureau of Statistics of China. 2001. *Urban Statistical Year Book of China (2001).* Beijing: China Statistics Press.

USAID. 2004. "Making Cities Work". *Southeast Asia Brief.* Retrieved 15 March 2004 from <http://www.makingcities work.org/urbanWorld/southeast-asia>.

US Census Bureau. 2005. "About Metropolitan and Micropolitan Statistical Areas". Washington, D.C.: U.S. Census Bureau). Retrieved 14 September 2006 from <http://www.census.gov/population/www/estimates/aboutmetro.html>.

Vining, Daniel R. 1986. "Population Redistribution Towards Core Areas of Less Developed Countries, 1950–1980". *International Regional Science Review* 10(1): 1–45.

Wang, Daben. 2002. "An Analysis on Urban Low-income Groups in Shanghai and Countermeasures". Paper presented at the eighth National Conference on Population Science. Beijing.

Wang, Guixin and Yin, Yongyuan. 2000. "*Shanghai Renkou Yu Kechixu Fazhan Yanjiu" (A Study on Shanghai's Population and Sustainable Development).* Shanghai: Shanghai University of Finance and Economics Press.

Wang, Guixin. *et al.* 2002. "Shanghai Dadushiquan Renkouxianzhuang Qushi Ji Guoneiwaibijiao Yanjiu" (A study on the current situation, trend and the domestic and international comparison of the population of Shanghai metropolitan region). Unpublished Manuscript. Population Research Institute of Fudan University, Shanghai.

Warr, Peter. and Isra Sarntisart. 2002. *The Role of Urban Regions in Power Reduction.* Bangkok, Retrieved 8 September 2004 from <http://angkor.com/2bangkok/2bangkok/Skytrain/index.shtml>.

Webber, Melvin. 2000. "The Joys of Spread City". In Roger Simmonds and Gary Hack (eds.), *Global City Regions: Their Emerging Forms.* London: Spon Press, pp. 277–81.

Webster, Douglass and Larissa Muller. 2002. *Peri-Urbanisation: Zones of Rural — Urban Transition.* Palo Alto: Asia Pacific Research Centre. Stanford University.

Wescott, Clay and Doug Porter. 2002. *Fiscal Decentralisation and Citizen Participation in East Asia.* Manila, Philippines: Asia Development Bank.

Wiest, Dana. 2002. *East Asia and the Pacific Operational Practice Notes: Fiscal Decentralisation in Thailand.* Washington, D.C.: World Bank. Retrieved from <http://wbln0018.worldbank.org/External/Urban/UrbanDev.nsf/0/8092DB20 ECEC3F8885256937006EC6F9?OpenDocument>.

Wilkinson, Earl. 2002. *AIDS Failure.* Manila, Philippines: Book of Dreams Verlag.

Winslow, Robert. 2004a. "Indonesia". *Crime and Society: A Comparative Criminology Tour of the World.* Retrieved 7 May 2004 from <http://www-rohan.sdsu.edu/faculty/rwinslow/asia/indonesia.html>.

———. 2004b. "Philippines". *Crime and Society: A Comparative Criminology Tour of the World.* Retrieved 7 May 2004 from <http://www-rohan.sdsu.edu/faculty/rwinslow/asia/philippines.html>.

———. 2004c. "Thailand". *Crime and Society: A Comparative Criminology Tour of the World.* Retrieved 7 May 2004 from <http://www-rohan.sdsu.edu/faculty/rwinslow/asia/thailand.html>.

———. 2004d. "Vietnam". *Crime and Society: A Comparative Criminology Tour of the World.* Retrieved 6 May 2004 from <http://www-rohan.sdsu.edu/faculty/rwinslow/asia/vietnam.html>.

Wittoelar, E. 2001. "People Centred Cities in a Globalising World: Issues in Governance". In *Transport and Communications Bulletin for Asia and the Pacific, No. 71.* Retrieved 5 April 2004 from <http://wwics.si.edu/topics/pubs/urbangov.pdf>.

Wong, Tai.-Chee. 1999. "Urbanisation and Sustainability of Southeast Asian Cities". In Tai.-Chee Wong and Mohan Singh (eds.), *Development and Challenge: Southeast Asia in the New Millennium.* Singapore: Times Academic Press.

World Bank. 1985. *World Development Report 1985.* Washington, D.C.: IBRD.

———. 1996a. *Livable Cities for the 21ˢᵗ Century.* Washington, D.C.

———. 1996b. *World Development Report 1996.* Washington, D.C.: IBRD.

———. 2000. *Cities in Transition: World Bank Urban and Local Government Strategies.* Washington, D.C.

———. 2002. *Thailand Environment Monitor 2002: Air Quality.* Bangkok, Thailand.

———. 2003a. "Cities in Transition: Urban Sector Review in an Era of Decentralisation in Indonesia". *Dissemination Paper No. 7, Urban Sector Development Unit, Infrastructure Department, East Asia and Pacific Region.*

———. 2003b. *Indonesia Environment Monitor 2003.* Retrieved 15 March 2004 from <http://www.worldbank.or.id>.

———. 2003c. *World Development Report 2004: Making Services Work for Poor People.* Cambridge, MA: Oxford University Press.

World Bank (WB), Asian Development Bank (ADB), and United Nations Development Programme (UNDP). 2000. "Pillars of Development". In *Vietnam Development Report 2001: Entering the 21st Century.* Hanoi, Vietnam.

World Commission on Environment and Development (WCED). 1987. *Our Common Future.* London: Oxford University Press.

World Health Organisation WHO. (2003). *Health Service Delivery Systems*. Retrieved 4 November 2003 from <http://w3.whosea.org/eip/thf/english/tex%20english_pdf/CHA6_1.pdf>.

World Resource Institute (WRI). 1996. *World Resources 1996–97*. Washington, D.C.

Wu, Peter Cheng-Chong. 2005. "Daily Consumption in Global City: Food Markets at the Crossroads". In Reginald Ying-Wang Kwok (ed.), *Globalising Taipei: The Political Economy of Spatial Development*. London: Routledge.

Yusuf, Shahid and Weiping Wu. 2002. "Pathways to a World City: Shanghai Rising in an Era of Globalisation". *Urban Studies* 39 (7): 1213–40.

Zhang, Shanyu. 1999. "Recent Great Changes in Shanghai's Population Distribution". (In Chinese.) *"Renkou Yanjiu"* (*Population Research*) 23(5): 16–24.

Zhou, Yixing. 1991. "The Metropolitan Interlocking Region in China: A Preliminary Hypothesis". In Norton Ginsburg, Bruce Koppel and T.G. McGee (eds.), *The Extended Metropolis: Settlement Transition in Asia*. Honolulu: University of Hawaii Press.

Zhu, Baoshu. 2002. *Changshi Hua Zaituijin He Laodongli ZaiZhuanyi (The Further Promotion of Urbanisation and the Further Transfer of the Labour Force)*. Shanghai: East China Normal University Press.

Zuo, Xuejin. J. 2000. "China's Rural and Urban Employment in the Reform Era: Recent Trends and Policy Issues". In Peng Xizhe and Guo Zhigang (eds.), *The Changing Population of China*. Oxford: Blackwell Publishers.

Index